Nature's Year
in the Kawarthas

Nature's Year in the Kawarthas

A Guide to the Unfolding Seasons

Drew Monkman

Illustrations by Kimberly Caldwell

NATURAL HERITAGE / NATURAL HISTORY INC.

Nature's Year In the Kawarthas
Drew Monkman

Copyright © 2002 Drew Monkman

Published by Natural Heritage/Natural History Inc.
P.O. Box 95, Station O, Toronto, Ontario M4A 2M8

www.naturalheritagebooks.com

National Library of Canada Cataloguing in Publication

Monkman, Drew, 1952-
Nature's year in the Kawarthas : a guide to the unfolding seasons/Drew Monkman ; illustrations by Kimberly Caldwell.

Includes bibliographical references and index.
ISBN 1-896219-80-2

1. Natural history—Ontario—Kawartha Lakes Region—Guidebooks.
2. Seasons—Ontario—Kawartha Lakes Region—Guidebooks. 3.
Kawartha Lakes Region (Ont.)—Description and travel. 4. Kawartha
Lakes Region (Ont.)—Guidebooks. I. Caldwell, Kimberly, 1972- II.
Natural Heritage/Natural History Inc III. Title.

QH106.2.O5M65 2002   508.713'67   C2002-903578-3

Illustrations © Kimberly Caldwell
Design by Derek Chung Tiam Fook
Edited by Jane Gibson
Printed and bound in Canada by Hignell
Printing Limited, Winnipeg, Manitoba

Natural Heritage / Natural History Inc.
acknowledges the financial support of the
Canada Council for the Arts and the Ontario
Arts Council for our publishing program.
We also acknowledge the financial support of
the Government of Canada through the Book
Publishing Industry Development Program
(BPIDP) and the Association for the Export
of Canadian Books.

Dedication

For my wife, Michelle, my children, Philippe, Julia, Sarah and Sophia,

and my parents, Cy and Lois

Contents

Acknowledgements xii

Foreword xiii

Introduction xv

The Setting xvii

Calendar of Natural Events of Special Interest xix

Legend for Terms and Symbols xx

1. January—Silence and Survival 1

    January At a Glance 2

    Birds 3

    Mammals 7

    Fishes 9

    Insects and Other Invertebrates 11

    Plants 13

    Weather 17

    The Night Sky 19

2. February—Gateway to the Year 23

    February At a Glance 24

    Birds 25

    Mammals 28

    Fishes 31

    Insects and Other Invertebrates 32

    Plants 35

    Weather 36

    The Night Sky 39

3. March—Waiting for Spring-to-be 43

    March At a Glance 44

    Birds 45

    Mammals 51

Amphibians and Reptiles 53

Fishes 55

Insects and Other Invertebrates 55

Plants 57

Weather 60

The Night Sky 62

4. April—Frog Song and Sky Dancers 65

April At a Glance 66

Birds 67

Mammals 73

Amphibians and Reptiles 76

Fishes 80

Insects and Other Invertebrates 83

Plants 85

Weather 89

The Night Sky 91

5. May—The Promise of Spring Fulfilled 95

May At a Glance 96

Birds 97

Mammals 101

Amphibians and Reptiles 103

Fishes 104

Insects and Other Invertebrates 106

Plants 113

Weather 120

The Night Sky 122

6. June—Endless Days and the Urgency of Life 125

June At a Glance 126

Birds 127

Mammals 131

Amphibians and Reptiles 134

Fishes 137

Insects and Other Invertebrates 140

Plants 146

Weather 153

The Night Sky 155

7.   July—Summer At its Height 159

July At a Glance 160

Birds 161

Mammals 164

Amphibians and Reptiles 165

Fishes 166

Insects and Other Invertebrates 167

Plants 170

Weather 174

The Night Sky 178

8.   August—Summer Becoming Fall 181

August At a Glance 182

Birds 183

Mammals 188

Amphibians and Reptiles 189

Fishes 190

Insects and Other Invertebrates 190

Plants 196

Weather 200

The Night Sky 201

9.   September—Mists and Melancholy Joy 205

September At a Glance 206

Birds 207

Mammals 213

Amphibians and Reptiles 215

Fishes 217

Insects and Other Invertebrates 218

Plants 221

Weather 229

The Night Sky 230

10. October—The Time of Falling Leaves 235

October At a Glance 236

Birds 237

Mammals 241

Amphibians and Reptiles 243

Fishes 245

Insects and Other Invertebrates 246

Plants 248

Weather 252

The Night Sky 254

11. November—A Hush upon the Land 257

November At a Glance 258

Birds 259

Mammals 262

Amphibians and Reptiles 265

Fishes 267

Insects and Other Invertebrates 268

Plants 273

Weather 276

The Night Sky 277

12. December—The Sun Stands Still 281

December At a Glance 282

Birds 283

Mammals 290

Fishes 292

Plants 292

Weather 294

The Night Sky 296

Appendix 1: Where to Go? 299
    Map 307
Appendix 2: Additional Resources 308
Notes 311
Selected Bibliography 313
Index 316
About the Author 336
About the Illustrator 336

Acknowledgements

First and foremost, I wish to extend my sincere thanks to Kimberly Caldwell, whose superb drawings illustrate the chapters of this book.

I would also like to thank the following individuals who gave generously of their time to review the manuscript and to share their expertise: Jerry Ball, Dave Bell, Peter Burke, Mike Clark, Jack Davis, Peter Dawson, Al Dextrase, Ken Duncan, Fred Helleiner, Colin Jones, Peter Lafleur, Bill McCord, Marty Obbard, Mike Oldham, Doug Sadler and Don Sutherland.

Many other people also made significant contributions. They include: Paul Anderson, Kevin Asselin, Don Blizzard, Terry Carpenter, Pam Chellew, Gail Corbett, Brock Fenton, Tracy Holden, Peter Hulsman, Joanne Jackson, Audrey Keitel, Tom MacDonald, Nick Mandrak, Greg Maude, Erica Nol, Bob Petty, Tom Pratt, Chris Risley, Jacob Rodenberg, Peter Sorrill and Evan Thomas.

Throughout my lifetime, Nature has been both a keen interest and an avocation. While many have been most supportive of this work, the responsibility for any errors remains with me. Any such reported to the publisher or myself will be rectified in subsequent editions.

Foreword

If, like me, you have ever opened the door on a party, to be met by a sea of unknown faces, you will have felt quite daunted. A quick round of introductions does not help. You know you will almost certainly never remember most of the people another time when you run across them in a different context. In any case there isn't much point, unless you can establish some kind of meaningful relationship. Having a friend along who knows the people may help to make this possible.

It is much the same with Nature. There is so much to know and to remember.

In this book, Drew Monkman has offered to fill the gap and make the knowing and remembering easier. He offers points of contact hard to come by, at least in books. He makes it all so intimate, while presenting the great array of natural phenomena in an accessible way, taking you through a year in the rich Kawartha environment. He has drawn on many sources, double-checking their accuracy, but still making it all strongly personal.

But this book can do more, serving as an introduction to a lifetime of real understanding of, and intimacy with, the natural world. Few things can be more enjoyable, or rather more deeply rewarding, in an alienated world. It will knit up the broken connection so urgently needed in our lives—and by our world. This is essential if the Earth's innate riches are to be saved.

Doug Sadler
Peterborough, Ontario

NATURE'S YEAR IN THE KAWARTHAS

Introduction

One of the greatest pleasures to be derived from the regular observation of the natural world is to witness the passage of time, as one season slips into the next. The predictability of seasonal change comes from the reoccurrence every spring, summer, fall and winter of natural events that usually occur within a few days of the same date each year. Such events provide a reassuring counterbalance to the onslaught of change and uncertainty that characterizes modern life. In nature we can rest assured that the barely perceptible lengthening of a January day is leading to another spring and that every year, on or about March 26, the first Tree Swallows will appear over the Otonabee River.

Nature's Year in the Kawarthas is an almanac of key events occurring in the natural world over the course of a year in central Ontario. Although the focus is the Kawartha Lakes area and Peterborough County, the sequence and general timing of events apply to all of "Cottage Country" including Land O'Lakes, Haliburton and Muskoka. This book should be of interest to anyone who is curious about the outdoors, including naturalists, cottagers, canoeists, hikers and hunters. Much of the information should be useful to educators as well.

By using a month by month approach, the book is very much a supplement to the regular calendar. It shows you when to look for the first Hepatica, when to expect the first Eastern Bluebirds, when Spring Peepers start calling, when fall colours peak, and which constellations are visible each month. Like a celestial clock, events such as these tick off the time of the season. They also help us to become more aware of the continuity of seasonal progression. To a large extent, "seeing" is knowing what to expect. An awareness that Bald Eagles are a real possibility over a half frozen December lake greatly facilitates actually seeing them. In fact, the cornerstone of most plant and animal identification is knowing what to anticipate given the time of year and the habitat. A seasons-based approach to natural history therefore provides a way to mentally organize and retrieve information about plants and animals. Otherwise, much of the content of field guides and other nature books becomes little more than an impenetrable mass of data.

The events that constitute nature's annual cycle are practically limitless. In Peterborough County alone, there are at least 1,200 species of vascular plants, 55 mammals, 160 breeding birds, 17 amphibians, 16 reptiles, 86 butterflies, 29 damselflies and 55 dragonflies. Each of these species responds to the advancing seasons in a series of datable events. Obviously, no one book could ever cover all of these happenings for every species, if in fact they were even documented. Most of the dates used in this book are based on many years of observations by myself and other local naturalists; some dates, however, are "best estimates" because the dates have never actually been documented for this area, or I was not able to find them. For example, while arrival and departure dates for many bird species have been carefully recorded for many years, the dates involving mammal and insect activity are not as well known.

The science of observing and recording the annual cycle of "first events"—be they bird song, nesting, leaf-out or countless other events—is known as phenology. Keeping track of the dates of first happenings not only enhances the pleasure of seeking out those events, but provides a measure of order and predictability to nature. It also serves as a way of being attentive to all that surrounds us. Phenology helps us to see the land as a whole. It is interesting to compare for any given event, what other events are usually happening at the same time. For example, when Spring Peepers are calling in late April, American Woodcock are displaying, Walleye are spawning, American Elm is in flower, the ice has probably just gone out of our lakes, the sun sets shortly after 8:00 p.m. and Orion is low in the western sky.

Depending on the species, the time of "first occurrence" does not always repeat itself each year. Factors such as abnormal weather patterns or the influence of an "El Nino" can delay or hasten events. Climate change, in particular, appears to be having an effect on phenological dates, especially with respect to those events occurring in the early spring. As a general rule, the year-to-year variability of events decreases as the spring advances. For example, there is much more variability in the arrival dates of early spring birds as compared to those birds that arrive in May. Also, by its very nature, a "first event" means that the event in question may not yet be widespread or easy to observe. When a given species of bird returns in the spring, there are usually only a small number of individuals for the first week or so. Larger numbers may not arrive until later. For example, although the first Red-eyed Vireos arrive in mid-May, the bird is not common until late in the month.

American biologist and writer, Bernd Heinrich, suggests that "most of us are like sleepwalkers here, because we notice so little." For so many people, nature has been reduced to little more than pretty landscapes and all that "stuff" that rushes past on the other side of closed car windows. I hope that this book will help people become more aware of all that surrounds us in our part of the natural world and in this way develop both a greater sense of place and sense of season. I rarely feel the urge any more to explore the fauna and flora of far-off places when there are so many intriguing species here. And many of these I am only beginning to know. It seems to me that if we are ever going to take care of this planet, we have to start by knowing and caring about our own region. Human nature is such that in the end we will protect only what we love and love only what we know. The knowing, however, must go beyond simply putting names to what we find in nature. We need to understand the natural world as a dynamic entity of countless interrelationships, the complexity of which we can only begin to understand. The "knowing" also needs to be done in a context of place—in this case central Ontario and the Kawarthas, and in a context of time—the passing seasons.

The Setting for *Nature's Year in the Kawarthas*

The setting for this book is primarily Peterborough County, an area loosely referred to as the Kawarthas. It is bounded by Rice Lake and the town of Hastings in the south, Eel Lake (just west of Silent Lake Provincial Park) in the north, Pigeon Lake and the town of Bobcaygeon in the west and Crowe Lake (almost to the town of Marmora) in the east. From north to south, the townships which make up the County are Galway-Cavendish-Harvey, Burleigh-Anstruther-Chandos (North Kawartha), Havelock-Belmont-Methuen, Smith-Ennismore, Douro-Dummer, Cavan-Millbrook-North Monaghan, Otonabee-South Monaghan and Asphodel-Norwood. The main city is Peterborough, which is located in the southwest corner.

The County is almost evenly divided between two of Canada's principal physical regions. It sits on the southern edge of the Canadian Shield, a vast area composed of ancient Precambrian bedrock, and on the northern edge of the Great Lakes-St. Lawrence Lowland, a region underlain by younger sedimentary rock. In addition to the physical components, the other main feature of the Kawarthas is its watercourses, namely the Kawartha Lakes. These lakes are all located on the Trent-Severn Waterway and include Rice Lake, Lake Katchewanooka, Clear Lake, Stony Lake, Lovesick Lake, Buckhorn Lake, Chemong Lake, Pigeon Lake, Sturgeon Lake and Lake Scugog. They make up the Otonabee River watershed and drain into Rice Lake and the Trent River. Like the Muskokas, this is "Cottage Country" and images of fishing, swimming and boating immediately come to mind.

The North

As you drive north up onto the Shield, the first thing you notice is the change in the rock. Suddenly the limestone disappears and beautiful pink granite and other igneous and metamorphic rocks now border roadsides and lakeshores. With so much rock near the surface, the soil is thin and poor. Abandoned farms attest to the difficulty of carrying out agriculture. Because farming is impractical, most of this area is forested. Images taken by satellite clearly show a largely unbroken expanse of dark green on the Shield while the lowlands to the south show only scattered pockets of green. Although the northern Kawarthas were heavily logged in the past, they have now largely reverted to forest. This part of the Kawarthas tends to be cooler than the South and receives more snowfall.

The South

The land south of the Shield is quite fertile and has calcareous, loamy soils. Limestone, laid down 490 million years ago during the Ordovician period, overlies the basal Shield rock. Some of this limestone is visible in roadcuts near the edge of the Shield and along the banks of the Otonabee River. The original forest covering this area was composed primarily of Sugar Maple, American Beech, Yellow Birch, Eastern Hemlock and White Pine. Lesser amounts of White Ash, American Elm and American Basswood were also present. White Cedar, too, was and still is a very common tree of the southern Kawarthas. The best example of near-virgin woods that remains can be found in Mark S. Burnham Provincial Park, located just east of Peterborough on Highway 7.

As a result of glaciation, much of the Shield area was stripped of its soil by the advancing ice. Huge amounts of this glacial material were deposited, however, in the southern part of the Kawarthas giving the region its rolling, hilly character. Glacial landforms such as moraines, eskers and the famous Peterborough Drumlin Field are all common. Although much of the land is agricultural, there is also a large proportion of rough farmland and scrub.

The Diversity of Natural Habitat, Flora and Fauna

The mix of Shield country, lowlands and water courses gives the Kawarthas one of the richest assortments of habitat types in Ontario. These include mixed northern forests, largely deciduous southern woodlots, alvars (largely open expanses of flat, surface limestone), abandoned farmland, agricultural land and a variety of wetland types such as cedar swamp and marsh. More localized habitats include the botanically-rich Cavan Swamp, the crystalline limestone of Petroglyphs Provincial Park, the extensive bare rock, oak and juniper ridges of Kawartha Highlands Provincial Park and even a few tiny remnants of tallgrass prairie located near the Hiawatha Reserve on Rice Lake.

With such variety of habitat, the diversity of plants and animals is also one of the most extensive in the province. Some species, like Black Spruce, Moose and Common Ravens are typical of northern Ontario; others, like Bitternut Hickory, White-tailed Deer and Cerulean Warbler are more characteristic of southern Ontario.

Seasonal Occurrences of Natural Events of Special Interest

	Jan	Feb	Mar	Apr	May	Jun	Jul	Aug	Sep	Oct	Nov	Dec
1	BBB	BBB	BBG	GF						FF	GGB	BBB
2	GGG	GBB	BBB	BGG	GFF	F					F	FFG
3		FFF	FGB	BBG	GF				F	GGB	BBB	GF
4	GGG	GGG	GBB	BBB	BGG	FFF	FFF	FFF	GGB	BBG	GGG	GGG
5			FBB	BBB	GGG	FFF						
6			F	GBB	BBB	BGF	F			FGG	BBB	F
7				FF	GBB	BBG						
8				F	GBB	F		FGB	BBG	FF		
9					FB	BF	FFG	BBB	BBG	GGG	FF	
10		F	FGG	GGB	BBB	BBG	GGF	F				
11					FG	BBB	GGF	FFF	F			
12				FF	BBB	BBB	BBG	GGB	GFF	FF		
13					FFG	GBB	BBB	GGG	GGF	FFF		
14					F	FFF	FGB	BBB	BGG	GFF		
15								F	FFG	BBG	F	

Key to Event Calendar

1 eagle watching
2 owls calling
3 waterbird migration
4 bird diversity at feeders
5 amphibian chorus
6 fish spawning
7 spring wildflowers
8 warbler migration

9 shorebird migration
10 dawn bird chorus
11 orchids in bloom
12 butterfly diversity
13 dragonfly diversity
14 insect chorus
15 fall colours

Level of Activity

Levels: F (fair)   G (good)   B (best)

Legend for Terms and Symbols Used in Bird Arrival and Departure Charts

Early month—from the 1st to the 10th
Mid-month—from the 11th to the 20th
Late month—from the 21st to the 30/31st

Departures—refers to the time when a species becomes generally absent or greatly reduced in numbers. In the fall in particular, many species migrate through our area over an extended period of time because of birds coming through from further north. It is therefore difficult to know exactly when "our" birds—those individuals that have bred in the Kawarthas—actually leave.

Arrivals—refers to the time of year when a species usually begins arriving in steady numbers. Some arrivals quickly pass through our area (e.g. Blackpoll Warbler), some linger here for several weeks or more before continuing north or south (e.g. most White-crowned Sparrows), some remain to breed here (e.g. Baltimore Oriole) and still others arrive from the north to spend the winter here (e.g. Northern Shrike). Species that linger in the Kawarthas before continuing north or south have an arrival and departure date for both the spring and the fall. These include many species of ducks, shorebirds and sparrows.

* (irregular visitor)—indicates a species that does not turn up every year. When they do visit our area, the arrival and departure dates can vary greatly depending on the year. Typical arrival and departure dates have been given. These species include many owls and the so-called winter finches.

w (winters)—indicates a species that spends the winter in the Kawarthas although part of the population may leave the area and migrate south. A typical example is the Blue Jay. A large percentage of jays migrate south but many also remain to spend the winter here.

b (breeds)—indicates a species that breeds in the Kawarthas although most of the birds that we see in the spring are only passing through on their way to more northern and/or western breeding grounds. A typical example is the Hooded Merganser.

How to Use This Book

In order to best meet the reader's needs, interest and available time, the natural events included for each month are presented at four different levels of detail.

1. A brief introductory essay attempts to capture both the spirit and some of the main features of the month.

2. An "At a Glance" summary lists the key natural events occurring during the month in each of the main areas of our flora and fauna, namely birds, mammals, amphibians and reptiles, fish, invertebrates and plants. Information on weather and the night sky is also included.

3. Each of these eight areas is then examined in more detail starting with a list of highlights and the approximate time of the month when these highlights usually first occur. Some may occur all month long while others are more specifically associated with the early month, mid-month or late month.

4. A number of these highlights (those identified with the icon ◇) are then expanded upon in article form. Various tables are also used to summarize information.

5. A map of Peterborough County is located on page 307. The map shows the various viewing locations mentioned in the book.

6. To find information on a specific plant or animal, simply turn to the general index at the back.

Note from the Author

A new phenomenon, known as the West Nile virus, is appearing to intrude on the natural world in Ontario. Although known to be carried by certain birds and to be spread by mosquitoes, the virus and its impact are not yet fully understood. If large scale spraying of toxic insecticides becomes commonplace, however, the repercussions on human health, wildlife and ecosystems could be serious.

White-breasted Nuthatch.

CHAPTER 1

January—Silence and Survival

For those of the natural world, January is a deadly serious time; survival is the only consideration. For many animals this means a day-to-day struggle to eat enough to simply get through the long winter night. In January, sound is the exception and silence the rule. Granted, the quiet may be broken by the styrofoam squeal of frigid snow underfoot, by the rifle shot of swollen tree fibres bursting in the cold or by the tinkling calls of a flock of finches passing overhead. But these sounds are simply pauses in a world of silence. Even the January moon shines with a cold-hearted light that only accentuates the stillness of the land.

But only to the casual hurried observer is the landscape lifeless. On a snowy morning, a troop of chickadees may suddenly appear at the forest edge, tirelessly peering and probing for dormant insects. Nearby, a White-breasted Nuthatch works its way down a tree trunk while a Downy Woodpecker taps softly at the rough bark. In the distance, White-tailed Deer browse quietly on basswood saplings, their grey winter hair matching the dim, grey-washed hues of the leafless hardwoods. The deer stop momentarily, startled by the hammer-like blows of a Pileated Woodpecker excavating a resonant old maple for dormant ants. We marvel at how each species in its own unique way has adapted to surviving winter. To the curious and attentive observer, there is wonder in the countless strategies used by plants and animals to withstand or retreat from the snow, wind and cold. Seen or unseen, awake or sleeping, life is all around us.

January At a Glance

Bald Eagles winter in the Kawarthas. Small numbers of Common Goldeneye and Common Mergansers spend the winter here, as well. Great Horned Owls are becoming increasingly vocal. A flight of "winter finches" occurs most years, and northern owl species are always a possibility.

A number of species including beavers, foxes and coyotes mate during January. Male Moose and White-tailed Deer lose their antlers. Deer "yard up" in northern parts of our area. Black Bears give birth to two cubs.

Amphibians and reptiles are in hibernation. Occasionally you will see a mink, otter or duck surface with a hibernating frog in its mouth.

Many fish such as bass, bullheads and carp are essentially dormant and may even partly bury themselves in the lake bottom. Species that remain active such as Yellow Perch and Walleye provide great ice fishing.

Insects can be found overwintering in all stages of their life cycle—as eggs, larvae, pupae (cocoons) and adults. Blackfly larvae, for example, are easy to find in open sections of winter streams. The galls of the Goldenrod Gall Fly are a common sight.

Herbaceous evergreen plants such as Wintergreen and Christmas Fern stand out in snow-free areas. Pines are shedding their cones. This is a good time to learn how to identify trees by the characteristics of the twigs and buds.

The daily maximum temperature averages about -4° C and the minimum about -15° C. At mid-month, the sun rises around 7:45 a.m. and sets at about 5:00 p.m. We quickly become aware of the increased daylight in late afternoon.

The Winter Six—Orion, Taurus, Gemini, Auriga, Canis Major and Canis Minor—rule the January sky. The Big Dipper is upright, low in the northeast. Watch for the Northern Lights. They are most impressive in winter.

Birds

January Highlights

All Month Long

- In our forests, mixed flocks of foraging chickadees, nuthatches and woodpeckers bring life to the seemingly empty winter landscape.

- Birds use a variety of strategies to survive the cold of winter. ◇

- The numbers of some winter birds vary greatly from one year to the next. These species are known as winter irruptives and include many of the finches and owls. ◇

- Courtship preoccupies Great Horned Owls this month.

- Ruffed Grouse often appear in silhouette as they feed at dusk and dawn on aspen buds.

- Even during the winter, woodpeckers defend feeding territories through a combination of drumming and calling. The loud "wuk-wuk-wuk" cackle of the Pileated Woodpecker can often be heard on winter mornings.

- Rarities and stragglers that have "forgotten" to migrate south sometimes show up at feeders.

- Bald Eagles can often be seen at Young's Point, in the vicinity of Petroglyphs Provincial Park and at the dumps at Kasshabog Lake, Haultain and Apsley. Be sure to arrive early before the dumps open for business.

- Small numbers of Common Goldeneye and Common Merganser can usually be found all winter long on the Otonabee River between Peterborough and Young's Point. Rarities such as the Barrow's Goldeneye turn up some years and may stay all winter.

- Small flocks of American Robins overwinter in Peterborough most years. When there is an especially heavy wild fruit crop, such as in the winter of 1998-99, the number of winter robins increases greatly.

- Flocks of winter finches such as redpolls and crossbills call constantly as they pass overhead. Just like songs, most bird calls are sufficiently distinctive to allow you to identify the species.

- If the weather is mild and sunny, some species such as European Starlings, White-breasted Nuthatches and Black-capped Chickadees will occasionally break into song.

Surviving the Cold

Birds use a variety of strategies to survive cold winter days and nights. We often see birds puffing up their feathers. This is because air pockets in the feathers provide excellent insulation. At night, many species take shelter from the wind in the boughs of evergreens. It has even been shown that the dominant birds in flocks roost in the deepest, most sheltered parts of the evergreen, while the least dominant birds are relegated to areas more exposed to the wind.

Probably the most important line of defence, however, is getting enough to eat during the day in order to maintain fat reserves. Fat is burned to produce heat through shivering. Opposing sets of muscles tug at each other causing the entire body to quiver, even while the birds sleep. Some species such as chickadees also have the ability to drastically lower their internal body temperature at night in order to use up their fat reserves at a lower rate. They also forage less on very cold days and spend more time in their roosts.

Birds such as nuthatches and bluebirds are known to crowd into hollows and even

American Robin in mountain-ash.

nesting boxes at night. By huddling together, they are able to share their own body heat. Grouse also like the idea of a warm shelter completely protected from the wind. On cold nights, they will literally dive into deep, soft snow drifts to take advantage of the shelter provided by the snow.

Winter Irruptives

The numbers of some winter birds fluctuate widely from year to year. These species are referred to as winter "irruptives," and the years in which they are particularly common are called "flight years." Most irruptive species breed in northern Canada and winter only intermittently south of the boreal forest. Among passerines (perching birds), the main irruptive species are the Bohemian Waxwing, Cedar Waxwing, Northern Shrike, Pine Grosbeak, Evening Grosbeak, Red-breasted Nuthatch, Pine Siskin, Common Redpoll, Hoary Redpoll, Purple Finch, American Goldfinch, Red Crossbill and White-winged Crossbill. Other irruptives include Black-backed Woodpecker, Three-toed Woodpecker, Gray Jay, Boreal Chickadee, Rough-legged Hawk, Northern Goshawk, Northern Hawk Owl, Snowy Owl, Boreal Owl and Great Gray Owl.

For winter finches, the cause of this phenomenon is thought to be a shortage of food in the breeding range. This shortage follows the end of "masting." Masting refers to a year in which seed production on trees is extraordinarily high. It tends to occur over a large area so that nearly all of the trees of a given species such as White Spruce or White Pine are masting at the same time. The abundance of food allows birds to lay more eggs than usual and fledge more young successfully. However, in a low food year following masting, the larger than usual numbers of seed-eating birds must migrate elsewhere to avoid starving. Unfortunately for birders, the occurrence of masting is unpredictable and dependent on a variety of weather factors.

Small mammals such as voles, mice and lemmings also have cyclic population fluctuations, themselves related to the masting years. When their numbers are high, owls fledge more young than usual, but when mammal numbers crash, they must move elsewhere to find food. Snowy Owls, for example, move south when lemming populations crash on the tundra.

In practice, the occurrence of winter irruptives is never as regular and predictable as birders would like. Winter finch invasions are especially complex. Scientists do agree, however, that the severity of the winter is not an important factor nor do all finches respond in the same way to the same conditions. The same unpredictability is characteristic of raptor invasions. The interactions between raptors and their prey are especially complex and mammal cycles are not fully understood. It is a myth, too, that northern owls are forced south because of unusually cold weather or deep snow cover. These birds are fully adapted to winter conditions and, if prey populations are high, the owls stay on their northern territories. The good news is that there is some kind of irruption every winter. If the Common Redpolls and Snowy Owls don't come, the Bohemian Waxwings and Great Gray Owls may. Every winter sees at least several irruptive species in our area.

Black-capped Chickadee.

The Great Gray Owl is probably the most impressive and visible raptor to make periodic flights into our area. Large invasions have occurred in the winters of 1978-79, 1983-84, 1995-96 and 1996-97 and were well-documented by Doug Sadler, a local naturalist and writer. In the winter of 1995-96, Sadler received reports of an astonishing 330 different Great Grays in an area including Peterborough County, west to Lake Simcoe and north and eastward into Haliburton and Hastings counties. He estimated, however, that at least 15% of these birds became known traffic casualties. Tim Dyson, an experienced bird bander who specializes in raptors, was able to band a large number of the owls. Dyson recalls seeing seven birds along one stretch of road with an incredible five birds in view at one time! His banding efforts provided valuable information on the health and age of the birds and helped to show, for example, that most of the owls had been fledged in 1994 and were in good physical condition.

Table 1.1: **Ontario's 10 Most Common Feeder Birds For 1999-2000**[1]

1.	Black-capped Chickadee	6. White-breasted Nuthatch
2.	Blue Jay	7. European Starling
3.	Downy Woodpecker	8. Common Redpoll
4.	Mourning Dove	9. American Goldfinch
5.	Dark-eyed Junco	10. Northern Cardinal

Mammals

January Highlights

All Month Long

- Moose and White-tailed Deer shed their antlers. This shows that the antler's role as a tool of defence is minimal, since predators such as wolves pose the greatest threat during the winter months, well after the antlers have fallen. By spring, the antlers have usually been completely devoured by small mammals seeking calcium and other valuable minerals.

- Deer "yard up" in conifer swamps such as in the Peterborough Crown Game Reserve. With less and less testosterone being produced, males are not nearly as aggressive as in the fall and form bachelor groups.

- On mild winter days when the temperature climbs above 4° C, bats sometimes emerge from hibernation and take "cleansing flights" to get rid of bodily wastes.

- Coyotes continue to be quite vocal during the winter months. Howling is most pronounced before the hunt and serves to gather the pack together. The animals are generally quiet after a kill.

- Mice, shrews, voles and moles remain active all winter long, as they make a living in the sub-nivean space between the earth and snow. Red Squirrels also use tunnels under the snow that lead from the home tree to a food stash or possibly another tree. During very cold weather, the squirrels remain in these tunnels. ◊

- Mice may come to feed beneath bird feeders at night. They, in turn, sometimes attract owls!

- Beavers are doing more in winter than just gnawing on sticks. Mating takes place this month or next. To tell whether a winter lodge is active, look for a dark hole at the top of the lodge where the snow has been melted away by the warmth of the occupants inside.

- Porcupines often take up residence in a large Eastern Hemlock, Tamarack or pine and will spend the winter munching away on the inner bark of the branches. Because of their short legs, they must avoid expending too much energy travelling through deep snow from one tree to another. ◊

Early January

■ Black Bears give birth to two or three cubs no larger than chipmunks. The cubs are hairless, sightless and toothless but flourish on the sow's rich milk.

Late January

■ The romantic season begins for Red Foxes and Coyotes and will last through the first half of February.

Happenings Under the Snow

Much of the mammal activity in winter is actually happening in the sub-nivean space under the snow. The temperature here remains just below 0°C even when air temperatures at the surface are much colder. In this dark, damp habitat, the snow becomes crystalline and can be easily excavated by voles, mice and shrews, which form large networks of trails. You can see these trails in field grass after the snow melts. Little do these mammals know that owls can actually hear them moving under the snow. They are especially vulnerable when in the vicinity of "ventilator shafts." These are special shafts constructed by voles in order to allow fresh air into the sub-nivean space when carbon dioxide levels become too high. It is amazing to watch an owl such as a Great Gray pounce on a seemingly lifeless expanse of snow and fly off with a vole in its talons. Although owls do represent a very real danger, the biggest threat to small mammals comes from the possibility of inadequate snow cover. If the snow does not arrive soon enough after the onset of subfreezing temperatures, many will perish.

Porcupines in Winter

The adaptations of animals that stay above the snow are just as interesting as those that dwell below. Porcupines, for example, want nothing to do with deep snow; their legs are simply too short. Often the Porcupine will select a favourite Eastern Hemlock, Tamarack or White Pine and feed almost exclusively in the same tree all winter. The foliage as well as the tender inner layer of bark (cambium) are both eaten. Porcupines will often start eating at the top of the tree and proceed along the limbs, leaving only clumps of growth on the ends. The animal cuts off twigs and small branches, eats the choice foliage and lets the rest fall to the ground. Hemlock boughs scattered on the ground are often a sign of porcupine activity. The tips of the boughs are cut off on a 45-degree angle in typical rodent fashion. The cuts are rough and show incisor teeth marks across the end. The effects of browsing on the tree are often visible from a considerable distance. Piles of scat under the tree are another telltale sign that a Porcupine is at home. Winter scat is very fibrous and often has a cashew-like shape.

During particularly cold weather, Porcupines will den up in a hollow within the tree or in a nearby rock crevice. Large piles of scat accumulate in and around the den and may actually provide insulation and discourage other animals from taking over the shelter. Porcupines stay close to the denning site all winter long in order to conserve energy.

Fishes

January Highlights

All Month Long

- Bass lie dormant under logs, weeds or rocks until the light and warmth of spring restore their energy and appetite. Smallmouth Bass virtually starve themselves over the winter. This is one reason why so few bass are ever caught by anglers at this time of year. There is also evidence that bass congregate in schools during the winter months.

- Bullheads may bury themselves in the mud of lake bottoms.

- Carp also settle into the mud bottom of a river or lake and remain partly covered by the mud all winter.

- Anglers pursue a variety of species in winter including Walleye, Yellow Perch, Northern Pike, Whitefish, Lake Trout and, in some lakes, Splake and Rainbow Trout. However, with the exception of Lake Scugog, ice fishing in the Kawarthas is restricted to northern Peterborough County. ◊

- This is a period of high fish mortality, especially for young fish. During the winter months, there is a shortage of food of appropriate size such as plankton.

Early Month

- In northern Peterborough County (division 15), the fishing seasons opens on January 1 for Northern Pike, Walleye, Brook Trout, Brown Trout and Lake Trout. The Splake and Rainbow Trout season is open all year except for December 24.

Ice Fishing

Although many fish species are essentially dormant during the winter, others remain active and continue to feed. These include Black Crappie, Walleye, Yellow Perch, Northern Pike, Whitefish, Brook Trout, Lake Trout, Rainbow Trout and Splake. However, other than Lake Scugog in Victoria County, the Kawartha lakes themselves are closed to angling in the winter. Ice fishing in this area is restricted to lakes in northern Peterborough County such as Pencil and Jack lakes. There are also a number of lakes which are open all year for Splake and Rainbow Trout fishing.

As a general rule, fishes in winter stay close to the bottom, usually within 15 to 30 centimetres. Being cold-blooded, they congregate where the water is warmest and where activity requires the least energy. Most species also frequent the shallower sections of lakes. For example, Northern Pike and Walleye are usually in less than 10 metres of water. Both of these species patrol weed beds in the winter where they hunt perch and other forage fishes. Walleye feed most heavily at dusk, during the night and again at dawn. Fishing is often best just after ice-up and then again at the end of the season.

Lake Trout, too, are usually found near the bottom. However, they will at times feed close to the icy ceiling of the lake. Phytoplankton levels are high here because sunlight penetration through the ice permits photosynthesis to take place. Zooplankton feed on the phytoplankton and baitfishes such as Lake Herring feed on the zooplankton. Herring in turn is a favourite food of Lake Trout.

Yellow Perch.

Insects and Other Invertebrates

January Highlights

All Month Long

- With a little searching, it is possible to find insects in various stages of their life cycle. The larvae of cattail moths, blackflies and Goldenrod Gall Flies and the egg masses of the Eastern Tent Caterpillar are just a few of the insects to be found. ◇

- Honeybees are the only insects to maintain an elevated body temperature all winter. They accomplish this by clustering together in a thick ball within the hive and eating stored honey to provide the necessary energy.

- Under the frozen surface of wetlands, most aquatic insects are still fairly active. Crayfish, too, continue to feed throughout the winter in our streams and rivers.

Discovering Insects in Winter

A winter walk or cross-country ski outing can be made all the more enjoyable by keeping an eye open for evidence of insect activity. It is even possible to see a few active insects themselves right in the heart of winter. For example, the beige seedheads of cattails are often home to moth larvae such as the Cattail Borer Moth. Seedheads harbouring cattail moths become especially conspicuous in late winter because the heads of most other cattails have completely blown away. Silk trails laid down by the larvae bind the down and the seeds together and keep the seeds from dispersing. This gives the seedheads a tight, compacted appearance. If you tear apart one of these seedheads, you are likely to find several larvae inside. They measure about six millimetres in length and are yellowish with brown stripes on the back. They will quickly start to move around if held in the warmth of your hand. Cattail moth larvae are a popular winter food of Black-capped Chickadees and Downy Woodpeckers. The adult moths emerge in early summer and can be seen on July evenings landing on cattail flowerheads to lay their eggs.

Blackfly larvae are also active during the winter months and can be found in all types of running water habitats from small trickles to large rivers. The larvae are several millimetres in length and resemble tiny beige worms. They are slightly thicker at the bottom end, giving them a punching-bag appearance. The larvae's abdomen is hooked securely to a silk pad attached to the substrate. The head bears fan-like structures which capture organic particles in the water such as algae and bacteria. The fans are regularly thrust into the mouth and wiped clean of food. Look for blackfly larvae on boulders, rocks, pebbles, logs and branches in shallow stretches of smoothly flowing water. The larvae will pupate into adults in the spring. Typically, over 30,000 flies will emerge from a square metre of stream bottom in good blackfly habitat!

In dead or dying trees, look for extensive patterns of grooves in exposed wood, on the wood under loose bark, or on the underside of the bark itself. These excavations are made by bark beetles and are located precisely at the point where the inner layer of bark and the outer layer of wood meet. Depending on the species of beetle, the grooves can appear just on the wood, just on the bark or on both surfaces. Galleries of uniform size are formed by the adult female beetle burrowing and laying eggs as she goes. When the eggs hatch, the weevil-like larvae tunnel out perpendicularly from the mother's burrow. These galleries increase in width since the larvae themselves are growing. The young pupate at the end of these side tunnels and emerge to the outside through round holes chewed through the bark. The whole pattern often looks like a big centipede with the larval tunnels forming the legs.

The space under loose bark often houses Grass Spider eggs as well. Look for a mass of sticky, white silk about two centimetres across. There is a little sac within the silk that contains the eggs of grass spiders. If you open the sac and put the eggs in a bottle, you may be able to see the young spiders hatch out.

If you are in field or field edge habitat, the most evident sign of insect activity is usually the ball-like enlargements on the stems of goldenrods which contain the larva of the Goldenrod Gall Fly. These are present in almost every patch of goldenrod.

On cherry trees, often found along edges of fields, you may find shiny brown rings about two centimetres long that encircle the twigs. They have a varnished appearance and are only slightly larger in circumference than the twig itself. These rings contain the eggs of the Eastern Tent Caterpillar which makes the conspicuous silken tents on cherry and apple trees in the spring. If you are not able to identify cherry trees in winter, look for small trees with large, black growths on the branches. The growths result from a viral infection known as Black Knot.

Eastern Tent Caterpillar egg masses on cherry twig.

Plants

January Highlights

All Month Long

- Evergreen woodland plants such as Wintergreen, Pipsissewa and Christmas Fern stand out in wind-blown areas or where the snow has melted away.

- Because of their thick bunches of needles, conifer branches intercept and hold the falling snow. This results in far less snow reaching the ground underneath the trees.

- White Spruce cones retain large quantities of ripe seed over the winter. This makes the White Spruce a favourite food source of winter finches such as crossbills.

- Winter trees and shrubs present a surprisingly wide spectrum of colours.

- Twigs and buds merit special attention this time of year. Because their characteristics are different for each species of tree, quick and accurate identification can be made on this basis.

- Like birds and animals, wildflowers use different strategies to survive winter. Annuals, biennials and perennials have all developed their own unique adaptations.

Pipsissewa.

The Colour of the Winter Landscape

To the practised eye, the January landscape is not nearly as drab as it might appear. Winter trees and shrubs actually present a wide spectrum of colours. These are not the rich colours of fall or the soft pastels of spring but they do proclaim the time of season just the same. Wetland edges give us reds, purples and oranges; hardwood forests are a study in greys, whites and yellows, while stands of conifers present the various greens. The following list gives an idea of the colour diversity seen even in winter:

- the bronze-green winter foliage of White Cedar
- the yellow-green of White Pine

- the blue-green of White Spruce
- the dark green of Balsam Fir
- the red twigs of Red-osier Dogwood and several willows
- the yellows and oranges of willow twigs, beech leaves and the bark of Bigtooth Aspen and Yellow Birch
- the purple crowns of distant White Birch
- the pale white-green of Trembling Aspen
- the creamy-white of White Birch
- the smooth, light grey of American Beech
- the mid-greys of White Ash and Sugar Maple
- the black-grey of Black Cherry

Winter Tree Identification

First of all, the term "twig" refers to the portion at the end of each branch that constitutes the previous year's growth. A twig's point of origin is marked by a distinctive, ring-like node around the branch and a change in the colour of the bark. Twigs tend to be smoother and more richly coloured than the rest of the branch. The buds are formed during the summer and contain the leaves and

Snow on spruce branches.

flowers for the coming year's growth. These leaves and flowers actually exist in miniature inside the buds. A bud may contain leaves only, flowers only, or both. The preformed flowers and leaves can be easily seen by picking apart the buds of the Horse Chestnut.

Buds can be on the side of the twig (lateral buds) or at the end (terminal buds). Because buds almost always form in the angle between the stem and the stalk of the leaf, both leaves and buds have the same arrangement on the twig. This arrangement can be either alternate or opposite. Buds are usually enclosed by overlapping scales called bud scales, and below each bud there is usually a leaf scar. This is the attachment point where last year's leaf grew from the twig. In the leaf scar, tiny dots can be seen. Known as bundle scars, these are the remains of conducting tubes that ran from the twig into the leaf. A small hand lens is useful for examining leaf and bundle scars. Like the characteristics of the buds, the leaf and bundle scars are important features in tree and shrub identification.

Honeysuckle, ash, maple, lilac, viburnum, elderberry and dogwood are the principal tree and shrub genera with opposite leaves and buds. Just about all of the others are alternate. The following mnemonic—which unintentionally sounds like a rallying call for animal rights—may be helpful in remembering these seven genera: HAM LIVED! (each genus except Lilac corresponds to one letter in the mnemonic; Lilac corresponds to LI).

My favourite winter buds are those of the Balsam Poplar. When rolled between your fingers, the fragrant, resinous buds exude the smell of spring, a season in which the smell of Balsam Poplar is everywhere. Other attractive buds include the plump, glossy-red buds of the American Basswood, the mealy, sulphur-yellow buds of the Bitternut Hickory and the large, sticky buds of the Horse Chestnut.

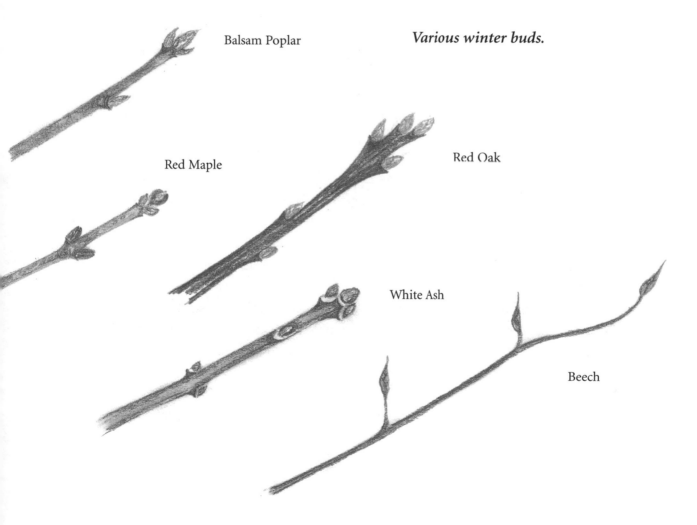

Balsam Poplar

Various winter buds.

Red Maple

Red Oak

White Ash

Beech

Plant Strategies for Winter Survival

Plants, like animals, have developed special strategies for winter survival. Wildflowers display some of the most diverse adaptations. Just as garden plants, can be annuals, biennials or perennials, the same is true for wildflowers. Annuals complete their life cycle in a single growing season and prefer open, full-sun environments. They are especially abundant in sites that have been recently disturbed. Some common native annuals include Common Ragweed and Beggar Ticks. The majority of annuals, however, are non-native and include Green Amaranth, Lamb's Quarters, Crab Grass and various mustards. With the first heavy frosts, most annuals die leaving only their seeds to survive the winter. The seeds will not germinate until they have been frozen for an extended period of time. This prevents fall germination and certain death from the cold. The seeds are long-lived and can remain dormant in the soil for years. The annuals of one group, known as winter annuals, set seed in the fall and survive the winter as a prostrate rosette of ground-hugging leaves which flower in the spring, produce seed and start the cycle again. The Daisy Fleabane is an example of a native winter annual.

Biennials take two years to produce their seeds. The first year is spent putting down roots and forming a rosette. This ring of prostrate leaves survives under the snow and sends up a stem early in the spring allowing for a quick start on the growing season. Biennials inhabit open, full-sun environments such as old fields and include the native Black-eyed Susan and Evening Primrose as well as common aliens such as Queen Anne's Lace, Common Mullein and Common Burdock. Relatively few species of plants are biennials.

The vast majority of our wildflowers are perennials. Although the above ground parts of many perennials die in the fall, the plant continues to survive below the ground, usually as a root, rhizome or tuber. Perennials often have a prominent tap root or a dense, fibrous root system. A rhizome is a root-like underground stem which produces new roots and stems allowing the plant to spread. A tuber is a short, thick underground stem. These various root-like structures continue to produce new plants for many years. After early domination by annuals and biennials, perennials soon take over field habitats. Asters, goldenrods and milkweeds are three of the most common native perennials in fields. In our woodlands, two of the best-known groups are the trilliums and orchids. In the case of many spring ephemeral wildflowers such as trilliums, the leaves and flowers that will appear in the spring have already been preformed in miniature within a bud at the tip of the underground rootstalk. Their cells are compacted and unexpanded and require only water uptake and warm spring weather to fully expand above ground (see May).

The Weather

January Highlights

All Month Long

- Snow directly shapes the composition of our plant and animal life and is the cause of many fascinating adaptations. ◇

- The weather can be mild with frequent thaws. Warm weather that arrives late in the month is known as the January Thaw.

- During evening twilight, the sky is often purple-mauve in the East and red-pink in the West.

- Our lakes are at a uniform 4° C except just below the ice surface, where the water is near the freezing point.

- We become aware of the lengthening days. Most of the daylight is gained at the end of the day in January rather than in the morning. In fact, in the first week of January dawn begins at its latest for the entire year.

Table 1.2: **January Weather Averages, 1961-1992** [2]

Daily Maximum	-3.8° C
Daily Minimum	-14.6° C
Extreme Maximum	11.7° C
Extreme Minimum	-37.9° C
Rainfall	16.0 mm
Snowfall	39.3 cm
Precipitation	49.5 mm

How Snow Affects the Natural World

Snow has a huge impact on plants and animals. By forming an insulating layer over the ground, it protects certain species while making life much more challenging for others. Deep snow makes walking and feeding difficult for White-tailed Deer but helps Snowshoe Hares to more easily reach the buds of saplings. Both plants and animals show amazing adaptations to life in a snow-covered environment. Some of these adaptations are primarily anatomical while others are behavioural. Birches, for example, have flexible trunks that bend with the weight of ice and snow without breaking. They usually spring back up when the snow melts. Snowshoe Hares and weasels turn white in the winter, thereby gaining the advantage of camouflage. The hares have also developed large feet or "snowshoes" and can therefore travel on top of the snow. Ruffed Grouse grow combs on the sides of their toes which give the birds better support when walking on the snow. Moose, on the other hand, are equipped with long, stilt-like legs that reach down through the snow to the firm ground below while keeping the animal's belly above the snow surface.

There are equally important changes in behaviour. Small mammals such as mice, voles and shrews live under the snow where they find shelter in a relatively warm environment with temperatures that rarely fall much below 0° C. Wolf packs generally choose to travel on frozen lakes in winter because lake snow becomes compacted by the wind, making walking easier. Snow forces White-tailed Deer to migrate to "deer yards" where the branches of coniferous trees intercept and hold much of the falling snow, thereby facilitating walking and feeding.

Because snow and cold drastically limit food availability, many animals hibernate or sleep through much of the winter or migrate to areas where more food is available. Studies have shown that most animals can withstand the cold as long as they have access to sufficient food. Both bird and mammal migration is much more a response to the lack of suitable food than to the onset of cold weather. Elk and caribou are notable mammal migrators; among birds the principal migratory species are the insect-eaters and ground feeders. I have often seen large flocks of healthy American Robins flying about on frigid winter days at temperatures of -25° C or colder. As long as they can find sufficient food such as berries to fuel their bodies, they do not appear to suffer from the cold. There are also many cases in which insect-eaters that winter in the tropics have been able to survive an Ontario winter by dining on suet at a backyard feeder.

Table 1.3: **Approximate Twilight, Sunrise and Sunset Times (EST)**

Date	Twilight Begins	Sunrise	Sunset	Twilight Ends
Jan. 1	7:16 a.m.	7:49 a.m.	4:45 p.m.	5:18 p.m.
Jan. 10	7:15 a.m.	7:48 a.m.	4:54 p.m.	5:26 p.m.
Jan. 20	7:11 a.m.	7:43 a.m.	5:06 p.m.	5:38 p.m.
Feb. 1	7:01 a.m.	7:32 a.m.	5:22 p.m.	5:53 p.m.

The Night Sky

January Highlights

All Month Long

- Major constellations and stars (shown in italics) visible (Jan.15, 8:00 p.m. EST) -

  Northwest: Cassiopeia and Pleiades high in sky; Andromeda (with M31 galaxy) just above, Great Square of Pegasus setting due W; Draco just below Ursa Minor

  Northeast: Gemini (with *Castor* and *Pollux*) high in sky; Big Dipper standing upright low in sky; Ursa Minor (with *Polaris*) to its left; Leo (with *Regulus*) rising over E horizon

  Southeast: dominated by Orion (with *Betelgeuse* and *Rigel*), Taurus (with *Aldebaran*) high to its right, Canis Major (with *Sirius*) low to its left, Auriga (with *Capella*) high above

  Southwest: an area called the "Water" of large, but dim constellations; Pleiades at zenith

- The night sky changes over the course of the four seasons. Each season has its representative constellations. Knowing them adds a great deal to our enjoyment of nature. ◇

- The winter sky provides a great opportunity to become familiar with the Big Dipper, Little Dipper and Cassiopeia. They are the starting points for learning the other constellations. ◇

- The early winter full moon rides higher in the sky than at any other season and passes nearly overhead at midnight. Coupled with the reflective quality of snow, moonlit winter nights shine with an unforgettable brilliance. It's a great time to go for a walk or ski.

- The Winter Six and their assortment of bright stars light up January evenings. Look for Orion, Taurus, Gemini, Auriga, Canis Major and Canis Minor.

Early January

- Quadrantid meteor shower takes place January 2-3. The point of origin is just east of the head of Draco.

A Sky Hike Through the Seasons

It comes as a surprise to many people, including many naturalists, that the night sky changes from one season to the next. The various stars and constellations come and go in much the same way as the hummingbirds fly south in the fall and the trilliums bloom in the spring. Exactly where in the sky you will see a given constellation, however, depends not only on the time of year but also on the hour of the night. All of this is due to the spinning of the earth and to our orbit around the sun. All that is really needed to explore the procession of stars and planets across the sky is the most-owned but least-used optical aids in the world—a pair of binoculars. Having some basic knowledge of the main features of the night sky and how the sky changes over the course of the four seasons engenders within us a deeper respect and appreciation for the wonder and fragility of life on earth.

Getting to Know the North Sky

The first step in learning the main stars and constellations is to become familiar with Ursa Major and its asterism, the Big Dipper. Ursa Major, Ursa Minor (Little Dipper) and Cassiopeia are known as circumpolar constellations because they appear to rotate around the North Star (*Polaris*) which is located almost exactly at the pole of the sky. They will guide you to other constellations because they are above the horizon and visible all year long. Most constellations disappear below the horizon for part of the year. There is no use looking for Orion in late spring or Leo in November.

Ursa Major (Big Bear) and the Big Dipper can always be found in the northern sector of the sky. The Dipper consists of seven stars and forms the tail and body of the Bear. To "see" the rest of the bear, look for two curves of stars. The curve in front of the Dipper's bowl forms the head and fore paw of the bear while the curve below the bowl forms the hind leg. The handle of the Dipper is the bear's tail. The two outer stars of the Dipper's bowl are known as the Pointers because they point directly to *Polaris*, the North Star. Starting at the Pointer star at the bottom of the bowl, imagine a line connecting to the upper Pointer. Project this line five times and you will have found *Polaris*. There are no other bright stars near *Polaris*. This technique works at any time of the night and at any season of the year.

Although *Polaris* is not particularly bright, it is unique. When you are facing *Polaris*, you are facing almost due north. South is therefore directly behind you, east is to your right and west is to your left. At our latitude, *Polaris* is also approximately half way up in the sky. It appears to remain stationary while Ursa Major and the other constellations seem to rotate around it. *Polaris* is also the first star in the Little Dipper's handle. This is helpful to know because the Little Dipper is a rather dim constellation.

The other well-known circumpolar constellation is Cassiopeia. Its five bright stars form an easy-to-remember "M" or "W" shape. To find Cassiopeia, imagine a line that starts where the Big Dipper's handle joins the bowl, extends through *Polaris* and continues the same distance to Cassiopeia.

The north sky.

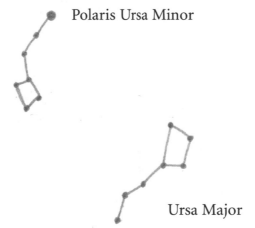

Cassiopeia

Polaris Ursa Minor

Ursa Major

Northern Cardinal in song.

NATURE'S YEAR IN THE KAWARTHAS

February—Gateway to the Year

February opens to what is traditionally the coldest week of the winter. Ice, snow and frigid temperatures usually reign supreme. Ironically, this is also the time we amuse ourselves with stories of a sleepy-eyed rodent emerging from its hole to gauge the prospects of spring. Although we cannot take the story literally, Groundhog Day does mark the mid-point of winter and, in earlier days, it was a time to take stock that you had half your hay, root crop and firewood left in order to comfortably make it to spring.

February is maybe the best month to enjoy winter. Sunset is not until 5:30 p.m. which allows for long afternoons to spend outdoors. Snow cover is more substantial as well. For some, there is the romance of the "big winter storm." It starts with an atmosphere of anticipation and the prospect of real excitement. There is the exhilaration of being out in the wind and snow and, afterwards, a spirit of camaraderie as friends and neighbours help each other dig out.

But winter can begin to weigh heavy on our psyche this month. At first glance, spring doesn't appear to be coming any time soon. Yet no matter how well-entrenched snow and ice may seem, February is indeed the "gateway to the year" and the promise of spring does begin to reveal itself this month. Forget what the calendar is saying and simply look, listen and smell. Already, there is a very noticeable stretch in daylight, American Crows and Horned Larks are returning and the first real bird song since last summer can be heard. Starlings are whistling and cackling, chickadees are singing their "fee-bee" song and even cardinals are calling once again, caught up in the urge to reaffirm their pair bonds. Our noses, too, are alerted to the coming change of season, often by the smell of a skunk out searching for a mate on a damp February night. And, in only a few more weeks, Red-winged Blackbirds will have returned to local marshes and the first Pussy Willow catkins and Wild Leeks will have emerged.

February At a Glance

Horned Larks and American Crows return to the Kawarthas. They are traditionally the first migrant arrivals of the year and mark the coming of "pre-spring." Great Horned Owls are calling and sometimes on their eggs by month's end. Bird song begins once again with cardinals and chickadees leading the chorus.

Male skunks emerge from their dens to find a mate. Their tell-tale scent is one of the first "datable" events of the new year. Male White-tailed Deer reform their bachelor groups. Deep snow can make this the most difficult time of year for deer. Mating time begins for squirrels, wolves, raccoons and minks, and will last until the end of March.

Burbot, also known as Ling, spawn under the ice in "writhing balls."

Snow Fleas can be common on woodland snow on mild, sunny days. Watch for what looks like spilled pepper!

Winter is a great time to become acquainted with lichens; on mild days, they actually photosynthesize and grow. The tan, papery leaves still clinging to young American Beech trees are a common winter sight.

Groundhog Day, February 2, marks the mid-point of winter. The first week of the month is, on average, the coldest week of the year. The average daily temperatures for the month are a maximum of -2° C and a minimum of -14°. The increased daylight becomes very noticeable in February. In mid-month, the sun is up by about 7:15 a.m. and sets by about 5:40 p.m. Days now are almost as long as in October.

Orion, Taurus, Gemini, Auriga, Canis Major and Canis Minor continue to dominate the southern and southwestern sky. The Big Dipper stands upright, low in the northeast.

Birds

February Highlights

All Month Long

■ Bird song begins once again as pair bonds are established or renewed. White-breasted and Red-breasted Nuthatches, Brown Creepers, Black-capped Chickadees, Mourning Doves, European Starlings, Northern Cardinals, House Finches and Purple Finches are some of the birds singing by mid-month. Mild, sunny mornings are the best time to hear all of these birds. ◇

■ Woodpeckers begin to drum more frequently to advertise ownership of territory.

Barred Owls sometimes leave their breeding territory during the winter and may even turn up in city parks and woodlots.

■ Male Common Goldeneyes intensify their courtship behaviour, bobbing their heads and whistling loudly.

Early February

■ Horned Larks (Prairie race) return. They are traditionally the first migrant arrivals of the year and mark the coming of "pre-spring." Along with Snow Buntings, these are birds of open, agricultural land. ◇

Mid-February

■ Ravens begin their aerial nuptial displays, diving and twisting like corkscrews over Shield country.

■ It somehow seems appropriate that Valentine's Day coincides with the return of bird song and avian love. In fact, the chickadee's three-note whistle is often represented as "Hi Sweetie."

Late February

■ Giant Canada Geese that have wintered along the Great Lakes and southwards begin arriving back in the Kawarthas.

■ Crow numbers increase as returning migrants bolster the ranks of those birds that never left. Watch for long, scattered flocks often flying at high altitudes.

■ Common Goldeneye and Common Merganser numbers increase.

- Abnormally warm weather conditions in the last week of February will bring in robins as well as blackbirds and waterfowl. This appears to be happening more often now as a result of climate change.

Table 2.1: **February Arrivals**

The arrival and departure tables provide an overview of most of the bird species migrating in or out of the Kawarthas each month of the year. However, some of the less common species are not included. Resident species (i.e. birds that are present all year round) such as Mourning Doves and House Sparrows are also not covered in the tables.

mid- month:	"Prairie" Horned Lark
late month:	"Giant" Canada Goose, Common Goldeneye (w), Common Merganser (w), Herring Gull, American Crow (w)

Renewing Pair Bonds

For many of our resident birds, the first step in the breeding cycle begins in February. This is the formation or reaffirmation of a pair bond between a male and female. With long-lived species such as geese, cranes and some owls, the same pair of birds may remain together in a monogamous relationship for life. For other species, a pair may stay together for several successive breeding seasons (Tree Swallows, Mourning Doves), for one entire breeding season (most songbirds) or for only a single nesting (House Wrens). In some species, such as American Robins, pairing arrangements seem to vary with individual birds.

Even in the case of birds that have a lifelong pair bond, the attachment weakens during the fall and early winter. The birds may be indifferent or even aggressive to each other during this time. By late winter, however, a reaffirmation of the pair bond begins. This is especially apparent in cardinals. Although the male and female remain together throughout the year, the bond is relaxed in the non-breeding season. But, starting in February, the male starts to sing regularly once again and both sexes often feed together. The male White-breasted Nuthatch is also becoming much more interested in the female with which he shares the same territory throughout the year. He sings in her presence, bows before her, fluttering his wings and cocking his tail, and may even bring her food. Male Black-capped Chickadees sing their "fee-bee" song much more often starting in mid-winter. This serves to attract a new mate or to strengthen the pair bond with an existing partner; some chickadees actually remain mated for life. Chickadee flocks begin to break up as spring approaches, and pairs take up residence on nesting territories.

Pine Siskins and Red-and White-winged Crossbills are three other species that sing and even nest in the middle of winter. These birds are highly nomadic winter visitors to the Kawarthas. Given sufficient food supplies, they will nest in any season of the year. The White-winged Crossbill has a particularly loud, chattery song that it often sings from the top of conifers. Listen for this species in areas where White Spruce, Tamarack, Eastern Hemlock and Balsam Fir are plentiful. They are most common in years with big crops of cone.

Although crossbills may turn up anywhere on the Shield, you can often find them in the Peterborough Crown Game Reserve, along County Road 507 to Gooderham, in the vicinity of Chandos Lake and along the Jack Lake Road south of Apsley. Crossbills often land right on the road to pick up grit which they ingest to help grind up their diet of conifer seeds. Although there has never been a crossbill nest found in Peterborough County, there is no reason why the birds would not nest here. In fact, crossbills and siskins were observed gathering nesting material in February and March of 1999. One Pine Siskin nest was found in April of 1986.

The strengthening of the pair bond is also evident in larger birds. The first species of the year to begin breeding activity is the Great Horned Owl. Male Barred Owls also become more vocal during this period. Barred Owls are highly territorial and will respond to imitations of their call and to tapes. Even during the day, they will often call back to you and sometimes fly in and land close by. Some Barred Owls leave their territory during the winter, seemingly to search for food. They are sometimes seen in parks and other wooded areas within towns and cities. There are often winter reports of Barred Owls in the City of Peterborough.

Courtship behaviour is also evident in Red-tailed Hawks during the late winter. Males and females start to perch close together, often in the same tree. They may also soar close to each other in wide circles and the male may even present the female with food. This is referred to as "courtship feeding."

Ravens also mate for life and stay together throughout the year. However, there is still a courtship period every winter as a first step in the reproduction process. During courtship behaviour, the birds can be seen soaring with wingtips nearly touching. The male may perform aerial acrobatics, sometimes actually tumbling in mid-air. These behaviours usually occur in the vicinity of the nest, which is generally located on a rock ledge or in a large conifer.

The courtship display of male ducks such as goldeneyes is especially interesting to observe at this time. The males can be heard uttering a loud, whistling call as they throw their head back and point their bill up in the air in an effort to impress the female. There are usually up to 50 of these beautiful black and white ducks along the Otonabee River during the winter months.

Horned Larks and Snow Buntings

By mid-February, "Prairie" Horned Larks (*Eremophila alpestris praticola*) are arriving back in the Kawarthas; along with American Crows, they are the first returning migrants of "pre-spring." Larks can often be seen along roadsides in open agricultural country and on fields recently spread with manure. Their tingling song is given in flight and can be heard even on the coldest days. The notes have a high-pitched, crystal quality which seems to complement the winter landscape. Horned Larks begin nesting in these same fields in late March.

Snow Buntings are another species of open fields. They arrive in late fall from the Arctic and spend the entire winter in our area. In the early winter, Snow Buntings are quite brown, but by spring their plumage has worn to mostly black and white. In all plumages, their large white wing patches, distinctive call and unique flight behaviour immediately identify them. Snow Buntings are amazing to watch in flight as they swirl and veer in unison, functioning more like a single bird than like a flock of 50. They always appear restless and continually land and take off again. When Snow Buntings alight on a snow-covered field, their mostly white colouration provides remarkable camouflage and the birds literally disappear from sight. Snow Buntings usually do not come to feeders but are sometimes attracted to seed scattered on the ground in areas adjacent to open fields. They also have a habit of landing on television antennas and on treetops in open areas. Most Snow Buntings leave the Kawarthas in March, usually before the snow melts.

Mammals

February Highlights

All Month Long

- Look for River Otters in winter around areas of flowing water such as streams and rivers.

- Gray Squirrels mate in February and can often be seen streaming by in treetop chases.

- Mating time also begins for Raccoons, Striped Skunks and American Mink. Mating activity will last until the end of March. ◇

- Bats that are overwintering in attics and other dry building environments will sometimes emerge from hibernation to try to find water. They usually die soon after.

Early February

- Don't waste your time looking for Groundhogs. No sane "woodchuck" is out of hibernation yet, and the last thought in their mid-winter dreams is whether the February sky is clear or cloudy!

Mid-February

- Male Striped Skunks roll out of their dens any time from mid-February to early March and go on a long prowl looking for females with which to mate. The smell of a skunk on a damp, late winter night is a time-honoured sign of spring and one of the first "datable" natural events of the new year.

Late February

- In years of deep snow, late winter is the most difficult part of the year for White-tailed Deer and Moose. ◇

- Wolves mate between now and the middle of March. Each mated pair can produce up to six pups.

Mammals on the Make

The so-called "dead of winter" is anything but dead for many of our mammals. Many species must mate at this time for their young to be born in April or early May when food becomes more plentiful and conditions in general are more conducive to raising a family. This is the case for some of our best known mammals—Gray Squirrels, "Eastern" Wolves, Coyotes, Red Foxes, Raccoons, Striped Skunks and American Mink—all of which have a gestation period averaging about two months. Because mammals tend to be so secretive, most mating activity goes on without our knowledge. There is one indicator, however, that everyone knows—the smell of a skunk on the prowl on a mild February or March night—one of the reliable first "datable" natural events of the new year. For some rural dwellers, the dog getting sprayed is practically a sign of spring!

A skunk can spray up to a distance of four metres and with surprising accuracy. The smell is so potent that it can cover six square kilometres. The active ingredient in the spray is butyl mercaptan, a compound which was used in World War I to make mustard gas!

Skunks often overwinter communally in groups of up to 12 individuals, most of which are females. Being polygamous, the male mates with all the females in the den before heading out to look for love elsewhere.

Striped Skunk on the prowl.

White-tailed Deer in Winter

Deer do not cope especially well with winter. In Ontario, White-tailed Deer are at the northern fringe of their range. They lack the anatomical adaptations such as long legs that moose have developed. When there is more than 50 centimetres of soft snow on the ground, deer are seriously handicapped and must expend large amounts of energy simply walking from one point to another. They have, however, adapted in terms of their behaviour. Every year most deer migrate to special wintering areas where the snow cover is thinner and browse is available. In agricultural lands, this wintering site may be a cedar swamp or flood plain or simply the south-facing slope of a woodlot or field. In more northern locations, many deer move into larger sites known as "deer yards." This is an area of mostly coniferous tree cover. Conifers offer browse, protection from the wind and less snow to contend with because much of it remains caught in the branches. The deer spend many hours lying under the protective boughs of these conifers. Deer yards are crisscrossed with a network of trampled trails used by the animals to move from the shelter of the softwoods to hardwood browse sites. These trails further decrease the amount of energy that the animals need to expend. The largest deer yard in the Kawarthas is the Peterborough Crown Game Reserve north of Stony Lake.

The winter diet of deer consists mainly of deciduous buds and twigs, conifer branches and both coniferous and deciduous saplings. Some of the preferred species include White Cedar, Eastern Hemlock, Canada Yew, Staghorn Sumac, Red Maple, White Ash, Yellow Birch, American Basswood and Apple. On south-facing slopes, deer are able to find various grasses and other plants exposed through melting. If corn is available, it is also a very popular food item. In deer yards, however, most of the new twig growth on woody shrubs may have been consumed by late winter; the animals sometimes end up relying on older twigs which have a much lower food value. This becomes a serious problem when snow forces the animals into the deer yards early in the winter, or when deep snow confines them to already overbrowsed areas. Even during an average winter, deer still lose up to 25 per cent of their body weight.

Surprisingly, a deer's food demands decrease during cold weather, because its metabolic activity slows down. During extended cold periods, deer will enter a state of semi-dormancy, sometimes called "hibernation on the hoof." This is an adaptation to survive the relative lack of food and the adversity of winter weather. Food demands can decrease by 30%. The animals will also bed down for much longer periods of time.

Even with these adaptations, if appropriate browse becomes too scarce, the doe will actually resorb the developing fetus into her body, and no fawn will be born in the spring. Weakened deer may also fall victim to coyotes and wolves or even to dogs that are allowed to run loose. This is a serious problem during winters with deep, prolonged snow cover and when the snow is crusty. Fawns may be the first to fall victim to predators because most of their food has been directed to body growth. They have little time to build fat reserves in the fall. Adult bucks, weakened by the frantic activity of the rut, may also be at risk.

In years of severe food shortage and only as a last resort, humans sometimes provide deer with supplementary or emergency feeding. This may involve cutting browse for the deer or, in extreme situations, providing mixed grain. It is wise to contact the Ministry of Natural Resources before going ahead with such measures. Providing the wrong type of food can actually kill the deer.

Fishes

February Highlights

All Month Long

- Burbot, also known as Ling or Freshwater Cod, spawn under the ice on rocky lake bottoms. Spawning activity occurs throughout February and into early March. ◇

Love Under the Ice

The Burbot, one of the lesser known of Ontario's fish, actually waits until the depths of winter to begin spawning. Also known as the Ling, Freshwater Cod or Lawyer, the Burbot is an elongated fish with a single barbel on the chin. Along with a few landlocked populations of Atlantic Tomcod in the Maritimes, the Burbot is the only surviving freshwater member of the cod family. Spawning takes place under the ice at night on rocky lake and river bottoms in anywhere from 30 centimetres to 3 metres of water. The fish form "writhing balls" of about a dozen intertwined individuals which actually move across the lake bottom. No nest is constructed and there is no parental care provided to the eggs or the young.

The Burbot was long regarded as an undesirable fish because of its strange appearance and predacious feeding habits. In fact, large scale eradication programs have taken place in the past to try to reduce Burbot numbers. Now, however, the Burbot is being promoted as an excellent eating fish. This is being done in an attempt to take pressure off Walleye and Lake Trout populations. Ice fishermen usually catch Burbot after dark in the same winter habitats as Walleye and Lake Trout. Burbot can be found in most of the lakes in the Kawarthas.

Insects and Other Invertebrates

February Highlights

All Month Long

- On mild, sunny days, check the snow around the base of large trees for Snow Fleas. What looks like spilled pepper may begin to jump around right before your eyes!

- Wingless scorpion-flies and wingless winter crane flies can often be found walking in the snow on cloudy winter days with mild temperatures. The latter is very slow moving, has long legs and is amazingly spider-like in appearance.

Late February

- Wingless scorpion-flies and wingless winter crane flies can often be found walking on the snow on cloudy winter days with mild temperatures. The latter is very slow moving, has long legs and is amazingly spider-like in appearance.

- In late February and through much of March, stoneflies emerge from creeks and rivers, and hundreds can sometimes be seen crawling on the adjacent snow.

Snow Fleas

The Snow Flea is probably the best known of the winter insects. On a mild, sunny day in February or March, carefully examine the snow adjacent to open ground where leaves and grass have been exposed through melting. The base of a tree along the edge of a sunny trail or field is a good place to try. What may initially appear like soot or pepper scattered on the snow will suddenly start jumping about in front of you! The organisms in question are Snow Fleas—wingless, pinhead-sized insects belonging to the order *Collembola*, the springtails. By using a magnifying glass or the "wrong end" of your binoculars, you may be able to see why springtail is such an appropriate name. A careful examination will reveal a tail-like structure folded under the hind end which, when released, catapults the tiny insect out of sight (actually just several centimetres away).

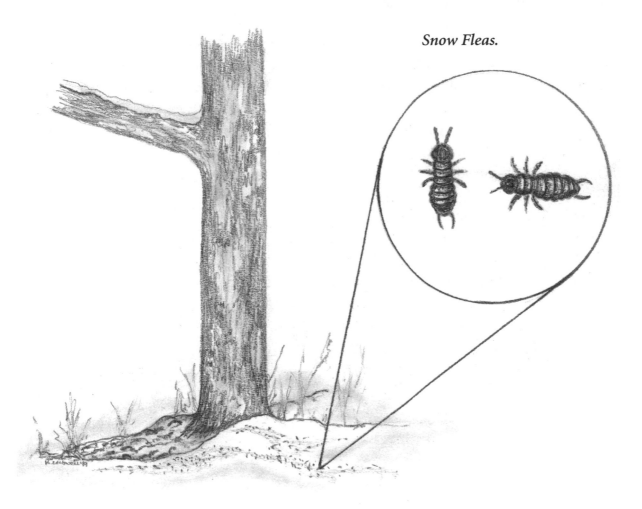

Snow Fleas.

Snow Fleas inhabit the soil and leaf litter in astonishing numbers and may actually be the most abundant insect species. Some estimates run as high as ten million individuals per acre. They are vegetarians and consume leaf mold, algae and pollen. In the winter, they like to take advantage of the warm microclimate present on the snow's surface where the temperature can be substantially higher than the surrounding air. The Snow Fleas you see may be eating organic material present on the snow or simply travelling across the snow cover from one site to another. At night, they return to the shelter of the leaf litter.

Winter Stoneflies

Another insect to watch for in mid-to-late winter is the winter stonefly. On mild, sunny days, adult stoneflies can often be seen crawling over the snow in areas close to running water. Winter stoneflies have a particularly interesting life history. After hatching in the spring, the stonefly nymphs bury themselves in the stream bed and spend the whole summer lying dormant in the mud. They become active again in the fall and feed and grow quickly for several months. Sometime during mid-to-late winter, the nymphs migrate to shallow riffles and stream banks, where they transform into adults and leave the water to find a mate. Adult stoneflies are weak flyers and do not stray far from the water's edge. After mating, the females return to the stream to lay their eggs.

One species commonly seen along Jackson Creek near Peterborough is the Small Winter Stonefly. On bright, mild days, it can often be found in large numbers right on the walking trail adjacent to the creek. It is black, measures about 8 millimetres in length and its wings are folded flat over its back. It also has two prominent tails (*cerci*). Since stoneflies are able to survive only in clean, moving water, their presence is an indicator of good water quality. In parts of the United States, winter stonefly numbers are monitored each year in order to gauge the health of streams.

Winter Stonefly.

Plants

February Highlights

All Month Long

■ On mild winter days when sufficient moisture is available, lichens are able to carry out photosynthesis and to actually grow. ◇

■ Young American Beech trees retain many of their tan, papery leaves for the entire winter. ◇

■ Several species of shrubs still have fruit "on the vine," even in mid-winter. These include Highbush-Cranberry, Staghorn Sumac and Maple-leaved Viburnum. Because the fat content of these fruits is quite low, they are seldom eaten by birds or squirrels until all other food sources fail. For example, I rarely see birds eating sumac fruit until March!

Lichens

Of all the conspicuous organisms in the natural landscape, lichens are probably the most overlooked. Winter can be a good time to get to know this interesting division of the Fungi kingdom. One reason why lichens are so amazing is that they often grow in the most inhospitable places possible—like on sun-scorched rocks and on the bare bark of trees. These incredibly hardy organisms consist of an alga and a fungus living together as a single unit. In this well-known symbiotic relationship, the alga photosynthesizes food both for itself and for the fungus. The fungus in return provides the alga with mineral nutrients and with water, which it rapidly absorbs from the air. Lichens survive the cold of winter by drying out to the point of becoming brittle. If temperatures climb above freezing, however, and if sufficient moisture becomes available, they can photosynthesize and grow even in winter.

Some of the most common lichens in the Kawarthas are those belonging to the genus *Parmelia*. They are pale grey or light green leaf lichens that typically grow on trees, logs and rocks. Some species of

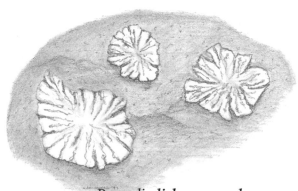

Parmelia **lichen on rock.**

Parmelia are pollution-tolerant and can easily be found on the bark of urban trees. *Parmelia* lichen are used by Ruby-throated Hummingbirds and Eastern Wood-Pewees in the construction of their nests. A winter ski outing along a rock ridge or through a conifer swamp can be a convenient time to look for some of the other common lichens. These include Lungwort, Rock Tripe, Powder Horn Lichen, False Pixie Cup and the familiar British Soldiers. *Forest Plants of Central Ontario* (see bibliography) is a good general guide to our lichens.

Winter Beech Leaves

Anyone who has spent time in the winter woods will have noticed that some of the smaller deciduous trees hold on to their dead leaves. This is especially true for young American Beech trees although Sugar Maple, Ironwood (Hop-hornbeam) and even mature oaks often retain a number of their leaves, as well. The bleached, ghostly leaves of the beech, however, are the main show. Unlike other species, beech leaves do not twist completely out of shape but maintain much the same form as in the summer. They are especially beautiful on a winter morning when the sun's rays pass directly through them. Dead beech leaves were used to stuff mattresses in pioneer times because they are not only soft but also springy and long-lasting. Why some trees hold their leaves throughout the winter remains a mystery. It is safe to assume, however, that some advantage accrues to the tree by doing so. Almost all of the leaves will have fallen from the trees by the time the leaves emerge in the spring.

Weather

February Highlights

All Month Long
- Days are now as long as in October. More than an hour has been gained since Dec. 21. Daylight is with us until almost 6:00 p.m.

Early February
- The first week of February is, on average, the coldest week of the winter.
- Groundhog Day, February 2, marks the mid-point of winter. ◇

Late February
- Late winter thaws regenerate the human spirit!

Young American Beech with previous summer's leaves still attached.

Table 2.2: **February Weather Averages, 1961-1990**

Daily Maximum	-2.4° C
Daily Minimum	-13.6° C
Extreme Maximum	12.5° C
Extreme Minimum	-37.8° C
Rainfall	22.1 mm
Snowfall	33.4 cm
Precipitation	55.1 mm

Groundhog Day

Even though the first week of February is statistically the coldest week of the winter, tradition steers our thoughts to spring at this time and to the escapades of the Groundhog. This familiar member of the squirrel family is supposed to arise and to rule on the arrival date of spring. If it sees its shadows, the timid animal will immediately dive back into its burrow and winter will continue for six more weeks. If there is no shadow, spring will soon be at hand. Unfortunately, as most people know, the Groundhog is a true hibernator and sleeps right through the whole event. In fact, while humans may be celebrating the prospect of an early spring, the woodchuck is curled up underground and getting by on only one breath and four heartbeats per minute!

The Groundhog Day tradition is linked both to Roman times and to the Christian celebration of Candlemas Day. In mid-winter, the Romans burned candles to Februa, the mother of Mars, asking for her intercession in bringing about an early, clement spring. The burning of candles later became part of the Christian Candlemas celebration which also takes place on February 2. Although it commemorates the purification of the Virgin Mary, Candlemas has long been associated with the idea of forecasting the coming of spring. An old English poem states:

> "If Candlemas Day be fair and bright,
> Winter will have another flight."
> If Candlemas Day be cloud and rain,
> Then winter will not come again."

Many early peoples believed that animals had the ability to forecast the weather; they therefore looked for portents to tell if spring would be early or late. The badger became the Candlemas forecaster in England. Although English badgers are dormant much of the winter, they do occasionally come out of their "setts" and can be seen grooming themselves. It is therefore likely that people would have seen badgers at this time of year. It is also probable that the early English settlers who came to North America mistook the Groundhog for a type of badger and simply transferred the weather forecasting tradition onto the shoulders of our sleep-loving rodent.

Table 2.3: **Approximate Twilight, Sunrise and Sunset Times (EST)**

Date	Twilight Begins	Sunrise	Sunset	Twilight Ends
Feb. 1	7:01 a.m.	7:32 a.m.	5:22 p.m.	5:53 p.m.
Feb. 10	6:51 a.m.	7:21 a.m.	5:35 p.m.	6:05 p.m.
Feb. 20	6:37 a.m.	7:06 a.m.	5:49 p.m.	6:18 p.m.
Mar. 1	6:21 a.m.	6:50 a.m.	6:02 p.m.	6:31p.m.

The Night Sky

February Highlights

All Month Long

- Major constellations and stars visible (February 15, 8:00 p.m. EST)

  Northwest: Pleiades high in W; Cassiopeia in mid-sky; Great Square of Pegasus at horizon; Andromeda (with M31 galaxy) just above it

  Northeast: Gemini (with *Castor* and *Pollux*) near Zenith; Auriga (with *Capella*) to its left; Big Dipper standing upright low in the sky; Little Dipper (with *Polaris*) to its left; Leo (with *Regulus*) to its left

  Southeast: Gemini near Zenith; Canis Minor (with *Procyon*) below Gemini; Canis Major (with *Sirius*) due S

  Southwest: dominated by Orion (with *Betelgeuse* and *Rigel*); Taurus (with *Aldebaran*) high to its right; Canis Major (with *Sirius*) low to its left; Auriga (with *Capella*) high above

- All winter long, Orion dominates the night sky.

- Leo, the constellation of spring, holds sway over the early morning sky as we head for work. Its promise of spring somehow makes the cold and darkness easier to endure.

Orion, the Constellation of Winter

No other constellation is as conspicuous and easy to remember as Orion, the Hunter. Maybe this is because Orion is one constellation that actually looks like its namesake. The belt, sword, shield and club are all easy to see and imagine. Of the four bright stars that form Orion's shoulders and knees, two are particularly impressive. *Betelgeuse*, which forms the left shoulder, is a reddish supergiant, 600 times the diameter of the sun. In the original Arabic, *Betelgeuse* is usually translated as "armpit of the great one." This seems like an apt name for one as boastful and vain as Orion! The lower right corner of Orion's torso is occupied by *Rigel*, a magnificent bluish-white star 50,000 times as luminous as our sun. For fans of science fiction, it is interesting to note that *Rigel* was an occasional destination of the starship "Enterprise" in the popular television series, "Star Trek."

The most fascinating aspect of this huge constellation, however, is the Orion Nebula. In order to find it, locate the three faint stars that make up the "sword" hanging from Orion's belt. If you examine the middle star closely, you will notice that it appears hazy. This is the Orion Nebula, the brightest of all the nebulae in the night sky. The nebula's indistinct, cloud-like appearance is visible through binoculars but becomes spectacular in even a small telescope. On a dark, clear night, far from the city lights, a small scope will allow you to see "bays and rifts" of stellar material intertwining themselves around four stars. This is known as the Trapezium. Parts of this greenish cloud of gas and dust are actually contracting to form new stars. Because of this, the Orion Nebula is often referred to as a star nursery. It measures about 26 light years across and is located about 1,500 light years from Earth.

For thousands of years, Orion has been identified as a person by cultures all over the world. The most well-known Orion legend, however, comes to us from Greek mythology. The Greeks saw Orion as a boastful hunter who claimed that no animal could overcome him. The spiteful goddess Hera therefore sent out a scorpion which succeeded in biting Orion on the heel and killing him. She then placed Orion in the sky for eternity as a warning to others. His two hunting dogs, Canis Major and Canis Minor, were placed alongside their master as well as the hare, Lepus, that they were pursuing. Scorpius, however, was placed on the opposite side of the heavens so that the two constellations would never appear together in the night sky.

Like the Big Dipper, Orion is useful in locating other stars and constellations. The belt acts as a pointer in two directions. To the right, it points to *Aldebaran* in Taurus, the Bull, and then on towards the Pleiades. To the left, the belt points to *Sirius* in Canis Major; *Sirius* is the brightest of all the stars. A line extended from *Rigel* through *Betelgeuse* points to Gemini, the Twins.

Spring

Song Sparrow singing in Red Maple.

Red Squirrel nipping maple twig to start a sap flow.

CHAPTER 3

March—Waiting for Spring-to-be

March is a time of waiting—waiting for spring-to-be. Our patience, however, is starting to wear thin. Whenever we think that winter is finally ready to give up her reign, we are hit by yet another blast of cold and snow. March is essentially a tug-of-war between winter and spring. And anything and everything goes—wind, snow, frigid cold, freezing rain, thundershowers, near-summer warmth. For this seems a month without rules.

March doesn't always flaunt the signs of spring. Many are subtle and reveal themselves only to those who actively search them out. But despite what the day-to-day weather may be doing, many indications of the impending change of season simply can't be missed. The sun now is higher, brighter and warmer; we have daylight from six a.m. until early evening; Leo, the constellation of spring, looms high in the east; the daytime sky is full of noisy flocks of crows, and local wetlands are brightened by Pussy Willow buds as they reveal their insulating tufts of white hairs. The first true spring migrants are only a mild spell away; a period of warm weather will bring in a flood of ducks and at least half a dozen species of songbirds.

In March, our sense of smell is reawakened by the spicy fragrance of sun-warmed Balsam Poplar resin, by the delicious aroma of boiling maple sap and by the pervasive odour of the thawing earth. Our ears are reacquainted with bird song as Red-winged Blackbirds, American Robins and a dozen other migrants once again advertise ownership of nesting territories. Our taste buds are treated to maple taffy, hardened over snow. All our senses tell us that the warmth and intense activity of "high spring" are coming. But let's not rush the season. Each stage of spring's arrival needs to be savoured, because it will be over all too soon.

March At a Glance

The first songbirds return this month with Red-winged Blackbirds and robins leading the way; bird song increases accordingly. Large numbers of waterfowl can be found on open sections of lakes and rivers. The first Tree Swallows return to the Kawarthas. This is also a great month to hear a variety of owls.

Mammals with a short gestation period mate this month. These include Chipmunks, Muskrats, Red Squirrels and Groundhogs. Wolves, Coyotes and Red Foxes may bear their young by month's end.

This is a good time to learn or review the calls of our frogs and toads. They are distinctive and easy to remember.

Snow Fleas are often abundant on the woodland snow. Stoneflies become more common, as well. Mourning Cloak butterflies are sometimes seen flying on warm days. Swarms of midges and the arrival of March Flies are a sure sign of spring.

Sugar Maples are tapped this month. The catkins of Pussy Willows and aspens break through their bud scales. Lilac and Red-berried Elder buds are swelling noticeably and the first Coltsfoot may bloom. The leaves of Wild Leek poke through the snow.

Just about any kind of weather can be expected this month. The lengthening days and the increased warmth and brightness of the sun are especially apparent. Daily maximum temperatures now average 3° C and minimums -7° C. The mid-March sun rises at about 6:25 a.m. and sets at about 6:20 p.m.

The spring sky offers more brilliant stars and constellations than any other season. Although the winter constellations are still visible, the signature constellation of spring is Leo. The Big Dipper stands high in the northeast.

Birds

March Highlights

All Month

- Male crows give courtship displays which include fluffing up their body feathers, bowing repeatedly and singing softly.

- The first songbirds return this month. Among the most anticipated are American Robins, Eastern Bluebirds, Eastern Phoebes, Red-winged Blackbirds, Eastern Meadowlarks and Song Sparrows. Bird song increases accordingly. If you don't already know the songs of these common birds, this is a great time to start learning them. ◇

- Open sections of local lakes and rivers are host to thousands of northward-bound ducks, impatiently awaiting the departure of the ice. Little Lake, Lake Katchewanooka and Gannon's Narrows are popular stopover points. ◇

- Starlings and House Sparrows are already laying claim to nest boxes. Pairs of noisy Canada Geese are staking out nesting territories on still-frozen ponds. Common Ravens and Gray Jays are busy incubating their eggs.

- This is usually the best time of the year to listen for owls. As many as four or five species can sometimes be heard. If out owling late in the month, you may also hear the first Ruffed Grouse, Common Snipe and American Woodcock. ◇

- Late winter and early spring is the only time of the year when large numbers of Red-winged Blackbirds are found in the city. They even come to feeders during this period.

Early March

- This is the only time of year that spotting a robin generates real excitement. There is, however, an irksome question. Is the bird a true migrant or simply an over-winterer? The situation is especially complicated in Peterborough, where small numbers of robins regularly spend the winter. However, migrant or not, an early March robin is always a welcome sight.

- Great Horned Owls are usually on their eggs by now. Biologists now believe that early nesting allows the young owls to be ready to learn their hunting skills in late spring when prey is most plentiful and the majority of prey animals are young themselves and therefore inexperienced at avoiding enemies.

Mid-March

■ Pairs of Red-tailed Hawks begin soaring over their woodlot territories.

Late March

■ Small flocks of Tree Swallows, the first true insect eaters to return to the Kawarthas, can usually be seen flying low over the Otonabee River and Little Lake in the last few days of March. ◇

■ Bald Eagles leave the Kawarthas, probably for northern Ontario. Many local naturalists believe, however, that eagles will soon become a regular breeding species in the Kawarthas. As of 2001, one Bald Eagle nest was known of in the area.

■ Snow Geese are now annual visitors to the Kawarthas during spring migration. Both the blue and white phases occur here. They are often found among Giant Canada Geese. Tundra Swans, too, are turning up more regularly, possibly because of a change in their migration route.

■ Sandhill Cranes return and can sometimes be heard calling at dawn and dusk and seen performing their courtship dance. It includes head bobbing, bowing and leaping into the air.

Table 3.1: **March Arrivals and Departures**

early month

arrivals:	Bufflehead (w), Hooded Merganser, Ring-billed Gull, Herring Gull, Northern Saw-whet Owl (w), American Robin (w), Red-winged Blackbird
departures:	Pine Grosbeak*

mid-month

arrivals:	Pied-billed Grebe, Great Blue Heron, Tundra Swan, Mallard (w), American Black Duck, Wood Duck, Ring-necked Duck, Greater Scaup, Northern Harrier, Red-shouldered Hawk, Red-tailed Hawk (w), American Kestrel (w), Killdeer, Eastern Bluebird, Song Sparrow, Eastern Meadowlark, Brown-headed Cowbird, Common Grackle
departures:	Golden Eagle

late month

arrivals:	Turkey Vulture, Snow Goose, Gadwall, Northern Shoveler, Northern Pintail, American Wigeon, Green-winged Teal, Blue-winged Teal, Redhead, Lesser Scaup, Canvasback, Cooper's Hawk(w), Sandhill Crane, American Woodcock, Common Snipe, Belted Kingfisher (w), Northern Flicker, Eastern Phoebe, Tree Swallow, Golden-crowned Kinglet (w), American Tree Sparrow (w), Rusty Blackbird

| departures: | Bald Eagle, Glaucous Gull*, Great Black-backed Gull, Iceland Gull*, Snow Bunting. As well, Rough-legged Hawks, Snowy Owls* Great Gray Owls and Northern Hawk Owls |

* depart in early spring but dates are difficult to pinpoint or data are incomplete.

Bird Song Returns in Force

The dreary silence of winter has definitely lost its grip by early March. Although not the full medley of April and May, there is now a wide selection of bird song to be heard on mild, pleasant mornings. The songs of Northern Cardinals, Blue Jays, Killdeer, Mourning Doves, Song Sparrows, House Finches, Common Grackles, Brown-headed Cowbirds, Red-winged Blackbirds and American Robins as well as soon-to-depart Dark-eyed Juncos and American Tree Sparrows announce the debut of another season of avian romance. March is therefore a great time to memorize the songs. Since the number of species singing this month is still fairly small, learning the various vocalizations is manageable. If you can remember these songs, you'll be better able to detect the new voices which will join the soundscape in April and May.

Some Tips on Learning Bird Song

There is a great deal of satisfaction to be derived—and frustration to be avoided—by recognizing at least the common bird songs. Even before the leaves come out you will probably hear three or four times as many birds as you will see; with practice, they can all be identified by song. To the practised ear, a chorus of bird song is like a symphony in which you recognize each of the individual instruments. However, to memorize bird song as pure sound is extremely difficult for most people. For most of us, including myself, it is much easier to convert the songs to a mnemonic or memory-aid. Fortunately, most of this work has already been done for us. The Red-breasted Nuthatch sounds like a child's toy horn; the American Bittern sounds like an old pump, and the Rose-breasted Grosbeak sings like an "American Robin who has taken voice lessons." The mnemonics that work best for me are the English "translation" variety. The best known of these include the "teacher, teacher, teacher" of the Ovenbird, the "drink your tea" of the Eastern Towhee and the "who cooks for you" of the Barred Owl. Some birders even make up their own mnemonic for a given species.

There is no doubt that some species sound similar to others. However, when you take into consideration the context of the song—habitat, time of year and the bird's behaviour—the choice usually comes down to one species. The context is the secret trick that birders use to make what might otherwise seem like extraordinary acoustic identifications.

A pair of Red-tailed Hawks.

NATURE'S YEAR IN THE KAWARTHAS

Start by learning the songs of the species that are most common in your own backyard. These will probably include the American Robin, Mourning Dove, House Finch, House Sparrow, Blue Jay, American Crow, European Starling and Black-capped Chickadee. I find that tapes are very helpful and regularly listen to them in the car for review purposes. Initially, you may wish to make up your own tape that includes only the most common species. You may even want to add the mnemonic of your choice to the soundtrack. By consulting a variety of different field guides and reference books, you can come up with a fairly complete list of mnemonics.

When I hear the right birds at the right time in the expected places then I know that the natural world is operating as it should and that, despite the myriad obstacles of migration, the birds of spring have once again returned.

The Waterfowl Spectacle Begins

One of the highlights of March is the large number of waterfowl that congregate along the Otonabee River, at Gannon's Narrows, on Little Lake, Lake Katchewanooka, Upper and Lower Buckhorn Lakes and Rice Lake. The birds use bodies of open water as feeding and staging grounds before pushing further north. Even on Little Lake, which lies in the heart of Peterborough, it is not uncommon to find over 500 individual birds at a time and up to 20 species. For local naturalists and bird enthusiasts, viewing migratory waterfowl in late March and early April has always been a rite of spring. Not only are the birds in immaculate breeding plumage, but they are often quite close to shore and therefore easy to observe. Some of the ducks that are present in the largest numbers include Ring-necked Duck, Hooded Merganser, Common Merganser, Common Goldeneye, Lesser Scaup, Bufflehead and Mallard. In addition, Pied-billed Grebes are usually seen. In recent years, small numbers of Snow Geese have also been annual visitors to the Kawarthas during spring migration. Tundra Swans, too, are being recorded here more often.

You may also wish to visit Presqu'ile Provincial Park near Brighton for their annual Waterfowl Viewing Weekends. These take place on the last two weekends in March. Some years, over ten thousand waterfowl are present including small numbers of Tundra Swans. Several duck species that occur uncommonly in Peterborough County can be seen in abundance at Presqu'ile. These include Canvasback, Redhead and Greater Scaup. All three are prairie nesters, which use larger lakes for staging. Spotting scopes are set up for use by the public, and experts are on hand to answer questions and to help with identification.

Lesser Scaup

Pied-Billed Grebe

Wood Duck

Hooded Merganser

Common waterbirds seen during migration in the Kawarthas.

Listening for Owls

Owls also make their presence known in March. Nesting Great Horned Owls hoot from woodlots, Eastern Screech-Owls sing their long "whinny" from wooded habitats mostly south of Peterborough and, further north, Barred Owls hoot and scream from mixed coniferous and deciduous forests. These resident species are joined this month by Saw-whet Owls; some are only passing through on their way north while others will remain here to breed. Their single-note whistle, which is monotonously repeated without any interruption, can often be heard on March nights. Some years there are also Snowy Owls still lingering in the area and, more rarely, Northern Hawk Owls and Great Gray Owls. These northern visitors are almost never heard calling, however.

If you go out listening for owls, choose a route that covers both southern and northern parts of the County. Screech-Owls are most common along the Indian, Ouse and Otonabee rivers near Rice Lake, while Barred Owls can be found in the Jack and Chandos lakes area. It is also best to wait for a night with little or no wind and until it is late enough for traffic noise to have decreased. Sometimes tapes will help to encourage owls to call. Both Barred Owls and

Eastern Screech-Owls will often fly in quite close in response to a tape recording of their call. If you are out "owling" late in the month, you may also hear the peenting call of the first American Woodcock, the winnowing noise of a Common Snipe overhead or the drumming of a Ruffed Grouse.

Return of the Insect Eaters

As April approaches the first of the true insect eaters arrive back in the Kawarthas. Tree Swallows and Eastern Phoebes lead the way. The vanguard of a half dozen or so Tree Swallows usually turns up over Little Lake or the Otonabee River. For five consecutive years, I found my first Tree Swallows of spring on exactly March 26th in front of the Bata Library at Trent University. The birds fly low over the water's surface searching for midges and other early flies. If the weather is abnormally warm, however, the swallows tend to disperse away from the water and are harder to find. For a species coming all the way from Florida, it is amazing how their arrival always occurs within a few days of the same date every year.

Phoebes announce their arrival by their distinctive raspy song. They are usually heard calling from shoreline trees near areas of open water. Soon after, they move onto their nesting territories, usually around cottages and other rural buildings. People sometimes confuse the song of the Black-capped Chickadee with that of the Eastern Phoebe. Although the chickadee does sound like it is whistling "fee-bee," the Black-cap's song is a clear, two-toned whistle, quite unlike the raspy notes of the phoebe.

Mammals

March Highlights

All Month Long

- Chipmunks emerge from their cozy dens and venture out into the yet snow-covered forest to find a mate. Fallen trees and sunlit woodland clearings are often good places to see them.

- Male Muskrats range far and wide looking for love. Males will attempt to mate with as many females as they can find, and this often results in vicious fights with other males. Muskrats are often found dead on the road in the spring, when their wanderings bring them into the path of automobiles.

- March is also the mating season for other mammal species with a short gestation period. Among these are Striped Skunks, Groundhogs, Eastern Cottontails, Snowshoe Hares, European Hares, Red Squirrels and both Northern and Southern Flying Squirrels.

- By following a few simple rules-of-thumb, your chances of actually seeing mammals first-hand can be greatly improved. ◇

Early March
- Watch for Red Squirrels chasing each other through the tree tops. The male is usually the one doing the chasing in this season of squirrel romance.

Mid-March
- When the sap starts to run, Red Squirrels can sometimes be seen biting Sugar Maple twigs and branches. It turns out that they are actually harvesting maple syrup by starting a sap flow, waiting a day or so for the water in the sap to evaporate and then returning to eat the syrup.

Late March
- Wolves, Coyotes, Red Foxes and Gray Squirrels bear their young any time between late March and the end of April.

- Moose suffer from tick infestations in the winter. Tick larvae burrow under the skin, where they consume the animal's fat and cause tremendous irritation. In an attempt to get rid of the ticks, the animals rub, scratch and bite their hide causing major hair loss. Some years, large numbers of Moose end up dying from hypothermia in late winter and spring.

Tips on Observing Mammals

Although mammals are usually harder to find and observe than other animals, there are ways to improve your chances. One of the most effective methods is to simply sit quietly in your car for 15 or 20 minutes in an area where two or more habitat types come together. This may be where a woodlot borders on a marsh or near a field that is bisected by a shrub or fence row.

Fence rows are especially good for Red Fox and Coyote, because the fence "breaks up" the animals' body structure and provides camouflage. Use binoculars to scan the fence row from your car. A beaver dam is also a good place to watch, since it forms a natural travel corridor for many species of mammals wishing to cross a pond or stream.

Another means of seeing mammals is to drive slowly along back roads at dusk, shortly after dark or at dawn. Agricultural areas are often good for White-tailed Deer, Coyotes, Red Fox, Raccoons and Striped Skunks. In order to see the shyer mammals such as members of the weasel family, large tracts of relatively undisturbed habitat are usually more productive.

Amphibians and Reptiles

March Highlights

All Month Long
- Amphibians and reptiles will remain ensconced in their winter retreats for a few more weeks yet. This is a good time, however, to learn the calls of our nine local frogs as well as the American Toad. They are all quite distinctive and easy to remember. ◊

Late March
- If the weather has been exceptionally mild, the first frogs usually begin calling, turtles emerge from hibernation and Eastern Garter Snakes become active.

Learning Frog and Toad Calls

During an average year, the appearance of the first frogs is still a few weeks away. Exceptionally warm weather, however, will speed things up. Both 1998 and 1999 had abnormally mild winters and early springs; the first Spring Peepers and Chorus Frogs were heard calling during the last few days of March in both of these years. Usually, however, mid-April is the time when frogs begin their annual spring chorus. Take some time this month to learn their calls. A number of commercial tapes are now available and, by using the memory aids listed on the next page, you will find the calls easy to remember.

Table 3.2: **Call Descriptions of the Amphibians of the Kawarthas**

Common Name	Call Description
(Eastern) American Toad	long, high-pitched musical trill lasting up to 30 seconds
Gray Treefrog	musical, slow, bird-like trill lasting 2 or 3 seconds
(Northern) Spring Peeper	short, loud, peep, repeated once a second; not unlike a high-pitched toy horn
(Midland) Chorus Frog	short, trill-like "cr-r-e-e-e," sounding like a thumb drawn along the teeth of a comb; repeated every few seconds
Wood Frog	short, subtle chuckle, like ducks quacking in the distance
(Northern) Leopard Frog	short, rattling "snore" followed by guttural chuckling ("chuck-chuck-chuck") like wet hands rubbing a balloon
Pickerel Frog	low-pitched, drawn-out snore, increasing in loudness over a couple of seconds
Green Frog	a short, throaty "gunk" or "boink," like the pluck of a loose banjo string; usually given as a single note
Mink Frog	rapid, muffled "cut-cut-cut," like a hammer striking wood. A full chorus sounds like horses' hooves on cobblestone.
Bullfrog	deep bass, two- or three-syllable "rrr-uum" or "jug-o-rum."

Hints for remembering some of the common frog calls.

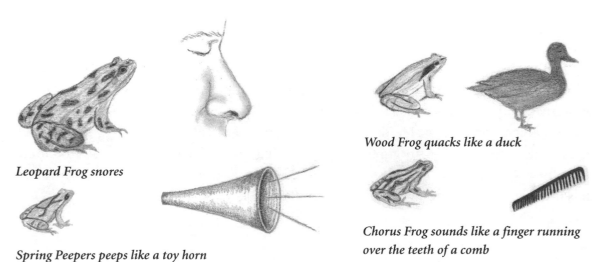

Leopard Frog snores

Spring Peepers peeps like a toy horn

Wood Frog quacks like a duck

Chorus Frog sounds like a finger running over the teeth of a comb

Fishes

March Highlights

All Month Long

- Lake Trout eggs hatch this month and next.

- Winterkill may occur in shallow lakes when the ice stays late, and there is deep snow cover. Under these conditions, insufficient sunlight is able to penetrate the ice and snow to allow photosynthesis. Most of what oxygen available is used up by bacteria to break down decaying vegetation. Large numbers of fish therefore die of asphyxiation.

- For many fishes, activity levels begin to increase following winter dormancy.

- Walleye and Northern Pike begin staging near spawning areas. Movement to these areas is triggered in part by increased flow rates as a result of snowmelt in late winter and early spring.

Late Month

- The winter fishing season for Walleye and Northern Pike in northern Peterborough County ends on March 31.

Insects and Other Invertebrates

March Highlights

All Month Long

- Stoneflies can still be found crawling on the snow near streams.

- Snow Fleas, looking like a powdering of black pepper, become more common.

Late March

- When the temperature climbs above 10° C, the first Mourning Cloak, Compton Tortoiseshell and Eastern Comma butterflies may make their debut spring flights.

- A sugar bush can be a great place to observe insect activity in March. Flowing maple sap attracts a wide variety of insects including bees, ladybird beetles, tortoiseshell butterflies, March flies and noctuid moths. Like tortoiseshells, several species of noctuid moths overwinter as adults.

■ The first swarms of mating midges can be seen over conifers along lakes and rivers. ◊

Swarming Midges

Looking out over a lake or river on a sunny spring day will often reveal large numbers of tiny, black insects flying about. Others can usually be seen floating dead on the water's surface. These harmless, mosquito-like flies are midges, and we can thank them for fuelling the early migration of Tree Swallows that are arriving at this time. Midges spend most of their life as larvae in the mud bottom of bodies of water. After transforming into a pupa, they rise to the water's surface where the adult midge emerges from the pupal case and flies off.

The real entertainment, however, is happening on shore. Dense clouds of tens of thousands of midges swarm over the top of prominent objects such as coniferous trees. Along the Otonabee River, the insects are most often seen on sunny afternoons and usually over cedars. These swarms allow male and female midges to find each other for mating. The swarm itself is composed almost entirely of males who are awaiting the arrival of females. Like the silk moths, the males have large, feather-like antennae which can detect the sound of an approaching female. The female produces an "erotic" flight buzz which attains just the right pitch when she reaches sexual maturity. When the female flies into the swarm, the males move towards her like iron shavings to a magnet. One male will attach himself to her and mate; mating frequently is completed within a matter of seconds. The female will then leave to lay her eggs.

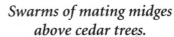

Swarms of mating midges above cedar trees.

Take time to observe the movements of the swarm. As long as there is no wind, the insect cloud remains more or less at the same height, although it will briefly move sideways. When a breeze comes up, the swarm moves lower but soon rises again as the winds subsides. These movements often suggest a plume of smoke or the synchronized wheeling of a tightly-knit flock of shorebirds or starlings. The swarm seems to function as if controlled by a single brain.

Much remains to be explained about this behaviour so watch closely, make sketches and take notes. There is no need to worry about being bitten because midges do not bite. In fact, the adults of many species do not appear to feed at all; their life expectancy is only a day or two.

Plants

March Highlights

All Month Long

- Our noses are the first to notice changes in Balsam Poplar. On warm days, you can often smell the familiar fragrance of the resin-like gum that coats the buds. The resin is softened by the strengthening sun. This softening allows the bud-scales to open at the proper time, and in turn permits the leaves to emerge.

- Depending on the species, willows are acquiring a deeper honey-bronze or wine-red colour, while Red-osier Dogwoods are flushed with a more exuberant red. Colour changes are often reported in birch and aspens as well. These changes may result from sap rising in the plants.

- The March winds spread pollen from the male cones of White Cedar. These same winds also disperse the winged seeds of the White Birch. The small wing allows the seed to be carried great distances.

- Lilac, Red Maple, Silver Maple and Red-berried Elder buds swell this month and become quite noticeable.

- Twigs from many trees and shrubs will leaf out early if brought inside and placed in water near a bright window.

Early March

- The furry catkins of Pussy Willows and aspens poke through bud scales and become a time-honoured sign of spring. ◇

Mid-March

- Sugar Maple trees are tapped around the middle of March to make Canada's world famous syrup. ◇

Late March

- Coltsfoot, with its dandelion-like flowers, may bloom if the weather is warm enough.

- Skunk Cabbage also blooms in March but has yet to be found in the Kawarthas. With climate change, however, it may eventually expand its range into this area. ◊

- Wild Leek leaves poking through patches of late-March snow are often the first sign of new herbaceous plant growth. Leeks do not flower, however, until early summer. By this time, the leaves will have died and fallen off since the heavy shade of the forest will have made photosynthesis impossible. ◊

- If the weather is warm, male catkins on alder bushes start to swell into yellow and purple garlands. They release golden puffs of pollen when jostled.

- Silver Maple and Red Maple flowers may begin to appear.

First Flowers

Although subtle in nature, change is afoot in our tree and shrub communities even in March. One species that attracts a great deal of attention at this time is the Pussy Willow. By mid-March, the Pussy Willow's bud scales open up and the furry catkins appear. These well-known signs of spring are actually clusters of tiny flowers densely covered with silky white hairs when immature. Catkin is a Dutch word meaning "little kitten," obviously a reference to the flower's soft, kitten-like appearance. The female catkins of the Pussy Willow eventually become very long and are visited by bees and ants for their nectar. These same insects visit the male catkins for their sweet-smelling pollen. Aspen catkins are also starting to emerge now and initially look quite similar to those of the Pussy Willow. Warm weather will also cause the male catkins of the Speckled Alder to swell this month.

Male Catkins

Buds when the scales first open

Female Catkins

Pussy Willow catkins.

Table 3.2: "First Bloom" Calendar For Selected Trees, Shrubs and Herbaceous Plants

For each of the spring and summer months, the "first bloom" calendar gives the approximate time when some of the better-known species usually begin to flower. The year-to-year variation in weather, however, may accelerate or slow the flowering process.

mid-March	Pussy Willow
late March	Silver Maple, Red Maple, aspens

At the Sugar Bush

A discussion of March would not be complete without mentioning the Sugar Maple. The ritual of tapping maple trees is centuries old. A visit to the sugar bush is also a wonderful way to witness spring's arrival. Blanketed in snow when trees are tapped, the forest floor will have become a bare carpet of brown when the sap flow finally stops. On warm days in March and April, pressure in the trees increases, causing a sap flow from all directions, not just from the roots up. The flow is enhanced by night temperatures below 0° C. It has been proven that tree trunks actually swell and shrink with the changing temperature. Sugaring proceeds in fits and starts depending on the vagaries of the weather, and can last from a week to nearly a month.

Squirrels will often nip off the tree's buds or bite through the bark on twigs in order to start the sap flowing. However, since it is almost entirely water, the squirrels will wait until the water in the sap evaporates and leaves behind a deposit of "syrup" which they readily consume. Birds such as chickadees as well as a variety of insects are also attracted to these sap flows.

Wild Leeks and Skunk Cabbage Lead the Way

In our woodlands the Wild Leek is the first herbaceous plant to show new growth in the spring. Its large leaves often pop up right through the remaining snow of late March. Taking advantage of the unobstructed sunlight flooding the forest floor, leeks use this opportunity to maximize photosynthesis and store the resulting sugars in underground bulbs. When the forest trees leaf out and cast a heavy shade, the leaves die and fall off since they are no longer useful. The rest of the plant, having stored the necessary energy, continues its cycle by flowering in early summer and producing seeds.

Over much of southern Ontario, Skunk Cabbage also blooms in March. The flowers are in a ball-shaped cluster inside a green and purple-brown hood. The plant's metabolic activity alone is often sufficient to melt the snow in a narrow circle around the hood! The foul, skunk-like smell of Skunk Cabbage actually attracts bees and flies for the purpose of pollination. This inhabitant of damp ditches and wetland edges is not found in the Kawarthas, although it does grow not far to the south of here. If the warming trend in our climate continues, however, Skunk Cabbage may soon become established in our area.

Weather

March Highlights

All Month Long
- There do not seem to be any weather rules this month; just about anything can be expected.
- The sun's heat melts the snow surface during the day so that it freezes into a hard crust at night. Some years it becomes hard enough to walk on.
- Dark objects such as fallen leaves and tree trunks absorb sunlight and transform it into heat. This heat melts the surrounding snow, allowing the object to sink down. Since debris that has accumulated in the snow over the course of winter is usually dark, it absorbs heat. This, in turn, helps to melt the snow around the debris.
- Melting snow uses up heat from the surrounding air, making the air feel cooler than you would expect.

Early March
- Exceptionally warm weather may result in short-distance migrants like robins and Red-winged Blackbirds arriving early. ◇

Late March
- The spring equinox falls on or about March 21st. For the next six months, we can enjoy days that are longer than nights.
- The snow cover is usually gone by late March, but occasional snow flurries are still to be expected. When snow comes after the robins return, it is sometimes called "Robin's Winter."

Table 3.3: **March Weather Averages, 1961-1990**

Daily Maximum	3.0° C
Daily Minimum	-7.4° C
Extreme Maximum	22.5° C
Extreme Minimum	-30.9° C
Rainfall	40.7 mm
Snowfall	22.1 cm
Precipitation	66.3 mm

Warm Spring Weather and Bird Migration

As climate change continues to be felt, March weather in recent years (especially 1998, 1999 and 2000) has often been much milder than usual. Although the early arrival of warm weather has an impact on bird migration, it does not affect all species equally. Short-distance migrants such as robins and Red-winged Blackbirds tend to arrive ahead of schedule. In the winter of 1998, Red-winged Blackbirds were already on territory and singing by the last week of February, fully three weeks early. The exceptionally warm weather continued unabated throughout the spring that year and allowed these same species to nest much earlier than usual.

Long-distance migrants, however, appear to be unaffected by this early warmth and presumably leave the tropics at the normal time. Even during abnormally warm and early springs, the many warblers that winter in Central and South America arrive back in Ontario at their usual time in May. Extremely cool weather, however, does have a definite stalling effect on migration and can result in arrival dates being later than average. This was the case in the cool spring of 1997, when tropical migrants were nearly two weeks behind schedule, because cold weather and unfavourable winds stopped them from advancing any further north than the lower Great Lakes.

Table 3.4: **Approximate Twilight, Sunrise and Sunset Times (EST)**

Date	Twilight Begins	Sunrise	Sunset	Twilight Ends
Mar. 1	6:21 a.m.	6:50 a.m.	6:02 p.m.	6:31 p.m.
Mar. 10	6:05 a.m.	6:34 a.m.	6:14 p.m.	6:43 p.m.
Mar. 20	5:47 a.m.	6:16 a.m.	6:26 p.m.	6:55 p.m.
Apr. 1	5:25 a.m.	5:54 a.m.	6:41 p.m.	7:10 p.m.

The Night Sky

March Highlights

All Month Long

- Major constellations and stars visible (March 15, 8:00 p.m. EST)

  Northwest: Andromeda (with M31 galaxy) is setting; Cassiopeia just above to the right; Pleiades above to the left; Taurus (with *Aldebaran*) due W

  Northeast: Boötes (with *Arcturus*) low in sky; Virgo (with *Spica*) just above E horizon; Big Dipper standing upright fairly high; Little Dipper (with *Polaris*) to its left

  Southeast: Leo (with *Regulus*) rules over the SE sky

  Southwest: dominated by Orion (with *Betelgeuse* and *Rigel*); Taurus (with *Aldebaran*) high to its right; Canis Major (with *Sirius*) low to its left; Canis Minor (with *Procyon*) due S; Auriga (with *Capella*) high above Orion; Gemini (with *Castor* and *Pollux*) to left of Auriga

- No other season offers as many bright stars and constellations as spring. There are no less than 11 first magnitude stars visible. ◊

- The signature constellation of spring is Leo. Like Orion, it is one of the few constellations that actually looks like what it is supposed to represent. ◊

- At the spring equinox, both the moon and sun rise due east and set due west.

- The full moon closest to the spring equinox rises later each subsequent night than at any other time of year. This is because the moon's orbit (the ecliptic) makes the greatest angle with the horizon in the early spring. This is just the opposite of what happens at the fall equinox during the Harvest Moon. The moon rises about 80 minutes later from the night of the full moon, to the night after. On average, the moon rises only 50 minutes later every day.

Bright Spring Stars!

No other season offers as many bright stars and constellations as spring. There are no less than 11 first magnitude stars visible. Two of the most dominant stars of the spring sky are *Arcturus*, in the constellation Boötes, and *Spica*, in the constellation Virgo. *Arcturus* is a yellow-orange star and, among stars visible from the latitude of Peterborough, is second only to *Sirius* in brightness. *Spica* is a bluish star and not quite as bright. The Big Dipper, which is now almost at the zenith, can help you locate both of these stars. Follow the curve of its handle (going away from the bowl) and "arc to *Arcturus*" and then "speed on" to *Spica*.

By following the curve of the Big Dipper's handle in the other direction, it is easy to locate *Regulus*, the brightest star of the Leo constellation. If you look to the southwest, the winter stars such as *Betelgeuse, Rigel, Sirius, Procyon, Aldebaran, Capella, Castor* and *Pollux* are still very prominent. And, by staying up after midnight, you can even get an early glimpse of the upcoming summer constellations.

In earlier times, it was often the custom to plant or harvest crops when a particular star first appeared above the eastern horizon just before sunrise. The first appearance of *Spica* was the signal that the planting of wheat should begin.

The Lion Constellation

Leo is the flagship constellation of spring. It is found high in the southern sky from early April to late June. The easiest way to find this large but rather dim constellation is to find its brightest star, *Regulus*. First of all, face north to locate the Big Dipper and the two stars that form the end of the Dipper's bowl closest to the handle. Extend an imaginary line southward from these two stars to the next bright star you encounter. This is *Regulus*.

Having found *Regulus*, face south in order for the Lion to appear right side up. You can now locate the remaining parts of the beast. Leo is best imagined as sitting on his haunches. His head, mane and forepaws are formed by an asterism known either as the Sickle or as a backward question mark. Ancient peoples throughout the world recognized this constellation as a large animal. The Greeks and Romans saw it as a lion, the Chinese perceived a horse, and it is thought that the Incas saw it as a puma.

The spring sky looking southeast.

Yellow-bellied Sapsucker drumming on a drain pipe.

NATURE'S YEAR IN THE KAWARTHAS

CHAPTER 4

April—Frog Song and Sky Dancers

April is the time of amphibian love, when marshes, swamps and woodland ponds reverberate with the calls of countless frogs consumed by a mating frenzy. Salamanders, too, join the fray as they venture over ice, rock and road to make their way back to ancestral breeding ponds. High overhead a snipe flies in wide, reckless circles, its wings creating a haunting tremolo sound. From a nearby thicket, the nasal "beep" of the woodcock is constantly repeated until the bird suddenly launches itself into the air and begins its spectacular sky dance.

On an April morning, the chorus of robins, cardinals and Mourning Doves is so loud that you have to get up and close the bedroom window. Forests resonate with the drumming of grouse and the courtship hammering of woodpeckers. Evening Grosbeaks call from overhead as they search out swelling buds on which to feast. On our lakes, we hear yet another April music—the tinkling of black candle ice, the clamour of ice piling up in ridges and the roar of waves rolling under the disintegrating frozen surface. Walk through the forest and your nose will recognize the time of season by the smell of the sodden, thawing earth and decaying leaves. And, for those of us old enough to remember, April will always be synonymous with the smell of grass fires.

New plant life, too, vies for our attention this month. The yellow flowers of Coltsfoot push forth among roadside stones and debris. Almost overnight, the tree tops appear less open as dormant buds swell and thicken. The flowers of maples, poplars, elms and alder stand out against the grey-brown landscape and provide a foretaste of what is to come; because, more than anything, April is a time of great expectation. In only a few weeks, the explosive growth of buds, flowers, shoots and leaves will totally transform the landscape. The extraordinary surge of life that we see and feel everywhere frees us of our late winter blahs and whets our appetite for the pleasures of May.

April At a Glance

April is a month of ardent bird song and courtship displays such as the nightly sky dance of the American Woodcock. Migration grows with the arrival of rails, swallows, kinglets, sparrows and the first shorebirds and warblers. Waterfowl numbers peak early in the month and huge flocks of Tree Swallows are often seen over the Otonabee River. Resident birds and earlier migrants are busy nesting. Canada Geese bound for James Bay pass over in high, long "v" formations.

Raccoons, as well as most members of the weasel family give birth this month. Male groundhogs arise from their six-month siesta to search out a mate. Otter watching is often at its best.

Local wetlands come alive with the clamorous calls of Spring Peepers, Chorus Frogs, Wood Frogs and Leopard Frogs. Salamanders breed in woodland ponds on wet, mild nights. Turtles emerge from hibernation and Eastern Garter Snakes mate.

Walleye, White Suckers, Northern Pike, Muskellunge and Rainbow Trout spawn this month. There are great opportunities to actually see the fish spawning.

Watch for the early butterflies such as the Mourning Cloak, the Eastern Comma and, by month's end, the Spring Azure. Swarms of mating midges are a common sight as is a variety of flies and bees. Warm air from the south often brings in migrant Green Darner dragonflies.

A variety of maples, poplars, willows, alders and elms flower this month. The flowers and swelling leaf buds give trees a hazy appearance. The first wildflowers and sedges bloom. Watch especially for Coltsfoot and hepatica.

Daily maximums now average 12° C and minimums 0° C. Most lakes are ice-free by April 20. Flooding, however, is a possibility. We turn our clocks ahead one hour on the first Sunday of the month. In mid-April, sunrise is at about 6:30 a.m. and sunset near 8:00 p.m.

The spring sky is dominated by the constellation Leo. Orion and Canis Major are low in the west while Boötes is rising in the northeast. The Big Dipper is high in the northeast.

Birds

April Highlights

All Month

- The muffled drumming of Ruffed Grouse is one of the most characteristic sounds of April.

- Woodpeckers are also very noisy this month. Listen especially for the courtship drumming of Yellow-bellied Sapsuckers on dead, dry trees or metal surfaces.

- Half-crazed cardinals and robins sometimes peck aggressively at windows and car mirrors in an attempt to drive the "invader"—their reflected image—out of their nesting territory. Fortunately, after about five or six weeks, hormonal changes will have made the birds less aggressive, and they soon forget the problem.

- The courtship flight of the American Woodcock provides nightly entertainment. Common Snipe, too, can be heard both day and night "winnowing" over their wetland territories. ◊

- Ospreys, American Robins, Common Grackles and Blue Jays are a few of the species already nesting this month. Jays go through a veritable personality change during the nesting season and become uncharacteristically quiet and secretive.

- The pace of migration accelerates noticeably with the arrival of wading birds, swallows, sparrows, kinglets and, by month's end, the first warblers. Most tropical migrants, however, will not reach the Kawarthas for another few weeks.

- Northward-bound Dark-eyed Juncos and American Tree Sparrows filter through our area. Juncos in particular can be quite abundant for several weeks, even in city backyards.

- Common Loons return and take up residence on our lakes as soon as the ice goes out.

- This is the peak calling month for Barred Owls.

Early April

- Waterfowl numbers usually peak on Little Lake, Buckhorn Lake, Lake Katchewanooka and various other large, open bodies of water. ◊

Mid-April

- Huge flocks of migrating Tree Swallows are seen over the Otonabee River and adjacent areas including downtown Peterborough. They are also abundant around the locks in Hastings, Lakefield, Buckhorn and Bobcaygeon. ◇

Late April

■ The first flocks of "Northern" Canada Geese (Southern James Bay sub-species) pass over. They can be distinguished from flocks of our local "Giant "Canada Geese by the larger numbers in the flock and the higher altitude at which they usually fly. ◇

■ The hunting season for Wild Turkey begins at the end of April and generally lasts until the end of May.

Table 4.1: **April Arrivals and Departures**

early month

arrivals: Common Loon, Horned Grebe, Red-necked Grebe, Double-crested Cormorant, Ruddy Duck, Osprey, Merlin, Greater Yellowlegs, Brown Creeper (w), Winter Wren, Vesper Sparrow, Fox Sparrow, Dark-eyed Junco (w)

departures: Northern Shrike, Bohemian Waxwing*

mid-month

arrivals: American Bittern, Sharp-shinned Hawk, Common Moorhen, Sora, Virginia Rail, Pectoral Sandpiper, Yellow-bellied Sapsucker, Purple Martin, Barn Swallow, Northern Rough-winged Swallow, Ruby-crowned Kinglet, Hermit Thrush, Brown Thrasher, Pine Warbler, Yellow-rumped Warbler, Chipping Sparrow, Swamp Sparrow, Field Sparrow, White-throated Sparrow, Savannah Sparrow

departures: Snow Goose, Redhead, Northern Pintail, American Wigeon, Northern Shoveler, American Black Duck (b), Mallard (b), Gadwall, Hooded Merganser (b), Greater Scaup, Canvasback, American Coot, Herring Gull (b), American Tree Sparrow, Fox Sparrow, Common Redpoll*

late month

arrivals: Green Heron, Broad-winged Hawk, Lesser Yellowlegs, Upland Sandpiper, Caspian Tern, Chimney Swift, Blue-headed Vireo, Bank Swallow, Cliff Swallow, Northern Waterthrush, Eastern Towhee (Note that Northern Canada Geese are passing through).

departures: Blue-winged Teal (b), Ring-necked Duck (b), Common Goldeneye, Bufflehead, Common Merganser (b), Merlin (b)

Sky Dancers

Two species that command considerable attention in April are the American Woodcock and the Common Snipe. The courtship flights of these birds have earned them the name "sky dancers." From early April to late May, the nasal "peent" of the woodcock is a common sound in damp, open habitats bordered by second-growth forest and wetland. The peenting begins in the twilight period after sunset. As darkness falls, the calls become more numerous until the bird suddenly bursts into the air and climbs in wide circles to an altitude of about 100 metres. Because the woodcock's three outer wing feathers are extremely stiff and narrow and spread apart during flight, the air rushing through causes them to vibrate producing a high twittering sound. The twittering stops, however, as the bird begins its zigzag descent; it is replaced by liquid, warbled notes that the woodcock actually sings. The warbling grows louder and louder, as the bird approaches the ground. It then ends abruptly, and the final portion of the descent is silent. The woodcock usually lands close to the same spot from where it took off. It then walks stiff-legged in the direction of the nearby female and once again begins the peenting sound. A few minutes later, the poor bird—which must be close to exhaustion—launches into yet another flight.

Woodcock-watching on a calm April night with Spring Peepers calling in the background is an event not to be missed. Because the darkening sky makes it difficult to actually see the woodcock in flight, try to face west so that the bird will stand out against the lighter, western sky. After it takes off, you can move closer to the take-off point. By remaining quiet and staying low, it is sometimes possible to get a close look at the bird when it lands. The nuptial flights usually stop when it becomes completely dark, although some woodcock display even during the night when there is a full moon. The birds will also display again at dawn. Woodcocks usually continue their nuptial flights until late May, well after mating has taken place.

If the area is wet enough, you may also hear the courtship flight of the Common Snipe. Actually seeing the bird can prove more difficult, because it never seems to be where the sound is coming from. The male snipe flies in wide, horizontal circles above the ground and regularly droops or dives, its tail fanned. With each dive, the outer tail feathers vibrate and make a strange tremolo sound known as winnowing. The common origin of the woodcock and the snipe is evident in the similarities in their displays. Snipe, however, court actively all day long, not just at dusk and dawn Local areas to visit for woodcock and snipe include the Trent University Wildlife Sanctuary and the fields south of the Peterborough Airport. The Miller Creek Conservation Area is usually a good location for snipe. Almost any overgrown field along a marshy area bordered by trees and shrubs, however, may have both of our sky dancers.

The Waterfowl Spectacle Continues

Waterfowl numbers on the Kawartha Lakes usually peak in mid-April giving this area a growing reputation for impressive waterbird concentrations, especially during the spring migration. In order to get a more accurate picture of the species and numbers involved, a mid-April waterfowl count has been carried out in recent years. Depending on the amount of ice cover in the Kawarthas and the conditions further north, a great deal of variability in waterbird numbers has been noticed from one year to the next. When spring is early, species such as Ring-necked Duck and Hooded Merganser will have moved on by mid-April, whereas later migrants such as Lesser Scaup and Bufflehead will be more common.

Some of the locations covered by the count include the south end of Pigeon Lake, Gannon's Narrows, Buckhorn Lake, Deer Bay, Lovesick Lake, Clear Lake, Lake Katchewanooka, the Otonabee River and Rice Lake. Miller Creek Conservation Area, Lakefield Marsh and various temporary ponds such as flooded corn fields are also surveyed for "puddle ducks." A run-off pond south of County Road 2 at Mather's Corners just north of Rice Lake has been quite productive in recent years. The combination of water and corn stubble often attracts Wood Duck, Northern Shoveler, Northern Pintail, American Black Duck, Mallard, Blue-winged Teal and Green-winged Teal.

Table 4.2: **Annual Spring Waterfowl Count Totals for Selected Species**

Species	1997	1998	2001
Common Loon	22	20	44
Pied-billed Grebe	50	4	9
Wood Duck	60	57	84
Green-winged Teal	5	17	74
Blue-winged Teal	9	10	11
American Black Duck	40	36	116
Mallard	226	205	512
American Wigeon	83	67	211
Ring-necked Duck	3698	1294	6824
Lesser Scaup	289	812	923
Greater Scaup	32	15	50
Bufflehead	890	1077	1608
Common Goldeneye	650	275	1736
Common Merganser	1374	775	3710
Hooded Merganser	1205	16	369

Observing a raft of ducks.

It is important to note the conditions for the "count" day. The 1997 count was held on April 13 during an abnormally cool, late spring, while the 1998 count was held on April 11 during an abnormally warm, early spring. The 2001 took place on April 13 and conditions were ideal for concentrating large numbers of birds. Lakes were open in the south but still mostly frozen in the north.

A total of 18,601 waterfowl were counted in 2001, compared to 6082 in 1998.

Swallows By the Thousands

Early in April, a fascinating avian spectacle takes place along the Otonabee River. Like a living cloud, thousands of northward-bound Tree Swallows swirl this way and that as they make their way up this river highway. The Otonabee serves as a natural corridor funneling the birds towards summer nesting grounds. The mass of birds often spills over onto adjacent streets including the heart of downtown Peterborough. On April 11, 1999, at least 5,000 Tree Swallows were observed swarming over Water Street between Trent University and Hilliard Street. The swallows feed heavily on tiny, mosquito-like midges that emerge from the water

Tree Swallows migrating along the Otonabee River.

at this time and provide the necessary energy for migration. Some midge species appear almost immediately after ice-out and are able to fly at temperatures close to freezing. Even after migration, large numbers of swallows often congregate over bodies of water during periods of cool weather. They seem to be able to find the necessary food there to sustain themselves.

The swallows' early arrival is not without its dangers. The birds must often face freezing temperatures, wind and snow. I have seen swallows on several occasions cowering behind headstones at Little Lake Cemetery in an attempt to find refuge from winter's last show of force. Although spring storms undoubtedly kill some birds, most manage to survive. There are even reports of these hardy swallows eating berries or picking flotsam off the river ice.

Sorting out the Canada Geese

A large flock of Canada Geese flying over in spring is a thrilling sight and a time-honoured sign of the changing seasons. The main passage of geese usually occurs in the last week of

April and the first week of May. But to complicate matters, there are at least two separate populations of Canada Goose seen in the Kawarthas. The most familiar subspecies is the Giant Canada Goose (*Branta canadensis moffati*) which was reintroduced into southern Ontario in the late 1960s after coming close to extinction. The Giant Canada returns in late February and March from its wintering grounds on the Great Lakes and in the northern United States. It can be seen in local wetlands in the spring, noisily advertising and defending its nesting territory.

Large, high-altitude flocks of geese seen in late April and early May, however, and then again in early October, are usually another subspecies, the so-called Southern James Bay or Northern Canada Goose (*Branta canadensis interiori*). A smaller bird, it nests around the fringes of the Hudson Bay Lowlands and winters mostly in the Tennessee Valley. Peterborough County is on the eastern edge of its migration route. The Southern James Bay subspecies has been at low population levels since the late 1980s (less than 100,000 birds) although the decline appears to have stabilized. Part of the decline in the population may be due to large numbers of Giant Canada Geese flying north to James Bay in the early summer to moult. These "moult migrants" may be competing with the northern nesting birds for scarce food resources. The main cause of the decline, however, is most likely related to over-abundant numbers of Snow Geese. By the late 1990s, the mid-continent population of Snow Geese was estimated at over four million birds. As a result of sheer numbers, the Snow Geese have destroyed vast areas of crucial salt marsh habitat along the western shores of James Bay and Hudson Bay. This may explain why gosling mortality among Canada Geese is so high; many of the young Canadas are starving. An extended hunting season for both the Giant Canada Goose and the Snow Goose is now in place in an attempt to reduce their numbers.

There also seems to be an increase in a third subspecies. Hutchins' Canada Goose (*Branta canadensis hutchinsii*) is quite small and especially distinctive when beside a Giant Canada Goose. There were three local reports of these birds in the spring of 1999, and there will undoubtedly be more in the future.

Mammals

April Highlights

All Month Long
- Otter viewing is at its best in early spring. When our lakes begin to open up, the animals often eat on the edge of the ice and are therefore more visible. Two young are

born this month or next. ◇

- Other members of the weasel family also bear their young this month. American Mink, Martens, Fishers as well as Short- and Long-tailed Weasels all contribute to the mammalian population boom of spring. Raccoons also become parents.

- Local Black Bears emerge from hibernation this month. ◇

Mid-April

- The first bats come out of hibernation and take flight on mild evenings. Females move to nursery sites, where they will give birth next month.

- Last spring's Beaver cubs are driven from the parental pond and forced to wander widely in search of a new territory.

- Young Muskrats are also obliged to leave home. Many unfortunately become roadkill.

- Porcupines switch from a diet of tree bark to one of new leaves and buds. Aspen catkins and Sugar Maple buds are favourite foods at this time of year.

Otter Viewing

In recent years, River Otters have become a fairly common sight in the Kawarthas. April is one of the best times to see these entertaining members of the weasel family. During the spring break-up, Otters can often be observed eating or frolicking on the ice beside open stretches

River Otter on the ice with a fish.

of water. They bring fish, frogs, crayfish and other prey items up onto the ice to eat. It is not uncommon to see an otter rolling on the snow or ice as it plays with some poor fish or frog before devouring it.

During the winter months, cross-country skiers occasionally see the tracks and "toboggan-like" slides of otters. When otters travel on snow, they tend to bound a few steps and then slide, pushing themselves with their short legs. It is well known that otters will also slide down hills, sometimes directly into open water. The otter's zest for life, if such can be said of a wild animal, is legendary. As one writer has remarked, "Otters are extremely bad at doing nothing. They are either asleep or entirely absorbed in some activity."

Otters are wide-ranging animals and don't necessarily remain in the same territory. Some locations where they are seen fairly often, however, include Gannon's Narrows and Lily Lake, a kilometre east of Ackison Road in Peterborough. At Gannon's Narrows, it is possible to see otters over the entire winter since the current keeps the water open. You may even see a Bald Eagle keeping them company!

Bears Emerge from Hibernation

Black Bears become active again this month. Male bears are the first to emerge from their winter dens, followed by barren females and females with yearling cubs. Mothers with new cubs are the last to emerge. A bear will have lost 15 to 40 percent of its fall weight by the time it comes out of hibernation and will continue to lose weight for several more weeks as well. It will not fully gain its weight back until berries become abundant in the summer. Although the Black Bear may appear somewhat emaciated in the spring, its coat is surprisingly luxuriant, having grown all winter.

In April and May, bears are forced to adopt a mostly vegetarian diet. They graze heavily on grass and even eat dandelions because of their high nectar content. Before the leaves come out, bears will also consume large amounts of Balsam Poplar buds. There are reports that the gummy sealant on the buds may act as a laxative and help to restore the animal's digestive system after the winter fast. When the aspens leaf out, the bears also eat huge quantities of the new, tender leaves. It is not uncommon to see a mother bear with her two yearling cubs munching away right in the top of an aspen. The best time to look for bears is in the morning at first light or at dusk. This animal seems to be increasing locally, particularly in areas south of the Shield such as Dummer and Asphodel townships.

Amphibians and Reptiles

April Highlights

Mid-April
- Local wetlands come alive with the clamorous calls of Spring Peepers, Wood Frogs and Chorus Frogs. ◇
- Salamanders breed in woodland ponds and can be observed crossing roads on wet, mild April nights. ◇
- Turtles come out of hibernation.
- Eastern Garter Snakes become active once again and begin to mate in "knots of snakes."

Late April
- Leopard Frogs add their voices to the amphibian chorus already well under way. Although far less common, it is also possible to hear the first Pickerel Frogs.
- Late April through early May is a good time to look for Five-lined Skinks. They can often be found under flat rocks on bare, granite outcroppings on the Shield.

The Amphibian Chorus Begins

At a time of year when many people spend their evenings glued to play-off hockey on television, there is an equally entertaining spectacle happening down at your local wetland. Countless thousands of frogs are caught up in the act of procreation, and the show is well worth taking in. The calls, given only by the male, serve to attract females and, in the case of some species, to advertise ownership of territory. When a receptive female arrives, the male clasps her waist from the back and spreads his sperm onto the eggs as they are voided from her body. All of the species that breed in early spring anchor their egg masses well below the surface, where they will not be killed by freezing on a cold night.

The frogs of early spring usually begin to call around the middle of April when night-time air temperatures have warmed to at least 8° C. When spring weather is particularly cool, however, the amphibian chorus can be delayed. Such was the case in 1992 when warmer weather did not arrive until month's end. The first species to break the long silence of winter is usually the Chorus Frog. Only about two centimetres long, it has a rising trill that sounds quite similar to a finger being drawn along the teeth of a comb. A few days later, the similar-sized Spring Peeper makes its entry. The peeper is one species in nature that more than lives up to its name. It produces an incredibly loud, high-pitched chirp or "peep" that seems about 100 times bigger than the tiny fellow producing the sound. A full chorus of peepers at close proximity is almost physically painful to the ears. I find that even hours afterwards, the peeper chorus can continue to resound in my head. The number of individual peepers calling can seem truly astounding.

In more wooded areas, the aptly named Wood Frog starts calling at the same time as the peeper. Looking like a masked thief, this handsome frog produces a short chuckle, almost as if it were doing an imitation of ducks quacking. More than one person has been tricked into believing that a flock of mallards has just landed. Finally, before the end of the month, the first Leopard Frogs are usually heard. Their call is usually described as a rattling "snore," followed by a series of guttural chucks. Some people compare the sound to that of wet hands rubbing a balloon.

Wood Frog.

Frog calls are loudest during the first few hours of darkness and fall off after midnight. Chorus, Wood and Leopard Frogs also call a great deal during the day. The best weather conditions for hearing a full chorus are mild, damp, windless nights that follow a period of rain. Evenings with light rain falling are especially good. If the weather has been excessively dry or cold over the preceding days, the frogs may not be quite as vocal.

Actually seeing a peeper call while thousands of its brethren produce a deafening chorus all around you is certainly one of the most memorable experiences of early spring. All you really need are patience and a good flashlight. Some of the frogs may fall silent when you first approach, but if you wait quietly the urge to sing will once again get the better of them. Softly rubbing two stones together or making a hushed, high whistle will sometimes jumpstart the calling as well. To see the frogs, scan the water, the floating plant debris and the lower sections of vegetation. Keep in mind that Spring Peepers and Chorus Frogs are only the size of a bumblebee and drably coloured. Fortunately, both species distend their throat into an easily visible vocal sac which serves to amplify the sound. The vocal sacs of the Wood Frog are on the sides of the body. Wood Frogs usually call as they float in the water while peepers often sing from vegetation just above the water level. The most difficult species to see is the Chorus Frog. Even smaller than a peeper, this is one species that can elude even the most determined amphibian watcher.

Some specific locations for hearing amphibians include the Miller Creek Conservation Area, the wetlands along County Road 24 north of County Road 18, the University Road swamp just north of County Road 4, the Mackenzie House Pond (entrance off Pioneer Road) behind Otonabee College at Trent University and the Snelgrove Creek wetland at the bottom of Creamery Road just south of County Road 1.

Salamander Watching

At about the same time that the Spring Peepers start calling, another ancient rite is taking place in our wetlands and woodland ponds. On mild, rainy April nights, thousands of salamanders are making their way over snow, ice, rock and pavement to breed in their ancestral ponds. Running a gauntlet of skunks, raccoons and automobiles, the salamanders are probably following an imprinted memory of their birthplace with its specific odours of mud and decaying vegetation. The three species most often seen are the Spotted Salamander (sometimes referred to as the Yellow-spotted), the Blue-spotted Salamander and the Eastern Newt. The first two species are members of the mole salamander genus, *Ambystoma*, and measure about 10 to 14 centimetres in length. The Spotted can sometimes reach 19 centimetres.

Salamander mating begins with a sort of underwater dance in which large groups of males gyrate and rub up against the females. If the female is willing, the pair will leave the group and the male will deposit a spermatophore (a small, jelly-like packet of sperm) on underwater debris. The female becomes fertilized by taking the spermatophore into her genital opening. Later, she will deposit from one to three gelatinous clumps of eggs on underwater vegetation. About six weeks later, tiny, gilled tadpole-like larvae are born which will leave the water by summer's end. By using temporary ponds and wet areas, salamander eggs and larvae are usually spared predation by fish and turtles. However, there is a tradeoff. The salamanders must breed very early in the season to assure there is

Spotted Salamander.

enough time for the larvae to transform into air-breathing terrestrial salamanders before the water dries up in summer.

To see salamanders first-hand, wait for a mild, rainy night in early to mid-April when the first frogs start calling. Temperatures of at least 8° C along with rain seem to provide the best conditions for breeding activity. Armed with a strong flashlight or headlamp and warm, waterproof clothing, slowly drive along back roads that pass through woodlands and treed, swampy areas. By watching carefully, you should be able to see the salamanders on the road. You should then park your car and get out and walk—evolution has not yet prepared salamanders to cope with the weight of car tires! Birchview Road on the east side of Clear Lake and Millage Road on the south shore of Lovesick Lake are two locations which are often good. During the day, you may sometimes find them under logs near woodland ponds. In boggy areas, especially where sphagnum moss is common, watch for the uncommon but striking Four-toed Salamander. Always take along a camera when you go looking for salamanders. They make for amazing photographs.

Table 4.3: **Average Breeding Periods for Frogs and Toads in the Kawarthas**

Common Name	Breeding Period
(Northern) Spring Peeper	mid-April to late June
(Midland) Chorus Frog	mid-April to early May
Wood Frog	mid-April to early May
(Northern) Leopard Frog	late April to late May
Pickerel Frog	late April to late May
(Eastern) American Toad	early May to late May
Gray Treefrog	mid-May to late June
Mink Frog	mid-May to late June
Green Frog	mid-May to late July
Bullfrog	mid-May to late July

Snake Spaghetti

When it comes to a mating frenzy, Eastern Garter Snakes have few equals. The males emerge from the winter hibernaculum before the females who remain hidden until the eggs within their bodies are ready for fertilization. When the female makes her appearance, all of the males in the vicinity will converge on her in a spaghetti-like mass of snake. Mating sometimes occurs even on the low branches of bushes. The males are attracted by a seemingly irresistible pheromone produced by the egg yolk. Only one of the males, however, will actually succeed in impregnating the female. He thwarts future suitors by leaving a gelatinous plug in the female's vent. The female can actually store sperm for up to seven years. She is able to use the stored sperm to fertilize her eggs should mating become impossible in some future year. This sometimes happens when population levels are low as a result of snake mortality. Locally, Mark S. Burnham Provincial Park is usually a good place to see Eastern Garter Snakes in the spring.

Fishes

April Highlights

All Month Long

- April is the fish watching month par excellence! Spring is in the air and "in the water." Soon after the ice goes out, many species of fish move towards the sun-warmed shallows in search of food. A large number of species also spawn at this time.

Mid-April

- Rainbow Trout leave Lake Ontario and move upstream to spawn in the shallow riffles of streams on the Oak Ridges Moraine. They are a spectacular sight as they jump up the fish ladder on the Ganaraska River in Port Hope.

- Walleye lay their eggs in rocky, fast-flowing stretches of rivers and along shoals in lakes. They are best seen after dark so take a strong flashlight. At the same time or shortly after, hordes of suckers also spawn in fast-flowing waters as well as in streams. ◇

Late April

- Northern Pike spawn in flooded areas when the water is between 4° and 11° C. Muskellunge spawn on emergent vegetation at water temperatures of 9° to 15° C. ◇

- Yellow Perch, too, will reproduce in April if the water is warm enough. They spawn right after the suckers and deposit their gelatinous mass of eggs on woody debris in the water.

- Trout season in southern Peterborough County (division 6) opens on the last Saturday of the month.

Northern Pike and Muskellunge

Northern Pike spawn in the early spring shortly after the ice goes out. By mid-to-late April, pike move into weedy, shallow bays and flooded marshy areas to scatter and then desert their eggs. They will sometimes spawn in water so shallow that half the fish sticks out into the air! If you quietly walk or canoe along a marshy shoreline or flooded area, you may see what looks like a sleek, miniature submarine cruising along the edge of a cattail bed or between grassy hummocks. This is almost certainly a pike searching for a suitable weed bed on which to scatter eggs or sperm. Pike are a common fish in Chandos Lake and have also established themselves in lakes such as Cordova, Belmont and Crowe.

A short time later, when the water has warmed to between 9° C and 15° C, Muskellunge can be seen spawning in similar habitat. In the Kawartha Lakes, Muskies prefer to spawn along the edge of beds of emergent plants such as cattails. The eggs are deposited over

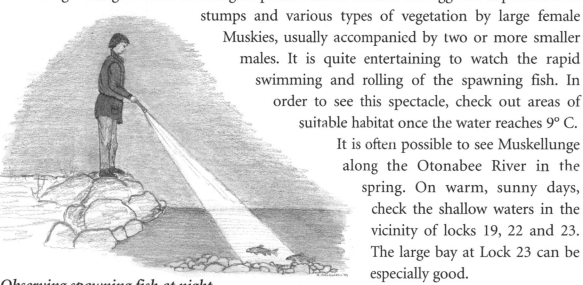

stumps and various types of vegetation by large female Muskies, usually accompanied by two or more smaller males. It is quite entertaining to watch the rapid swimming and rolling of the spawning fish. In order to see this spectacle, check out areas of suitable habitat once the water reaches 9° C. It is often possible to see Muskellunge along the Otonabee River in the spring. On warm, sunny days, check the shallow waters in the vicinity of locks 19, 22 and 23. The large bay at Lock 23 can be especially good.

Observing spawning fish at night.

Walleye and White Suckers

Starting sometime around the middle of April, when water temperatures reach 7° C, Walleye begin to spawn. In the Kawarthas, there are two different spawning modes. Some populations breed exclusively in fast-flowing water over gravelly and rocky bottoms. In fact, spawning Walleye can be seen in the fast water areas below almost any dam in the Kawarthas. Other populations spawn on shoals in large lakes such as Pigeon, Chemong and Clear. In the latter two lakes, the fish spawn primarily along the eastern shorelines.

The spawning period can last up to three weeks. After the eggs are deposited by the female and fertilized by the male, they are subsequently deserted. Because the growth of the young is based on water temperature, the best reproductive success occurs in years when the Walleye spawn a little later than usual, and there is a steady warming of water temperature without any significant cold periods. Extremely cold water can kill the fry. The spawning period can last up to three weeks.

Spawning activity makes for excellent fish-watching. Although some fish can be seen during the day, large numbers are usually observed only at night, when the actual spawning takes place. The fish are most active after dark and you will therefore need a strong-beamed flashlight or portable spotlight. The Walleye's eyes glow when a light is shone upon them. At Lock 19 in Peterborough, the gravel-covered spawning beds are located below the lock and dam along both shores. Other locations to see Walleye include Gannon's Narrows, the causeway across Chemong Lake and the rapids below the pedestrian bridge in Young's Point. In years past, the Water Street power dam near Langton Street in Peterborough was also a great spot for Walleye-watching. "All you could see were thousands of big eyes," recalled one area resident.

When you are watching Walleye, also keep an eye open for small, chubby fish that are spawning closer to shore in shallower water. These are Trout-Perch and, as their name suggests, they have characteristics of both the trout and perch families. They are an important food fish for many game species.

Walleye spawning.

Shortly after Walleye have begun spawning, White Suckers join the fray. They move up from lakes in the spring to deposit their eggs and sperm in fast-flowing sections of rivers and streams. Sometimes the schools can be so dense that a small stream may appear to be wall-to-wall fish, as they splash and scramble by the thousands over rocky rapids. The sucker is a prolific spawner, depositing an average of 50,000 eggs. As in the case of the Walleye, no attempt is made to care for the eggs.

Suckers are also one of the most easily watched spring spawners. The fish can be easily seen both day and night. Like Walleye, they spawn by the thousands at Lock 19 in Peterborough as well as in countless small streams throughout the Kawarthas. Suckers are a favourite spring food of bears, which have no trouble catching them in shallow water.

Insects and Other Invertebrates

April Highlights

All Month Long

- Early butterflies such as tortoiseshells and anglewings are sometimes seen flying, basking or feeding at sap flows. Watch in particular for Mourning Cloaks and Eastern Comma (winter form). ◇

- To attract these early butterflies to your yard, try putting out mashed bananas with the skin split.

- Woolly Bear caterpillars become active once again after overwintering as larvae curled up in some protected nook or cranny. They resume eating leaves for a short while and then pupate in a cocoon made from their own hairs. About two weeks later, they emerge from the cocoon as white Isabella Moths.

- Swarms of midges are a common sight near bodies of water.

- Large, pregnant queen wasps are often seen on warm days in early spring.

- On warm days mosquitoes of the *Culex* genus may appear. They have overwintered as adults.

- In areas where birch and aspen grow, watch for The Infant, an early spring geometer moth with orange and black hindwings. At a distance, this day-flying moth appears mostly orange and resembles a skipper butterfly.

Late April

■ If the weather is warm, the first Spring Azure and elfin butterflies are seen by month's end. There is always a chance, too, of finding a rarity like the Early Hairstreak; one was seen in 1999.

Butterflies of Early Spring

On a warm spring day when temperatures climb above 15° C, you may be surprised to see a butterfly in flight or feeding on sap oozing from a freshly cut tree stump. In fact, several species of our butterflies overwinter in the adult stage and become active again even before the last snow melts and the first flowers bloom. Species of the genus *Nymphalis* (the tortoiseshell butterflies) and, to a lesser degree, *Polygonia* (the anglewings) overwinter in the Kawarthas. They choose protected hideaways such as hollow trees or logs, woodpiles and the shelter afforded by loose boards on barns and sheds. One species, the Compton Tortoiseshell, is often found around cottages. Here it finds a good variety of wintering spots including the family outhouse!

Tree sap is probably the most common source of butterfly food in early spring. Butterflies are attracted to sap oozing from recently cut stumps, from broken branches and from tree taps at the local sugar bush. The Yellow-bellied Sapsucker is also an important ally of butterflies at this time of year. When sapsuckers return in April, they immediately begin to

Mourning Cloak Butterfly basking in spring sun.

drill their characteristic series of horizontal, pit-like holes in trees. Trembling Aspen, Red Maple, White Birch and Eastern Hemlock are commonly selected. The sapsucker feeds both on the sap itself and on the many small insects that the sap attracts. Butterflies, too, take advantage of this nectar-like liquid. Later in the spring, Ruby-throated Hummingbirds also drop by.

The most common butterfly species seen at this time of year is usually the Mourning Cloak. This large tortoiseshell butterfly has purple-brown wings edged with yellow. It will often feed with its wings wide open, thereby allowing a good view of the wing colour. In early spring, the sunny edges of mixed and deciduous forests as well as wooded cottage neighbourhoods are usually the best places to see butterflies. They also like to sit on roads in order to absorb heat.

Plants

April Highlights

All Month Long

- A pastel wash of swelling buds spreads over the landscape giving distant trees a soft, hazy appearance.
- Although White Spruce cones begin to open in the early fall, most of the seeds are dispersed in the spring.

Early April

- Coltsfoot send forth their dandelion-like flower heads.

Mid-April

- Male alder catkins grow into long, hanging tails that shed puffs of bright yellow pollen when touched.

Late April

- The first woodland wildflowers bloom. ◇
- By month's end, most of the wind-pollinated trees are in full bloom. Willows and maples have the best of both worlds in that they may also be pollinated by insects. ◇
- Farmers are cultivating their fields and usually planting the first hard corn, oats and spring wheat by the end of April.

Table 4.4: "First Bloom" Calendar For Selected Trees, Shrubs and Herbaceous Plants

early April	Coltsfoot, Red Maple, Speckled Alder, aspens, willows
mid-April	American Elm
late April	Manitoba Maple, Leatherwood, Bloodroot, Blue Cohosh, Trailing Arbutus, Dutchman's Breeches, Marsh Marigold, violets, hepaticas, dandelions, Peduncled Sedge, Distant Sedge, Plantain-leaved Sedge, Mountain Rice Grass

The First Trees in Flower

Almost without our knowing it, the flower buds of maples, poplars, willows, alders and elms are gradually transforming the April landscape. Well before the leaves appear, their flowers will already have released pollen to the spring winds. Because insect activity is so unpredictable during the cool days of April, most early-flowering species depend on the wind for pollination. The first tree off the mark is the Silver Maple whose flowers appear in March. Its fat, showy clusters of flower buds are red but the flowers themselves are greenish-yellow. Both male and female flowers appear on the same tree. About a week later, Red Maples blossom and brighten the landscape with crimson red flowers. Packed in tight clusters, male and female flowers usually appear on different branches of the same tree. Young trees, however, often produce only male or female flowers but not both. It is interesting to note that these female trees turn yellow in the fall, while the male trees turn red. The third maple to flower in April is the Manitoba Maple, a somewhat aberrant member of the clan. Not only does it have ash-like, compound leaves, but the pollen flowers and seed flowers appear on completely separate trees. The male flowers are at the end of long, slender stalks. This design probably facilitates pollination by the wind. Most maples, however, are both wind and insect-pollinated.

Elm flowers, looking like so many brown raindrops hanging from the branches, also add new colour to early spring's palette. The small, wind-pollinated flowers are clustered in loose tassels. Elms have perfect flowers consisting of both male and female parts. The seeds will mature and fall away even before the leaves reach their full size.

A large number of early-flowering trees produce their flowers in long, caterpillar-like catkins. This is the case for the willows, poplars and alders. Catkin-bearing trees are usually pollinated by the wind, although willows also benefit from some pollination by insects. The male flowers of the Speckled Alder are one of the most beautiful signs of spring in local wetlands. In the warm April sunshine, they swell into eight-centimetre-long purple, red and yellow garlands, releasing their pollen in golden puffs when jostled. The female flowers are nestled in small, erect catkins that become cone-like in appearance when the seeds are ripe. Old female cones from previous years can usually be found on the trees. Male and female alder catkins are borne on the same tree and are visible during the winter.

As for poplars, the pollen and seed catkins are located on separate trees. This has both advantages and disadvantages for the species. In most trees, self-pollination from male flowers on the same tree is possible, if not necessarily desirable. Female poplars, however, can produce seeds only if there is a male poplar nearby. This adaptation assures the production

Flowers of several early-blooming trees.

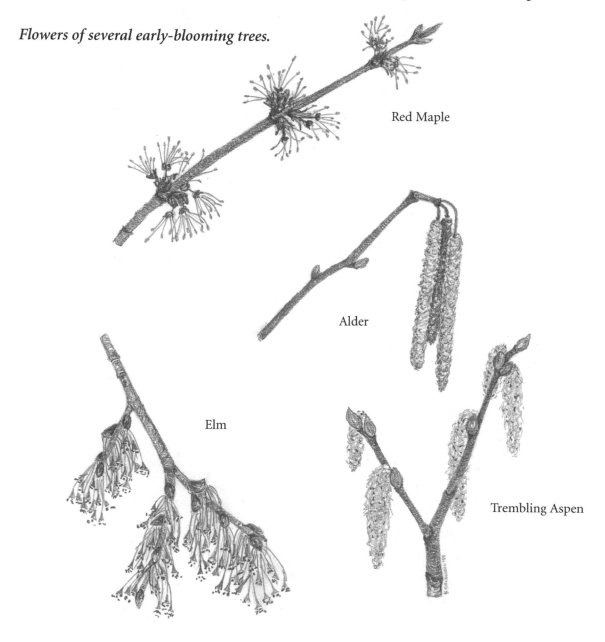

Red Maple

Alder

Elm

Trembling Aspen

of seeds with more genetic variability, because self-pollination results only in a repetition of the same genetic code. Just to be safe, poplars hedge their bets by reproducing to a very large extent through root suckering.

Willows are similar to poplars in that a given tree is either male or female. They differ, however, in that both wind and insects play a role in pollination. Depending on the species, the catkins appear well before the leaves or at the same time. The most famous of our willows is, of course, the Pussy Willow. In the early stages, male and female Pussy Willow catkins look very similar but by April, the differences become apparent. The male catkins are larger and covered with small, yellow flowers.

Coltsfoot: Perfectly Adapted to Early Spring

For most herbaceous plants, early spring temperatures are too cold for plant growth and for the survival of tender tissues like flowers. One species that has evolved to overcome this problem is the Coltsfoot, a plant similar to the dandelion in appearance. Its flowers are borne on scaly stalks that have evolved to protect the plant from most occurrences of severe cold. Initially, the plant sends up just flowers; only later in the spring will the leaves appear. This non-native plant is common along roadsides in well-drained gravel. In Peterborough, the south side of Parkhill Road just east of Brealey Drive is usually a good location for Coltsfoot.

Coltsfoot growing along a roadside.

Table 4.5: "Leaf-out" Calendar for Selected Trees, Shrubs and Herbaceous Plants

For each of the spring and summer months, the "leaf-out" calendar gives the approximate time when the better-known species come into leaf. As with flowering, the year-to-year variation in weather may accelerate or slow down the process of leafing out. Micro-climate can also have an effect. For example, cities tend to be warmer than outlying areas so city trees are usually in leaf first.

late April	currants, Red-berried Elder

Finding Early Spring Blooms

One of the best places to see woodland wildflowers, sedges and grasses is Mark S. Burnham Provincial Park, located just east of Peterborough. This is also an excellent location for early flowering shrubs such as Leatherwood and Red-berried Elder. Other good sites for spring botanizing include the various Trent University nature areas, the Heber Rogers Conservation Area on Clear Lake and Peter's Woods Provincial Park near Centreton in Northumberland County. Many species of interest, however, can be found in any large woodlot or forested area anywhere in the County. To find Trailing Arbutus, try locations on the Canadian Shield such as Petroglyphs Provincial Park. The plant tends to grow in exposed sandy areas, often near pine.

Weather

April Highlights

Early April

- Snowstorms and flooding are often part of the weather picture early in the month.

- We move our clocks ahead one hour on the first Sunday in April. Sunrise is suddenly about an hour later than the day before; this means getting up in the dark once again if you're an early riser.

Late April

- Most lakes in the Kawarthas are usually ice-free by April 20th. In recent years, however, the ice has been going out earlier. ◇

Table 4.6: **April Weather Averages, 1961-1990**

Daily Maximum	11.5° C
Daily Minimum	0.2° C
Extreme Maximum	29.7° C
Extreme Minimum	-15.0° C
Rainfall	56.2 mm
Snowfall	7.8 cm
Precipitation	66.3 mm

Ice-out

On our lakes, winter is slow to loosen its grip. The retreat of the ice occurs in fits and starts as spring warmth grows but then falters. Eventually, however, spring wins out and by April 20, most area lakes are open. The process, however, is more complicated than you might think. From below, the ice is being melted away by the relatively warmer meltwater flowing into the lake along the shoreline. From above, the ice is eroded by the warmth of the spring sun. When the snow cover on the surface melts, the deterioration of the ice picks up speed. Solar radiation penetrates into the ice creating tiny cracks. Meltwater infiltrates downwards through these cracks creating vertical columns. Ice that has been deteriorated in this manner is known as candled ice because it looks remarkably similar to a layer of vertically packed candles. With so much water present in the ice, the ice cover appears quite dark in colour. And then, within 24 hours, the ice is gone. But where? It hasn't sunk below the surface of the lake because ice is lighter than water. Nor has it been carried out by winds or currents. The decomposing ice pack has essentially collapsed and any remaining solid ice has melted away in the slightly warmer lake water. This fascinating process is also accompanied by its own music; listen especially for the crystal tinkling of candle ice and the roaring noise of waves as they roll under the ice surface.

Table 4.7: **Approximate Twilight, Sunrise and Sunset Times**

Date	Twilight Begins	Sunrise	Sunset	Twilight Ends
Apr. 1	5:25 a.m. EST	5:54 a.m. EST	6:41 p.m. EST	7:10 p.m. EST
Apr. 10	6:08 a.m. DST	6:38 a.m. DST	7:52 p.m. DST	8:22 p.m. DST
Apr. 20	5:50 a.m.	6:21 a.m.	8:04 p.m.	8:35 p.m.
May 1	5:32 a.m.	6:04 a.m.	8:18 p.m.	8:50 p.m.

Daylight Saving Time starts on the first Sunday in April. Set your clocks ahead one hour.

The Night Sky

April Highlights

All Month Long

- Major constellations and stars visible (April 15, 10:00 p.m. DST)

  Northwest: Taurus (with *Aldebaran*) due W; Cassiopeia is low in the sky; Pleiades are to its left

  Northeast: Big Dipper standing upright fairly high; Little Dipper (with *Polaris*) to its left

  Southeast: Leo (with *Regulus*) rules over the SE sky, Boötes (with *Arcturus*) and Virgo (with *Spica*) are almost due E

  Southwest: Orion (with *Betelgeuse* and *Rigel*) is low in W; Taurus (with *Aldebaran*) high to its right; Canis Major (with *Sirius*) low to its left; Canis Minor (with *Procyon*) above *Sirius*; Auriga (with *Capella*) high above Orion; Gemini (with *Castor* and *Pollux*) to left of Auriga

- Easter is celebrated on the Sunday after the first full moon following the spring equinox. The Christian Easter was preceded by an old pagan festival celebrating fertility and new growth. The enduring message of Easter has always been the celebration of new life.

- The date on which Easter is celebrated reminds us of how closely human events used to be tied to the phases of the moon. Knowing the different phases adds one more dimension to appreciating the rhythms of the natural world. ◇

- Early spring is the best time of the year to see a lunar halo. Look for it on evenings when the temperature is a few degrees above freezing. The halo appears like a silvery ring around the moon and is caused by the prism-like nature of high-altitude ice crystals.

Late April

- The Lyrids meteor shower can be seen in the northeast April 20-22.

Learning the Phases of the Moon

Easter, the oldest celebration in the Christian church, usually takes place in April. It provides an excellent example of the close links between many religious traditions and the cycles of the natural world. Not only are there the nature-related themes of rebirth and renewal, but the actual date on which Easter is celebrated is determined by the phases of the moon. Easter always occurs on the first Sunday after the full moon following the spring equinox.

Many of us are unfamiliar, however, with the comings and goings of the moon. It is just "somewhere up there," its movements are largely ignored and its amazing surface is only rarely looked at closely. Like the sun, the moon rises in the east and sets in the west. It follows roughly the same path through the sky as the sun and is actually visible during the day as much as during the night. But, unlike the sun, the moon rises each day an average of 50 minutes later than the day before. It takes the moon about 29 1/2 days to go through the full cycle of eight distinct phases:

1) *new moon*: The new moon rises and sets with the sun and stays close to it during the day. The sun shines on the far side of the moon during this phase making the moon invisible.

2) *waxing crescent*: It rises and sets shortly after the sun and can be quite striking in the evening twilight, low in the west. Earthshine (sunlight reflected off the earth, onto the moon and back again) dimly illuminates the moon's surface to the left of the crescent. Looking like the rounded part of a D, the waxing crescent is "Developing" towards the full moon.

3) *first quarter*: This is the familiar "half moon." It is called "first quarter" simply because the moon has completed one-quarter of the cycle from one new moon to the next. A quarter moon is in the sky about half the day and half the night. This is the best moon phase for looking at the moon's surface through binoculars. The shadows cast by the mountains and craters highlight the vast flat plains that the ancients called "maria," believing them to be seas.

4) *waxing gibbous*: The word gibbous means "like a hump." The waxing gibbous moon rises late in the day and shines most of the night, interfering with stargazing.

5) *full moon*: The beautiful full moon rises at sunset and sets at sunrise. It often appears like a huge orange ball as it climbs above the eastern horizon in the evening. A spring night lit up by a full moon and accompanied by a frog and woodcock displaying is an occasion not to be missed. Other birds, too, such as Killdeer, Mourning Dove and various sparrows often call sporadically at night when the spring moon is full.

6) *waning gibbous*: The waning gibbous moon rises after sunset and starts to take on the shape of a C. The moon is "Crumbling" away.

7) *last quarter*: Rising in the middle of the night, the last quarter moon doesn't interfere with stargazing until after midnight.

8) *waning crescent*: What is left of the crumbling moon rises and sets just before the sun and stays in the sky most of the day. A crescent moon at dawn or dusk seems to glow with peacefulness and connect us to a simpler, less frantic time.

If you are like many people and still have trouble telling whether or not the moon is waxing or waning, the following poem that I composed for my students may be of help.

"Light on right, moon soon bright.
Night on right, moon soon out of sight."

"Light" refers to the illuminated part of the moon; "bright" refers to the full moon; "night" refers to the dark part of the moon, and "out of sight" refers to the new moon.

Indigo Bunting at feeder.

NATURE'S YEAR IN THE KAWARTHAS

CHAPTER 5

May—The Promise of Spring Fulfilled

All of the promises that Nature has been making since the winter solstice are fulfilled in May. The birds of spring arrive en masse, leaves and flowers burst out all around us and any hint of winter is soon lost in the warmth and the sunshine. Although it seems foolish to talk of a favourite month, for anyone who takes pleasure in watching the seasons unfold May has no equal. In fact, if you want to fall in love with the natural beauty and diversity of the Kawarthas and have only a fortnight to spare, choose the last two weeks of May.

Not that all is idyllic. May advances in fits and starts depending on the vagaries of the weather. Cold weather is no stranger to the month nor are days of mid-summer heat. But, when the warm weather does arrive, it triggers change at a dizzying pace. This can be frustrating for anyone who is attempting to observe everything new that is happening.

May begins with tree branches bare to the sky and ends with the freshness of new leaf as a green veil is drawn down upon our forests and fence rows. But as the trees leaf out, the spectrum of pastel greens, whites, browns and reds offers a colour spectacle equal to that of fall—at least to those who take the time to appreciate the subtleties, nuances and changes occurring from one day to the next. Woodlots are carpeted with rafts of White Trilliums, fields glow with dandelion gold and lilacs bow heavy with blossom. Although lilac may be the sweetest fragrance of the month, Balsam Poplar is the most pervasive.

Southerly winds this month push avian migrants north to devour the billions of insects feasting on the rapidly developing green canopy. Many of these birds make brief appearances in our backyards as they make their way to nesting grounds further north. The serene piping of White-throated Sparrows and the exuberant song of the Ruby-crowned Kinglet often provide the background music for several days as we toil in our gardens, full of expectations for the new season. The arrival of the birds of spring is no less than a reaffirmation of life.

May At a Glance

May is the finest month of the year for birding. Songbird migration peaks, northward-bound Canada Geese continue to pass over. Expect "your" hummingbirds back early in the month as well.

A host of mammals give birth this month, fox-watching is at its best and, if you want to see Moose, head up to Algonquin Park. Female White-tailed Deer drive their male fawns from last year away as they prepare for fawning.

The American Toad, as well as nearly all of our local frog species, can be heard calling at some time this month. Garter and Northern Water Snakes mate and Midland Painted Turtles basking in the sun are once again a common sight.

This is a great time of year for fish-watching! Members of the sunfish family usually begin to spawn, as do many of the non-game species such as the beautiful Iowa Darter. Walleye and pike season opens and fly-fishing for Brook Trout is at its best.

Blackflies and mosquitoes make their presence known this month but so do graceful dragonflies and damselflies as well as a variety of beautiful "spring ephemeral" butterflies. June beetles crash into screen doors by night and tent caterpillars forage in trees by day.

Almost all of our native trees leaf out, providing a beautiful spectacle of pastel colours. Serviceberry, cherry and Lilac flowers brighten roadsides, while trilliums and other spring wildflowers carpet woodlots. Dandelions are everywhere.

The last frost occurs this month and cool weather and even snow are still possible. Near-summer warmth, however, is more typical. The average daily temperatures are a maximum of 19° C and a minimum of 6° C. In mid-May, the sun rises at about 5:45 a.m. and sets around 8:35 p.m.

The spring sky is still dominated by the constellation Leo. Look for Arcturus, the brightest of the spring stars and Spica, a star of the constellation Virgo. The Big Dipper is high in the northeast.

Birds

May Highlights

All Month

- Spring migration is at its busiest this month with the arrival of the long-distance migrants from the neo-tropics. May is synonymous with birding at its best. ◇

- On calm nights with low cloud cover, it is often possible to hear the contact calls of migrants as they pass overhead.

- With many species nesting, baby birds are inevitably found and believed to have been abandoned. Rarely is this the case. The cardinal rule is to leave them alone!

- Migrating Rose-breasted Grosbeaks and Indigo Buntings are becoming increasingly common at sunflower feeders, so keep your feeders stocked up at least until the end of the month. Grosbeaks will sometimes return to feeders later in the summer with their young in tow.

Early May

- Skeins of high-flying Northern Canada Geese pass over as they make their way to James Bay.

- Loons, either alone or in pairs, are often seen flying due north in the early morning. Knowing the meaning of loon "language," both vocal and behavioural, adds a great deal to our enjoyment of these magnificent birds. ◇

- Hummingbirds return from Central America and make a beeline to our feeders. Their natural food at this time of year includes tree sap oozing from Yellow-bellied Sapsucker drillings. Hummingbirds also eat the many insects that are attracted to these sap flows.

Mid-May

- Songbird migration is at its peak. Migrating warblers, vireos, thrushes, tanagers, orioles and flycatchers are most abundant between May 10th and 25th—exactly at the right time to take full advantage of the legions of insects that are emerging. Locally, Jackson Park and the adjacent rail-trail is a good spot to see and hear migrants, but get there early, preferably before 8:00 a.m.

Late May

- Non-breeding Giant Canada Geese start to migrate north to James Bay to moult.

Flocks of a hundred birds or more are sometimes seen. This "moult migration" continues until mid-June. Once there, they go through a complete wing moult which renders them flightless for a short period.

May Arrivals and Departures

early month

arrivals: Least Bittern, Least Sandpiper, Solitary Sandpiper, Spotted Sandpiper, Common Tern, Black Tern, Whip-poor-will, Ruby-throated Hummingbird, Red-headed Woodpecker, Eastern Kingbird, Great Crested Flycatcher, Least Flycatcher, Warbling Vireo, Yellow-throated Vireo, House Wren, Marsh Wren, Wood Thrush, Veery, Gray Catbird, American Pipit, Black-and-white Warbler, Yellow Warbler, Palm Warbler, Nashville Warbler, Blackburnian Warbler, Cape May Warbler, Black-throated Green Warbler, Black-throated Blue Warbler, Chestnut-sided Warbler, Northern Parula, American Redstart, Prairie Warbler, Cerulean Warbler, Magnolia Warbler, Golden-winged Warbler, Ovenbird, Scarlet Tanager, Grasshopper Sparrow, White-crowned Sparrow, Lincoln's Sparrow, Rose-breasted Grosbeak, Bobolink, Baltimore Oriole

departures: Red-necked Grebe, Horned Grebe, Ruddy Duck, Greater Yellowlegs, Pectoral Sandpiper

mid-month

arrivals: Long-tailed Duck, White-winged Scoter*, Eastern Wood-Pewee, Philadelphia Vireo, Red-eyed Vireo, Blue Jay (w), Sedge Wren, Swainson's Thrush, Bay-breasted Warbler, Wilson's Warbler, Tennessee Warbler, Common Yellowthroat, Clay-coloured Sparrow, Indigo Bunting

departures: Solitary Sandpiper, Ruby-crowned Kinglet (b), American Pipit, Lincoln's Sparrow, White-crowned Sparrow, Evening Grosbeak*, Pine Siskin.

late month

arrivals: Semipalmated Plover, Short-billed Dowitcher, Dunlin, Semipalmated Sandpiper, Wilson's Phalarope, Whimbrel, Black-billed Cuckoo, Common Nighthawk, Yellow-bellied Flycatcher, Willow Flycatcher, Alder Flycatcher, Olive-sided Flycatcher, Gray-cheeked Thrush, Cedar Waxwing (w), Blackpoll Warbler, Mourning Warbler, Canada Warbler

departures: White-winged Scoter, Long-tailed Duck, Lesser Yellowlegs, Yellow-bellied Flycatcher, Philadelphia Vireo, Swainson's Thrush, Gray-cheeked Thrush, Blackpoll Warbler, Cape May Warbler, Bay-breasted Warbler, Tennessee Warbler

The Neo-tropical Migrants Arrive at Last!

With May comes the biggest push of spring migration with nearly all of the long-distance migrants from Central and South America (the neo-tropics) arriving. It is possible to see more species at the height of migration in May than at any other time of year. Lengthening daylight causes the production of breeding hormones in birds and these increased hormonal levels in turn trigger migration. But weather, too, plays a key role. Large movements of birds are closely associated with warm weather so keeping an eye on the forecast can improve your birding success. Unlike fall migration, north winds and cool weather in the spring stall migration. The birds often wait in large numbers for warmer air and southerly winds to "push" them along. This phenomenon occurred during the exceptionally cool spring of 1997. Warblers usually observed only in early May were still backed up at Point Pelee on Lake Erie until the weekend of the 24th when warm weather finally arrived. As a general rule, however, neo-tropical migrants arrive on more predictable dates each year than those birds that winter in the continental United States.

Black-and-White-Warbler.

Most bird species migrate at night when there is less danger from predators. Migrants generally use the daylight hours for feeding and resting. If conditions are favourable, such as with the passage of a northward advancing warm front, birds will start migrating about one hour after sunset. It is quite common at this time to hear their contact calls as they fly overhead. Changing weather conditions during the night can also cause "groundings" of birds. When a northward moving warm front collides with a cold front, the warm air—and the birds in it—rises over the cold. The air cools, rain develops and the birds are forced to land. This means that rainy mornings in May can produce superb birding, especially when the rain is light and starts after midnight. On the other hand, long periods of fair weather with southerly winds allow the birds to fly well into the daylight hours and to disperse over a large area. Under these conditions there are no noticeable concentrations of migrants and spring migration is said to be "poor"—for the birders that is.

You don't have to go far afield either to see the birds of May. As long as there is sufficient cover, even city backyards can have their own coterie of migrants. Habitat edges are especially worth checking—woodlot edges, hedge rows, wooded roadsides, and the shrubby edges of wetlands. Some specific birding sites that are often productive include Jackson Park and Little Lake Cemetery in Peterborough, the trails on the Trent University Campus, Miller Creek Conservation Area, Sawer Creek Wetland, Squirrel Creek Conservation Area, Herkimer Point at Hiawatha, Young's Point (the large stand of White Pine on South Beach Road) and Petroglyphs Provincial Park.

Loon Language

The Common Loon is probably the best known bird of the Kawartha Lakes. Cottagers in particular are very possessive and protective of "their" loons and are understandably concerned about the birds' welfare. Knowing more about the loon's mysterious visual displays and soulful calls allows us to appreciate the birds even more.

Common Loons have at least four distinct calls. The "wail" is a wolf-like call lasting about two seconds. It is given by both sexes and is used to summon a mate or off-spring. The "tremolo" is a vibrating, laugh-like call which lasts only about one second and seems to indicate alarm. It is given when either sex is disturbed or senses danger. The "yodel" is a long and complex call that starts with a wail and then changes into a series of yodel-like undulations. It is territorial in nature and is given by the male. This call is most common in spring and is usually heard between dusk and dawn. Finally, both sexes will also use "hoots" which are short, soft, contact calls often given when the birds congregate in flocks.

Loons are also famous for their unique visual displays. "Bill-dipping" often occurs when two birds meet each other, especially in a flock, and may serve to reduce aggressive tendencies. When territorial skirmishes occur, loons will sometimes raise their body upright out of the water and tread with their feet. Males may also hold their wings out to the side and give the yodel call. Another visual display used by males during territorial conflicts involves extending the head and neck on the water. Once again the yodel call is often produced at this time.

Mammals

May Highlights

All Month Long

■ A large variety of mammals give birth this month. These include Beavers, Red Squirrels, Northern and Southern Flying Squirrels, Red Foxes, "Eastern" Wolves, River Otters, Porcupines, Groundhogs, Striped Skunks, Moose and White-tailed Deer.

■ Fox-watching is at its best. ◇

■ If you have never seen a Moose, now is the time to go up to Algonquin Park. They are quite common along the side of Highway 60 in May and June, attracted by puddles of salty snowmelt from winter road maintenance operations. An increasing number of moose is also being seen in Peterborough County, sometimes as far south as Haultain on Highway 28.

■ Before giving birth to their new fawns, female White-tailed Deer drive their male fawns from last year out of the area to avoid interbreeding.

■ The buck White-tail's antler growth accelerates dramatically as a result of the increased daylight. They tend to be almost secretive during spring and early summer, spending their time with other bucks and allowing the does a wide berth.

Mid-May

■ Moose give birth to one or two calves, almost always during the second half of May. An island is often the nursery of choice.

Late May

■ White-tailed Deer fawns are usually born in late May or early June. If conditions are good, two fawns will be born.

Fox-Watching

May and early June provide an excellent opportunity to observe Red Foxes. At this time of year when the young are born, it is relatively easy to observe the kits playing outside the den. The dens are often located in abandoned Groundhog holes or dug by the adults on a sandy slope, frequently at the edge of a woods or on a knoll. Fortunately for the mammal-watcher, the same den may be used for many years. The kits begin to come out of the den when they are about a month old. The female remains with the kits for the first month or so while the male does most of the hunting. She can often be seen outside the den, doing her best to tolerate the antics of her playful litter. It is best to approach the den slowly from a downwind direction and to stop often in order not to startle the animals. Foxes and other mammals can also be seen along road margins in the twilight period before sunrise as they scavenge for road-killed animals. Watch for the glimmer of the fox's green eyes in the headlights.

Fox cubs in front of den.

Amphibians and Reptiles

May Highlights

All Month Long
- Nearly all of our local frog and toad species can usually be heard calling at some time this month.

- Northern Water Snakes mate in May by entwining themselves around each other. They sometimes can be seen partaking in mating activity on low branches and in other vegetation near the water's edge.

Early May
- The long, fluid trills of American Toads can often be heard both day and night as they sing and mate in marshes and in temporary meltwater ponds. They can sometimes even be heard calling from backyard garden ponds. ◇

- Midland Painted Turtles basking in the sunshine are once again a common sight on logs and hummocks in local wetlands. ◇

Mid-May
- Gray Treefrogs, Green Frogs, Mink Frogs and Bullfrogs join the chorus.

Trilling Toads

The call of the American Toad is without a doubt one of the most pleasant and typical sounds of May. Like frogs, male toads defend territories and advertise their presence to females by singing. The long, high-pitched musical trill can last up to 30 seconds and can be heard both day and night. When more than one male are singing at a time, each individual will usually sing at a slightly different pitch. It is also possible to watch toads as they gather in marshes and in pools of temporary, shallow meltwater for a veritable mating frenzy. Mating activity lasts for only a few days, however, so you have to check the breeding sites soon after you hear the animals start calling. Males are easy to identify because they are half the size of females, and their inflated vocal sacs stand out prominently when they call. The males will literally throw themselves on everything that moves, including the observer's rubber boots! Once a female is found, the male holds on to her back for dear life until she lays her eggs which he will fertilize. Unlike frogs, toad eggs are in ribbon-like strings instead of big clumps.

Painted Turtle basking on a log.

Basking Turtles

Given all that turtles have to do in the short period between May and September—hunt, eat, grow, mate, lay eggs—it may seem somewhat bizarre that they spend so much time simply basking in the sun. The explanation lies in the fact that they are ecothermic (cold-blooded) and can raise their body temperature only by absorbing heat from their surroundings. A high body temperature is necessary in order to digest food and to be able to hunt effectively. Turtles accomplish this by crawling up onto rocks and logs and exposing their entire body—including spread-out toes—to the sun. By doing so, they can achieve a body temperature eight to ten degrees higher than the surrounding air. Female turtles are especially fond of basking at this time of year. Researchers speculate that this may help to speed up development of the eggs that they will be laying in a few weeks. In the relatively cold Canadian climate, basking may make all the difference in successful reproduction.

Fishes

May Highlights

All Month Long
- Many of our non-game species such as minnows, sticklebacks and darters spawn in the spring. ◇

Mid-Month
- The fishing season for Walleye and Northern Pike opens on the second Saturday of the

month in southern Peterborough County and the third Saturday in the north. The only exceptions are some fast-water areas which remain closed for one additional week to protect adult fish after spawning.

Late Month

- Members of the sunfish family such as Smallmouth Bass and Pumpkinseed begin to spawn.

- Fly fishing for Brook Trout is at its best. Because the water is still quite cool, the fish are often near shore and can sometimes be seen jumping for flying insects.

Getting to Know Our Non-game Species

The Kawarthas boast a large number of fascinating non-game fish species, most of which are largely unknown to the public. A perfect example is the beautiful Iowa Darter. Members of the perch family, darters are never seen swimming or resting in normal fish fashion but spend most of their time on the bottom. And, just as the name implies, these fish actually dart about from one spot to another. The Iowa Darter averages about six centimetres in length and frequents the shallow waters of lakes and rivers and occasionally, the

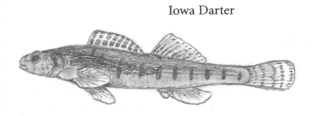

Iowa Darter

Several common non-game fish species.

fast-flowing sections of gravelly streams. Spring males are so vividly coloured that you might think you are looking at an escapee from a tropical fish aquarium. In May, they show blue or green bars between the brown stripes on the sides, are yellow underneath and have reddish lower fins. To top it off, the first dorsal fin is banded in blue and red.

The Iowa Darter is an ideal species for fish-watching because it spawns so close to shore.

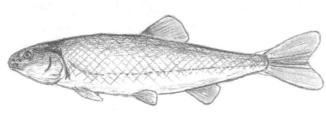

Creek Chub

The female darter deposits her eggs beneath undercut banks of lakeshores or along the shore of quieter sections of streams. The eggs are laid on fibrous roots or organic debris. There is no parental care of the eggs or young. Iowa Darters are found throughout the

Kawarthas. The best places to watch for them are in the quiet waters along the shore of a lake.

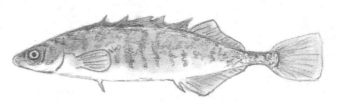

Brook Stickleback

Most species of the minnow family are also spawning this month. The Creek Chub, a popular bait minnow, spawns in clear streams when the water temperature reaches 16° to 21° C. The eggs are deposited in a mound-like nest of stones constructed by the male. Large Creek Chub can be seen in most streams, and it is possible to observe the male guarding the eggs from predators. This attractive minnow has a steely appearance and a very dark lateral stripe. Spawning males actually develop large, sharp tubercles on the head.

Insects and Other Invertebrates

May Highlights

All Month Long

- The first dragonflies and damselflies change from forbidding aquatic nymphs to gracious adult flying machines, ready to prey on other insects. The first species seen is usually the large and ubiquitous Common Green Darner. Early darners are often individuals that migrated south for the winter.

- This is the flight season for the "spring ephemeral" butterflies such as the Olympia Marble, Chryxus Arctic, the rare West Virginia White and several of the elfins. Start looking for them early in the month, especially if the weather is warm.

- Large, pregnant queen bumblebees forage at flowers and search out a suitable underground chamber in which to make a nest and start a new colony.

- When the water warms sufficiently, crayfish moult and then mate. Ninety-nine percent of the crayfish in the Kawarthas south of the Canadian Shield are Rusty Crayfish, an alien species introduced fro the United States. It is named for the reddish-brown patches on its carapace. Because of the Rusties success, native crayfish species south of the Shield have nearly disappeared.

- Zebra Mussels reproduce when the water temperature climbs above 12° C. Mature females can produce more than 40,000 eggs per year. ◇

Early May

■ Blackflies are usually at their worst about now. One square metre of a fast-running stream can produce over 30,000 in one season! ◇

Mid-May

■ At about the same time as the wild cherries bloom, mosquitoes become quite noticeable and pesky! Mosquitoes feed on the nectar of cherry blossoms and help to cross-pollinate the trees. ◇

■ The Spring Field Cricket serves up the first insect music of the year.

Late May

■ Adult June beetles emerge from the soil and crash into doors and windows at night.

■ Gypsy Moth and tent caterpillar infestations sometimes reach epic proportions in late May. ◇

■ Canadian Tiger Swallowtails and Black Swallowtails appear by month's end and are often seen "puddling" for salts along dirt roads.

■ Frothy, white masses of spittle become a common sight on the stems of plants in lush, weedy areas. They are created by spittlebug nymphs which suck juices out of the plant's stem and then excrete the excess. This creates a froth which envelopes the insect and probably provides protection from predators. Adult spittlebugs resemble leafhoppers.

Zebra Mussels

Zebra Mussels, small clam-like shellfish of Eurasian origin, have been steadily increasing in the Kawartha Lakes since the mid-1990s. Their yellowish-brown, D-shaped shells can grow up to five centimetres in length and are sharp enough to tear your skin off. Zebra Mussels attach themselves to solid objects such as submerged rocks and dock pilings in shallow, algae-rich water. Being filter-feeders, they are able to make a remarkable difference in water clarity. This allows for greater light penetration which can in turn impact on the entire ecological balance of the lake.

Mature female mussels can produce in excess of 40,000 eggs per year. The eggs are released when the temperature climbs above 12°C and hatch into free-swimming, microscopic larvae known as veligers. This larval stage accounts for the rapid spread of Zebra Mussels; they are able to survive in any residual water source and are often inadvertently introduced into another lake. Veligers drift with the currents for three or four weeks as they seek out a hard surface on which to attach themselves. They then transform into the typical clam-shaped mussel. Sexual maturity is usually attained within one year.

Many cottagers are unaware that Zebra Mussels will actually abandon a given area if food supplies dwindle. This behaviour often leads people to believe that the mussel population is declining. The mussels actually release themselves from whatever object they have been clinging to and drift in the current in hope of finding a richer feeding ground. But, if the food supply should once again increase, other mussels will soon show up to take advantage of it. Diving ducks such as scaup and Ring-necked Ducks eat large quantities of Zebra Mussels, but these ducks pass through our area for only a few weeks during migration and there are far more mussels than ducks! The long-term impact of Zebra Mussels on the Kawartha Lakes still waits to be seen.

Blackflies

In May, there is a price to be paid for the bird music and flowers that we enjoy so much. The price is called blackflies. Unlike the "good and bad" years of mosquitoes, blackflies are bad every year. There really is no escaping them. Blackfly larvae require cold, clear running water in which to develop. This sort of habitat is everywhere on the Canadian Shield making the northern Kawarthas a blackfly paradise. But, because the adults disperse widely after emerging from the pupae, avoiding areas with streams is not always a solution. Some species are considered "woodland" and others prefer more open country.

The first onslaught of blackflies develops from eggs that hatched the previous fall. The larvae grow slowly over the course of the winter and then spin cocoons in the spring in which they transform into adults. A bubble of air carries them to the surface, releasing a ready-to-fly adult when the bubble bursts. It is possible to see this "popping out" taking place. The freshly emerged adult usually buzzes around on the water's surface for a few seconds and then flies to a shaded area to rest and allow its cuticle to harden and dry. In other species of blackflies, the eggs overwinter and hatch in the spring. These species do not mature into biting adults until June or later. Fortunately for us, those adults that emerge in mid-to-late summer never reach the huge numbers of spring blackflies.

The majority of blackfly species produce only one generation of adults in a year. A given female, however, is able to produce eggs two or three times during her short lifetime. In some species the females already have fully developed eggs when they emerge as adults and do not require a blood meal at all. In most species, however, a blood meal is necessary in order to provide the required nutrients for egg development. It often takes two or three blood meals for the female to fill her gut, each meal taking three to five minutes of uninterrupted eating! Luckily, not all blackfly species feed on humans; some prey on birds or other mammals. It might also be some consolation to know that both male and female blackflies feed heavily on nectar to obtain the energy necessary for flying and mating. In the process, they inadvertently pollinate many species of plants.

Mosquitoes

When the cherries begin to blossom in mid-May, the appearance of the first mosquitoes is not far behind. Both males and females feed heavily on the nectar of cherry flowers. Like the blackfly, however, the female mosquito requires a blood meal for her eggs to develop properly.

Although there are 59 species of mosquitoes in Ontario, many do not bite humans and most produce only one generation of adults a year. The majority of the mosquitoes found in the Kawarthas belong to the genus *Aedes*. The larvae hatch from overwintering eggs laid in mud the previous year. In the spring, these muddy areas are flooded by melting snow and rainfall and create an ideal habitat—generally devoid of predators—for the larvae to develop. A warm, damp May assures quick growth and means the breeding pools will not dry up before the adult mosquitoes emerge. Some *Aedes* species breed only once while others, such as *Aedes vexans*, breed continuously from June until September. *Vexans* is usually only a problem in wet summers, however, because it requires muddy areas created by rainfall to lay its eggs on. For this species, the period from the time the eggs are laid until the adults emerge can be as little as four to five days under favourable conditions.

A species that is found typically in urban areas is *Culex pipiens*, also known as the Northern House Mosquito. They breed in any locations where water collects and stands still. These can include old tires, tin cans and even a glass of water left outside. They will also breed in heavily polluted water. The eggs develop into adults in about a week. *Culex pipens* are present from spring until fall. They overwinter as adult mated females which find shelter in locations where the temperature remains

Mosquito feeding on nectar at cherry blossom.

above freezing, such as cellars, sewers, well pits and even animal burrows. With warm spring days, these females seek a blood meal and begin the cycle again.

Despite the bother mosquitoes cause us, it is important to remember the central role they play in wetlands. Mosquitoes can be thought of as a pipeline channeling energy from decomposing plant matter on the pond bottom directly to the birds nesting in the dead tree above the same pond. Mosquito larvae convert the decomposed matter into living insect protein, fat and carbohydrates and serve as food for countless other animal species including fish and predatory aquatic insects. Adult mosquitoes provide food for numerous species of insectivorous insects such as dragonflies and for birds such as swallows and nighthawks. When people spray mosquito habitat, the energy pipeline is shattered.

Tent Caterpillars

As green foliage transforms the landscape, hordes of caterpillars are provided with an almost unlimited source of food. Tent caterpillars, in particular, can be very plentiful. We have two species in our area, the Forest Tent and the Eastern Tent Caterpillar. Only the latter actually constructs a tent. Eastern Tent Caterpillars emerge in mid-May from "varnish-coated" egg masses wrapped tightly around the twig of a cherry or apple tree. They spin a small silken tent in a crotch of the same tree and enlarge the tent as they grow. The caterpillars feed outside the tent during the day, using it only for resting. Even though they may completely defoliate their

Eastern Tent Caterpillar— note tent.

host tree, new leaves grow and the tree usually recovers. When fully grown, the caterpillars leave the tree and spin a cocoon in some sheltered location. By summer they will have transformed into nondescript, brown moths measuring about three centimetres across.

Forest Tent Caterpillars feed on a much larger variety of deciduous trees than their tent-making cousins. They can therefore defoliate large areas of forest in years when their population peaks. Like the Eastern Tent Caterpillar, they are a species native to Ontario.

About every 10 years, an outbreak occurs and can last for several years. Aspen are the preferred host trees although they will readily feed on other hardwoods as well. Even trees that have been completely stripped of their leaves usually refoliate in three to six weeks. These caterpillars are distinctive because of the keyhole-shaped markings on their back.

Although Forest Tent Caterpillars do not make tents, they do spin silken threads for pathways to and from their feeding sites on the trees. When the light is right, it is possible to see hundreds of these silk highways in the treetops. At maturity, the caterpillars spin white, silken cocoons on trees, fences, buildings and other structures. They remain in the cocoons for about ten days. By about the first week of July, they will have metamorphosed into fuzzy yellow or buff-coloured moths.

Forest Tent Caterpillar numbers are naturally regulated by factors such as late spring frosts which kill the larvae, bird predation—cuckoos love them—and parasitic and predatory insects. The most important predatory insect is the Tachnid Flesh Fly which may destroy over 80% of the larvae.

In order to control tent caterpillars on your property, the egg bands (overwintering stage) can be removed from the twigs by hand between July and the following spring. After hatching in the spring, look for black clusters of the caterpillars on the main stem, especially in the evening or on cool days. These can be pruned off or squashed.

Gypsy Moths

Gypsy Moths were accidentally introduced to North America from Europe in 1869 and have been present in Ontario since at least 1981. The caterpillars damage our forests by eating the leaves of hardwoods and even some conifers. They have a particular affection for oaks, poplars and White Birch. It is estimated that each Gypsy Moth caterpillar will consume about one square metre of foliage during its life! Infestations often last several years. Repeated defoliation weakens trees and makes them more susceptible to other stress factors such as drought and fungal infections.

The eggs are laid in July or early August and hatch in late April or early May of the following spring. The tiny caterpillars climb trees and hang from silk threads, often being blown by the wind to other trees. The caterpillar stage lasts for about two months. The most damage to trees is done by large caterpillars, usually in late June. In July, the caterpillars go into the pupal stage, at which time they transform into white moths. It is interesting to note that despite having wings, female Gypsy Moths cannot fly and must make the males come to them. They attract the male moths by releasing airborne chemicals called sex pheromones.

After mating, the female lays a buff-coloured mass of 200 to 1,000 eggs and covers the mass with hairs from her body for protection. Humans may inadvertently transport egg masses on such items as firewood, trailers and bicycles. This helps to explain the long-distance spread of the insect.

Homeowners can reduce Gypsy Moth numbers on their property by scraping the egg masses from trees and either burning or squashing them. When they are in the caterpillar stage, you can tie strips of burlap around the trunks of trees. The caterpillars will hide under these, especially on sunny days. The insects can then be collected and squashed or thrown into a bucket of soapy water.

Serious Butterfly-Watching Begins!

Butterfly activity in May depends a great deal on the weather. The warmer it is, the more species of butterflies will be active. Because species such as Mourning Cloaks and Eastern Commas overwinter as adults, they can usually be found on any warm day. Other species, however, require an extended period of warm weather in order to complete their metamorphosis into adults.

Table 5.1: **Some May Butterflies of the Kawarthas**

Canadian Tiger Swallowtail	Mourning Cloak	Juvenal's Duskywing
Mustard White	Dreamy Duskywing	Cabbage White
Chryxus Arctic	Eastern Pine Elfin	Eastern Comma
Spring Azure	Compton Tortoiseshell	Hobomok Skipper
Olympia Marble	Columbine Duskywing	West Virginia White (rare)
Northern Cloudywing	Hoary Elfin	
Henry's Elfin	Milbert's Tortoiseshell	

Many of the spring butterflies are most commonly found in the northern part of the Kawarthas. A number of them are also single-brooded, which means that there is only one generation flying per year. Habitat edges are best for butterfly-watching. This may be an area where a field and woodlot meet, at the edge of a marsh or along a road. Butterflies are also attracted to lilac flowers, sometimes in considerable numbers. Some specific locations you may wish to try for spring butterfly-watching include the Sandy Lake Road north of Havelock, Petroglyphs Provincial Park and the Galway-Cavendish Forest Access Road south of Lake Catchacoma. The latter is a good place to look for the West Virginia White.

Table 5.2: Common May Dragonflies and Damselflies

dragonflies:	Common Green Darner, American Emerald, Hudsonian Whiteface, Four Spotted Skimmer
damselflies:	Boreal Bluet, Eastern Forktail

Plants

May Highlights

All Month Long

- Although not as flamboyant as the colours of fall, spring offers an equally beautiful flush of colour. From the white blossoms of serviceberry and cherry trees to the lime greens of distant woodlands, the season paints the landscape with a gentle warmth all its own. ◇

- Dandelions bloom in profusion, turning some fields almost as yellow as goldenrod will in September. Within days the yellow flowers are replaced by white seed heads. ◇

- A number of native sedges, rushes and grasses bloom in the spring at about the time the leaves are coming out. Look for Pennsylvania Sedge, Woodland Poa grass and Wood Rush. ◇

- Poison Ivy often makes its presence known. ◇

- For most of May, trees such as ash and oak look the same as they did all winter. They will not leaf out until the end of the month.

- Late spring frosts may destroy blooms or injure flower buds so that the bloom is deferred or never develops at all.

- *Agrocybe dura,* or Cracked Top Mushroom, is a common spring species that appears on lawns in May and early June. It is cream or tan in colour, with a small cap. *Panaeolus foenisecii,* or Brown Hay Cap, is also a very common lawn mushroom from spring through fall. When fresh, the whole mushroom is dark chocolate brown. Morrels also fruit in the spring and make for delicious eating, especially with fresh Brook Trout!

- For farmers, this is the busiest time of the year. Hard corn and soybeans are sown in May and, towards the end of the month, white beans are being planted.

Early May

- Along roadsides and rail-trails, watch for the light brown stems of Common Horsetails rising from the ground in large colonies. You can see the spore cones on the tips of some of the stems.

Mid-May

- Deciduous woodlots display a profusion of spring ephemeral wildflowers including Spring Beauty, Yellow Trout Lily, Large-flowered Bellwort and, of course, White Trillium. Their life cycle is controlled by the rhythms of the forest canopy. ◇

- Most trees are in leaf by the middle of the month.

- Sugar Maples appear light yellow from the thousands of yellow flowers in bloom. Within a week or so, they fall to leave a yellow confetti on sidewalks, driveways and roadsides.

Late May

- The spring ephemeral wildflower display draws to a close. Trees have leafed out, and the forest floor is shrouded in shade.

- Trembling Aspens and dandelions release their seeds and fill the air with their white "parachutes." Elms, Norway Maple and Silver Maple also shower the ground with their seeds.

- Allergies from grass and tree pollen (especially birch) can be bad. Birch pollen is nearly as irritating as ragweed. Most pollen is released in the morning between 8:00 a.m. and noon, when the anthers dry and burst open. Grass pollen levels rise towards the end of the month and remain high until late July.

Table 5.3: **"First Bloom" Calendar For Selected Trees, Shrubs and Herbaceous Plants**

early May	Leatherleaf, Sweetgale, Fly Honeysuckle, Red Trillium, Marsh Marigold, Spring Beauty, Yellow Trout Lily, Early Meadow Rue, Large-flowered Bellwort, Prairie Buttercup, Kidney-leaved Buttercup, Prickly Gooseberry, serviceberries
mid-May	Pin Cherry, Red-berried Elder, Common Lilac, White Trillium, Red Trillium, Painted Trillium, Wild Strawberry, Pussy Toes, Early Saxifrage, Two-leaved Toothwort
	Flower cones appear on pine, fir and spruce.
late May	Striped Maple, White Ash, Choke Cherry, Tartarian Honeysuckle, Red-osier Dogwood, Hobblebush, Showy Orchis, Early Coralroot, Pink Ladies'-slipper, Yellow Ladies'-slipper, Ram's-head Orchid, Fringed Polygala, Jack-in-the-Pulpit, Wild Columbine, Barren Strawberry, False Solomon's Seal, Mayapple, Common Buttercup, blueberries, currants, hawthorns, mustards

A selection of spring ephemeral wildflowers.

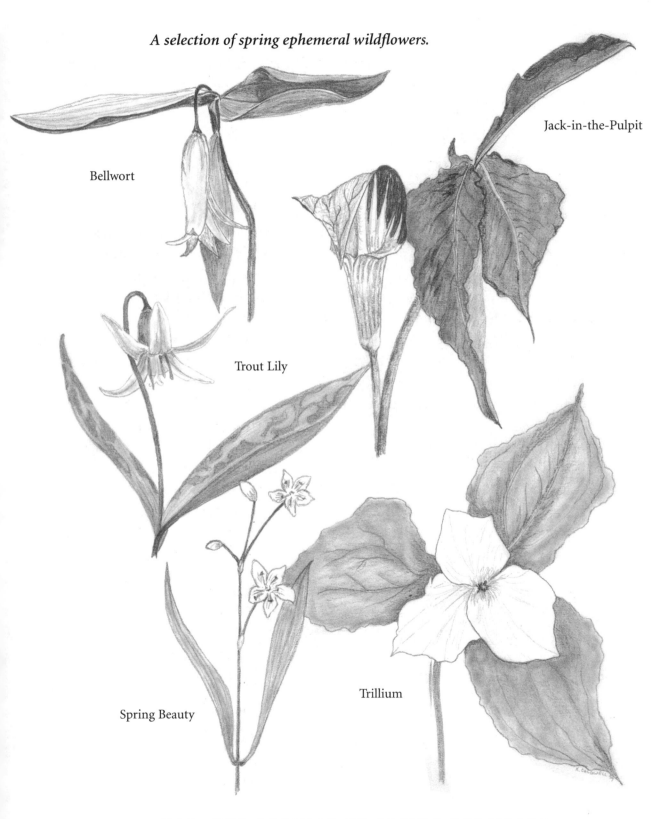

Bellwort

Jack-in-the-Pulpit

Trout Lily

Spring Beauty

Trillium

Table 5.4: "Leaf-out" Calendar for Selected Trees, Shrubs and Herbaceous Plants

early May	Tartarian Honeysuckle, Pin Cherry, Choke Cherry, Manitoba Maple, Norway Maple, Trembling Aspen, Common Lilac, willows
mid-May	Sugar Maple, Bigtooth Aspen, Tamarack
late May	Red Oak, White Oak, American Basswood, American Elm, White Ash, Red Maple

The Colours of Spring

Although the fall colours inevitably receive the most press, there is an equally beautiful showing of colour in the spring. A wash of pastel greens, reds and yellows appears over forest and woodland as buds begin to open and flowers and leaves emerge. The Trembling Aspen is one of the first trees to leaf out, along with many of the willows. About a week later, the Bigtooth Aspen becomes quite noticeable with its unique silver-grey foliage. In the city, Manitoba Maple and bright lime-green Norway Maple lead the way. At about the same time, Sugar Maples take on a characteristic light yellow appearance as thousands of tiny flowers open in the warm May sunshine. Another beautiful tree of spring is the Tamarack. Its soft needles are a gentle light green, every bit as beautiful as the smoky gold that they become in late October.

White, too, is signature colour of May. Like so many of the woodland plants that bloom this month, white blossoms also adorn our most conspicuous native shrubs. Early in the month, serviceberries stand out like white beacons against the slowly greening landscape. These small trees grow in clumps and are common along roadsides and field edges. We tend to notice them only in the spring, however, when their beautiful masses of white, five-petal flowers burst forth. Belonging to the genus *Amelanchier*, they go by a number of different

Tamarack coming into leaf.

common names, including shadbush—because they flower at the same time as shad fish from the Atlantic Ocean invade the rivers of New England, Juneberry—because their fruits ripen in June, and serviceberry—because their flowering coincided with funeral services held by early settlers in the spring to bury people who had died during the winter; winter burial was impossible because of the frozen ground. The fruits of serviceberries are very popular with wildlife and have usually all disappeared by early summer.

By mid-May, Choke and Pin Cherries join the parade and add their own splashes of white. They tend to grow in the same habitat as the serviceberries. Cherry leaves are unique in that they are tinged with bronze-orange when they emerge.

A Few Words About Dandelions

If not the most loved, perhaps the most common plant to flower in May is the dandelion. Introduced from Europe, dandelions provide copious amounts of pollen and nectar to insect visitors. Botanists speculate that when dandelions are at their flowering peak, almost all of the insects abandon other plants in order to take advantage of the feast offered by these yellow-flowered aliens. This almost certainly has a negative effect on the ability of these other plants to set seed and could theoretically force them to eventually shift their flowering dates. Early in the spring, when the only meadow plants in flower are a few dandelions, it is fascinating to sit and watch how insects such as bumblebees are attracted to them. Insects see the flowers as shining points of ultraviolet light set against a green background which they perceive as grey. The bees will suddenly change their flight path and head directly to the dandelions like iron shavings to a magnet. Ultraviolet light is invisible to humans.

Dandelions also have a number of other interesting attributes. The spring leaves are delicious in a salad, and the flowers are largely responsible for the first honey of the season, thanks to the abundant pollen and nectar they provide to honey bees. The flowers are also a favourite spring food of Black Bears.

An Overlooked Treasure: Grasses, Sedges and Rushes

Probably the most overlooked group of plants, even by naturalists, are the grasses, sedges and rushes. This is unfortunate because, to many people's surprise, grasses do have flowers, the flowers are surprisingly colourful and there is a great deal of diversity in their size and design. Several problems, however, exist for the amateur naturalist. Most plant books base identification on characteristics of the mature fruit. However, fruit matures later in the season

(June for many sedges and July or August for most grasses) so early spring identification is more difficult. Once you get to know the species well, identification based on flower or vegetative traits becomes possible. It is also necessary to use the scientific names when dealing with these plants and to forget about common names. For grasses and sedges, there is no accepted standard source for common names, and many species have no common names at all.

Carex lucorum sedge.

Quite a large number of sedges, grasses and rushes flower in the spring. The earliest species are often in well-drained upland woods like Mark S. Burnham Park. Pennsylvania Sedge (*Carex pensylvanica*) is a common spring-flowering sedge species locally. It is replaced by the very similar *Carex lucorum* on the Canadian Shield in more northern parts of the county. Both species grow in open woodlands. Two other rather common spring-flowering sedges are Plantain-leaved Sedge (*Carex plantaginea*), a distinctive broad-leaved sedge of upland woods such as Mark S. Burnham Provincial Park, and Pedunculate Sedge (*Carex pedunculata*), a smaller species with reddish bases and pedunculate spikes (flower stalks). The latter occurs in a variety of woodland habitats.

Common spring-flowering grasses include Woodland Poa (*Poa alsodes*), a species of upland woods, and Mountain-rice (*Oryzopsis asperifolia*) which grows in a variety of wooded and semi-wooded situations. A less common species is Sweet Grass (*Hierochloe odorata*). It can be found along roadsides and on open, often sandy ground. Sweet Grass is also known as Vanilla Grass.

Although most rushes flower in late summer, two local wood rushes, *Luzula multiflora* and *Luzula acuminata*, are spring-flowering. The former is the earlier of the two to flower. Both grow in woodlands.

Poison Ivy

Poison Ivy also attracts considerable attention in the spring but not because of its flowers. May seems to be the time of year that so many of us end up with its infamous rash. There are three easy ways to distinguish Poison Ivy from other three-leaved plants. The middle leaflet has a much longer stem than the other two, the leaflets droop downward, and at least one of the leaflets is almost always asymmetrical—the left side and right side are different. For example, one side may have three "teeth" and the other side none. There is great variability in leaf size and shininess and in the sort of habitat where the plant is found.

About 70% of people are quite allergic to Poison Ivy while the other 30% may eventually become susceptible after repeated exposures. A rash from Poison Ivy can be contracted in a number of ways. These include exposure to smoke from burning the plants, simply touching an unbroken leaf or even petting the family dog after he has gone for a romp through the plants. If you do walk through a patch of Poison Ivy, be sure to wash your socks and pants because the oil remains dangerous for up to a week.

Living by the Rhythms of the Forest Canopy

Most people who enjoy nature would agree that the spring ephemerals—woodland herbaceous plants with a short blooming period—are the most beautiful and finely adapted segment of the yearly floral calendar. This group includes Spring Beauty, Mayapple, Blue Cohosh, Yellow Trout Lily, Jack-in-the-Pulpit, Bloodroot, Squirrel Corn, Dutchman's Breeches, violets, toothworts, hepaticas and trilliums. They are nearly all restricted to deciduous forests and woodlots, because their life cycle is attuned to the rhythms of the forest canopy. For this group, the time available to complete seed maturation is very short. Once the forest canopy closes, the light available on the forest floor for photosynthesis falls to 1% of the level at the top of the canopy. In the deep shade of the inner forest, plants struggle to produce enough food even for their own needs, let alone have food left over for the process of seed maturation. Nor can these plants get around the light problem simply by blooming earlier. Flowering is limited by the temperature of the soil and the air; frost in particular is a serious threat.

Plants must also face the challenge of attracting pollinators to carry out cross-pollination. Cool, damp weather reduces insect activity to almost zero and, should the cold continue, can seriously jeopardize the possibility of seed production. In mid-spring, there are relatively few pollinators to go around, even at the best of times. Flowers initially attract the attention of pollinators by their shape, colour and scent. They then offer up "floral rewards" of nectar and pollen. Some species, like Jack-in-the-Pulpit and Red Trillium, use their colour and putrid odour to deceive pollinator flies into thinking that they are pieces of rotting meat. The majority of woodland plants, however, are not overly specialized and attract a broad array of insects. Most flower for only about two weeks but, being long-lived perennials, their seed success in any one year is less important than their success over a multi-year period.

In order to be ready to take full advantage of the short photosynthetic season available in a deciduous forest, spring woodland plants actually preform their flowers in miniature the year before. The flowers form in a bud at the tip of the underground rootstalk but their cells are compact and unexpanded. Expansion into full, above-ground flowers is mostly the result of water uptake when warm spring conditions arrive. Leaves are preformed in a similar manner, but their full expansion still requires some new photosynthesis to take place. New photosynthesis is also necessary for seed maturation and to provide stored food reserves for next year's growth. Most woodland trees and shrubs also preform their leaves and flowers. An easy way to see this is to pick apart a large bud of a Horse Chestnut tree. The two tiny pairs of leaves and grape-like flower cluster are quite recognizable.

Once their seeds have matured, almost all of the spring ephemerals use woodland animals to spread their seeds. These include small mammals, birds and especially invertebrates such as ants.

Weather

May Highlights

All Month Long
- Don't put your winter parka away just yet. May can serve up anything from mid-summer heat to chilling wind, rain and even snow.

- Our lakes receive a much-needed breath of oxygen during the so-called spring turnover. ◇

- Damp, mild mornings resonate with life. The air is rich with the fragrance of Balsam Poplar resin, a characteristic smell of spring in the Kawarthas. Around farms and houses, the smell of lilac blossoms and mown grass mixes nicely with the Balsam.

- There is generally a period of summer-like weather. This brings about an explosive greening of the landscape and all of the related effects on our fauna. Trying to keep up with all the "firsts" of the season can be a frustrating experience!

Early May
- May 5 is the mid-way point of spring.

Mid-May
- On average the last frost in the Kawarthas occurs about May 18. Frost will generally not occur again until September, giving our area an average of 135 frost-free days.

Late May
- Lake temperatures usually permit "comfortable" swimming by month's end but, as with all aspects of the weather in the Kawarthas, there is great variability from year to year.

Table 5.5: Weather Averages, 1961-1990

Daily Maximum	18.7° C
Daily Minimum	6.0° C
Extreme Maximum	31.7° C
Extreme Minimum	-3.7° C
Rainfall	70.4 mm
Snowfall	0.1 cm
Precipitation	70.8 mm

The Spring Turnover

After the ice retreats from lakes in the spring, a critically important phenomenon occurs. The lake is allowed to "breathe" for the first time since the previous fall. Aquatic plants, however, which create oxygen through photosynthesis, do not do the job on their own; they contribute only a small amount of this essential gas. Fortunately, there is a brief period in the spring and fall when oxygen from the air above can enter the lake. At these two times of year, all of the water in the lake is at more or less the same temperature. This permits a thorough mixing of the water. On windy days, wave action on the surface creates currents which extend from the surface right to the bottom of the lake. Oxygen from the air mixes with the water and is carried throughout the lake by these currents.

But, as summer approaches, the surface water heats up considerably while the water deeper down remains at 4° C. Because warm water is lighter than cold water, the two do not easily mix and currents cannot penetrate the colder layer below. Oxygenation of this lower level therefore stops. Virtually no mixing of the two water masses will occur until the fall, when the upper level of the lake once again cools down to the same temperature as the water below.

Table 5.6: Approximate Twilight, Sunrise and Sunset Times DST

Date	Twilight Begins	Sunrise	Sunset	Twilight Ends
May 1	5:32 a.m.	6:04 a.m.	8:18 p.m.	8:50 p.m.
May 10	5:19 a.m.	5:52 a.m.	8:28 p.m.	9:01 p.m.
May 20	5:07 a.m.	5:41 a.m.	8:39 p.m.	9:14 p.m.
June 1	4:57 a.m.	5:33 a.m.	8:50 p.m.	9:26 p.m.

The Night Sky

May Highlights

All Month Long

- Major constellations and stars visible (May 15, 10:00 p.m. DST)

  Northwest: Gemini (with *Pollux* and *Castor*) in mid-sky; Cassiopeia low in N; Auriga (with *Capella*) to its left

  Northeast: Ursa Major high in sky; Ursa Minor (with *Polaris*) below it; Boötes (with *Arcturus*) high to right of Dipper; Corona Borealis just below Boötes

  Southeast: Boötes (with *Arcturus*) in mid-sky; Virgo (with *Spica*) low to its right; Leo (with *Regulus*) high in the South

  Southwest: Leo (with *Regulus*) high in the South; Gemini (with *Pollux* and *Castor*) to its right

- Every spring and fall, migrant birds use the stars as an important source of directional clues. ◇

Early May

- The Eta Aquarids meteor shower peaks on May 5. It radiates from the Aquarius constellation low in the southeast and is most visible after midnight. Aquarius rises around 12:30 a.m. on May 5.

Using the Stars to Navigate

A series of classic experiments performed by Stephen Emlen, a behavioural ecologist, showed how migrant birds take directional information from the stars. Using caged Indigo Buntings in a planetarium, Emlen projected the spring sky on the planetarium ceiling and found that the birds oriented in the proper migratory direction. When he rotated the stellar patterns, the birds shifted their position as well. As young birds mature, it is believed that they learn to recognize the area of least apparent stellar movement, namely the area around the North Star. When Emlen created a "false sky" rotating around *Betelgeuse* (in the constellation Orion), the birds acted as if *Betelgeuse* was the North Star. The stars, of course, are only one source of navigational information. Other cues used by birds include visual landmarks, smells, ultraviolet light, infrasound, solar movements, barometric pressure, wind direction, the earth's magnetic fields and even the wave patterns of the tides.

Summer

Fritillary and hairstreak butterflies feeding on milkweed.

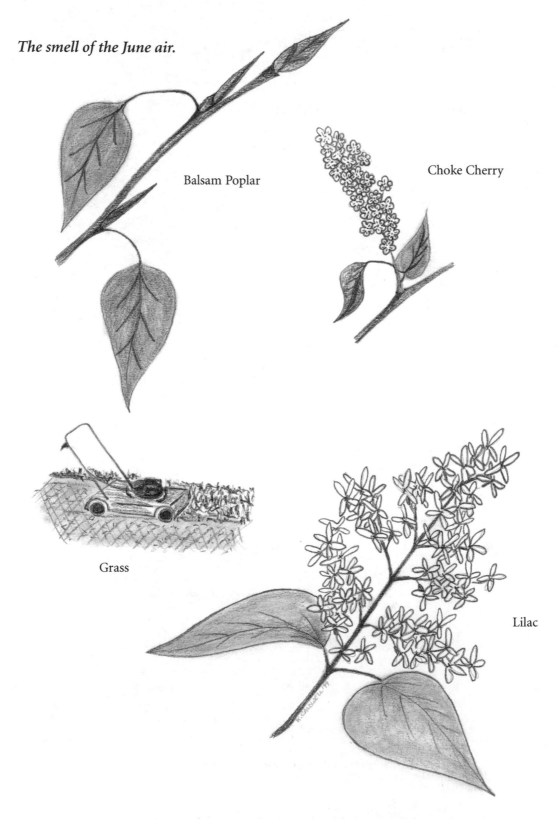

The smell of the June air.

Balsam Poplar

Choke Cherry

Grass

Lilac

CHAPTER 6

June—Endless Days and the Urgency of Life

In June the world is brand new. Never in the year is the foliage fresher, the kaleidoscope of greens more vivid, the smells of the natural world more alluring and the urgency of life more palpable. Growth and procreation are the order of the day. June's long days convey a sense of unending time. Hal Borland spoke of June as "long, sweet days we bought and paid for with long, cold nights and short bitter days at the dark turn of the year."[1]

This is a wonderful time of year to enjoy all that our senses can perceive. The smell of the early June air, especially on a damp morning, conveys the essence of a green world. It is a compelling perfume with accents of Balsam Poplar, lilac, cherry and freshly mown grass. Rising early on a June morning is worth the effort for the fragrance of the air alone. On our farms, a signature scent of June is freshly-cut hay curing in the sun. It is claimed, that from a downwind location, you can smell a hayfield a mile away.

Although June brings new opportunities for the naturalist, this is a time of relative calm after the hectic days of May. There is still much to be seen, but the pace of change has slowed, especially since spring migration has finally ended. Insects receive more attention, some for their beauty but others for their nuisance factor! Plants, too, take over the spotlight with highly-sought species such as orchids blooming throughout the month.

In June we have the sense that this time of long days and short nights will last forever. The sun arches high overhead giving more than 15 hours of daylight. On or about the 21st of the month, we celebrate the summer solstice as the sun rises and sets farther north than on any other day of the year and thereby signals the imperceptible transition into summer.

June At a Glance

With migration completed, June is the month of peak nesting activity. Bird song is also at its strongest and most diverse. Like many species, Chimney Swifts and Ruby-throated Hummingbirds are putting on elaborate courtship flights. Breeding Bird Surveys are carried out all over North America.

Beavers are active at dawn and dusk and easy to observe. Bats give birth to a single young this month. Watch for White-tailed Deer fawns as well as baby Groundhogs, Raccoons, Striped Skunks and Red Foxes.

June nights resound with a chorus of Gray Treefrogs, punctuated by the calls of Bullfrogs, Mink and Green Frogs. Turtles are laying their eggs and are commonly seen along roadsides and in other sandy locations.

Bass, Carp, Pumpkinseeds and Bluegills are spawning and make for interesting fish-watching.

The insect world explodes wide open this month. Both damselflies and dragonflies abound and, by month's end, the year's largest variety of butterflies is on the wing. Swallowtails and White Admirals are particularly noticeable. Giant silk moths, sphinx moths and fields of fireflies provide entertainment by night.

The annual roadside flower parade kicks off with mustards, buttercups and daisies leading the way. The white blossoms of hawthorns, dogwoods and viburnums are also a common sight this month. In coniferous and mixed woodlands, species such as Bunchberry, Clintonia and a wide variety of orchids are in flower. The yellow pollen from pines and other conifers dusts land and water.

With more than 15 hours of sunlight, June days seem never-ending. The summer solstice marks the beginning of summer on or about June 21. The average daily temperatures are a maximum of 23℃ and a minimum of 10℃. In mid-June, the sun is up at about 5:30 a.m. and sets at about 9:00 p.m.

The night sky is dominated by the Summer Triangle and the Milky Way. Arcturus is high overhead. The Big Dipper is high in the northwest.

June is also the month of garden tours, the first strawberries and the sweet smell of the first cut of hay.

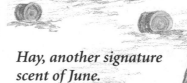

Hay, another signature scent of June.

Birds

June Highlights

All Month

- This is the time of peak nesting activity for many species including migrants from the tropics. ◇

- June, through early July, is a critical time for loons. The birds are very vulnerable to disturbance by humans as they attempt to nest and care for their chicks. ◇

- Male hummingbirds can be seen doing their pendulum courtship flight, almost as if suspended from a string. They fly in wide arcs above and to both sides of the female.

- Breeding Bird Surveys are carried out to monitor the number of species and individual birds that are nesting along a given route. ◇

- Osprey eggs usually hatch during the first half of June. The young are fed constantly by the female throughout the month with fish supplies provided by the male. The young fledge about 52 days after hatching.

Early June

- The last migrants pass through in the first week of June. Migrant shorebirds often linger in the Kawarthas until early June, as well.

- In downtown areas, Chimney Swifts are putting on quite a show. Pairs can be seen and heard in courtship flight as they raise their wings and glide in a V position. Swifts nest in colonies on the inside walls of old chimneys such as at the old Central School on Murray Street in Peterborough. On May 23, 2001, at about 8:30 p.m., between 300 to 400 swifts were seen "dancing on the air and forming spirals" above the school before being swallowed up by the chimney.

- Bird song is at its strongest and most diverse. The best listening is just before sunrise during the "dawn chorus." In the city, robins lead off the chorus starting well before any hint of light. ◇

Mid-June

- Many species of ducks such as Mallards begin moulting.

Late June

- Baby loons hatch in the last week of June or the first week of July. ◇

early month	
arrivals	late-May migrants such as flycatchers may still be arriving
departures	Semipalmated Plover, Semipalmated Sandpiper, Least Sandpiper, Dunlin, Wilson's Phalarope, Magnolia Warbler (b), Wilson's Warbler

Nesting at its Peak

By the second week of June, spring migration has finished and the nesting season has moved into high gear. Most neo-tropical migrants have laid their eggs by the end of May and have young in the nest by the second week of June. Our resident birds as well as early-spring migrants may be starting a second brood by now. Many species such as American Robins,

Eastern Bluebirds and Mourning Doves have two and occasionally three broods in a season. Most songbirds spend about two weeks incubating their eggs and another two weeks feeding the young before they leave the nest. For example, the incubation period for robin eggs is 12 to 14 days, with the young leaving the nest about 14 to 16 days after hatching. Many species will also make attempts at renesting if their nest is destroyed or if predators eat the eggs or young. In fact, it is very common in May and June to see a crow being pursued by a frantic smaller bird such as a grackle or robin. The eggs and young of other birds make up a large part of the diet of American Crows, Blue Jays and even Common Grackles themselves at this time of the year.

Chimney Swifts in courtship flight over downtown Peterborough.

Protecting Our Loons

Loons are especially vulnerable at this time of year. The birds are incubating their eggs for most of the month and are easily scared off their nests by human disturbance. This can result in nesting failure due to cooling of the eggs or predation by gulls or Raccoons. Boaters can help to protect loons by staying away from the wilder areas of lakes where the birds are nesting and by slowing down when travelling along shorelines. Boats can scare the incubating bird off the nest, and the waves can swamp the nest and drown the eggs. Because anglers often fish for bass along shorelines where loons nest, it is especially important that bass tournaments not be held at this time.

The babies hatch in late June or early July and almost immediately leave the nest. Once again, boat waves can cause the chicks to become separated from their parents and to easily fall prey to predators. Human disturbance also means that the parents are forced to spend more time keeping track of their chicks which allows less time to hunt for food. The chicks will not be able to catch food for themselves for at least six weeks.

On some lakes, where appropriate nesting habitat for loons is in short supply, cottagers are building nesting platforms. These floating structures sit low in the water and look like a small island. When placed in a quiet, sheltered cove, they are proving quite successful in attracting loons. Instructions for building nesting platforms can be obtained from Bird Studies Canada.[2] Although the Ontario loon population is still quite healthy, the number of young being produced is in decline.

Counting Breeding Birds

A male bird singing in the same location during the May, June and July breeding season usually signifies the presence of a breeding pair. For this reason, surveys of the abundance of breeding species are conducted at this time of the year. The Breeding Bird Survey (BBS) is a major information source for population changes of terrestrial birds along roadsides in North America. About 95 BBS routes are done each year in Ontario. Volunteers survey their route by car, starting 30 minutes before sunrise. Birds are identified mostly by song at 50 stops located 0.8 kilometres apart. I have been doing a route between Lasswade and Havelock since 1994 and generally record about 65 species.

Data from Breeding Bird Surveys indicate that nearly one in five Canadian species shows a significant decline, while only one in 10 shows a significant increase.[3] The decline is especially bad in the case of some species that winter in the West Indies and in Central and South America. Not surprisingly, there appears to be a basic link between bird and forest; the massive removal of forest on much of the wintering area and the fragmentation of forests on the nesting grounds are having a very negative impact. A case in point is the Wood Thrush. Wood Thrush numbers have decreased to 25 per cent of population levels in the 1960s. Fragmentation is an especially serious problem in the southern half of Peterborough County. In fact, it is one of the least suitable landscapes in southern Ontario for nesting forest birds such as Wood Thrushes and Ovenbirds. There is a real need to encourage restoration and the linking of forest tracts in this area.

The Dawn Chorus

Even if you are not yet ready to undertake a Breeding Bird Survey, you should at least make a point each spring of taking in the "dawn chorus." This refers to the fervent bird song that takes place each morning before the sun comes up. If you are to hear the whole show, you should be outside at least one hour before sunrise, preferably with a folding chair, a thermos of coffee, a flashlight and a notebook. Get comfortable and start taking note of the time at which the first individual of the various bird species sings. The first songsters are usually the robins but, depending on the type of habitat, other species may sing intermittently all night. The exuberance of the various songsters usually peaks at about one-half hour before sunrise with an almost deafening climax. Picking out the individual species at this time becomes quite a challenge! The intensity falls off rapidly once the sun rises above the horizon but there is still lots to be heard until at least eight o'clock. If you want to make the dawn chorus experience into even more of a celebration.

Here is a list of some of the most common and noticeable June songsters listed by the habitat type(s) in which they most often occur:

wetlands:

Tree Swallow, Gray Catbird, Eastern Kingbird, Common Yellowthroat, Northern Waterthrush, Yellow Warbler, Swamp Sparrow, Red-winged Blackbird, Common Grackle

deciduous forests:

Great Crested Flycatcher, Least Flycatcher, Blue Jay, Black-capped Chickadee, Veery, Warbling Vireo, American Redstart, Ovenbird, Black-and-white Warbler, Red-eyed Vireo, Rose-breasted Grosbeak

evergreen and mixed forests:

Hermit Thrush, Pine Warbler, Yellow-rumped Warbler, Black-throated Green Warbler, Purple Finch

fields, meadows and fence rows:

Killdeer, Eastern Kingbird, Song Sparrow, Savannah Sparrow, Field Sparrow, Red-winged Blackbird, Eastern Meadowlark, Bobolink, Indigo Bunting, American Goldfinch

brushy areas, open woodlands and roadsides:

Mourning Dove, Great Crested Flycatcher, Eastern Kingbird, Northern Flicker, Blue Jay, House Wren, Brown Thrasher, Gray Catbird, American Robin, Warbling Vireo, Red-eyed Vireo, Chestnut-sided Warbler, Yellow Warbler, Common Yellowthroat, Song Sparrow, Chipping Sparrow, Northern Cardinal, Baltimore Oriole, Indigo Bunting, American Goldfinch

lakesides and cottages:

In addition to many of the species listed above (depending on the type of habitat surrounding the lake) you may also hear Common Loon, Osprey, Ring-billed Gull, Herring Gull, Barn Swallow, Purple Martin, Eastern Phoebe

suburban neighbourhoods:

Mourning Dove, Blue Jay, American Crow, Tree Swallow, Black-capped Chickadee, American Robin, Red-eyed Vireo, Yellow Warbler, Common Grackle, European Starling, Chipping Sparrow, Song Sparrow, Northern Cardinal, House Finch, House Sparrow

urban downtown:

Ring-billed Gull, Rock Dove, Chimney Swift, Barn Swallow, Common Nighthawk, European Starling, House Finch, House Sparrow

Mammals

June Highlights

All Month Long

- Throughout the spring, Beaver are very active at dawn and dusk and easy to observe.

- Female White-tailed Deer have a tendency to "rule the woods" when their fawns are young and vulnerable. The buck's antler growth has now reached the halfway point of development.

- Observing bats can be a fascinating activity, especially on warm June evenings. By understanding some of the strategies that moths use to avoid becoming a bat's meal, the whole predator-prey relationship seems much more evenly balanced. ◇

- Black Bears can sometimes be found in hay fields, grazing on clover and alfalfa.

- Bears mate from early June to early August with the peak period between mid-June and mid-July. In what probably is done to show dominance and sexual readiness, bears will bite and claw the bark of trees to a height of almost two metres above the ground. They will also rub against the tree with their haunches and in doing so leave behind a scent mark.

Early June

- Mother chipmunks force their young to leave the den and to find their own territories. This dispersal causes a lot of chipmunk "chuck-chucking" in the woods!

- Baby Groundhogs emerge from burrows. Watch for baby Raccoons, Striped Skunks and Red Foxes, too.

Mid-June

- Little Brown and Big Brown Bats give birth to a single young, usually in mid-to-late June. Spring and summer roosts are often located in and around buildings.

Observing Bats

Late spring and early summer is an excellent time of the year to observe bats feeding. Let the presence of insects be your guide. Try to find a strong, isolated white light in a rural area, preferably near a body of water. These lights often attract large numbers of insects, which in turn attract bats. If there are few insects present, move on to another light. Bats forage most heavily starting at dusk and continue for about an hour. It is also possible to see species such as Little Brown Bats feeding over water just after dusk. Some lakes and rivers seem almost alive with foraging bats. As darkness falls, however, it becomes very difficult to see the animals. In this situation a bat detector (an instrument that allows you to listen to echolocation calls) is very useful. You soon become aware that there are far more bats than you expected and just "listening in" on the action can be most exciting.

Observing bats is even more interesting if you know which species of bats are present and if you have some understanding of how the insects themselves are "coping" with the presence of these airborne marauders. Little Browns, Big Browns and Red Bats often forage together at the same light but flight differences and size can help us to actually identify which species is which. The Reds have a rapid and direct flight which is quite different from that of the other two. Little Brown Bats are smaller and have an erratic, fluttering flight. The Big Brown also shows this same general flight pattern, but it is much larger than either of the other two species.

Bats feeding at street light.

In the relationship between bats and their prey, things are not as one-sided as it appears. Insects have developed a number of strategies to avoid becoming bat food. For example, a pair of ears that are sensitive to the bat's echolocation calls allow some moths to detect the presence of bats long before the bats detect them. They simply fly off in another direction. However, if these same insects are surprised by a bat at close quarters, they will merely fold their wings and dive directly into the vegetation

The adaptations of some tiger moths (family *Arctiidae*) are especially interesting. They not only have ears for listening to bats but they produce their own ultrasonic sounds which serve as a defence mechanism. These sounds may advertise the fact that the moths are poisonous (as larvae, many *Arctiidae* feed on milkweed), thereby serving as an acoustic version of the Monarch Butterfly's bright colours and slow, conspicuous flight. The sounds may also startle the bats, since they are not emitted until the bat is within one metre of the moth. A bat's diet, however, is not restricted to moths. They tend to be fairly opportunistic feeders and will eat whatever insects are available. For Little Brown Bats, staple foods include caddisflies, mayflies, mosquitoes and especially midges.

Amphibians and Reptiles

June Highlights

All Month Long
- Painted Turtles and Snapping Turtles are often seen along roadsides and other sandy locations laying their eggs. ◇
- The Green Frog's banjo-like "poink" is a widespread sound both day and night. In more northern wetlands, Mink Frogs join the chorus with their constant "hammering."
- Ringneck and Milk Snakes lay their eggs this month and next.

Early June
- Just as tiny Spring Peepers are winding their chorus down, huge Bullfrogs herald approaching summer with their deep, garrumphing "jug-o-rum" calls.
- Five-lined Skinks, Ontario's only lizard, mate in early June and are therefore more active and visible. Look for them on sunny, bare bedrock outcroppings with deep cracks such as at Petroglyphs Provincial Park. Skinks are now on the threatened species list.

Mid-June
- The Gray Treefrog chorus of melodious, bird-like trills reaches its peak. ◇

Late June
- Red-backed Salamanders lay their eggs in rotten logs. The young actually go through the larval stage in the egg. The eggs are guarded by the adults throughout the summer.
- Young Spring Peepers and Wood Frogs complete their development and emerge from ponds. They can often be found in damp, shaded locations on the forest floor.

Five-lined Skink—note Wild Columbine in foreground.

Egg-laying Turtles

Starting in early June, turtles are a familiar sight along many of our roads and rail-trails. Midland Painted Turtles, followed later in the month by Snapping Turtles, search out nesting sites this month, preferably with well-drained, loose, sandy soil or fine gravel. The female scrapes out a hollow with her hind legs to a depth of about 10 to 15 centimetres. Painted Turtles lay five to ten white eggs, elliptical in shape and about two centimetres long. Snapping Turtles lay anywhere from 15 to 30 spherical eggs that look remarkably like ping-pong balls. They are about 2.5 centimetres in diameter and white and pink in colour. Although most turtles lay only one clutch of eggs, Painted Turtles will occasionally lay two clutches. When the female turtle has finished laying, she uses her hind legs to fill in the hole and then drags her shell over the nest to cover up any signs of her presence. She then returns to the water, and if she is lucky she will avoid getting run over by a car!

Curiously enough, the eventual sex of the baby turtles depends on the temperature at which the eggs are incubated. Cooler temperatures (22°C-26°C) result in all males being born, while warmer temperatures (30° C and greater) result in females. There is still a great deal that remains to be discovered about this bizarre phenomenon.

Unfortunately, turtle eggs stand a very poor chance of surviving the 90-day incubation period. Predators such as raccoons, skunks and foxes usually discover the nests within a matter of hours, dig up the eggs and enjoy a hearty meal. They leave behind a familiar sight of crinkled, white shells scattered around the nest area. Since the number of these predators

Snapping Turtle laying eggs at roadside.

has increased considerably in recent years, very few turtle nests go undiscovered. Cool weather can also be a problem, especially for Snapping Turtles. If the weather is not warm enough, the eggs will not be sufficiently incubated and therefore will not hatch. With such low reproductive success, it is a good thing that Snapping Turtles are long-lived and may lay eggs over a 50-year period or more.

Those eggs that are lucky enough to survive will usually hatch in late summer. If the weather is warm, the young turtles will leave the nest immediately. If the fall weather is abnormally cool, however, the young may stay in the nest until the following spring. They are able to withstand winter temperatures to several degrees below zero Celsius thanks to glycogen in the body fluids, which acts like an antifreeze.

The Music of June Nights

The most familiar night-time sound of the month of June is the bird-like trill of the Gray Treefrog. People are often surprised to learn that the "bird" trilling from high in a tree is actually a frog. From late May to the end of June, male treefrogs gather at shrubby ponds and swamps and call vociferously from overhanging branches. The calls serve to advertise ownership of a territory, albeit a small one, and to attract females. The females arrive a night or two after the males and choose a partner largely on the calibre of his singing. The males will remain at the pond for several weeks in the hope of breeding with other, later-arriving females.

Many cottagers are familiar with treefrogs as the nocturnal visitors that gather around the porch light. Their sticky toe-disks allow them to literally walk up and down the walls and windows. A treefrog will often sit for hours without moving, seemingly oblivious to its surroundings. And then suddenly, with no forewarning, it will have jumped a metre or more, landed safely and be stuffing a hapless moth into its mouth. You can also see treefrogs by following their trill with a flashlight. Gray Treefrogs continue calling intermittently throughout the first half of the summer, especially when the weather is warm and humid.

Gray Treefrog on cottage wall.

Fishes

June Highlights

All Month Long

- Common Carp begin spawning. They can be observed throughout much of the summer thrashing on the surface of shallow rivers, lakes, bays and backwaters. The fish may frequently jump right out of the water. Carp were introduced to North America from Europe in the late 1800s.

- The Brook Stickleback spawns in early summer. Like all sticklebacks, the male actually constructs a nest of small sticks and bits of vegetation. He then induces one or more females to lay eggs in the nest. Despite his small size, the male is very aggressive in guarding the eggs.

Early June

- Muskellunge season throughout Peterborough County opens on the first Saturday of the month.

- Pumpkinseed and Bluegill are spawning and display fascinating mating behaviour. ◇

- Smallmouth, Largemouth and Rock Bass as well as Black Crappies and Brown Bullheads are also spawning. Male bass can be seen guarding their shallow-water nests, which are often located in the vicinity of docks. ◇

Late June

- Bass season throughout Peterborough County (divisions 6 and 15) opens on the last Saturday in June.

Spawning Sunfish

The two species of sunfish found in the Kawarthas are the Pumpkinseed and the Bluegill. The former is native to this area while the latter was introduced. It is not uncommon for these closely-related fish to hybridize. Male Pumpkinseeds construct their nest in the shallow water of lakes and ponds in May or June when water temperature reaches about 13° C. The nests are actually built in colonies ranging from just a few to as many as 10 to 15. The male sweeps away gravel and other debris from the bottom with his caudal fin, almost as if he were using a whisk brush. At the same time, he holds his side fins out and pushes water forward so as to remain stationary. The male sunfish, like the male bass, is very aggressive at spawning time and will chase off intruders by charging and even biting.

The females remain in deeper water until the nests are completed. The male will actually swim out and "greet" an approaching female and try to drive her into his nest. If he is successful in attracting her, there is a fairly elaborate courtship between the pair, in which the two fish swim in a circular path, side by side, with their bellies touching. As the female expels the eggs, the male fertilizes them with his sperm. Not only will females often spawn in more than one nest but more than one female may also use the same nest.

Although the female quickly leaves the nest after spawning, the male remains to vigorously defend the eggs and fry. The eggs hatch in two to three days and one nest may produce several thousand young. Male Pumpkinseeds will actually nip at bathers' legs or feet if they come too close to the nest.

Bluegills have similar reproductive behaviour, although they breed later in the spring, when the water warms to at least 19° C. Their colonies are larger, sometimes numbering 40

*Bluegills spawning—
note "cuckolder" male
in background.*

or 50 nests. Female Bluegills produce an average of 12,000 eggs! Like the Pumpkinseed, the male Bluegill is a doting father and will guard the fry for several days after they hatch. However, not all Bluegill males are territorial and defend a nesting site. Some males rely on a different mating strategy. Known as satellite or "sneaker" males, they are smaller in size and will actually slip into a territorial male's nest when the female is spawning there. The "cuckolder" will then release his sperm at the same time as the larger territorial male does. Although territorial males out-reproduce sneaker males in a given year, the sneaker males become sexually active at an earlier age.

There are excellent opportunities right in Peterborough to observe sunfish and bass spawning behaviour. Watch for these fish along the shoreline of quieter portions of the Otonabee River as well as in the canal section in town. Pumpkinseed, Rock Bass and Smallmouth Bass nests can even be found in the canal below the Liftlock.

Spawning Bass

Many cottagers are familiar with the sight of a large bass spawning in the shallow water at the end of the dock throughout much of June. Their aggressive nature at this time of the year is well-known, especially to bathers who may have experienced an unexpected thump on the leg. Bass actually provide an excellent opportunity for fish-watching, because there is much of interest to be observed. Both the Smallmouth and Largemouth display similar spawning behaviour. The most important difference is that the former chooses rocky, gravelly sites to spawn while the latter prefers a mud bottom, often where water-lily roots have been exposed by the constant tail-sweeping of the male. Spawning takes place when the water temperature reaches 16° C to 18° C, usually sometime in June. The male constructs the nest at a depth of about one metre. He uses his caudal fin to "sweep" a shallow depression, free of loose silt and debris. The male and female then engage in pre-spawning rituals that involve rubbing and nipping each other. Eventually, the two rest on the bottom of the nest, where the female deposits the eggs and the male releases his sperm. The female is subsequently driven off by the aggressive male. As many as three different females, however, may deposit eggs in the same nest. The male remains to jealously guard the eggs and later to protect the young fry. After they hatch, the young bass swim in a school close to the nest with the male close by. He continues to do this for about two weeks.

Insects and Other Invertebrates

June Highlights

All Month Long

- Adult mayflies, of which there are 300 Canadian species, emerge from lakes and streams and form large mating swarms, usually early in the morning or in the evening. For many of us, seeing mayflies in the spring evokes memories of fishing expeditions past.

- Damselflies and dragonflies become very common and will remain so all summer. Sometimes, thousands of individuals of a single species of dragonfly will emerge on the same day and fill the air. Synchronous emergence may be an adaptation to maximize the chance of a dragonfly's finding a mate of the same species. ◊

- Aquatic insects are very active and plentiful, making this a great time of year for pond studies.

- Spider eggs hatch and the spiderlings "balloon" to new locales on filaments of silk borne by the wind. Bushes are sometimes covered with this silk.

- Several butterfly species that are usually found only in the United States may appear in our area during migratory years. Species such as the Common Buckeye may first show up in June, establish a small colony and last through several generations into early September.

Early June

- The first Monarch Butterflies return to our area. When Monarchs leave Mexico, many fly to the Gulf states or Florida where they breed and lay eggs. Most of the spring Monarchs we see are the butterflies that emerge from these eggs. Some, however, are the next generation.

- Giant silk moths are attracted to bright, white lights. Sphinx moths, June beetles and even Giant Water bugs keep them company. ◇

Late June

- Warm, late spring nights are wonderful for insect-watching. Most familiar are the fireflies with their magical Morse code flashes of yellow light. However, an astute observer can also find camel crickets, flower fly larvae and fungus-feeding beetles. ◇

- Butterfly-watching is at its most productive in late June and early July since the greatest number of different species is aflight at this time. Swallowtails, White Admirals and European Skippers are especially noticeable. Blue-black, day-flying Virginia Ctenuchid moths are also a common sight. ◇

Droves of Dragonflies

Some species of late spring and early summer dragonflies undergo "synchronous emergence." Thousands of individuals of the same species emerge on the same day and, following a period of about 24 hours in which they are relatively inactive, they seem to be everywhere as they forage together and presumably search out mates. For two days in late May of 1999, tens of thousands of Beaverpond Baskettail dragonflies patrolled the roads, fields and lawns along the east shore of Clear Lake near Young's Point. Driving along Birchview Road there were dragonflies as far as you could see! Synchronous emergence may be an adaptation to maximize the chances of a dragonfly's finding a mate of the same species.

Table 6.2: **Common dragonflies and damselflies of late spring and early summer**

dragonflies:	Common Green Darner, Lancet Clubtail, Racket-tailed Emerald, Beaverpond Baskettail, Calico Pennant, Dot-tailed Whiteface, Common Whitetail, Chalk-fronted Skimmer, Four-spotted Skimmer, Twelve-spotted Skimmer
damselflies:	Marsh Bluet, Hagen's Bluet, Eastern Forktail, Ebony Jewelwing

Giant Silk Moths

June is the month of the spectacular giant silk moths. These insects, which can measure up to 15 centimetres in width, include the well-known Luna and Cecropia Moths. Both are found in the Kawarthas. The male silk moths have large, feather-like antennae which serve to locate a female. The female moths release airborne sex attractants called pheromones. These are emitted in infinitesimally small quantities. The male's antennae are designed to maximize the surface area that can come into contact with the molecules. This explains why they are so much larger than the female's antennae. This most amazing chemical communication system allows a male to find a female at distances of up to five kilometres!

Probably the best known of the silk moths is the Cecropia. After fertilization, the female Cecropia will lay 100 or more eggs in a cherry, birch or maple. The Cecropia caterpillar will reach nine centimetres in length by mid-August and then spin a spindle-shaped cocoon in which it will spend the winter and exit as an adult in the spring. It is interesting to note that adult silk moths exist for the sole purpose of reproduction; in fact they don't even eat! Some of the other silk moths that can be found in the Kawarthas include the Polyphemus, the Promethea, the Luna, and the small, but spectacular, Io Moth.

Io and Cecropia moths on light pole.

Fireflies in June meadow.

The Io is generally the most common silk moth species.

Although silk moths may turn up just about anywhere, they are most common in rural areas. They are usually found from early to mid-June although the Cecropia is sometimes seen in late May in years when warm weather arrives ahead of schedule. Silk moths are most active after 10:00 p.m. on warm, still nights. They are attracted to bright white lights, often in locations near water such as marinas and resorts. Look for them flying around the light, resting on the light pole or sitting on the ground. The south shore of Stony Lake has often been a good place to find them. Be sure to take your camera along as well because these moths are not only extremely beautiful but they are very cooperative and will even allow themselves to be picked up and moved to a more suitable location for a picture. Royal moths such as the Imperial, sphinx moths like the Big Poplar and other insects such as June beetles and Giant Water bugs may also be found at these same lights.

Firefly Magic

A meadow alive with fireflies is one of the most beautiful sights of early summer. Hovering like tiny helicopters, their flight projects an unhurried, calming quality. A member of the beetle family *Lampyridae*, fireflies possess a special organ in the abdomen which produces light. The light switches on when the insect flies upward and switches off when it descends. Like the songs of male birds, the light serves to attract a female. When a female of the same species sees the male's flash, she responds with her own luminous signal. Through a series of signals and responses, the two beetles come together and mate. Because different species of fireflies have different flash patterns, the female is attracted only by the proper sequence of flashes. It is interesting to note that this light is created without any heat being generated.

Don't let the month finish without an evening of firefly-watching. Fireflies are most visible between dusk and midnight, especially in damp, open areas with bushes and long grasses. They are particularly numerous at the end of the month. One place you might try is the first field at the Miller Creek Conservation Area.

Butterfly-Watching At Its Best

One of the most pleasurable nature activities in summer is butterfly-watching. More species can be seen in late June and early July than at any other time of the year. Unlike birding which often requires getting up at the crack of dawn, dealing with less than perfect weather and straining your eyes and your neck muscles for a momentary flash of colour in the dense foliage, butterfly-watching is a much more civilized affair. Butterflies fly only during warm, sunny weather and are rarely on the wing before eight o'clock. Many birders are now expanding their horizons and turning their attention to butterflies once the spring migration is over. As more and more people are discovering, butterflying can quickly become an obsession, especially if you also enjoy photographing them.

About 80 species of butterflies have been found in the Kawarthas, which represents about half of the butterflies occurring in Ontario. The rich diversity we enjoy is mostly the result of "sitting on the edge" of the Canadian Shield. Thanks to our geographic location, we have species here that are typical of both more southern and more northern regions. Activities such as monitoring numbers, recording behaviour and keeping lists of species encountered add a great deal to our understanding of local *lepidoptera.*

To find a given species of butterfly, it is necessary to know the time of year it flies and the kind of habitat it prefers. As a general rule, most species prefer sunny locations with lots of flowering plants. Joe-Pye Weed, milkweeds and dogbanes are particularly popular. Once you start paying attention, the abundance of some species such as the European Skipper and the Northern Crescent is amazing.

Although butterflies can turn up anywhere, including in vacant urban lots, the following locations deserve special attention. In the southern part of the County, the Trent University

Table 6.3: A list of some common early-summer Butterflies

Northern Cloudywing	Summer Azure	Common Ringlet
Cabbage White	Viceroy	Canadian Tiger Swallowtail
Milbert's Tortoiseshell*	Arctic Skipper	Question Mark*
Juvenal's Duskywing	Silvery Blue	Monarch
Clouded Sulphur	Northern Pearly-eye	Mustard White
American Lady*	Peck's Skipper	Mourning Cloak
European Skipper	Great-spangled Fritillary	
Acadian Hairstreak	Eyed Brown	* numbers vary greatly from year to year.
Red Admiral*	Tawny-edged Skipper	In 2001, Red Admirals and American
Hobomok Skipper	Atlantis Fritillary	Ladies were extremely common.
Banded Hairstreak	Little Wood-Satyr	
White Admiral	Dun Skipper	
Long Dash Skipper	Northern Crescent	

campus is excellent. Try the Promise Rock Trail, the Lady Eaton Drumlin and beside the canal east of the South Drumlin. Other productive areas include the Miller Creek Conservation Area, the Kiwanis—Jackson Park Rail-Trail, Parkhill Road West where it runs through the Cavan Swamp east of Highway 7A and the old C.N. railroad bed between the Drummond and Cameron Lines south of Highway 7 east. In the north, be sure to visit Petroglyphs Provincial Park. Two excellent habitats to survey in the park are the margins of the lakes and

Canadian Tiger Swallowtails at mud puddle.

wetlands and any of the open areas near the glyph site itself. Also worth trying are the Warsaw Caves Conservation Area, the Jack Lake Road south of Apsley, the Sandy Lake Road north of Twin Lakes and the Galway-Cavendish Forest Access Road off County Road 507 south of Lake Catchacoma.

Like many species these days, butterfly populations are under pressure as a result of threats such as habitat destruction and pesticide use. In order to understand how they are faring, it is necessary to gain better base line knowledge about butterfly numbers. Consequently, butterfly counts have been held since 1974 in many localities across North America. Similar to the Christmas Bird Counts, they are a social event as much as a learning experience and monitoring device.

Just as with the Christmas Bird Count, a 24-kilometre diameter circle is demarcated so as to include the widest variety of butterfly habitats. The circle remains the same from year to year. Small parties of observers are each given a different part of the circle to cover, and they spend the day identifying and counting all of the butterflies seen. Because some species such as the European Skipper are often very abundant, best "guesstimates" are sometimes necessary. Even though this method of counting may not be the most mathematically sound, it does provide a rough sense of the relative abundance of different species within a given area, especially when the results are examined over a number of years.

On June 27, 1998, the first Peterborough County butterfly count was held. The circle was centred on Stony Lake in order to include habitat both on and off the Canadian Shield. Both the number of species and the number of individual butterflies were quite impressive. The count also confirmed suspicions that Petroglyphs Provincial Park is a veritable paradise for butterfly-watching!

Plants

June Highlights

All Month Long

- With over 15 hours of sunlight daily, plant growth proceeds at amazing rates. White Ash shoots may grow two centimetres a day.

- Fresh, immaculate June leaves cover the entire spectrum of green. The new growth on spruce trees is especially attractive in its bright lime attire.

- More than 20 species of orchids bloom this month. Among them are the spectacular lady's slippers, Dragon's Mouth and Rose Pogonia. ◇

- Early June through mid-July is the best time to check out the intriguing plants of sphagnum bogs.

- A spring bloom of blue-green algae occurs in our lakes and is often quite noticeable. The algae feed on inorganic nutrients such as phosphorus (and possibly nitrogen) brought into the lake by spring runoff. The species typically involved in spring is *Aphanizomenon flos-aquae*, a filamentous alga. Its population begins to climb when the lake stratifies following the spring turnover.

- All kinds of grasses bloom this month. Among these are the forage grasses like Orchard Grass, Timothy and Meadow Fescue.

- On local farms, corn and soybeans are still being shown, and both spring wheat and barley are up.

- When the weather is dry enough, usually with drying north winds, the first cut of hay will take place. Unfortunately, this often results in the death of baby birds such as Bobolinks, Eastern Meadowlarks, Savannah Sparrows and Northern Harriers, all of which commonly nest in hay fields.

Early June

- A large variety of wildflowers of coniferous and mixed woodlands is in flower. These include Bunchberry, Goldthread, Fringed Polygala and Starflower. Most are pure white. ◇

- The annual roadside flower parade begins with mustards and buttercups blooming first. They are followed later in the month by Ox-eye Daisies, Viper's-bugloss, Goat's-beard and Bladder Campion. Almost all of the roadside denizens are exotic (non-native) species.

- The white flowers of hawthorns, dogwoods and the first viburnums brighten fields and wetland edges.

- The seeds of elm, poplar, willow and Red Maple are usually ripe by now. Elm and poplar seeds are short-lived and should be planted as soon as possible.

Mid-June

- Balsam Poplars, along with a variety of willows, release their airborne seeds. The seeds are carried long distances by long, white silky hairs. This "fluff" collects on lawns and on the surface of wetlands. Silver Maple and American Elm seeds whirl to the ground, borne on tiny wings.

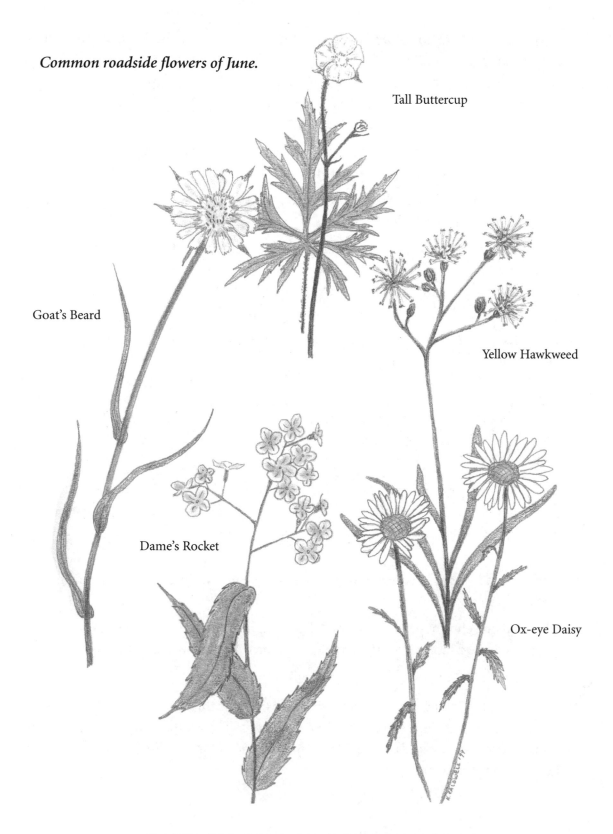

Common roadside flowers of June.

Tall Buttercup

Goat's Beard

Yellow Hawkweed

Dame's Rocket

Ox-eye Daisy

- Serviceberries, also known as Juneberries, are the first shrubs to boast ripe fruit. Silver Maple seeds are also ripe.

- The male cones of pines and Balsam Fir release their pollen. Decks, picnic tables and lake edges look as if they have been powdered with a yellow dust. ◇

- Black Cherries and Black Locusts bloom. Locust flowers are very aromatic.

Table 6.4: "First Bloom" Calendar For Selected Trees, Shrubs and Herbaceous Plants

early June	White Oak, Red Oak, American Beech, European Buckthorn, Starflower, Wild Sarsaparilla, Goldthread, Bunchberry, Yellow Clintonia, Twinflower, Canada Mayflower, Solomon's Seal
mid-June	White Pine, Black Locust, Black Cherry, Black Walnut, Alternate-leaf Dogwood, Highbush-Cranberry, Nannyberry, Bittersweet, Poison Ivy, Red Raspberry, Blackberry, Showy Lady's-slipper, Arethusa, Grass Pink, Rose Pogonia, Wood Lily, Blue Flag, Blue-eyed Grass, Goat's-beard, Dame's Rocket, Bladder Campion, Forget-me-not, Canada Anemone, Yarrow, Riverbank Grape, Yellow Hawkweed, Philadelphia Fleabane, Ox-eye Daisy, vetches, roses
late June	Catalpa, Common Elderberry, Staghorn Sumac, Spotted Coral-root, Common Milkweed, Viper's-bugloss, White Sweet Clover, Bittersweet Nightshade, Rough Cinquefoil, Birdsfoot Trefoil, Chicory, Wood Sorrel, Sheep Laurel, Tall Meadow Rue, St. John's Wort, cattails

Wild Rose.

Our Heritage of Orchids

For many naturalists, June is synonymous with orchids. More than 20 species of these exceptionally beautiful wildflowers bloom this month in the Kawarthas. In addition to their legendary beauty, finding orchids is very satisfying because they usually require some special searching. Unfortunately, they have disappeared from many of their former locations because people continue to pick them, seemingly unaware of how uncommon these plants are. The Kawarthas have long enjoyed a special status among orchid lovers, because the first book on Ontario's orchids was researched in this area and written by a Peterborough resident, Frank Morris, in 1929. Some of the most interesting passages are the vivid descriptions of orchid-searching trips to the Cavan Swamp, Stony Lake and other well-known locales near Peterborough. One becomes immediately aware of how much more plentiful the orchids were at this time and how much we have lost.

The lady's-slippers are probably the most renowned of our orchids, but they are by no means common. They have extremely complex flowers in which self-pollination is all but impossible. Bees enter the flower through the incurved split in the main pouch. They are forced to exit, however, by an opening at the top of the flower, and when they do so they inadvertently pick up pollen as they leave. If they visit another flower of the same species, they will follow the same path but unwittingly deposit pollen from the first flower, thereby assuring cross-pollination.

Showy Lady's Slipper.

The Kawarthas boast four species of lady's-slippers. Possibly the best known member of this genus is the Pink. It is usually found in dry upland sites, almost always in association with pine. Petroglyphs Provincial Park and the north shore of Stony Lake provide good habitat for this plant. The largest of our native orchids is the Showy Lady's-slipper. It measures up to 80 centimetres in height and occurs in open to semi-shaded wetland edges. Showy Lady's-slippers require ten years of growth from germination to the time they flower! Dry to moist calcium-rich sites are the preferred habitat of the Yellow Lady's-slipper. I have found these many times in the Warsaw area. The Kawarthas also have a fairly healthy population of Ram's-head Lady's-slippers, a species that has become quite rare provincially. This species prefers cold, undisturbed wetland edges, usually where White Cedar are present.

Naturalists also seek out three other species of orchids this month because of the unique design of their flowers and the special habitats in which they grow. They are the Dragon's Mouth (Arethusa), Swamp Pink (Calopogon) and Rose Pogonia. All three are usually found in fens and bogs, where they add beautiful splashes of pink to the landscape. These species are by no means easy to find, but the joy of discovery makes the search well worthwhile.

Wildflowers of the Coniferous Forest

Just as the spring ephemerals of the hardwood forest are characteristic of May, the flowers of the coniferous and mixed forests typify the month of June. With the exception of stands of White Cedar, habitats with a large proportion of coniferous trees are usually not as densely shaded as deciduous forests and the light conditions tend to be uniform over the entire year. Therefore, the plants associated with these habitats do not have the tight time constraints of the spring ephemerals to leaf out, blossom and produce seed. They must, however, be tolerant of low light conditions. Some species that are particularly fond of shade include Fringed Polygala, Canada Mayflower, Pink Lady's Slipper, Wood Sorrel, Bunchberry and Wintergreen. In fact, the photosynthetic processes of these plants are most efficient at low light levels.

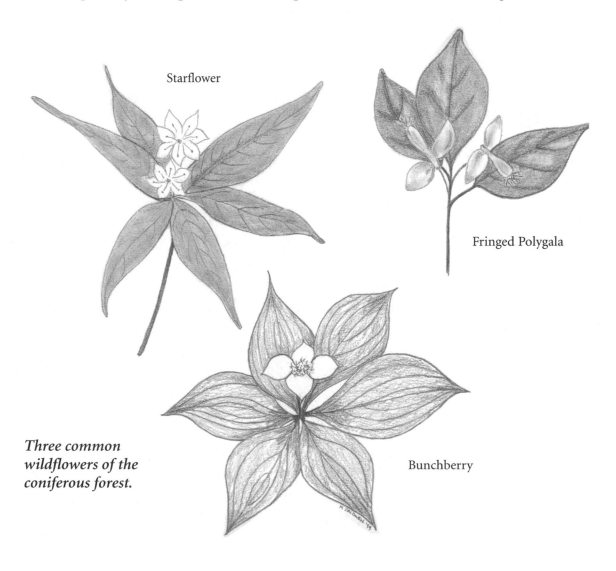

Starflower

Fringed Polygala

Three common wildflowers of the coniferous forest.

Bunchberry

These plants share other characteristics as well. They are all perennials and most of them produce immaculate white flowers. In addition, species that thrive in poor light conditions often grow in colonies by means of a subterranean network of rootstalks. Bunchberry is actually an "underground shrub" in that the stems are all attached underground by a common rootstalk. This strategy allows the plant to dispense with an energy-demanding trunk and branch system. Rather than wasting the little sunlight energy it receives, Bunchberry simply allows the ground to support the stems and leaves. Relatively few of the stems produce flowers, and the plant spreads mostly by underground rhizomes that eventually produce colonies of self-supporting clones. Canada Mayflower, Goldthread, Wild Sarsaparilla and Starflowers are just a few of the many plants that use this same strategy.

Unlike the spring ephemerals, the wildflowers of the coniferous forest have leaves that persist at least until the fall. Many, such as the Wood Sorrel and Twinflower, have evergreen leaves that contain sugar compounds which act like antifreeze. They allow the leaves to survive the rigours of winter and to immediately begin photosynthesis in the spring.

A Dusting of Yellow

For a few brief days in mid-June, a mysterious dust descends from the sky turning flat surfaces a lemon colour and making the shores of lakes and streams appear as if a strange yellow alga has bloomed. This unique phenomenon is a result of the many White and Red Pines that dominate the landscape of much of the Kawarthas and release their pollen in late spring. The pollen grains are uniquely designed for wind pollination and actually contain two air bubbles. Although usually more pronounced on Shield lakes, these pollen showers also occur right in the City of Peterborough.

White Pine is typical of many of our conifers with regard to pollination. The male or "pollen cones" are catkin-like in appearance and grow in clusters near the base of new shoots. They are usually located in the lower part of the crown of the tree. After the pollen is shed, these cones wither and fall away, often dropping from the trees like a veritable rain shower and covering the ground beneath the trees. The inconspicuous female cones become receptive to the wind-blown pollen at precisely the same time as the pollen grains are being shed. The female cones, however, stay on the tree much longer.

Most conifers require one summer season for the seed cones to mature but in the case of pines, two summers are necessary. White Pine cones are mature by September of their second year. The seeds are released when the cone scales open. Take the time to go out and closely examine the male and female cones of our conifers. Their colour, shape, texture and location vary widely from one species to the next but they all share a special beauty.

Weather

June Highlights

All Month Long

- With more than 15 hours of sunlight, June days convey a sense of unending time.

- Weather is much more like summer than like spring. The daily mean temperature is almost as warm as in August.

Late June

- Summer officially begins on or about June 21 with the summer solstice. The sun rises and sets farther north than on any other day of the year. It also stands higher in the sky at noon and casts shorter shadows than on any other day. In the Kawarthas, the June sun is at its highest at about 1 p.m. ◇

Table 6.5: **Weather Averages, 1961-1990**

Daily Maximum	23.2° C
Daily Minimum	10.0° C
Extreme Maximum	34.4° C
Extreme Minimum	- 0.7° C
Rainfall	71.1 mm
Snowfall	0.0 cm
Precipitation	71.1 mm

The Summer Solstice

A pivotal celestial event takes place this month. On or about June 21, we witness the summer solstice, the longest day of the year and the first official day of summer. At the solstice, Earth cruises past the point in its orbit that results in the greatest tilt of the Northern Hemisphere toward the sun. The sun rises and sets at its furthest point north and therefore traces its highest and longest arc through the sky. Sunlight strikes our part of the globe more nearly perpendicularly than at any other time of year and therefore heats the Earth much more efficiently. And all life responds!

People always and everywhere have celebrated the summer solstice. We can only imagine

The June sun is nearly directly overhead at noon.

the rituals that took place at Stonehenge or in the Big Horn mountains of Wyoming, where native Americans constructed a wheel of stones with 28 spokes and a clear summer solstice sunrise alignment. We may never recapture the complete meaning behind these places, but by witnessing the solstice ourselves, we can easily imagine the power transmitted into people's lives at such ceremonies. More and more people are once again celebrating the spiritual and symbolic dimensions of both the summer and winter solstices.

The solstice is best observed from a height of land that provides an unobstructed view of the northeast. Armour Hill in Peterborough is an excellent observation point. There is also a large steel cylinder which precisely indicates direction. Try to note the exact point where the sun rises and, if you wish, where it sets. At the beginning of each of the other seasons, repeat these observations. You will be astonished at the difference in rising and setting points of the sun with each new season. You can, of course, make these same observations from your own home or cottage. Knowing the exact north and south points of the sun's annual swing is just one more way people can live more fully in the place they call home. With each passing year, there is a great sense of satisfaction as you watch the sun advance to a specific point on the horizon—and no further—and then double back and retrace its steps southward.

Date	Twilight Begins	Sunrise	Sunset	Twilight Ends
June 1	4:57 a.m.	5:33 a.m.	8:50 p.m.	9:26 p.m.
June 10	4:53 a.m.	5:29 a.m.	8:57 p.m.	9:33 p.m.
June 20	4:53 a.m.	5:29 a.m.	9:01 p.m.	9:37 p.m.
July 1	4:57 a.m.	5:34 a.m.	9:01 p.m.	9:37 p.m.

The Night Sky

June Highlights

All Month Long

■ Major constellations and stars visible (June 15, 10:00 p.m. DST)

Northwest: Ursa Major high in sky; Ursa Minor (with *Polaris*) to its right; Leo (with *Regulus*) to its left

Northeast: "Summer Triangle" made up of *Vega* (in Lyra), *Deneb* (in Cygnus) and *Altair* (in Aquila); Cassiopeia low in N

Southeast: Boötes (with *Arcturus*) high in sky; Sagittarius at E horizon and above it, the brightest part of the Milky Way

Southwest: Virgo (with *Spica*)

■ The summer stars have arrived. The three stars of the Summer Triangle, *Vega*, *Deneb* and *Altair*, can be seen low in the eastern sky soon after dark. *Vega* is the second brightest star in the evening sky.

■ The most easily recognizable constellation associated with the stars of the Summer Triangle is Cygnus, the Swan. *Deneb* marks the swan's tail. The great bird hovers on outstretched wings with its long neck pointing southward.

■ Look high overhead for *Arcturus*, the star that heralded the arrival of spring. It is now the brightest star in the sky.

■ Starting in June, the Milky Way is at its most spectacular. ◇

■ The June moon rises about 30 degrees south of due east and sets 30 degrees south of due west.

The Milky Way

Anyone with an interest in the night sky looks forward to the period from late spring to early fall for a veritable rite of summer stargazing—observing the Milky Way. It is the most beautiful feature of the night sky during these warm nights and should not be missed. Shaped like a spiral wheel, the Milky Way is our home galaxy, and our solar system is located on one of the spiral arms about two-thirds or 25,000 light years out from the centre. The Milky Way is brightest in the area of the constellation Sagittarius, which lies in the southeast. This is because the centre of the galaxy is actually located behind the stars of Sagittarius. There are also dazzling parts of the Milky Way in Cygnus and in Perseus. In June, Perseus is not visible until about 1 a.m. You can either stay up late or wait until later in the summer when Perseus rises earlier.

To best appreciate the Milky Way, try to choose a clear, moonless night when the temperature gets down to at least 15° C. Warm, humid nights tend to produce a lot of haze, and the mosquitoes often become a major irritant. There is no need to have a telescope. A pair of binoculars will transform the gauzy "river of milk" seen by the naked eye into thousands and thousands of individual stars.

The summer sky looking northeast.

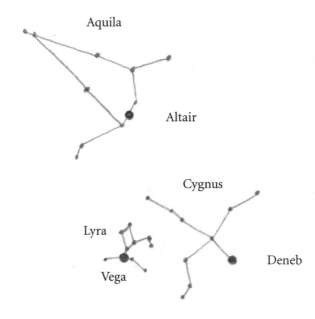

Aquila

Altair

Cygnus

Lyra

Vega

Deneb

Indigo Bunting singing beside a strawberry field.

CHAPTER 7

July—Summer at Its Height

The preparations and toil of spring begin to bear fruit in July. Eggs arc now fledged birds; flowers have become ripe berries and seeds; tadpoles have grown into small frogs, and the once-green roadsides are now a riot of colour and floral diversity. Where several weeks ago there were mostly whites and yellows, the intense colours of high summer have added blues, oranges, pinks and magentas to the roadside palette.

July is a treat for all of our senses. The warm, humid air is often replete with the sweet smell of milkweed flowers, while the fragrance of flowering basswood trees draws bees and other insects by the thousands. Our palates, too, are well-served in July as strawberries, raspberries, tomatoes and the first sweet corn ripen. Although the annual cycle of bird song is winding down now, the serene, haunting song of the thrush gives beauty to early summer evenings. The voices of Bullfrogs, Whip-poor-wills and Common Nighthawks take over as darkness falls.

This, the warmest month of the year, brings hot, humid and thundery weather. Afternoons shake and tremble with intense thunderstorms whose gift of rain is often too short and violent to be of much benefit to the thirsty soil. The fact that the sun is rising and setting a little farther to the south each day largely goes unnoticed as we go about enjoying the summer weather. But like a cruel joke, the first thing that happens once true summer has finally arrived is fall migration. The vanguard of southward-bound shorebirds is already starting to arrive in our area and, by month's end, the first warblers will be departing. And so the wheel of the year continues to turn, allowing us very little time to simply sit back and admire the fresh, new world around us—the intimations of autumn are already beginning to make themselves known.

July At a Glance

Early July is a time of fledgling birds and the contact calls of parents and young. Soon, however, nesting duties will be completed. Many species begin moulting and bird song decreases noticeably. Blackbirds flock up and roost in large, clamorous flocks. Swallows start congregating on wires. The first southward-bound shorebirds are already arriving here from the far north.

Baby Skunks and Raccoons are often seen along roadsides. Roadkill increases accordingly. Black Bears mate and leave characteristic tree rubbings.

Bullfrogs, Green Frogs and Mink Frogs call until late month. Countless young frogs and toads transform into adults and leave their natal ponds. Snapping Turtles are still laying eggs and Garter and Water Snakes are giving birth.

American Basswood in flower.

Sunfish, Rock Bass, Yellow Perch and young Smallmouth and Largemouth Bass provide fish-watching opportunities throughout the summer. They are often common around docks.

Cicadas start to fill the void left by the decrease in daytime bird song. Grasshoppers are suddenly very noticeable and dragonfly and damselfly numbers peak. For butterfly-watchers, fritillaries steal the show this month. Deer and horseflies provide something to swat at while swimming or portaging a canoe.

Roadside flowers are at their most colourful and diverse. Ox-eye Daisies and, later, White Sweet Clover and Queen Anne's Lace prevail. Wetland flowers such as Purple Loosestrife are blooming. Ripe berries adorn the cherries, honeysuckles and dogwoods. Basswood trees and milkweeds flower and attract a multitude of insects. The scent of both these species fills the air.

This is our warmest month with hot, humid and often thundery weather. The average daily temperatures are a maximum of 27° C and a minimum of 13° C. In mid-July, the sun rises at about 5:45 a.m. and sets around 8:55 p.m.

The Summer Triangle and Milky Way continue to dominate the night sky. Pegasus, the signature constellation of fall, becomes visible. The Big Dipper is high in the northwest.

Birds

July Highlights

All Month Long

- Starlings flock up and roost in huge, noisy swarms. The birds are particularly loud in the evening when they move to roosting sites in city shade trees. ◇

- Family groups of Common Mergansers are often seen feeding and travelling along shorelines on lakes in the northern Kawarthas. Because broods of mergansers sometimes combine, it is not uncommon to see a female with a parade of over 20 young in tow.

- Hummingbirds are a constant source of wonder and delight as they visit our gardens and feeders all summer long. ◇

- Cottage roads can be good for birding during the summer. Watch especially for trees and shrubs with ripe fruit where birds maybe feeding and for brushy areas which afford lots of cover. If you hear contact calls, stop and "pish."[1]

Early July

- Bird song is noticeably muted by early July. Mates have been found, claims to territory settled and many young already fledged. In many ways, this is the turning point of the avian year since fall migration for some species has already begun.

- Veeries, Wood Thrushes and Hermit Thrushes, however, still sing their clear, serene songs on early summer evenings. Later in the evening, the echoing call of the Whip-poor-will and the nasal "peenting" of the Common Nighthawk are sometimes heard. Both of these species have declined in numbers in the Kawarthas.

- Southward-bound migrant shorebirds start appearing at local sewage lagoons.

Mid-July

- With nesting duties completed, many species of birds begin moulting.

- Caspian Terns start showing up in our area. Most of these birds are slowly making their way from Lake Huron breeding colonies down to Lake Ontario.

- Swallows start congregating on telephone wires, especially in the vicinity of farms.

- Red-winged Blackbirds, Common Grackles and American Crows reform flocks.

Late July

- Northern Waterthrushes, Yellow Warblers and the first Bank and Rough-winged Swallows are migrating south by month's end.

- American Goldfinches nest from late July through early August.

- By the end of the month, shorebird-watching is usually quite good at local sewage lagoons and at Presqu'ile Provincial Park.

- Fall waterfowl migration is slowly getting started. Already Mallard and Blue-winged Teal numbers are increasing on sewage lagoons and large wetlands. Like the wigeon and pintail that will start arriving in August, these birds are probably arriving from points much further west.

- Young Ospreys leave the nest in late July or early August but return for feeding and roosting for about seven days. They can usually be found in the vicinity of the nest for some time after that, as well.

Table 7.1: **July Departures and Arrivals**

early month

arrivals	Least Sandpiper, Lesser Yellowlegs

mid-month

arrivals	Solitary Sandpiper, Semipalmated Sandpiper, Pectoral Sandpiper, Greater Yellowlegs, Caspian Tern, Ring-billed Gull, (juvenals disperse from Great Lakes breeding colonies into Peterborough County)

late month

arrivals	Blue-winged Teal (b), Mallard (b)
departures	Northern Waterthrushes and Yellow Warblers begin to head south, especially those birds that did not successfully raise young. Some individuals of these two species do remain, however, until mid-August.

Shorebirds are the first "fall" migrants.

Semipalmated
Sandpiper

Pectoral Sandpiper

Least Sandpiper

Post-breeding Flocks

Starting in July, blackbird flocks become a common sight in both urban and rural areas. In the city, huge flocks of European Starlings roost in large trees and make their presence known by their clamorous calls and frequent flights from one tree to the next. In local wetlands, large flocks of Red-winged Blackbirds and Common Grackles start to form this month. Starlings, too, are usually present in these flocks. Many of the swallows also gather in post-breeding flocks by mid-July. They often roost at night in some of our larger marshes such as at Miller Creek and Buckley Lake.

There are a number of probable advantages in forming flocks. First of all, there is safety in numbers. If a large group of birds flocks together, the chance of any one individual being killed by an enemy is lower than if that individual roosted in a small group or singly. When predators attack a flock, they try to single out a bird on the edge of the group and pursue that one individual. However, most flocks change shape constantly, expand and contract in size and generally make it very difficult for the predator to remain focused on one bird.

Birds also appear to gain information about good feeding sources by following other birds in the morning when they leave the roost. While the birds are eating, it takes only a few individuals to watch for enemies. That allows the vast majority of the birds in the flock to spend their time feeding and preening rather than having to constantly watch for danger.

Amazing Hummingbirds

The number of hummingbirds coming to feeders usually increases in early July when fledged young begin to accompany the female on feeding excursions. Finally, the hard-working female has some time to catch her breath, having built the nest, incubated the eggs and taken full responsibility for feeding the nestlings—all without any help from the male.

If you happen to have a hummingbird feeder, you may wonder why the birds spend so much time sitting quietly on a perch, seemingly "doing nothing." They are in fact going through the process of emptying their crops. The crop is a part of a bird's digestive system that stores food immediately after it is taken in. Before being able to feed again, the hummingbird has to wait for its crop to become about half empty as sugar water or nectar is passed into the rest of the digestive system. The process takes approximately four minutes. This also helps to explain why, over the course of an hour, the bird makes about 15 feeding trips. At this high feeding rate, the hummingbird's kidneys need to work extremely efficiently. It has been calculated that hummers void over 75 per cent of their body weight daily. This is about the same as a human voiding 75 litres of water a day!

Mammals

July Highlights

All Month Long
- Baby Striped Skunks, Groundhogs, Red Foxes and Raccoons are often seen along roadsides, in campgrounds and even in suburban backyards.
- Roadkill on our highways is very noticeable. The carnage is partly due to the large number of young mammals which must range widely in search of food and/or a new territory. Since highway traffic is also heaviest during the summer months, collisions with animals are inevitable.
- Bats are seen more often since the young are now starting to fly.

Mid-July
- Food becomes very plentiful towards the middle of the month when countless berries ripen. Among the most important for mammals are blueberries, raspberries and cherries. With luck, you may see a bear foraging for berries in the early morning or late evening. ◇

Abundant Food

Summer provides abundant food for mammals, especially in the form of insects and plants. Skunks, for example, feed primarily on insects in early summer. The digs they make are sometimes a source of frustration for suburban lawn owners. By late July, however, the ripening wild cherries, raspberries and blueberries provide an additional source of food for skunks as well as for foxes, bears and raccoons. In fact, Black Bears begin to put on large amounts of weight only once berries become available. Whether the sow will have the reserves of fat necessary to give birth to a cub the following January depends largely on how plentiful the berries are during the summer months. The large berry component of mammalian diet makes the scat (droppings) almost impossible to identify at this time of the year. It appears in all sorts of shapes and configurations. By July, aquatic vegetation is also plentiful and provides a large portion of the sodium requirements of large mammals such as Moose.

It is also important to mention that the influx of cottagers to the Kawarthas in summer means a lot more food for mammals in our local dumps. Quite often, bears visit dumps, especially in the evenings and early mornings.

Amphibians and Reptiles

July Highlights

All Month Long

- Green Frogs and Bullfrogs call until late July, when the amphibian chorus comes to an end. ◇

- Young frogs transform into adults and leave their natal ponds. Tiny Wood Frogs, Spring Peepers and American Toads can usually be found in moist areas of the forest floor from July through September.

- Salamander larvae also mature into the adult phase in July or August. Mole salamanders such as the Spotted and Blue-spotted take up residence in subterranean retreats. Occasionally, they resurface on rainy nights and may be seen crossing roads.

- Snapping Turtles continue to lay eggs into early July, particularly during cool summers.

- Watch for the uncommon Map Turtle basking on rocks in large lakes such as Stony. They often do their sunbathing one on top of the other. Map Turtles frequent deep water and are very shy.

- Eastern Garter Snakes and Northern Water Snakes give birth in July and August. The young of both these species are born live and may number as many as 50 in a brood. The baby snakes measure 12 to 22 centimetres at birth and must fend entirely for themselves from the moment they are born.

The Conclusion of the Frog Chorus

The frog chorus that began in April comes to an end by late July with Green Frogs and Bullfrogs closing the show. These species are very territorial and their calls serve both to attract a female and to advertise ownership of a piece of real estate to other males. Green Frogs and Bullfrogs will defend their territory vigorously, even to the point of wrestling with an intruding male. Along with Mink Frogs, both of these species lay their eggs in mats which float on the surface of the water. Unlike the other frogs, their tadpoles must over-winter at least one year and often two years before they reach the adult stage.

Fishes

July Highlights

All Month Long
- Rock Bass, Pumpkinseed, Bluegills, Yellow Perch and young Smallmouth and Largemouth Bass provide fish-watching opportunities throughout the summer. Look for them in the vicinity of docks, vegetation and other shoreline structure.

- Many species such as Muskellunge, Brook Trout and Lake Trout are moving towards deeper waters as the lake temperatures rise as a result of warm summer weather.

- Carp and bass may still be spawning in early July if the spring weather has been abnormally cool.

- Largemouth Bass feed voraciously in shallow, weedy bays. ◇

- Large schools of Spottail Shiners can be seen over sandy lake bottoms. They are a favourite prey of many game fish.

Summer Bass

Largemouth Bass frequent shallow, weedy waters in July, where they feed voraciously on prey such as frogs. This behaviour corresponds with the peak frog numbers since young Leopard Frogs are just now transforming into adults. Bullfrogs are also vulnerable in early summer, since their mating behaviour can attract the attention of large bass and Muskies. For many people, their best fishing memories are of warm, calm summer evenings casting for bass with a surface lure that mimics a frog. The bass's appetite for frogs appears to diminish somewhat later in the summer, possibly because Leopard Frogs become more terrestrial and frequent damp meadows and fields. Another favourite summer fish with anglers is the Smallmouth Bass. It is famous for its superb fighting abilities and its readiness to strike at bait throughout the summer months.

Insects and Other Invertebrates

July Highlights

All Month Long

- For the lepidopterist, the fritillary butterflies steal the show this month.

- A wide variety of dragonflies and damselflies is on the wing. ◇

- Deer flies and horseflies are very common. ◇

- Most of the tiny, delicate flies attracted to cottage and campground lights at night are midges. They resemble mosquitoes but lack the biting mouth-parts.

- The tent caterpillars that were so common on the cherry trees in May have now pupated and become small brown moths. Before they die the females lay a "varnish-coated" egg mass around cherry and apple twigs. The eggs will hatch next May.

- Water striders and whirligig beetles are a common sight on the Kawartha lakes all summer long. Being true bugs, striders impale their prey with their beak and then suck out the contents. Some species are scavengers while others are predators. Whirligig beetles can whirl around on the surface unmolested by fish because of the fact that they literally stink! Abdominal glands produce an array of defensive chemicals, some which smell like rotting diapers.

Early July

- Meadows light up with thousands of fireflies.

Mid-July

- Cicadas start to fill the void left by the decrease in daytime bird song.

- Grasshoppers and crickets are suddenly very noticeable.

Getting to Know Our Dragonflies and Damselflies

It is hard to go anywhere near water in July and not notice dragonflies and damselflies. Belonging to an ancient order of insects called *Odonata*, watching these creatures is like looking into the Earth's past. In their huge eyes we are seeing life as it existed millions of years ago. Because of their relative abundance and the fact that most can be readily identified in the field, they are an attractive insect group to study. Our knowledge of the Kawarthas' dragonflies and damselflies, however, dates only from 1993 when a small group of local naturalists began keeping detailed records of their sightings. At least 86 species of *Odonata* have been recorded so far in Peterborough County but more species are almost certainly present.

Dragonflies in "wheel" position.

One of the most interesting and noticeable dragonfly behaviours is mating. The extraordinary acrobatics that they go through are definitely worth watching. There are three stages of *Odonate sex*. First of all, the male bends his abdomen beneath him in order to transfer sperm from his genitalia at the tip of the abdomen to the secondary sex organs located near where the abdomen and thorax meet. Secondly, the male forms a "tandem" with the female by grabbing her behind the head with claspers located at the tip of the abdomen. Finally, the pair alight and form a "wheel" position. The female bends the tip of her abdomen around until her genitalia (located at the tip) are brought into contact with the male's secondary sex organs. He then may use special "scoopers" to clear out any sperm that another male may have deposited in the female. This helps to assure that only his genes will be transferred to future generations. Having cleaned house, the male injects his sperm into the female, and the wheel position is broken. Because the male wants to make sure that a rival suitor does not impregnate the female, males of most species will stay around and actively guard her until she has finished laying her eggs. In some species, including most of the damselflies, the male actually retains the female in his hold until egg-laying is complete.

On warm, sunny days, wetlands such as Miller Creek Conservation Area are excellent spots for dragonfly watching. Don't forget to take your binoculars along to help with identification.[2]

Deer and Horseflies

Just as May is infamous for its blackflies and June for its mosquitoes, July's claim to fame is the notorious deer fly. Deer flies can be identified by their black-spotted wings and by the annoying habit of buzzing persistently around the victim's head. It is believed that the ancestral host of deer flies was the deer, which, like humans, the flies attack high on the body. Deer flies are daytime biters and are less deterred by repellents than mosquitoes and blackflies. We can at least be grateful that only the females bite. Nectar is the food of choice of the seldom-seen male.

Horseflies (*Tabanus spp.*), which are larger and usually grey or blackish, belong to the same family as the deer fly but tend to bite lower on the body, preferring the legs. They are less common and generally not a serious pest to humans. Horseflies are among fastest flying insects.

Table 7.2: **Some Common Mid-Summer Butterflies**

Least Skipper	Great Spangled Fritillary	Red Admiral*
Dun Skipper	Atlantis Fritillary	White Admiral
Mulberry Wing Skipper (local)	Silver-bordered Fritillary	Viceroy
Black Swallowtail	Meadow Fritillary	Northern Pearly-Eye
Mustard White	Baltimore Checkerspot (local)	Eyed Brown
Cabbage White	Question Mark*	Little Wood-Satyr
Clouded Sulphur	Compton Tortoiseshell*	Common Wood-Nymph
Orange Sulphur	Mourning Cloak	Monarch
Acadian Hairstreak	Milbert's Tortoiseshell*	Banded Hairstreak
American Lady*		

*designates a species that fluctuates greatly in number from one year to the next

Plants

July Highlights

All Month Long

- Roadside flowers are at their most colourful and diverse. Ox-eye Daisies, and later White Sweet Clover and Queen Anne's Lace prevail. ◇

- A profusion of ferns adorns fields, wetlands and forests this month. By now, they usually show all of their key characteristics and can therefore be identified with more confidence.

- The Dunce Cap mushroom, *Conocybe lactea*, whose quarter-sized white cap occurs at the top of a long delicate stem, is probably the most characteristic summer mushroom on lawns. It is especially common when temperature and humidity are high. The well-known Field Mushroom, *Agaricus campestris*, also appears on lawns during the summer. It is mostly white to pale tan.

Early July

- Common Milkweed flowers and its rich, sweet scent fills the early summer air. ◇

- Several species of orchids bloom, including Rose Pogonia, a wetland plant.

- Prairie species such as Butterfly Milkweed and Wild Bergamot flower. ◇

- By July, many of the flowering shrubs of May and early June are yielding ripe fruit. The crimson berries of the Red-berried Elder are the first to mature. On most plants, hungry birds will have devoured them all.

Mid-July

- Wetlands deliver a full spectrum of colour as a variety of shrubs and herbaceous plants is now in bloom. ◇

- Basswood trees flower and attract a multitude of bees which feed heavily on the tree's nectar and pollen. The basswood's gentle fragrance is transferred to the bee's honey and wax.

- Wild raspberries and blackberries are usually ripe and ready to be enjoyed.

- Purple Loosestrife blooms prolifically.

Late July

- The branches of cherries, honeysuckles and dogwoods bow with ripe berries.

- Ghostly-white Indian Pipe blooms in the heavy shade of hardwood forests. ◇

Common roadside flowers of July.

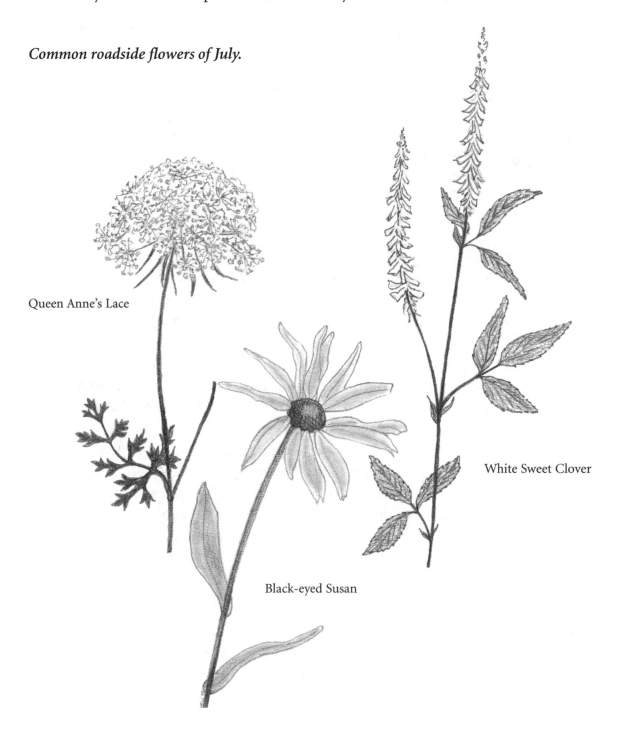

Queen Anne's Lace

Black-eyed Susan

White Sweet Clover

Table 7.3: "First Bloom" Calendar For Selected Trees, Shrubs and Herbaceous Plants

early July	Swamp Milkweed, Harebell, Black-eyed Susan, Queen Anne's Lace, Early Goldenrod, Wild Bergamot, Butterfly Milkweed, Hairy Beardtongue, Orange Hawkweed
mid-July	Evening Primrose, Bouncing Bet, Spotted Jewelweed, Spotted Joe-Pye-weed, Spotted Coral-root, Pearly Everlasting
late July	Showy Tick-Trefoil, Boneset, Kalm's Lobelia, Indian Pipe, Rattlesnake-plantains, Grass-leaved Goldenrod

The Roadside Extravaganza

July roadsides are bordered with numerous brightly coloured flowers. The majority of these species are non-native perennials. Unlike woodland species, their bloom period is quite long, usually averaging around 45 days. Some plants, like Yarrow and Butter-and-Eggs, can actually produce flowers for over 100 days—from June through to October.

Ox-eye Daisies dominate early in the month, accompanied by an assortment of other species including Purple Vetch, Orange Hawkweed, Viper's-bugloss, Bladder Campion, Red Clover, Spreading Dogbane, Common Milkweed and Philadelphia Fleabane. Towards the middle of the month, White Sweet Clover is usually the predominant plant. Also present in large numbers now are Queen Anne's Lace, Black-eyed Susan, Purple-flowering Raspberry, Yarrow and various cinquefoils and St. John's-worts. By the end of July, Queen Anne's Lace will have taken over as the predominant roadside flower. Many individuals of the other species, however, are still in bloom and some new plants have become much more conspicuous. These include Bouncing Bet, Smooth Hawk's-beard, Musk Mallow, Chicory, Evening Primrose, Common Mullein, Fireweed, various thistles, knapweeds and the first goldenrod. Pearly Everlasting is also flowering in the northern parts of Peterborough County in late July and in some areas, such as on the limestone plain just south of Burleigh Falls, Wild Bergamot is in bloom.

Sweet and Sticky

In early July the air is fragrant with the sweet scent of milkweed flowers. The smell, of course, serves to attract insects, whose feet inadvertently pick up the flowers' sticky pollinia. These are small packets containing pollen. With luck, the pollinia will be transferred to the stigma of another plant's flower, and the pollen grains will fertilize the flower. If the insect is not strong enough, however, it can actually become trapped by the pollinia bodies and remain stuck to the flower. It is not uncommon to see dead insects on milkweed flowers that have met their demise in this manner. Judging by the relatively small number of seed pods that appear on the plants in late summer, it would seem that comparatively few flowers become pollinated.

Our Prairie Past (and Future!)

Peterborough is, or at least was, a "prairie town." Samuel Strickland, an early settler to this area, described the natural ecosystem of Scott's Plains (Peterborough's original name) as that of a tallgrass prairie. Much of the downtown area of present-day Peterborough was an "oak savannah"—in other words a prairie-like habitat interspersed with oak trees. This type of habitat covered large sections of southern Ontario from Windsor to as far east as Trent River. Tallgrass prairie is a mixture of native grasses such as Big Blue Stem, and wildflowers such as Black-eyed Susan, Wild Bergamot, Wild Lupine, Indian Paint Brush and Butterfly Milkweed. Native peoples camped in these prairie meadows, deliberately burning them to keep woody plants from becoming established. This allowed the prairie plants to thrive.

When white settlers first arrived, it is estimated that about 150 square kilometres of the area south of Rice Lake was tallgrass prairie. In fact, the native name for Rice Lake was "the lake of the Burning Plains," most likely referring to the fires that would have been set to kill woody plants. There were also a number of prairie sites along the lower Otonabee River near Hiawatha.

Since this time, however, almost all of the original prairie has disappeared. Only a few remnant sites remain, and these are all under five hectares in size. In order to bring back some of the Kawarthas' prairie heritage, a large-scale prairie restoration project was begun in the spring of 1998 on the Rainbow Restoration Site, an eight-hectare field located on the 2nd Line of South Monaghan Township. The site can be accessed via the Rainbow Cottages Resort. Seeds of five grasses and 24 other plants were collected from several of the remaining prairie sites in the Rice Lake area. These seeds were nurtured into seedling plugs and planted using a tobacco planter. Local prairie flora was used in order to protect the unique genetic diversity of this area.

Table 7.4: Typical Herbaceous Plants of the Rice Lake Tallgrass Prairie Ecosystem

The species are listed in the order in which they bloom:

Arrow-leaved Violet, Early Buttercup, Prairie Buttercup, Seneca Snake Root, Indian Paint Brush, Wild Lupine, Wood Lily, Canada Tick Trefoil, Wild Bergamot, Butterfly Weed, Cylindric Blazing-Star, Sky Blue Aster, Indian Grass, Big Blue Stem

Colourful Wetlands

A skein of colour also brightens our wetlands this month. Among the taller shrubs and herbaceous plants, white flowers prevail as Meadowsweet, Tall Meadow-rue and Common Elderberry are all in bloom. Cattails, too, are still blooming early in the month. Their tightly-packed, greenish-brown female flowers make up the plant's well-known sausage-like body. Above this is a "tail" of yellowish male flowers which eventually disappears in late summer. By mid-month, Swamp Milkweed, Spotted Joe-Pye-weed and Purple Loosestrife add pinks and reds to the colour spectrum just as the orange flowers of Spotted Jewelweed are starting to bloom.

Areas of open water are graced with Yellow Pond Lilies and various bladderworts with Fragrant White Water Lilies floating among them like china teacups. Along the edges of ponds and streams, the array of colours is completed by the blue spikes of Pickerelweed and the white flowers of Arrowhead. In acidic, bog-like habitats, you may also find Pitcher Plants blooming and, early in the month, Rose Pogonia Orchids and Sheep Laurel.

July Woodland Flowers

In our woodlands, particularly where conifers are present, a few wildflowers are still blooming. Some of the species to watch for include Wood Sorrel, Twinflower, Pipsissewa, Wintergreen and Shinleaf. By late July, clusters of the ghostly-white Indian Pipe can be found flowering in the deep shade of hardwood forests. It is leafless and contains no chlorophyll. Indian Pipe receives its nourishment from fungi in the soil which in turn draw their food from the roots of trees. Another parasitic plant that shares similar habitat is the Spotted Coral-root, a member of the orchid family which also blooms in summer.

Weather

July Highlights

All Month Long

- This is our warmest month, with hot, humid and often thundery weather. July is therefore prime lightning season. Almost three-quarters of lightning strikes occur between noon and 6 p.m. ◇

- Local lakes usually reach their warmest temperatures. The average is about 23° C. This

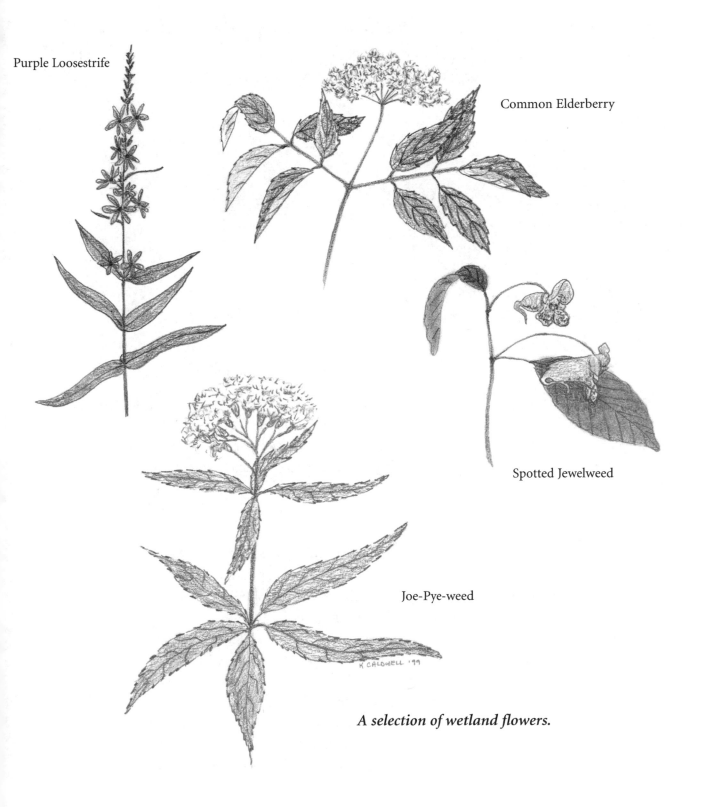

Purple Loosestrife

Common Elderberry

Spotted Jewelweed

Joe-Pye-weed

K CALDWELL '99

A selection of wetland flowers.

warm water sits on top of much colder water, almost creating two separate lakes. ◇

■ As the days once again grow shorter, we lose more daylight in the morning than in the evening. The sun doesn't set until almost 9 p.m. for most of the month, and twilight lasts until 9:30 p.m.

Table 7.5: **July Weather Averages, 1961-1990**

Daily Maximum	26.5° C
Daily Minimum	12.8° C
Extreme Maximum	36.1° C
Extreme Minimum	4.0° C
Rainfall	69.4 mm
Snowfall	0.0 cm
Precipitation	69.4 mm

Warmth, Sun, Rain and Thunderstorms

July is both our warmest and rainiest month. However, since precipitation in the Kawarthas is fairly evenly distributed throughout the year, the extra rain that falls in July is not usually appreciable. In fact, July is also the sunniest month of the year. With the sun, too, comes weather that is often hot and muggy. This is because almost half of our summer air masses originate over the Gulf of Mexico. Fortunately, the Polar and Pacific regions of the continent also send air masses our way in July. The air that originates in these locations tends to be drier and cooler.

The heat and humidity often lead to severe thunderstorms on July afternoons. As the air warms up over the course of the day, evaporation increases dramatically. The warm, moist air rises and forms white, fluffy cumulus clouds. However, if the moisture in the clouds increases too much, they will transform themselves into dark, flat-topped cumulonimbus, or thunderstorm, clouds. These clouds typically take on an anvil shape. The tops of the clouds build up a positive electric charge while the bottoms develop a negative charge. When the buildup of electrical charges becomes great enough, charges between parts of the cloud or between the cloud and the earth—which normally has a negative charge—are released as lightning. The huge amount of heat from lightning creates shock waves in the air that we call thunder. By remembering that thunder travels one kilometre in three seconds, the time between when you see the lightning and when you hear the "bang" will tell you how far away the storm is.

The American-based National Lightning Safety Institute advises that you should take shelter if the flash-to-bang is less than 30 seconds and remain inside for a full 30 minutes after the last rumble of thunder. This is because many lightning strikes occur at considerable distances from a storm system, even when clear skies are visible. In addition to lightning, thunder and heavy rain, thunderstorms can also be accompanied by hailstones, high winds and can cause locally extensive damage.

Two Lakes In One

The Kawartha Lakes usually reach their warmest temperatures—usually about 23° C—during the month of July. About five metres below the warm surface water, however, there is a much colder body of water that remains at 4° C all summer long. Anyone who has made a deep dive into a summer lake will attest to this fact. Because of the difference in water density, the two temperature zones do not mix. A summer lake is therefore best thought of as two separate lakes—a warm one on top and a cold one underneath. The area separating the two is referred to as the thermocline.

Oxygen levels in the cold water zone often become quite low in summer. There are a number of reasons for this. First of all, oxygen from the air has no way of entering these cold, deep waters. As was explained above, there is no mixing in summer between the oxygen-rich warm water zone and the cold water below. Secondly, because there is no light penetration into water this deep, there is no plant growth and, consequently, no oxygen is produced through photosynthesis. Finally, when algae from the surface waters die, they sink into the cold water zone. Valuable oxygen resources are used up in the process of decomposition.

Low oxygen levels have a major impact on fish and invertebrates living in the cold water zone. In order to find sufficient oxygen, they are sometimes forced upwards to the thermocline and can end up all crowded together in a narrow band of water. Lacking the necessary adaptations, they would not survive if they were to move into the warmer water above the thermocline. Low oxygen levels may eventually lead to the demise of species such as Lake Trout and Whitefish.

Table 7.6: **Approximate Twilight, Sunrise and Sunset Times (DST)**

Date	Twilight Begins	Sunrise	Sunset	Twilight Ends
July 1	4:57 a.m.	5:34 a.m.	9:01 p.m.	9:37 p.m.
July 10	5:04 a.m.	5:40 a.m.	8:57p.m.	9:33 p.m.
July 20	5:14 a.m.	5:49 a.m.	8:50 p.m.	9:25 p.m.
Aug. 1	5:28 a.m.	6:01 a.m.	8:37p.m.	9:10 p.m.

The Night Sky

July Highlights

All Month Long

- Major constellations and stars visible (July 15, 10:00 p.m. DST)

  Northwest: Ursa Major dominates the NW sky with Ursa Minor (with *Polaris*) to its right and Boötes (with *Arcturus*) to its left; Leo (with *Regulus*) at horizon

  Northeast: "Summer Triangle" made up of *Vega* (in the constellation Lyra), *Deneb* (in the constellation Cygnus) and *Altair* (in the constellation Aquila). Also look for Cassiopeia and the Milky Way; Great Square of Pegasus (low in NE)

  Southeast: Sagittarius (near horizon) and above it, the brightest part of the Milky Way

  Southwest: Boötes (with *Arcturus*) in mid-sky; Virgo (with *Spica*) to lower right

- The Summer Triangle and Milky Way dominate the night sky. The Milky Way is best seen from 11 p.m. to 1 a.m.

- Pegasus, the signature constellation of fall, becomes visible along the northeastern horizon in the late evening. Along with July's migrating shorebirds, the arrival of Pegasus reminds us to enjoy summer now because it will not last.

- Generally warm and pleasant weather makes for comfortable stargazing. ◇

- Being opposite the high-riding summer sun, the summer moon travels low in the southern sky. This means that summer moon shadows are much longer than those of winter.

Guidelines for Summer Stargazing

Although the summer sky is less brilliant than the sky of early spring, there are numerous constellations to see and the Milky Way is at its most impressive. Summer stargazing is all the more enjoyable because of the generally favourable weather. People also have more leisure time. The guidelines for satisfying summer stargazing are simple:

- Use binoculars. Any size will do, as long as you know how to focus them properly and how to hold them steady. A good idea is to always keep a pair in your car.

- Be sure to bring a star chart and a flashlight. The flashlight should be dimmed down either with a layer of red cellophane over the glass or with a coating of dark red nail polish. This will help your eyes to remain properly attuned to the darkness. You may even wish to buy an inexpensive penlight for this purpose.

- Try to get as far away as possible from light interference. Generally speaking, the further north or east you go in Peterborough County, the darker the skies.

- If at all possible, try to avoid the period covering four days before and after the full moon. The moon simply washes everything out.

- Be sure to take advantage of nights with low humidity. You can gauge the humidity by looking at the Milky Way. If the Milky Way is extra clear, you have a great night for stargazing.

- Rather than standing and bending your neck, you will be much more comfortable lying on your back with your head propped up with a pillow or life jacket. This position will not only allow you to hold the binoculars more steady but will avoid a bad case the next morning of "astronomer's neck." In a pinch, you can even lie on the hood of the car, using the windshield as a backrest.

The Summer Triangle

One of the main features of the summer sky is the Summer Triangle. To find it, use a sky chart along with the Big Dipper as your guides. All summer long, the Big Dipper is suspended high in the northwest. The two stars that form the end of the Dipper's bowl closest to the handle point almost directly to *Vega*, the brightest star of the Triangle. The other two stars in the Triangle are *Deneb* and *Altair*. *Deneb* marks the tail of Cygnus, the Swan, an easily recognizable constellation. The central stars of Cygnus are also known as the Northern Cross, a shape they closely resemble. *Altair* forms the head of Aquila, the Eagle, which looks like a giant bird soaring across the heavens on outspread wings and almost on a collision course with Cygnus. Although *Vega* is located in a rather small, unremarkable constellation (Lyra), it is the brightest star of the Summer Triangle and the second brightest star in the summer sky. Only *Arcturus*, which is now high overhead, is brighter.

Barn Swallows—note the shorter tail of the juveniles.

CHAPTER 8

August—Summer Becoming Fall

The frantic plant growth and animal activity of spring and early summer have now been replaced by a languid atmosphere of maturity and calm. But, despite weather which is often hot and sultry, August is very much "summer-becoming-fall." Bird migration is well underway, the first leaves are starting to change colour and roadsides are being transformed by a yellow surf of goldenrod. The avian chorus of only a few weeks ago has fallen silent and given way to an orchestra of crickets, grasshoppers and cicadas.

Our senses this month are piqued by the spicy fragrance of Wild Bergamot, by the delicious taste of fresh corn and tomatoes, by the calming sight of misty dawns and by the sounds of millions of insects caught up in the urgency to procreate. For many of us, there is also the all-too-familiar irritation in our eyes, nose and throat as ragweed pollen triggers another hay fever season.

Thoreau observed "how early in the year it begins to be late." Already, signs of fall are everywhere. On clear, cool evenings we hear the contact calls of migrant songbirds as they stream overhead against the backdrop of the Milky Way, while Snowy Tree Crickets call in perfect unison in the background. With late August comes the anticipation of bright, cool September weekends and the riot of colour that is just around the corner. In a cultural sense, August is much more the end of the year than is December; because, with Labour Day, our lives begin anew with everything from a new school year to the reconvening of myriad community activities.

August At a Glance

Bird song has almost ceased. Swallows continue to flock up on wires. Shorebird numbers at local sewage lagoons and mud flats swell to at least 10 species. Songbird migration is in full swing by mid-month, particularly for warblers. Flocks of migrating nighthawks can be seen in late afternoon and evening.

Wolves are quite vocal this month. Public wolf howls take place in Algonquin Park. A variety of mammals feeds heavily on late summer fruit and nuts. Little Brown Bats begin to congregate at mating and hibernation sites.

Baby turtles are born this month and next. Leopard Frogs are often abundant in fields adjacent to wetlands. Toads become more common on our lawns and gardens.

Many species of fish retreat to the deeper cooler water below the thermocline.

The calls of crickets, cicadas and grasshoppers dominate the soundscape. Monarch Butterflies and sulphurs are usually quite common this month, as are small, red dragonflies of the Sympetrum genus. Fall Webworm feeding webs are very noticeable. Yellowjackets are increasingly present and annoying.

Jewelweed, Purple Loosestrife and Joe-Pye-weed brighten local wetlands. The first fall colour starts to appear on Virginia Creeper, Red Maple and Staghorn Sumac. Goldenrod borders roadsides and covers fields in a sea of yellow. Ragweed is in flower, setting off the beginning of another hay fever season. Mushrooms are plentiful and add much-needed colour to our woodlands.

August weather is often hot and humid, so air quality warnings are commonplace. By month's end, misty dawns signal fall's approach. The average temperatures for the month are a maximum of 25° C and a minimum of 12° C. In mid-August, the sun rises at about 6:15 a.m. and sets at about 8:20 p.m.

The Summer Triangle and Milky Way still dominate the summer sky. On August 12, the Perseid meteor shower reaches its peak. The Big Dipper reigns over the northwestern sky.

There's lots to do this month, including the Rockhound Gemboree in Bancroft and the Buckhorn Wildlife Art Festival. Farmers are harvesting winter wheat, oats and barley. Photographers will find all sorts of fascinating insects and spiders on goldenrod this month.

Birds

August Highlights

All Month Long

- Swallows continue to flock up on wires. Most will have departed by month's end.

- Many songbird species are moulting and feeding heavily in preparation for migration. ◇

- Shorebird numbers swell to at least ten species. These birds often show up in wetlands in late summer, when low water levels expose the muddy, invertebrate-rich bottom.

- "Convocations of loons" are often seen on some of the larger lakes. ◇

- Other than the sporadic singing of a handful of species such as Eastern Wood-Pewees, Red-eyed Vireos, Indigo Buntings, Song Sparrows and Mourning Doves, bird song has almost completely ceased.

- There are excellent opportunities in this month for seeing songbirds as well as shorebirds. ◇

- Young Barred Owls leave or are ejected from their parents' territory. This territory sorting out is accompanied by a lot of calling.

Early August

- Blue Jays once again become quite vocal. Along with the "lisping" of Cedar Waxwings, the calls of jays are typical August sounds. ◇

Mid-August

- Songbird migration is in full swing by mid-month, with numerous warblers moving through. Listen for their contact calls as they pass overhead at night.

- Flocks of migrating Common Nighthawks can be seen from mid- to-late August. Watch for them in the late afternoon and early evening.

- Large groups of Killdeers can be found feeding in recently ploughed fields during the late summer and fall. Other species of shorebirds sometimes turn up as well.

Red-eyed Vireo singing high in an American Elm.

Table 8.1: August Departures and Arrivals

early month

departures	Common Tern, Bank Swallow, Northern Rough-winged Swallow
arrivals	Northern Pintail, Northern Shoveler, American Wigeon, Semipalmated Plover, Bonaparte's Gull

mid-month

departures	Upland Sandpiper, Black Tern, Yellow Warbler, Cerulean Warbler, Prairie Warbler, Northern Waterthrush
arrivals	Gadwall, Red-breasted Nuthatch (b)* (in flight years), Bay-breasted Warbler, Cape May Warbler, Tennessee Warbler, Wilson's Warbler, Purple Finch* (in flight years)

late month

departures	Least Bittern, Spotted Sandpiper, Semipalmated Sandpiper, Black-billed Cuckoo, Olive-sided Flycatcher, Barn Swallow, Cliff Swallow, Purple Martin, Veery, Golden-winged Warbler, Grasshopper Sparrow, Baltimore Oriole
arrivals	Ring-necked Duck (b), Merlin, Yellow-bellied Flycatcher, Philadelphia Vireo, Swainson's Thrush, Blackpoll Warbler

Preparing for Migration

It now seems that many of our birds have suddenly disappeared, since only a handful of species continue to sing. With the exception of the American Goldfinch and the Cedar Waxwing, most birds have finished nesting. Freed of the responsibility of caring for young, many species retire to the dense foliage of late summer, where they moult and gorge themselves on the plentiful food resources. As migration time approaches, birds must accumulate the necessary fat reserves to undertake the flight southward.

Moulting can take from 5 to 12 weeks to complete in most songbirds. Many warblers, for example, moult from their colourful breeding plumage to a much more drab "basic plumage." Ducks, swans and geese, however, change their feathers all at once in a period as short as two weeks. During this period they cannot fly at all. Many duck species are almost unrecognizable in their basic plumage and difficult to identify.

Convocations of Loons

On our larger lakes, it is not uncommon to see groups of ten or more loons together in mid-to-late summer. Parent birds actually leave their young unattended for several hours as they join these groups, which also include single birds, non-breeding pairs and pairs whose nesting attempts were unsuccessful. It is interesting to watch their intricate maneuvers as they dive and resurface in unison, rear up and flash their wings and appear to talk to each other in chuckles, clucks and croonings. The exact purpose of these gatherings is not fully understood, but they certainly appear to have a social function. They may be linked to preparations for migration, and there is even some evidence that pair bonds may be formed at this time. Aggressive encounters between birds are also seen. This phenomenon is observed every year by cottagers on Shield lakes such as Stony.

August Birding Opportunities

Birding can be excellent in August, especially in the second half of the month when both songbirds and shorebirds are migrating in large numbers. Shorebird species to be expected include Lesser and Greater Yellowlegs, Least, Semipalmated, Pectoral and Solitary Sandpipers and Semipalmated Plover. Short-billed Dowitcher, Baird's Sandpiper and Stilt Sandpiper also turn up regularly. Shorebirds are especially interesting because they allow the observer to get quite close and to take long, leisurely looks. If the sewage lagoons at Havelock, Lakefield and Port Perry are low on shorebirds, a drive to Presqu'ile Provincial Park is well worth the effort. The shoreline between Beach Four and Owen Point is a veritable shorebird mecca.

By mid-August, songbird migration is very much in evidence. Unlike the spring, fall songbird migration is a much more drawn-out process, with many species moving through our area over a period of a month or more. For example, the Red-eyed Vireo is a common migrant from the middle of August until the end of September. Most warbler species, too, will continue to move through the Kawarthas until at least the middle of September. Migration is initiated by the arrival of cool damp weather with northerly winds. Migrants often turn up along the margins of lakes, in the trees and shrubs along cottage roads, along shrubby fencerows and even in city backyards. Backyard birding is even good at night, when it is often possible to hear the contact calls of migrant birds. Some nights the sky seems filled with the chirps of thousands of southward-bound travellers.

As the month draws to a close, keep an eye open for large flocks of migrating nighthawks. It is not uncommon to see 20 or more of these birds flying like over-size swallows as they make their way south, "hawking" for insects as they go. These flocks are most often seen in late afternoon and early evening, particularly after a rainfall.

Migrating Common Nighthawks.

Exit Song—Enter Calls

Bird calls, as opposed to songs, now dominate the avian soundscape. By far the most prominent call heard in August and September is that of the Blue Jay. It can be heard in both urban and rural areas, and its vocalizations are extremely varied. Two common calls are a loud, harsh "thief, thief" and a low, throaty, whistled "too-weedle, too-weedle." Other bird calls typical of August are the cawing of crows, the "kree-kree" of Ring-billed Gulls and the high-pitched lisping of Cedar Waxwings. In some years, Red-breasted Nuthatch numbers increase considerably in late summer and their "toy horn" call becomes a common sound.

Mammals

August Highlights

All Month Long

- Wolves are quite vocal this month. The young in particular respond readily to human howls. There are now indications that wolves in Peterborough County are a different species from what was previously thought. ◊

- In August and throughout the fall, family groups of otters can often be seen feeding and frolicking in quiet lakes.

- A large variety of mammals gorge themselves on late summer fruit and nuts. Bears are especially fond of American Beech nuts and sometimes leave large piles of broken branches called "bears' nests" high in the crotches of trees where they have been feeding.

- Gray Squirrels may give birth to a second litter this month.

Late August

- Starting in late summer and throughout the fall, listen for coyotes calling. ◊

- Little Brown Bats begin to congregate in large numbers at mating and hibernation sites such as caves and old mine shafts.

Wolves and Coyotes in Peterborough County

Despite development and human encroachment, a small wolf population still exists in Peterborough County. The animals are most commonly seen crossing lakes in winter, particularly in northern areas. The actual identity of these wolves, however, is being questioned. The traditional view holds that the wolves of central Ontario and Algonquin Park are a small race of the Gray Wolf, but new genetic evidence indicates that Gray Wolves are absent from the entire area south of the French River. Through research done by Brad White of McMaster University and Paul Wilson of Trent University, it now appears that our wolves may be a northern race of the Red Wolf, a species that still survives in small numbers in the southern United States. The preferred prey of the Red Wolf is the White-tailed Deer. White and Wilson are even proposing a different name for this wolf, namely the Eastern Wolf (*Canis lycaon*). No doubt this view will be challenged. But, if their unique pedigree should hold true, maybe more will be done to protect the animals.

Coyotes, which are common in the Kawarthas, are closely related to this Eastern Wolf; consequently, the two species readily hybridize. In fact, all wolf and Coyote-like animals in Peterborough County contain, to varying degrees, both Coyote and Eastern Wolf genetic material. Depending on the habitat, one or the other is dominant. Even the wolves in Algonquin Park show some evidence of prior hybridization with Coyotes. It is often possible to see Coyotes by driving through agricultural land shortly after sunrise. Look carefully in grassy fields and along fence rows. Although "wild" dogs are also found from time to time in the Kawarthas, there is no genetic proof that they actually hybridize with either wolves or Coyotes.

Late summer and fall is also a great time to listen for their "yip-yip" calls. The pups are now in their "adolescence" and begin to practise their calling for the first time. They have a higher-pitched howl than the adults and also make bird-like squeaks and squeals. Listen for Coyotes just after dark or immediately before dawn. The patchwork of open land and wooded areas around the Cavan Swamp is often a good place to hear them.

Amphibians and Reptiles

August Highlights

All Month Long
- Leopard Frogs wander en masse from their wetland habitat to invade nearby fields. They feed heavily on the bounty of insects to be found there in mid-to-late summer.

- Wood Frogs and Spring Peepers are fairly easy to find in the lower, damper areas of woodlands.

- American Toads become more common on our lawns and gardens. Young Leopard Frogs and Green Frogs often show up as well

Late August
- The eggs of all of our turtle species hatch from late August to early October. In some cases, however, the young may actually overwinter in the nest. Emergence from the ground then occurs the following spring.

Fishes

August Highlights

All Month Long

- Lake, Brown and Brook Trout feed heavily in preparation for fall spawning.

- Many species of fish continue to seek out the deeper, cooler water below the thermocline. ◊

- Fishermen concentrate their efforts on bass this month.

Seeking Cooler Water

Prevailing weather conditions strongly influence fish activity in August. Generally speaking, many fish retreat to cooler depths this month. These species include Walleye, Muskellunge, Smallmouth Bass, Lake Trout and Brook Trout. In the deeper Shield lakes of the northern Kawarthas, Lake Trout now frequent the cool waters below the thermocline where they find temperatures of 10° C and colder that they prefer. Brook Trout also move down to cooler depths or move to spring water upwellings in streams. Both of these trout species are feeding actively in preparation for spawning in September and October.

Insects and Other Invertebrates

August Highlights

All Month Long

- The sounds of countless crickets, grasshoppers and cicadas fill the natural world. ◊

- Fewer species of butterflies are seen in mid-to-late summer. However, Monarch numbers increase in August and, by month's end, sulphurs are especially plentiful. Large numbers of butterflies can often be found in late summer in fields of flowering alfalfa.

- Milkweeds attract a variety of grasshoppers, beetles, bugs and caterpillars. Now is the best time to look for Monarch caterpillars. Also watch for the tuft-covered Milkweed Tussock Moth caterpillars and the red and black Large Milkweed Bug.

- The beautiful rhythmic sound of Snowy Tree Crickets provides a good estimate of air temperature. ◇

- Carolina Locusts are very conspicuous with their crackling flight and yellow-bordered wings. ◇

- The electric, buzzing sound of the cicada makes the mid-day heat seem even more torrid. ◇

- Fall Webworms are active and their nests are very noticeable.

- Yellowjacket wasps are increasingly common and annoying. ◇

- *Catocala* or underwing moths become fairly common. They are attracted both to white lights and to bait. Try a mixture of stale beer, mashed bananas, molasses and a shot of rum! Spread the concoction on tree trunks and check it after dark for moths.

Late August
- Small dragonflies of the genus *Sympetrum* (Meadowhawks) become quite common. In most species, the males are red and the females are yellow.

The Insect Chorus Hits Its Stride

From the middle of summer until the first frosts, the natural soundscape is dominated by the incessant calls of crickets, long-horned grasshoppers, locusts (short-horned grasshoppers) and cicadas. As with birds and amphibians, only the males call. The express purpose of their calls is to attract a female for the purpose of mating. As a general rule, we hear crickets and long-horned grasshoppers during both day and night while cicadas are vocal only during the day. Locusts, a group which contains our most abundant "grasshoppers," are somewhat less vocal.

Grasshoppers and crickets use the same technique, "stridulation," to produce their song. In much the same manner as a violin string being scraped by a bow, these insects rub one part of their body on another. In the technique used by long-horned grasshoppers and crickets, the forewings are rubbed together. The base of one wing has a hardened edge while the base of the other has a toothed area. Each time the hardened edge hits a tooth, a click is produced. Because the rubbing occurs so fast, the individual clicks blend together and sound like chirps or trills. In the case of short-horned grasshoppers (locusts), one of the hind legs is rubbed over a projecting vein, or scraper, on the forewing. Each hind leg has a row of about 80 fine spines which vibrate like the teeth of a comb.

To listen to crickets, grasshoppers and locusts, the best locales are marshes and meadows, particularly on a sunny afternoon or warm evening. At night, the shrubby edges of woodlands are also excellent. Tapes of their calls are now available.[1] If bird song has proven to be too easy, why not try your hand at identifying the crickets and grasshoppers by song? I wish you luck!

Crickets and Relatives

Around habitations, the crickets are the most common insect songsters. They have a louder and comparatively richer call than grasshoppers. The best known members of this group are the field crickets (*Gryllus* spp.), which are the typical black crickets. Most of the insect song we hear, however, comes from a smaller group known as ground crickets (Subfamily *Nemobiinae*). Less than one centimetre in length, this family of crickets creates a non-stop wall of sound both day and night.

Three key players in the August soundscape.

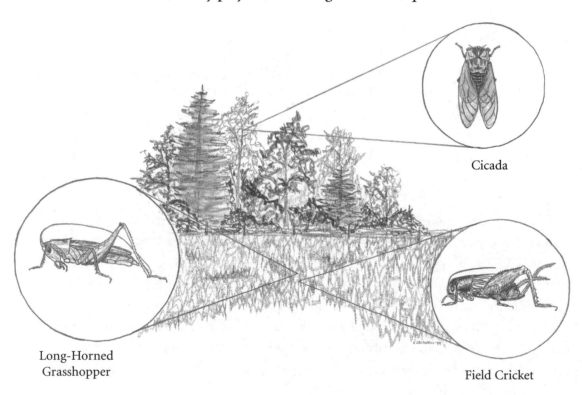

Cicada

Long-Horned
Grasshopper

Field Cricket

Tree crickets (Subfamily *Oecanthinae*) are another very vocal group and many species are excellent singers. Most sing with a prolonged trill, reminiscent of the American Toad. One species of particular interest is the Snowy Tree Cricket (*Oecanthus fultoni*) which is pale green in colour and sings mostly at dusk on warm evenings. Its rhythmic calling is one of the most beautiful nighttime sounds of late summer. Often several males will sing in perfect unison. This species is also known as the thermometer cricket because it is possible to calculate the air temperature by the frequency of its calls. By counting the number of chirps in seven seconds and adding five, the temperature in degrees Celsius can be estimated quite accurately. The favoured host plants of the Snowy Tree Cricket are raspberries and blackberries. Roadsides and other brushy areas adjacent to deciduous woodlots are often good places to listen for them.

Long-horned grasshoppers (Family *Tettigoniidae*) are not well-known as a general rule. They are a less active group, and their green colouration provides excellent camouflage. Despite their name, Long-horned grasshoppers are more closely related to crickets than to grasshoppers. The bush-katydids (*Scudderia* spp.) are included in this group, and several are both common and very vocal. The true katydids (Subfamily *Pseudophyllinae*), whose "katy-did, katy-didn't" is so well known in the eastern United States, are more southern in distribution and have not yet been recorded in Peterborough County. One species, however, has been found as close as Orono.

True Grasshoppers

The short-horned grasshoppers or locusts (Family *Acrididae*) inhabit open, dry areas and are quite variable in colour. Although most locusts are not vocal, some such as band-winged grasshoppers (Subfamily *Oedipodinae*) are very conspicuous in flight because of the crackling noise they produce and the eye-catching pale border on the dark hind wings. Walk along any dusty road or trail in August and you can't help but see and hear them as they fly up in front of you. In fact, they are often referred to as "road dusters" because of their dust-like colouration and the little puff of dust they create when they land. Our most common grasshoppers, the spur-throated grasshoppers (*Melanoplus* spp.), are also locusts. Species of this group are responsible for most of the grasshopper damage done to agricultural lands. One of the most common species in this area is *Melanoplus femurrubrum*, a generally yellow locust with red legs. They do not produce any audible sound.

Table 8.2: **Common Night-time Insect Sounds**

Like birds and frogs, insects can be identified by sound. In fact, comparing the insect calls to those of the frogs can be an effective way to remember them. The following suggestions will help with identification to at least the subfamily level.

tree crickets	a rich, long-lasting trill not unlike the American Toad
Snowy Tree Cricket	a soft, rhythmic treet, treet ... like a rich, gentle-voiced Spring Peeper
bush katydids	a short, electric, "teeth of a comb" sound like a Chorus Frog
ground crickets	a rapid but soft series of very high notes "tikitikitiki ..."

Cicadas

Without any doubt, the sound that best represents the arrival of high summer is the buzzing, "electric" song of the cicada. Adult cicadas call from tree trunks or posts by vibrating membranes at the base of the abdomen. Because they tend to sing loudest during the hottest periods of the day, it's a sound that seems to sap the energy right out of you. An amazing feature about cicadas is the number of years they spend in the ground as nymphs. Periodical cicadas (*Magicicada* spp.) spend either 13 or 17 years underground before emerging as adults. This group, however, does not extend as far north as Ontario. The most commonly heard species of cicada in our area is the Dogday Cicada, an insect probably named after the "dog day" heat of August.

Wasps

Wasps, too, are very active and visible in August. They are particularly skilled at nest-making and it can be fascinating to watch them work. Probably the most familiar are members of the genus *Vespula*, which are social wasps that nest in colonies. They include the very common Bald-faced Hornet, which makes the globular paper nests that are often located in trees. This black wasp with yellowish-white markings on the face needs to be treated with respect.

Anyone who tries to have a picnic in late August or September will almost certainly be visited by

Yellowjackets seeking out a sugar meal.

yellowjackets. They, too, are *Vespids* and are easily identified by the black and yellow bands or triangles on the abdomen. Yellowjackets usually nest in the ground, often in an abandoned animal burrow. They are particularly abundant after a dry, warm summer because these conditions allow the nests to flourish. At summer's end, there is a frantic search for food to feed the larvae still in the nest. Caterpillars are the larval food of preference but yellowjackets will also turn to human foods as a source of protein for the colony. Adults are also attracted to sugar in order to fuel the energy requirements of their own bodies. Most of the *Vespid* wasps succumb to the hard frosts of October; only mated queens survive the winter in order to start new colonies in the spring.

Table 8.3: Some Common Butterflies of Late Summer & Early Fall

Cabbage White	Orange Sulphur	Meadow Fritillary
Mustard White	Viceroy	Northern Crescent
Clouded Sulphur	Common Ringlet	Monarch

Underwing moth with hind wings spread to show patterning.

Plants

August Highlights

All Month Long
- Petroglyphs Provincial Park is a great destination for botanizing in August. Woodland Sunflower, Harebell and Showy Tick-Trefoil are just a few of the plants that are in bloom this month. Ferns and mushrooms also abound.

- Spotted Jewelweed, Purple Loosestrife, Spotted Joe-Pye-weed, Small-flowered Agalinis (*Gerardia*) and the uncommon but beautiful Cardinal Flower add oranges, purples, pinks and reds to wetland edges.

- Water levels often drop in late summer, revealing emergent shorelines. These sites are definitely worth exploring for many interesting plants such as the bladderworts.

- A profusion of ripe wild fruits can be found on various shrubs and small trees. ◇

- Many leaves now have a dusty, tattered look.

- There is often a very noticeable algal bloom in the Kawartha Lakes in August or September. Unicellular blue-green algae such as species of the genus *Microcystis* are commonly involved at this time of year. The surface water may turn almost completely green.

Early August
- Queen Anne's Lace continues to dominate roadsides. New floral arrivals include different species of goldenrods and thistles as well as Virgin's Bower and Wild Cucumber. ◇

- Some Red-osier Dogwoods once again produce flowers in mid-to-late summer.

Mid-August
- Ragweed is in bloom. Its pollen sets off the beginning of another hayfever season. Goldenrod is not the culprit. ◇

- By mid-month, mushrooms become quite common, especially after a period of rain. They add much-needed colour to coniferous and mixed forests.

- Red Maples along the edge of lakes and wetlands are the first trees to show splashes of fall colour. Virginia Creeper and Staghorn Sumac may also show colour change. ◇

Red-osier Dogwood often reflowers in August.

Late August

■ Goldenrods reach peak bloom at month's end and take over as the main roadside flowers. Some fields appear almost totally yellow!

■ Most species of ladies'-tresses orchids bloom in late summer as do Fringed and Bottle Gentian.

Table 8.4: "First Bloom" Calendar For Selected Trees, Shrubs and Herbaceous Plants

early August	Turtlehead, Cardinal Flower, Great Lobelia, Virgin's Bower, Wild Cucumber, Small-flowered Agalinis (Gerardia), White Snakeroot, Woodland Sunflower, Large-leaved Aster, Flat-topped White Aster, Grass-leaved Goldenrod
mid-August	Ragweed, Canada Goldenrod
late August	Bur-Marigold, Bottle Gentian, Calico Aster, Fringed Gentian, Grass-of-Parnassus, New England Aster, Nodding Ladies'- tresses

August Fruits

Almost all of our trees and shrubs bear ripe fruit by the end of August. Early in the month, blueberry picking is at its best. Later, the dark purple berries of the Common Elderberry and the white fruit of the Red-osier Dogwood will ripen and be quickly stripped off by birds. It is also common in August to see new flowers on some Red-osiers. Sugar Maple keys ripen and begin to fall this month along with the first acorns. By the end of the month, the purple-black berries of the European Buckthorn will also be ripe. This non-native species has dark green, glossy leaves and is by far the most common shrub in urban and agricultural areas. Native trees and shrubs have difficulty competing with it, especially along hedgerows.

A List: Some Native Shrubs and Trees Bearing Fruits

Choke Cherry, Pin Cherry, Black Cherry, Blackberry, Red Raspberry, Purple-flowering Raspberry, Bittersweet, Virginia Creeper, Riverbank Grape, Bunchberry and other dogwoods, Highbush-Cranberry, Maple-leaved Viburnum, Hobblebush, Nannyberry, Downy Arrow-wood, American Mountain-ash, Winterberry Holly, Mountain Holly, Red-berried Elder, Common Elderberry, Bristly Sarsaparilla, Staghorn Sumac, Poison Ivy, currants, serviceberries, blueberries, cranberries, honeysuckles,

Chokecherry in fruit.

The Roadside Parade Continues

In the first half of August many of the same flowers as in July continue to bloom. Roadsides are still dominated by Queen Anne's Lace and, further north, by increasing numbers of goldenrod such as Grass-leaved Goldenrod. The deep lavender of thistles and the bright yellow of Smooth Hawk's-beard are also common August sights. Most of the roadside denizens of July such as Black-eyed Susan, Evening Primrose, Bouncing Bet, and White Sweet Clover also remain common. New arrivals on the scene, however, are Wild Cucumber and Virgin's Bower. Their sprawling stems, covered in white flowers, can be seen draped over trees, brushpiles and fallen branches.

Blame Ragweed, Not Goldenrod!

Also, by month's end, Ragweed is in full bloom and its pollen has hay fever sufferers cursing with every sneeze. Goldenrod, which relies on insects to spread its sticky, heavy pollen, is not the culprit. Its bright, yellow flowers have evolved with the express purpose of attracting insect pollinators. The small, green flowers of the Ragweed, however, rely strictly on the wind to spread their light but irritating pollen. A single Ragweed plant can produce a billion grains of pollen and only three or four of the spike-covered pollen grains may be necessary to cause the onset of hay fever symptoms. Pollen density is highest during the morning hours.

Ragweed, the bane of hayfever sufferers.

A Hint of the Colour to Come

Along roadsides and rail-trails, Virginia Creeper is starting to show red leaves. Many of the Red Maples are also turning various shades of red and burgundy, especially those trees that grow around wetlands. This may be related to the effect of cool air settling on low-lying areas. By mid-month, especially during dry summers, many sumac and Red-osier Dogwood also begin to change colour. Noticeable, too, is the appearance of orange and yellow leaves on a number of Sugar Maples. At this early date, colour change in Sugar Maples is usually an indication of a severely stressed tree.

Weather

August Highlights

All Month Long

■ The heat and humidity are often accompanied by air quality warnings on television and radio. One of the most important pollutants is ground level ozone. When the Air Quality Index (AQI) for ozone climbs over 100, it causes serious respiratory problems. People with heart and lung disorders are at highest risk.

Early August

■ At this time of year, the "Dog Star," *Sirius*, rises in the southeast just before the Sun. Because the star is so bright, and its appearance often coincides with the hottest weather of late July and early August, this period became known as the "Dog Days" of summer.

Late August

■ Heavy morning mists, especially in valleys and over lakes, complement the beauty of the August sunrise. Coupled with the noticeably shorter days, they are yet another hint of impending autumn.

■ Lawns and meadows are soaked with dew most mornings.

Table 8.5: **August Weather Averages, 1961-1990**

Daily Maximum	25.1° C
Daily Minimum	11.7° C
Extreme Maximum	35.2° C
Extreme Minimum	0.0° C
Rainfall	81.1 mm
Snowfall	0.0 cm
Precipitation	81.1 mm

Table 8.6: Approximate Twilight, Sunrise and Sunset Times (DST)

Date	Twilight Begins	Sunrise	Sunset	Twilight Ends
Aug. 1	5:28 a.m.	6:01 a.m.	8:37 p.m.	9:10 p.m.
Aug. 10	5:39 a.m.	6:11 a.m.	8:25 p.m.	8:57 p.m.
Aug. 20	5:52 a.m.	6:23 a.m.	8:10 p.m.	8:40 p.m.
Sept. 1	6:07 a.m.	6:37 a.m.	7:49 p.m.	8:19 p.m.

The Night Sky

August Highlights

All Month Long

- Major constellations and stars visible (August 15, 10:00 p.m. DST)

  Northwest: Ursa Major in mid-sky, Ursa Minor (with *Polaris*) above to its right and Boötes (with *Arcturus*) to its left

  Northeast: Cassiopeia in mid-sky; Pegasus and Andromeda (with M31 galaxy) low to its right; Perseus near N horizon

  Southeast: "Summer Triangle" made up of *Vega* (in Lyra), *Deneb* (in Cygnus) and *Altair* (in Aquila)

  Southwest: Sagittarius at S horizon

- The Perseid meteor shower peaks on August 12. It radiates from the Perseus constellation in the northeast and is most visible after midnight. ◇

- The constellations Sagittarius and Scorpius boast numerous nebulae and star clusters that are visible with binoculars.

- By mid-to-late August, Orion is visible one hour before dawn on the eastern horizon.

Meteor Month

August 12 is usually the peak of the annual Perseid meteor shower, but viewing can also be good for a few nights before and after this date. Meteor watching is always best when there is little or no moon effect. However, even if there happens to be a bright moon at the time of the Perseids, a single observer should still be able to see at least a dozen meteors per hour. The shooting stars originate in the Perseus constellation, low in the northeastern sky just below Cassiopeia.

A meteor shower occurs when the Earth passes through a stream of debris left behind by a comet. In the case of the Perseids, the meteors originate from debris left by the comet Swift-Tuttle that was last seen in 1992. Most of the debris consists of particles the size of grains of sand which burn up and emit light as they speed through our atmosphere. No Perseid meteor has ever been known to actually hit the Earth as a meteorite. In 1997, however, an observer watching the Perseid shower saw a meteor so bright that it actually illuminated objects on the ground!

Meteor showers are best viewed from a dark location as far away from city lights as possible. If you watch from a suburban backyard, you are likely to see less than 15 per cent of the meteors visible from a dark site. Bring along a comfortable lawn chair and look up. As the night progresses, Perseus climbs higher and higher in the sky and is nearly overhead by dawn. At that point, the meteors streak down in all directions toward the horizon. The Perseid shower makes for a great group activity or "star party" because people can look in different directions and thereby cover the whole sky. Group totals of as many as 150 meteors per hour are possible.

Fall

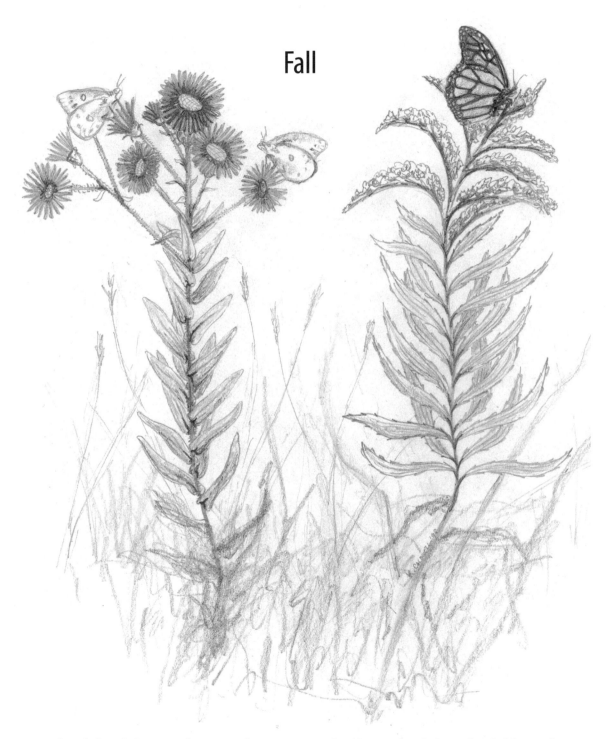

Clouded Sulphurs and Monarch on New England Aster and Canada Goldenrod.

The Blue Jay, a typical sight and sound of September.

CHAPTER 9

September—Mists and Melancholy Joy

With September comes the beginning of fall, a season of melancholy joy and sentimentality. It is both a time of new beginnings and wistful endings. Almost without our knowing it, many of our migratory songbirds will slip away this month. Listening to their calls in the night sky, one feels a certain sadness at their departure but also a sense of wonder in the mystery of bird migration.

A September dawn is ushered in by heavy dews, mist and sunshine softly filtered through countless spider webs. This is a month of yellows and purples when asters and goldenrods practically take over our fields and roadsides. We awake to the raucous calls of Blue Jays and crows, the gentle lisping of White-throated Sparrows and the subdued notes of migrating warblers and vireos foraging along hedgerows. During the day, the steady background chorus of crickets and grasshoppers is punctuated now and again by the lonely call of a Spring Peeper. A walk through Shield country on a warm afternoon charms our noses with the scent of Sweetfern, warmed by the late-summer sun. The smell of rotting, windfall apples and the fragrance of goldenrod also pervade the September air. Outdoor markets overflow with fresh fruit and vegetables which tantalize our taste buds as in no other month of the year.

On or about September 21, the sun crosses the Equator on its annual southward course, marking the official beginning of fall. In fact, the leaves of several species of trees will have almost reached their colour peak by the time the calendar gets around to acknowledging autumn's official arrival.

By the end of the month, the first flights of northern geese will be going over and sparrows will have replaced warblers as the most common migrants. Maples will set both city streets and country vistas ablaze with their oranges, reds and yellows.

September At a Glance

Fall songbird migration peaks, huge flocks of blackbirds invade corn fields and wetlands, migrating sparrows visit our gardens and Blue Jay calls dominate the soundscape.

Many mammals are fattening up this month or gathering and hiding food in preparation for winter. Bats and moose are mating and groundhogs usually begin their six-month hibernation.

Frogs continue to be quite common in damp woodlands, ditches and fields as they feed heavily. Peepers and treefrogs call sporadically during the day while turtle eggs that were laid last June begin to hatch.

This is a time of heavy feeding for many species of fish such as Walleye, Muskellunge and trout. Fishing can be excellent.

Spiders and insects put on a great show this month. Crickets call day and night, Monarchs depart for southern climes, wasps are especially numerous, spider webs are everywhere, and goldenrods and asters become veritable insect magnets.

Asters and goldenrods turn fields into a riot of yellow, white and purple, mushrooms abound in damp woodlands, Virginia Creeper and White Ash attain their most vivid reds and burgundies and, by month's end, fall colour in general approaches its height.

September is a time of heavy morning mists, the first frost and the fall equinox. Dusk is now two hours earlier than at the end of June. Average daily temperatures for the month are a maximum of 20° C and a minimum of 7° C. In mid-September, the sun rises at about 6:55 a.m. and sets at about 7:25 p.m.

The Great Square of Pegasus rules the September sky. The Big Dipper hangs low in the northwest and Cassiopeia dominates the northeast. The Harvest Moon usually occurs this month and bathes the early evening in moonlight.

Birds

September Highlights

All Month Long

- Large flocks of robins and blackbirds are commonplace. Plowed fields harbour American Pipits and Killdeers as well as the occasional Black-bellied Plover and Pectoral Sandpiper. ◇

- A trip to the shores of Lake Ontario can be very rewarding in September and October. Songbirds, shorebirds and hawks are all moving through in large numbers. ◇

- Fall migrants respond especially well to "pishing." This technique can bring birds in remarkably close. ◇

- Large numbers of Blue Jays make a mass exodus southward this month. Others will remain, however, to winter in the Kawarthas. Their calls are probably the most common bird sound of September.

- White-winged Crossbills sometimes arrive on the Shield in late summer as they follow ripening corn crops across the continent.

- Fall warblers challenge birders' identification skills. Actually, they are much easier to identify than most people think. ◇

Early September

- Fall songbird migration is at its peak. Warblers, vireos, thrushes, swallows and flycatchers depart for Central and South America in huge numbers. Keep an eye on the weather forecast because the passage of a cold front usually brings in large numbers of migrants. ◇

Mid-September

- Migrating White-throated Sparrows arrive in the Kawarthas and are a common sight at feeders for several weeks. They are joined later in the month by White-crowned Sparrows and Dark-eyed Juncos. Be sure to scatter sunflower seed on the ground.

- On sunny mid-September days when cumulus clouds dot the sky and the winds are from the northwest, watch for migrating Broad-winged Hawks. Because the birds are usually soaring at high altitudes, a concerted effort is usually necessary to pick them out. Over the Kawarthas, it is not uncommon to see 30 birds or more flying together.

- There are often large flights of thrushes around the middle of the month and their loud, plaintive calls are quite easy to hear in the night sky.

Late September

- The first southbound Northern Canada Geese go over as they make their way to wintering grounds in the Tennessee Valley. Our local Giant Canada Geese do not leave the Kawarthas until December or January and winter no further south than the middle Atlantic states.

- Large numbers of Turkey Vultures are sometimes seen as they make their way south.

- Although bird song is generally absent in the fall, some species will utter a half-hearted, tentative song on bright September and October mornings. Among those heard most regularly are American Robins, Eastern Meadowlarks, Purple Finches and White-throated Sparrows.

- The waterfowl hunt opens on September 25 and closes December 20. The Ruffed Grouse season begins at the same time but finishes December 31 or January 15, depending on where you hunt.

Table 9.1: **September Departures and Arrivals**

early month

departures	Least Sandpiper, Lesser Yellowlegs, Caspian Tern, Common Nighthawk, Chimney Swift, Eastern Kingbird, Tree Swallow, Wood Thrush, Bobolink, Mourning Warbler
arrivals	Lesser Scaup, Black-bellied Plover, White-winged Crossbill*

mid-month

departures	Broad-winged Hawk, American Kestrel (w), Sharp-shinned Hawk (w), Common Moorhen, Solitary Sandpiper, Whip-poor-will, Ruby-throated Hummingbird, House Wren, Great Crested Flycatcher, Eastern Wood-Pewee, Alder Flycatcher, Least Flycatcher, Warbling Vireo, Philadelphia Vireo, Cape May Warbler, Blackburnian Warbler, Canada Warbler, Chestnut-sided Warbler, Northern Parula, Wilson's Warbler, American Redstart, Indigo Bunting
arrivals	Red-necked Grebe, Blue-headed Vireo, Brown Creeper (b), Winter Wren (b), Ruby-crowned Kinglet (b), Golden-crowned Kinglet (b), American Pipit, Palm Warbler, Yellow-rumped Warbler (b), White-throated Sparrow (b), White-crowned Sparrow, Lincoln's Sparrow, Rusty Blackbird

late month

departures	Osprey, Virginia Rail, Sora, Northern Flicker, Yellow-bellied Flycatcher, Eastern Phoebe, Red-eyed

Rose-breasted Grosbeaks are nocturnal migrants.

Vireo, Blue Jay (w), Marsh Wren, Swainson's Thrush, Gray-cheeked Thrush, Brown Thrasher, Gray Catbird, Cedar Waxwing (w), Bay-breasted Warbler, Blackpoll Warbler, Black-and-white Warbler, Ovenbird, Scarlet Tanager, Rose-breasted Grosbeak, Brown-headed Cowbird

arrivals   "Northern" Canada Geese, Peregrine Falcon, Northern Saw-whet Owl, "Northern" Horned Lark (b), Orange-crowned Warbler, Dark-eyed Junco

Flocking Continues

A number of species form large flocks in the fall. These include American Pipits, American Crows, Ring-billed Gulls and a variety of blackbirds. Pipits are regularly seen in fields of winter wheat as well as fields that have been recently plowed. Large numbers of Rusty Blackbirds, Common Grackles, Red-winged Blackbirds and European Starlings often fill the trees of local wetlands. Corn fields also attract huge numbers of blackbirds in the fall, as well as Canada Geese.

American Robins, too, form flocks at this time of year. Joined by migrant robins from further north, they seem to take on the behaviour of a totally different species and appear possessed by a restless urgency. It is almost as if fall robins have rediscovered their ancestral wildness. Fall robins are only rarely seen on lawns, as they prefer to gorge themselves on berries. They are particularly fond of mountain-ash, dogwood, Black Cherry and European Buckthorn berries at this time of the year. Later in the fall, watch for large numbers of robins on wet days following the passage of a cold front. The birds often appear by the dozens on leaf-strewn roads, where they find earthworms forced out of the ground by the rain.

Flocks of Ring-billed Gulls are also a common sight, especially in agricultural areas and around schools. They wait like vultures on school roofs until the students come out for recess spilling popcorn and potato chips as they go. Actually, if it weren't for the gulls, the schoolgrounds would be a lot dirtier. In the evening, the gulls head to large bodies of water such as Rice Lake and Clear Lake to spend the night.

Pishing: The Birder's Secret Tool

Much of fall songbird migration tends to be a quiet and somewhat secretive phenomenon. The observer therefore needs to slow down, to look carefully and, especially, to listen. Although the birds are usually not singing in the fall, they are making contact calls and tend to be in mixed flocks that often contain very vocal chickadees. A rule of thumb of fall birding is to stop and take a close look any time you hear chickadees calling because there are usually migrants with them.

It is particularly useful to know how to entice the birds in for closer observation. The easiest and most effective technique is to imitate the distress call of a bird or small mammal. This technique, which is known as "pishing," can draw birds in like a magnet since they are curious about unusual sounds. It simply involves taking a deep breath and softly but quickly repeating the word "pish" as you let the air out in one, drawn-out exhale. The effectiveness of this technique varies somewhat depending on the species of bird but definitely works extremely well with chickadees and the nuthatches, kinglets, vireos and warblers that are often in their company. Chickadees and nuthatches are almost always the first species to come into view in response to pishing. Be sure to continue for at least another minute, however, because the other species are sometimes just a little slower to react.

Identifying the Fall Warblers

Many birders enjoy the challenge of identifying the fall warblers. In some ways, warbler-watching is actually better in the fall than in the spring. The daily stream of birds is steadier and less dependent on the idiosyncrasies of the weather. The migration period is also much longer, extending from late July, when the first Northern Waterthrushes and Yellow Warblers migrate through, until late October, when the last of the Yellow-rumped Warblers are seen.

When Roger Tory Peterson published his *Field Guide to the Birds*, he unfortunately set a negative tone regarding the identification of fall warblers. On two pages entitled "Confusing Fall Warblers," he presented the dingiest, drabbest and least remarkable of these birds, leading some people to believe that the entire warbler assemblage is exceedingly hard to identify after the end of June. Such, however, is not the case. Some species do not change at all (e.g., Ovenbird, American Redstart, Black-throated Blue Warbler) and many are just slightly altered from their spring plumage (e.g., Black-throated Green Warbler, Nashville Warbler, Canada Warbler). Immature birds present the biggest challenge, although one, the Chestnut-sided Warbler, is so distinctive that it's easier to identify than some spring adult species. As a general rule, adult warblers migrate earlier than the immatures. By mid-September, the majority of warblers seen tend to be young birds.

The secret to enjoying fall warblering is not to worry about identifying everything you see. Just let some of the LYJ's (little yellow jobs!) flit on by. You will see enough that is familiar to come up with a very respectable species total. Be sure to use the pishing technique, however. Fall warblers are very inquisitive.

A Matter of Weather

September is to fall what May is to spring. Migration is in full swing and, given the right conditions, birding can be spectacular. Even though some birds appear to migrate regardless of the weather, large movements of fall migrants usually occur just after the passage of a cold front. The northwesterly breezes provide tail winds which facilitate flight and help the birds to conserve energy. It can be notoriously difficult to predict, however, when migration conditions are going to be optimal since weather conditions at points far away from the Kawarthas are also having an influence. It is therefore important to get out regularly to maximize your chances of witnessing a large passage of birds.

Migrant White-throated Sparrows.

Sparrows of Passage

By mid-September, the gentle lisping calls of migrating White-throated Sparrows can be heard along edge habitats and in city and suburban backyards. They are joined at the end of the month by Dark-eyed Juncos and aristocratic-looking White-crowned Sparrows. If you haven't been feeding the birds all summer, now is the time to start. All three of these species will come faithfully every day to your yard as long as there is sunflower seed scattered on the ground close to adequate shelter. All three species definitely prefer feeding on the ground, although they will occasionally land on above-ground feeders. Sparrows also love unkempt gardens in which the perennials have gone to seed.

Despite our best attempts to keep them, however, almost all of the sparrows will have departed by mid-October as the urge to migrate pulls them southward. Only some of the juncos will remain to spend the winter in the balmy climes of the Kawarthas.

Mammals

September Highlights

All Month Long

- The members of the squirrel family are especially conspicuous in late summer and early fall. Chipmunks call repeatedly as they collect nuts and seeds to store in underground pantries. Gray Squirrels, too, are quite noticeable as they go about burying food in preparation for winter. Red Squirrels make caches of conifer cones that they nip off the trees. ◇

- White-tailed Deer are feeding heavily to build up fat that will supply up to a third of their winter energy needs. A gray-brown winter coat replaces the reddish summer coat in September, as well. With dense inner fur and long, hollow outer hairs, it is actually ten times thicker than the summer coat. The gray-brown colouration will offer excellent camouflage in the winter woods.

- Bucks expend considerable time this month rubbing their antlers against branches in order to peel off the velvet covering. The velvet has supplied nourishment to the growing antlers all spring and summer long.

- Sensing the shorter days, Beavers begin cutting down trees once again for winter food. Aspens are the preferred species.

- Little Brown and Big Brown Bats mate and take up residence in hibernation sites. Other bat species such as the Red Bats migrate south. ◇

Early September

- The hunting season for Black Bear starts on September 1 in northern Peterborough County and on September 15 in the south.

Late September

- Moose mate from late September to late October. Being such "romantic" beasts, they time the rut to coincide with the height of the fall colours.

- The hunting season for rabbits and hares opens on September 25 throughout Peterborough County and lasts until the end of February or March, depending on the district.

A Busy Time for Squirrels

September is a time of heavy feeding for many species of mammals as they prepare for the coming winter. The Eastern Chipmunk is one of the most noticeable mammals at this time of year. Its staccato *chuck-chuck* becomes a very common woodland sound as it collects nuts and seeds to store in underground pantries. The chipmunk is not a true hibernator and therefore must visit its pantries over the course of the winter. Dietary staples include hazelnuts, beech nuts and acorns as well as seeds from conifers and herbaceous plants. Berries and mushrooms are also eaten in large numbers.

The shortening daylight hours also trigger a change in the behaviour of Gray Squirrels. Their activity, too, becomes dominated by eating and storing food. To store food, Gray Squirrels dig a shallow hole, deposit a single food item and then cover it with soil. It has been demonstrated that squirrels do not actually remember where they hide their food. Relocating buried food is based on smell and even a degree of luck. Frequently, the food they find was buried by another squirrel. You may also see baby Gray Squirrels at this time of year. These are animals born in early August, when about a third of female Gray Squirrels have a second litter.

As for Red Squirrels, they are busy gathering cones, especially from spruces and hemlocks. The seeds in the cones will ripen in storage and be ready for winter consumption. They will also place apples or mushrooms on the fork of a twig to ripen or dry and be eaten at a later date.

The Groundhog, our largest member of the squirrel family, usually begins hibernation in late September or early October. When fall frosts kill much of the foliage on which the Groundhog feeds, the animal heads to its deep, winter burrow where it becomes dormant. It will survive on the fat that it has accumulated all summer long and not emerge until March. The Groundhog population appears to be decreasing in the Kawarthas, possibly as a result of increased predation by coyotes.

Bats On the Make and On the Move

It is quite common to see small groups of bats on September evenings. Some Ontario species such as Red, Hoary and Silver-haired Bats migrate south to the Gulf states. The more common Big Brown and Little Brown Bats, however, spend the winter months in Canada, although they do sometimes fly considerable distances to hibernation sites. The Little Brown Bat has been known to fly up to 800 kilometres to reach the abandoned mine or natural cave where it hibernates. On early fall evenings, these two species are often seen feeding in small groups or moving toward their wintering destinations. Three other bat species that hibernate in Ontario, albeit in smaller numbers, are the Northern Long-eared, the Eastern Pipistrelle and the Eastern Small-footed.

Male and female bats of both species swarm at hibernation sites in late summer before actually beginning hibernation at the end of September or early October. Mating activity is believed to be the main purpose of the swarming phenomenon. The closest known hibernation sites to Peterborough are an abandoned mine near Renfrew and a limestone cave along the Moira River near Belleville. It is interesting to note that, after mating, the sperm is stored in the female's body until spring, when ovulation and fertilization take place. The young are born in late spring or early summer.

Locally, large numbers of bats have been seen in late summer over the Indian River near the Warsaw Caves. The numbers peak about an hour after dark. Whether these are mating swarms or simply bats gathering to feed is not known. The status of the Warsaw Caves as an overwintering site also needs to be studied. It is possible that bats do hibernate in some of the smaller, less accessible caves. During the summer of 2000, a series of new caves were discovered in this area, and they apparently harbour a large bat population. From September to May, people should stay out of any caves or mine where bats are hibernating as disturbance costs the animals energy and is usually fatal.

Amphibians and Reptiles

September Highlights

All Month Long

- Frogs are still very common in fields, ditches and damp woodlands. Abundant spiders and insects provide plentiful food in these habitats.
- There are sometimes large "migrations" of frogs across busy roads. ◇
- Spring Peepers and Gray Treefrogs often call sporadically from woodland trees and shrubs. ◇
- Baby turtles are hatching.

Frogs on the Move

Frog populations are usually high in late summer and early fall since their ranks have been bolstered by large numbers of young-of-the-year frogs. Young Wood Frogs, Spring Peepers

Newly-hatched Snapping Turtle.

and American Toads can often be seen during a September walk through a damp woodland. Fields, ditches and wetland edges are alive this month with Leopard Frogs and Green Frogs. Many species, including Leopard Frogs, are starting to move from summering sites such as meadows and marshes to their hibernation sites in streams, ponds and rivers. Some species of frogs move considerable distances to reach their overwintering sites. Amphibians prefer to travel during warm, wet weather and particularly when the rain comes in the evening or at night. If conditions for "migration" have been too dry for a long period of time but then suddenly become suitable, the numbers of frogs on the move can be quite spectacular. When this migration involves crossing busy roads, large numbers of frogs are killed.

Fall Frog Song

It is not uncommon to hear Spring Peepers and Gray Treefrogs calling in the fall. The vocalizations tend to be sporadic, however, and given only by one or two individuals at a time. The calls also seem to be restricted to the daytime. Studies have shown that the frogs calling in the fall are mostly first-year males. The fact that the sun is lower in the sky (as in the spring) may initiate this calling.

Fishes

September Highlights

All Month Long

- Muskellunge and Walleye move to shallower water and feed heavily. Walleye in particular develop quite an appetite for frogs. Late September through November offers the best fishing of the year for these species.

Late September

- Brook Trout also feed heavily and start moving upstream in preparation for spawning. Males begin to acquire their nuptial colours. Opportunities to observe the fish are quite good. ◇
- The fishing season for trout closes on September 30 throughout Peterborough County.

Colour to Rival the Fall Leaves

Brook Trout are also voracious feeders in the early fall as they prepare to spawn. As the water's surface layer cools, trout move in closer to shore to feed and are therefore easier to observe. They also migrate upstream in the fall and can sometimes be seen stopping to sun themselves over submerged rocks or logs. The males begin to acquire the deep orange to purple-red underside that distinguishes them during the spawning season. A beautiful black border on the underside separates the white belly from the rich flank colour. The orange and red pigments are acquired from the bodies of certain crustaceans on which the trout prey. During the summer these pigments are stored in the muscles, giving them their distinctive pink colour. In the fall, however, the pigments become visible in the skin in males. As in birds, the colours may serve to make the male fish more attractive to the female, as well as being an indication of overall health and suitability as a mate. Spawning itself will take place any time from late October to late November.

Muskellunge.

Insects and Other Invertebrates

September Highlights

All Month Long

- Goldenrod and aster attract huge numbers of insects and provide excellent opportunities for close-up observation. Look for Honey Bees, wasps, long-horned beetles, soldier beetles, ambush bugs, Monarch butterflies and mantids, as well as syrphid flies, which mimic bees or wasps in appearance.

- Migrating Monarch Butterflies are often seen flying in a southerly direction as they make their way towards their Mexican wintering grounds. ◇

- The almost total absence of biting insects makes outdoor activities especially pleasant.

- Swarms of flying ants are a common sight, even within the city and in rural areas. Winged males, along with fully reproductive females, develop in later summer. After mating occurs, the females start a new colony or enter an established one. As for the males, they simply die soon after.

- Fall Webworm nests stand out noticeably. ◇

- Woolly Bear caterpillars are often seen crossing paths and roads in search of a site to overwinter. Watch also for Yellow Bear and American Dagger Moth caterpillars which are similar in size and also have a hairy appearance. ◇

- Dragonflies are still common, especially the various darners and the small red or yellow meadowhawks. Watch for Yellow-Legged and Whitefaced Meadowhawks in particular.

- Hornets and yellowjackets seem to be taking over. The workers (sterile females) spend less time at the hive feeding the young in early fall and more time looking after their personal needs for sugar and sweet liquids.

- Spider webs are everywhere. As in June, it is often possible to see spiderlings "ballooning" to new locales on filaments of silk borne by the wind.

Early September

- Sulphurs become the most common butterfly species seen.

- Monarch Butterfly numbers are at their highest. They begin to congregate at Presqu'ile Provincial Park, which is a jumping off point for their migration across Lake Ontario and on to Mexico.

- Although the song of the cicada fades away early in the month, crickets and grasshoppers continue to call fervently during the day. As temperatures become cooler, however, the amount of evening song is noticeably reduced.

September Butterfly Opportunities

Sulphur butterflies reach their peak numbers in the Kawarthas this month and are a common site in fields and along roadsides. The species most regularly seen is the Clouded Sulphur, although the Orange Sulphur is common as well. The latter is often seen over alfalfa fields. Males of both these species can sometimes be found "mud puddling," a behaviour in which they gather in large numbers around pools on dirt roads or even in sand traps on golf courses and probe the mud or sand with their tongues. It is believed that they are ingesting sodium present in solution in order to replace the sodium lost during mating.

Anyone with an interest in butterflies should make a point of attending the Labour Day Weekend Monarch Butterfly tagging demonstration at Presqu'ile Provincial Park. A tagger is on hand to answer questions about Monarchs and to show how the butterflies are tagged with a tiny adhesive sticker bearing a number and return address. Monarchs are especially common at Presqu'ile because they use this peninsula as a jumping off point before crossing Lake Ontario. Butterflies tagged at the park have been found in the pine forests of central Mexico, where the insects spend the winter. Monarchs are not the only migratory butterflies. Red Admirals, Painted Ladies and American Ladies all move southward in September as well. In years of abundance, both lady species can sometimes be found in large numbers this month, particularly along the northern shores of Lake Ontario and Lake Erie.

Ugliness in Architecture: The Fall Webworm

The webs of the Fall Webworm, a member of the tiger moth family, are a rather unsightly but common occurrence on trees in late summer. Their large, loose webs, which encase the ends of branches of broad-leaved trees and shrubs, house colonies of small, beige caterpillars covered with long hairs. The web is expanded to enclose new leaves as required. These webs often remain on the tree throughout the fall and winter and are easy to mistake for tattered old oriole nests. These caterpillars are often confused with the Eastern Tent Caterpillar since they both build a communal nest of webbing. Tent caterpillars, however, are active only in the spring and their nest is a triangular web located in the crotch of a fruit tree. Unlike tent caterpillars, webworm larvae leave the nest only when they are ready to spin a cocoon and pupate. The insects overwinter in the pupal form. Small, white webworm moths emerge in May, mate and lay their eggs on the underside of leaves. The eggs hatch in the summer and the cycle begins once again.

Fall Webworm nest and caterpillars—note that adult moths are present only in spring.

The damage to the tree or shrub is usually limited to the leaves within the web and rarely causes the tree any serious harm.

Woolly Bear caterpillar.

Woolly Bears on the Move

Another caterpillar often seen in September is the Woolly Bear. It is brown in the middle and black at both ends and is a favourite of school children because of its cuddly appearance. An old belief stated that, if the middle stripe is narrow, the winter will be mild. Judging by our winters in recent years, there must be a lot of narrow-striped Woolly Bears! These caterpillars overwinter in the larval form, curled up under a piece of loose bark, a rock or a log. In the spring, they feed briefly, spin a cocoon and emerge two weeks later as white Isabella Moths.

Two other hairy caterpillars are commonly seen at this time of year. Watch for the Yellow Bear and the American Dagger Moth caterpillar. The latter is a white caterpillar with five narrow, black hair "pencils" emerging from its back.

Plants

September Highlights

All Month Long

- The leaves of most our native trees and shrubs will begin to change colour this month. Understanding how and why this happens adds a great deal to our enjoyment of fall. ◇

- Goldenrods and asters turn fields a riot of yellow, purple and white. Goldenrods dominate early in the month, but asters reign supreme by month's end. ◇

- Other September wildflower specialties include False Dragon-head, Grass-of-Parnassus, Fringed and Bottle Gentians, Kalm's Lobelia, Gerardia, White Snakeroot and ladies'-tresses orchids.

- Wild Cucumber drapes its numerous branches, flowers and tendrils over shrubs, fences and fallen trees. The gray, silky plumes of the Virgin's Bower, its flowers now gone to seed, are also a common sight in these locations.

- A large variety of native grasses that bloomed in the summer can actually be best identified in the fall. This is because seeds rather than flowers are most important for identification. The fall is a wonderful time to study this generally neglected part of our flora.

- Many plant species are spreading their genes this month. The seeds of Common Milkweed, Fireweed and the various thistles are borne by parachutes of white floss. Sugar Maple samaras helicopter to the ground and Bur Marigold seeds hitchhike to new locales.

- Mushrooms are often most plentiful and diverse in September. A number of local species are edible. ◇

- White Pine cones become mature and most of the seeds are shed. Red Pine, White Cedar, Balsam Fir, White Spruce and Tamarack also begin to release their seeds.

- Winter wheat is usually planted in September.

Early September

- The seeds of the American Highbush-Cranberry, White Birch, and even White and Red Ash can be harvested at this time.

Mid-September

- Red Maples growing along the edges of lakes and wetlands reach their peak colour by mid-September or earlier.

- Even before the first frosts, ferns such as Bracken begin to turn brown and shrivel.

Late September

- Trees are not the whole show when it comes to fall colour. Virginia Creeper glows with scintillating reds while dogwoods offer beautiful burgundies. ◇

- By late September or the first week of October, the leaves in northern Peterborough County are usually close to their colour peak. Consider taking a "colour drive" to the Wilberforce or Glen Alda areas. Sugar and Red Maple colours in Algonquin Park

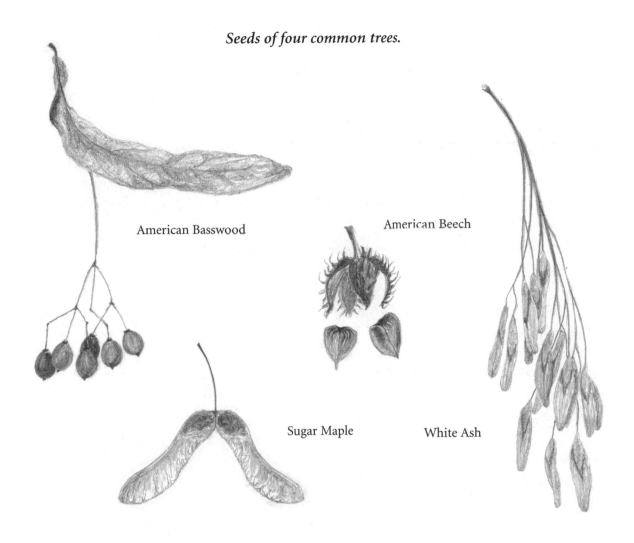

Seeds of four common trees.

American Basswood

American Beech

Sugar Maple

White Ash

generally reach their height about now as well. ◇

■ The appearance on lawns of the Shaggy Mane mushroom, *Coprinus comatus,* is a sure sign of fall. The brown or white cylindrical caps are very distinctive. The Stinking Parasol, *Lepiota cristata,* can also be quite common in autumn. This small, white mushroom has a strong, penetrating odour.

■ Old needles die and begin to fall off White and Red Pine.

■ Soybeans are harvested in late September and early October.

Table 9.2: "First Bloom" Calendar For Selected Trees, Shrubs and Herbaceous Plants

early September	Panicled Aster, Heath Aster, Hairy Aster
mid-September	Beechdrops

How and Why Leaves Change Colour

September is a wonderful time of year for enjoying the trees and flowers. Although it is not traditionally thought of as a month for wildflowers, our fields and roadsides are more colourful now than at any other time of year. The fall leaves, however, are nature's finest accomplishment this month. And even though we witness this spectacle every year, the spectrum and intensity of colours never cease to amaze.

A basic understanding of the mechanisms involved in how and why leaves change colour adds a great deal to our enjoyment of the fall colours. First of all, colour change is not simply a reaction to cold weather. While it is true that some years produce better colours than others, the intensity of the colours depends more on the amount of sunshine that the leaves receive than on cool temperatures or an early frost. Colour change and the shedding of the leaves are manifestations of a plant's preparation for winter. For a large broad-leaved tree, there would be a definite price to be paid for keeping its leaves. Not only would a tree run the risk of losing branches and entire limbs because the weight of ice and snow on the leaves, the organism would lose a great deal of water through transpiration. Since winter is essentially a time of drought in which water is locked up in the form of ice, the tree must minimize water loss and desiccation. One way it does so is by getting rid of its leaves.

Because the various minerals or "nutrients" that the roots absorb from the ground are available in very small quantities, trees must conserve them as much as possible. A very high proportion of these substances is contained in the leaves, where they are used in photosynthesis. As the days get shorter and the daily amount of light decreases, it is no longer economical for the tree to continue to produce chlorophyll, the chemical that captures the sun's energy and uses it in combination with water and carbon dioxide to produce the sugar-based substances that make up a tree. Trees have therefore evolved to initiate a "salvage operation" every fall, in which nutrients are removed from the leaves and stored in the woody tissues until the next spring. The nutrients will therefore be readily available to help manufacture a whole new set of leaves.

As the nutrients are removed, the leaves eventually lose their ability to manufacture chlorophyll. At this point a colour change in the leaves becomes apparent. Other pigments in the leaves which have always been there become visible, since they are no longer masked by the green pigment of chlorophyll. Carotene pigments provide the yellows and oranges, while anthocyanins give us the beautiful reds. The red pigments are created in the fall from excess sugars and seem to be brightest when there is lots of fall sunshine. These pigments may actually help to protect the leaves from cold. Some experts believe that the anthocyanins allow the leaves a little more time to rescue additional nutrients before the whole salvage operation shuts down and the leaves fall to the ground. The actual shedding of the leaves is achieved by the formation of a corky layer of cells at the base of each leaf stalk. Eventually, the leaf's connection with the twig is broken and it falls off in the wind or rain. At this melancholy time of year, it is comforting to think of the fall colours not as the demise of this year's leaves, but rather as the transfer of precious nutrients back to the parent tree to use in next spring's foliage.

Table 9.3: Autumn Leaf Colour

Colour is quite variable, even within the same species. White Ash, for example, can turn any colour from bronze-yellow to wine-purple. Male Red Maples usually turn red while female trees tend to be yellow. The following list outlines the most common colours:

reds, purples and burgundy	Red Maple, White Ash, Pin Cherry, Staghorn Sumac, Common Blackberry, Red Raspberry, oaks, dogwoods
pinks	Maple-leaved Viburnum, Choke Cherry, dogwoods
oranges	Sugar Maple, Red Maple, Staghorn Sumac, Bigtooth Aspen
yellows	Sugar Maple, Silver Maple, Red Maple, Norway Maple, Trembling Aspen, Bigtooth Aspen, White Birch, Balsam Poplar, Striped Maple, American Beech, Bitternut Hickory, Black Walnut, White Ash, American Basswood, Tamarack, elms, willows
browns and coppers	American Beech, White Ash, oaks

Asters and Goldenrods

This is the season of asters and goldenrods. Peterborough County hosts approximately 17 species in each of these plant groups. Although many of the asters are similar in appearance, knowing some of the more distinctive species adds interest to a September hike. In fields, meadows and along roadsides, look for the violet-coloured New England Aster and Smooth

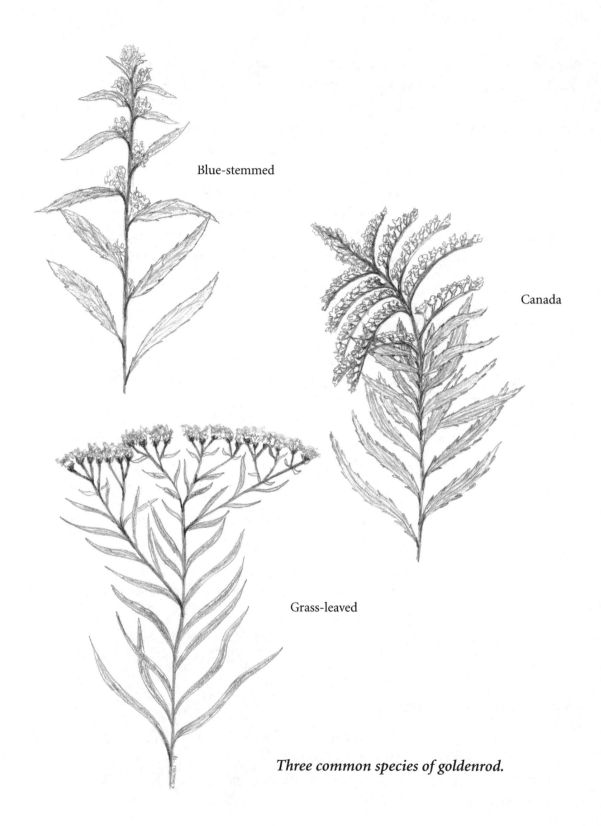

Blue-stemmed

Canada

Grass-leaved

Three common species of goldenrod.

Aster, and the white flowers of the Heath Aster, Panicled Aster and Calico Aster. In damp thickets, Purple-stemmed Aster is quite common along with Flat-topped White Aster.

As for the goldenrods, the most common species in dry, open areas are the Early Goldenrod and the Canada Goldenrod. In rich, open woods, look for Blue-stemmed Goldenrod and Zigzag Goldenrod. Bog Goldenrod is a common species of wetland borders. Many of the asters and goldenrods have different blooming periods and some are still in flower in mid-October. The particular mix of species also changes between the southern Kawarthas and Shield areas.

Mushrooms

In much the same way as wildflowers epitomize a spring woodland, mushrooms signal the coming of fall. When the weather becomes slightly cooler and we receive sufficient rain, the fruiting bodies of fungi become very abundant and appear in an incredible variety of shapes, colours and sizes. Some of the most interesting species appear in cool, shaded, mixed forests. Their incredible diversity and beauty add interest to a fall walk, and they are also a wonderful subject for photography. Although mushrooms have now been given their own kingdom (Fungi), they are still thought of as an element of our flora.

The fungi can be classified into several groups. These include the gilled fungi or "true mushrooms," which have the typical flat or rounded cap, the coral fungi, which are highly branched, the polypores, which look like wooden shelves or brackets protruding from a tree trunk, and the various jelly fungi, which are rubbery to the touch, extremely colourful and grow on wood. Maybe the most entertaining group, however, is the puffballs. Some species of giant puffballs can be as big as footballs and look like errant loaves of white bread. On the other hand, earthstars are small and dainty. They have a "ball" in the centre surrounded by star-like rays. The ball releases the spores from a small opening in the top when they are mature. A gentle touch will cause the spores to puff out in a plume of "smoke."

As a general rule, mushrooms do not adhere to a strict seasonal calendar. They often appear any time that the temperature and moisture conditions are right. Many species, such as the deadly Destroying Angel, can be found in the spring, summer and fall. Two groups that are closely tied to a specific season, however, are the morels, which appear in the spring, and the stinkhorns, which are associated with fall. During an average year, by far the greatest number of species and individual mushrooms is found in late summer through mid-fall. Mark S. Burnham Provincial Park can be a wonderful place to see mushrooms at this time of year, especially for polypores.

People often wonder how mushrooms can seemingly pop up overnight. In reality the fungus has probably been growing in the location for years but only when the conditions are right does it send up a fruiting body. Because the fruiting bodies are 90% water, they can grow extremely fast. The fungus simply pumps water into the preformed cells and away it goes! The portion of the mushroom that you don't see is the hyphae. They are thin, string-like threads, which form a mat in the ground or in decaying wood.

Mushrooms play a pivotal role as essential decomposers and recyclers of our ecosystems.

Trees Aren't the Whole Show

In addition to the fall beauty of our large deciduous trees, there are also beautiful colour changes happening at eye level and lower. Possibly the most impressive display is put on by the Virginia Creeper. Spiraling upward over fences, small trees and even telephone poles, this common vine glows with the brightest and deepest of reds. Closer to the ground, blueberry, strawberry and Poison Ivy leaves are also aglow in luminous reds; blackberry bushes and dogwoods provide a stunning display of burgundies and purples; Maple-leaved Viburnum offers delicate tones of pink; and dogbanes, grape and Purple-flowering Raspberry give us wonderful yellows. Bracken fronds add a scintillating blend of brown, yellow and gold, having lost their pedestrian green even before the first frost.

Seeing the Fall Colours

For most people, seeing the fall colours means seeing the Red and Sugar Maples. They usually reach their peak by the first week of October in the northern Kawarthas and a week or so later further south. Remember, however, that the maples are not the only show. The oaks, with their stunning burgundies and browns, and the aspens with their flaming yellows, also provide a beautiful display a little later in the month.

Although there is spectacular colour to be seen just about everywhere, two "colour drives" are especially good. The first is a loop starting at Apsley, going east through Lasswade, up to Glen Alda and back west again to Highway 28. The second is to take County Road 23 north through Buckhorn to County Road 507 and then on to Wilberforce. You can either go back the same way or return by way of Highway 28. In Algonquin Park, the maples usually peak about the last week of September. A drive up to Dorset (where you can climb the fire tower) and then back through Algonquin Park and Bancroft also makes for a great colour trip. Be sure to stop at the Eagle's Nest lookout at Bancroft. Throughout the fall colour season, a province-wide information line provides twice-weekly updates on the progression of the colours.[1]

Table 9.4: The Colour Timetable

The following are the approximate dates when some of the better-known species usually reach their colour peak. There is always variation, however, depending on the weather and the trees' exposure to sunlight.

late September	White Ash, Pin Cherry, Staghorn Sumac
early October	Red Maple, Sugar Maple, Black Walnut, American Basswood, American Beech, American Elm
mid-October	Red Oak, White Oak, Bitternut Hickory, Silver Maple, Trembling Aspen, Bigtooth Aspen, Balsam Poplar
late October	Tamarack, Norway Maple, King Crimson Maple (a cultivar of Norway Maple)

Weather

September Highlights

All Month Long

■ Heavy morning mists dance and curl over rivers, lakes and valleys. Cool morning temperatures cause water vapour in the air to condense and therefore become visible. The combination of mist, scintillating leaves and the rising sun give September dawns a beauty unequalled at any other time of the year.

■ September usually gives us some of the finest weather of the year. Gone is the high humidity of summer and the oppressive heat. For many of us, September is the month we shake off our summer lethargy and come back to life.

Early September

■ Despite what the calendar is saying, it already looks and feels like fall. Daylight and darkness are now almost equal in duration because we have been losing nearly three minutes of sunlight every day.

Mid-September

■ The first sub-freezing temperatures since the spring are usually recorded along with the first frost. Low-lying areas are especially vulnerable to frost.

Late September

■ The fall equinox takes place on or about September 21. Dusk is now two hours earlier than it was at the end of June.

Table 9.5: **Weather Averages, 1961-1990**

Daily Maximum	20.1° C
Daily Minimum	7.3° C
Extreme Maximum	33.3° C
Extreme Minimum	- 4.4° C
Rainfall	73.8 mm [74.8?]
Snowfall	0.0 cm
Precipitation	73.8 mm

Table 9.6: **Approximate Twilight, Sunrise and Sunset Times (DST)**

Date	Twilight Begins	Sunrise	Sunset	Twilight Ends
Sept. 1	6:07 a.m.	6:37 a.m.	7:49 p.m.	8:19 p.m.
Sept. 10	6:18 a.m.	6:47 a.m.	7:32 p.m.	8:02 p.m.
Sept. 20	6:30 a.m	6:59 a.m.	7:14 p.m.	7:43 p.m.
Oct. 1	6:43 a.m.	7:12 a.m.	6:53 p.m.	7:22 p.m.

The Night Sky

September Highlights

All Month Long

■ Major constellations and stars visible (September 15, 9:00 p.m. DST)

Northwest: Ursa Major low in sky, Ursa Minor (with *Polaris*) above, and Boötes (with *Arcturus*) below to left

Northeast: Cassiopeia in mid-sky with Pegasus (with the Great Square) and Andromeda (with M31 galaxy) to its right; Pleiades just above horizon

Southeast: Pegasus (with the Great Square)

Southwest: "Summer Triangle" made up of *Vega* (in Lyra), *Deneb* (in Cygnus) and *Altair* (in Aquila); Sagittarius near S horizon

- The Harvest Moon—the full moon closest to the fall equinox—usually occurs in September. For several days the moon rises close to the same time every evening. In earlier days, farmers would traditionally continue to work into the night, harvesting their crops by moonlight. ◇

- At the fall equinox, both the moon and sun rise due east and set due west.

- This is still an ideal time to explore the Milky Way. Autumn nights are some of the clearest of the year, it is dark early, and in the early evening the Milky Way is right overhead.

- Pegasus and its asterism, the Great Square, is the best-known constellation of the fall. ◇

The Moonlit Evenings of Harvest Time

Anyone familiar with the comings and goings of the moon knows that the full moon rises in the east just as the sun is setting. This is because the moon is always opposite the sun in the sky. On average, the moon rises about 50 minutes later on each subsequent day. Moonrise times around the fall equinox, however, do not follow this general rule. In September and October, the full moon rises an average of only 30 minutes later for several evenings in a row and seems to linger above the horizon as it follows a shallow angle up into the sky. The moon appears full or nearly full on all of these nights. The casual observer would almost think that September and October have a whole series of full moons!

In the fall, the moon's path is veering toward the north, from constellations like Scorpius towards Taurus and Gemini. As a result, the moon's night-to-night motion has a more northerly component than it does during the summer and winter months. This comes at the expense of the easterly component of its motion and results in the interval between successive moonrises becoming shorter than usual. All of this means, of course, that our evenings are bathed in moonlight. To busy farmers, these moonlit evenings are still a much-appreciated bonus of light. They allow the equivalent of two additional days of harvesting, hence the name Harvest Moon. In October, this phenomenon is called the "Hunter's Moon," the full moon following the Harvest Moon. Hunters of long ago took advantage of this moonlight to hunt game late into the evening.

The full moon also appears to be larger at moonrise than when it is riding high in the sky. This isn't because the moon is any closer than usual. It is simply an illusion. When measured or photographed, the moon is exactly the same size no matter where it is in the sky. Our eyes have much more experience judging the size of objects located straight ahead. We also tend to relate the size of the rising moon to the hills, trees and buildings that appear to be close by it. On the other hand, we tend to see things situated high above us as being smaller. This is also true for how we see the constellations. Cassiopeia, for example, looks much larger close to the horizon than high up in the sky.

Pegasus and the Great Square

The signature constellation of fall is Pegasus. Most people are more familiar with its asterism, the Great Square. In September, this huge constellation can be seen in the eastern sky. In Greek mythology, Pegasus was a winged horse born from seafoam. Three of the Great Square's four stars represent one wing of the horse, fastened strangely enough to the horse's rump. The fourth star of the Square is borrowed from Andromeda. It takes a lot of imagination to actually "see" a horse in this constellation. The Great Square, however, is a very striking figure. Once you know it, you won't forget it.

The Andromeda Galaxy

Using the Great Square as a guide, you can easily locate the Andromeda constellation and the adjacent Andromeda Galaxy. This is the most distant object the human eye can see without the aid of binoculars and appears as a faint oval of fuzzy light. Like our own Milky Way, it is a spiral galaxy containing hundreds of billions of stars and is our closest galactic neighbour. What is even more amazing, the light that allows us to see it left the galaxy two million light-years ago! Andromeda reminds us that, when we look into the night sky, we are looking into a gigantic time machine and seeing astronomical events that often took place eons ago.

The fall sky looking southeast.

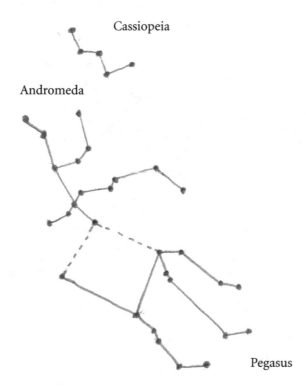

Cassiopeia

Andromeda

Pegasus

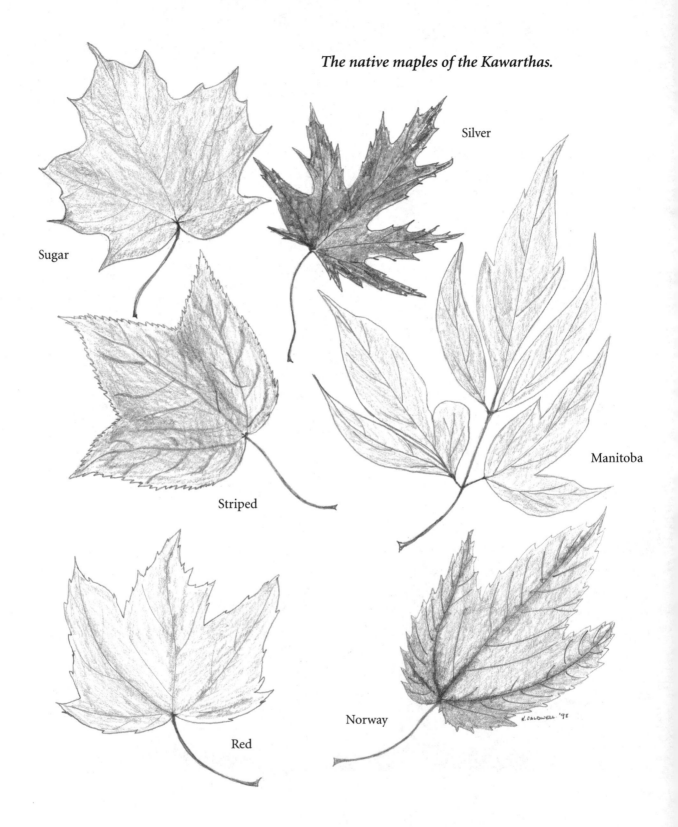

The native maples of the Kawarthas.

Silver

Sugar

Striped

Manitoba

Red

Norway

CHAPTER 10

October—The Time of Falling Leaves

October is ushered in by flaming leaves of red, orange and yellow and the conviction every fall that the colours must be " the most beautiful in years." The early October sun shines with warm benevolence and casts a hazy, surreal light. Crickets sing in meadows of aster and all is gentle and still. Winter seems far away. But, as experience has taught us, the beauty of early October is both temporary and fragile. So we try to hang on to these magnificent days before wind and rain scatter leaves and pre-winter descends upon us. Perhaps it is the ephemeral nature of October's loveliness that makes it so special.

The southward flight of many birds continues this month. Hardier species, such as geese, ducks and sparrows, are now making their journey. Many of the sparrows in particular will linger during their southward passage and become regular visitors to backyard feeders.

With the first heavy frosts, fields, roof tops and windshields are covered in silver. Leaves drop from trees like a light rain and vistas that were previously hidden by foliage once again become visible. This is the month of the rake. But there is a payoff for our labour in the familiar, spicy smell of the fallen leaves. It is a smell which seems to transport us back to childhood, evoking an instant flood of memories of autumns past. The taste of pumpkin pie and turkey also tells us the time of year, as do the far-off reverberation of shotguns and, at month's end, the wind whistling through the leafless trees.

As October draws to a close, the only leaf colour that remains is the yellow of poplars and Tamarack and the browns, oranges and burgundy of the Red Oaks. Corn fields and cattail marshes have become a sea of dull yellow. The fallen maple leaves have quickly lost their colour and turned a ubiquitous brown. With cold, wet weather and increasingly shorter days, it's not hard to imagine why the Celts chose this time of year to celebrate the various traditions that have become our Hallowe'en.

October At a Glance

Sparrow and waterfowl migration takes centre stage this month. Diving ducks start arriving on our larger lakes. Flocks of gulls, robins, blackbirds, crows and local geese are widespread. The variety of birds at feeders is greater than at any other time of the year. Beautiful thrush-like Fox Sparrows sometimes even turn up in our yards.

Groundhogs and jumping mice start their long period of hibernation. Chipmunks retreat to their dens. Porcupines begin their mating season. Buck White-tailed Deer make digs in preparation for the upcoming rut.

Turtles begin their annual period of hibernation. Spring Peepers call sporadically during the day. Frogs and toads are attracted to warm pavement on damp, mild nights.

Muskies feed heavily and provide excellent fishing opportunities. Lake Trout spawn, followed shortly after by Brook Trout.

Sulphur butterflies, Sympetrum dragonflies and various midges are just a few of the insects commonly seen this month. Snowy Tree Crickets can still be heard for much of October. Killing frosts, however, eventually bring the insect chorus to an end and terminate most insect activity.

The fall colours reach their zenith but after the peak colour of the first week, many trees quickly shed their leaves. The last of the asters bring the year's wildflower parade to a conclusion. At month's end, Tamaracks glow with a golden yellow. Most non-native trees and shrubs, however, are still green and fully-leaved.

This is the month of the first killing frosts and, usually, a period of Indian Summer. Average daily temperatures reach a maximum of 13° C and a minimum of 2° C. In mid-October, the sun rises at about 7:30 a.m. and sets at about 6:30 p.m. We turn our clocks back an hour on the last Sunday of the month.

The Great Square of Pegasus dominates the night sky. The Big Dipper is low in the north. Orion looms low in the south as we head for work in the early morning darkness. The Hunter's Moon bathes the early evenings in moonlight.

Birds

October Highlights

All Month Long

- Flocks of local Giant Canada Geese are a common sight as they fly to and from corn and soybean fields.

- Flocks of Eastern Bluebirds, sometimes numbering over 20 birds, roam the autumn countryside. In recent years, good numbers of fall bluebirds have been observed in the area between Warsaw and Norwood. Flocks of gulls, blackbirds, crows and robins are still widespread, as well.

- This is sparrow month. Watch especially for the beautiful, thrush-like Fox Sparrow feeding on the ground with White-throated and White-crowned Sparrows. White-throats can often be heard singing a short, half-hearted version of their well-known song.

- On balmy October days, male Ruffed Grouse can sometimes be heard drumming. Young grouse leave the family group at this time to establish their own individual territories. However, for completely unknown reasons, their wandering is often accompanied by strange behaviour. October grouse have been known to fly into walls, fences, windows and just about any other obstacle imaginable.

- A large variety of bird species is attracted to backyard feeders this month. ◇

- Bird species that are usually found only in southern or western parts of North America may inexplicably turn up in our area. This phenomenon occurs in September and November as well but October is the more usual month.

Early October

- Northern Canada Geese continue to fly over in large, high-altitude flocks during the first week of the month. ◇

- Golden-crowned and Ruby-crowned Kinglets, along with Yellow-rumped Warblers, pass through in large numbers and lisp gently from trees and shrubs as they search for food. The Yellow-rumps are a bellwether species in that they are the first warblers to arrive in the spring and the last to leave in the fall.

- Saw-whet Owls migrate southward through the Kawarthas.

Mid-October

■ Northern Saw-whet Owls migrate southward. ◇

■ Rough-legged Hawks arrive in the Kawarthas. Most will linger here for about a month.

■ Migrating diving ducks are congregating on the larger Kawartha Lakes such as Pigeon Lake. Watch for the large rafts of Common Goldeneye and scaup with lesser numbers of mergansers, scoters and sometimes Long-tailed Ducks.

Late October

■ The first "winter finches" often show up. These may include Pine Siskins, Common Redpolls, Evening Grosbeaks and Pine Grosbeaks. Unfortunately, an influx of these species is by no means an annual event and is difficult to predict. (see January)

Flocks of Red-winged Blackbirds are a common sight in fall.

Table 10.1: October Departures and Arrivals

early month

departures
: Double-crested Cormorant, American Bittern, Green Heron, "Northern" Canada Goose, Blue-winged Teal, Northern Shoveler, Northern Flicker, Blue-headed Vireo, Tennessee Warbler, Nashville Warbler, Magnolia Warbler, Black-throated Blue Warbler, Black-throated Green Warbler, Palm Warbler, Orange-crowned Warbler, Pine Warbler, Eastern Towhee

arrivals
: American Coot, Northern Saw-whet Owl (b), Hermit Thrush (b), Fox Sparrow, Lapland Longspur, Dunlin, White-rumped Sandpiper

mid-month

departures
: Pied-billed Grebe, Turkey Vulture, Wood Duck, Peregrine Falcon, Cooper's Hawk, Northern Harrier, Red-shouldered Hawk, Merlin, Black-bellied Plover, Belted Kingfisher (w), Common Yellowthroat, Chipping Sparrow, Field Sparrow, Vesper Sparrow, Savannah Sparrow, Eastern Meadowlark

arrivals
: American Black Duck (b), Redhead, Greater Scaup, Long-tailed Duck, Common Goldeneye, Bufflehead, Surf Scoter, Black Scoter, White-winged Scoter, Red-breasted Merganser, Rough-legged Hawk, Bald Eagle & Golden Eagle (passing through only), Herring Gull (b), Long-eared Owl (b), Northern Shrike, American Tree Sparrow, Snow Bunting, Pine Siskin*

late month

departures
: Horned Grebe, Red-necked Grebe, Green-winged Teal, Northern Pintail, Gadwall, American Wigeon, Sandhill Crane, Common Snipe, American Woodcock, Bonaparte's Gull, Brown Creeper (w), Winter Wren, Ruby-crowned Kinglet, Hermit Thrush, Eastern Bluebird, Swamp Sparrow, White-throated Sparrow, White-crowned Sparrow, Song Sparrow, Dark-eyed Junco (w), Lapland Longspur, Red-winged Blackbird, Common Grackle, Rusty Blackbird

arrivals
: Snow Goose, Canvasback, Ruddy Duck, Hooded Merganser (b), Pine Grosbeak*

Fall Geese

In recent years, we have seen a huge increase in the numbers of Canada Geese in southern Ontario. The vast majority of these are the non-migratory race, known as the "Giant" Canada Goose. In the fall, these birds feed heavily in local corn and soybean fields. They are often seen flying low over the city in groups of 10 to 40 birds as they make their way to and from feeding areas. The geese remain here until the lakes and rivers freeze up, forcing them to spend the rest of the winter along Lake Ontario or in the eastern United States. Their abundance has created a thriving fall goose hunt, especially on local farms.

The smaller "Northern" Canada Geese, which breed in the vicinity of James Bay, pass over the Kawarthas in large, high-altitude flocks during the last week of September and the first week of October. It has been suggested by some scientists that adopting a V- formation allows the geese to maintain visual contact with each other and to avoid collisions. The Native Peoples referred to this time of year as "goose-going days." Even now, people love to trade reports on the number and size of the flocks they have seen. In recent years, however, it seems that fewer flocks are being seen over this area. This may be related to declines in the number of Northern Canada Geese. However, on September 28, 2001, Anne Anthony counted more than 6,000 geese flying over the Coltesloe area east of Peterborough between 10:30 a.m. and 3:30 p.m.

Feeder Frenzy

Early October is often the busiest time of the year for activity at the bird feeder, especially if your yard has lots of trees and shrubs. On a typical day, White-throated and White-crowned Sparrows, along with Dark-eyed Juncos, feed quietly on the ground, while Black-capped Chickadees, White-breasted and Red-breasted Nuthatches, Blue Jays, Northern Cardinals, Mourning Doves, American Goldfinches and both House and Purple Finches come to the feeders. Robins call from fruit trees, Yellow-rumped Warblers and Golden-crowned Kinglets flit nervously among the foliage, while crows, blackbirds and gulls pass overhead. Two or three of the White-throated Sparrows will often break into a fuzzy fall version of their well-known "sweet Canada" song. As Doug Sadler observes, there is a "recrudescence of the life-force" that wells up in many birds and frogs in the fall and manifests itself as song, even though its reproductive purpose is for another season. If you are lucky, you may also be paid a visit by the most beautiful of the sparrows, the Fox Sparrow.

Wanderers from Afar

Local birders keep an eye open in the fall for marsh birds from the southern United States that sometimes drift northward. The most common of the post-breeding wanderers is the Great Egret. It appears to be slowly extending its range northward towards the Kawarthas. Cattle Egrets sometimes turn up as well and even Glossy Ibises are a possibility. Totally unexpected species from the western states and provinces may also show up. Because fall is the hurricane season in the United States, storms sometimes knock birds far off their migration route and they can end up just about anywhere. A good example of this phenomenon is a Broad-billed Hummingbird that somehow found itself at a hummingbird feeder near

Buckhorn in October of 1989. This species had never been recorded before in Canada and is usually found no further north than Arizona.

Saw-whet Owls

In the early 1990s, it was discovered that large numbers of tiny Northern Saw-whet Owls migrate through the Kawarthas during the month of October. Tim Dyson, a local bird bander and taxidermist, has banded over 100 of these fascinating birds in the course of a single fall. Banding is also done each year by Trent University at the Oliver Ecological Centre on Pigeon Lake. Although some Saw-whets spend the winter along the Great Lakes, most of the Ontario population winters in the southeastern United States.

The birds are caught at night by playing a tape of their whistle-like call. Curious by nature, the owl will approach the tape recorder and get caught up in a strategically-located mist net. On October 21, 2000, a Saw-whet Owl was banded at the Oliver Ecological Centre and released at 8:10 p.m. Exactly two and a half hours later, the same bird was recaptured 60 kilometres further south near Port Hope on Lake Ontario. If the bird flew the distance non-stop and was captured immediately, the time difference would indicate an average flight speed of 24 km/hr. Obviously, these birds don't waste any time when migration is on their mind. Cool clear nights with light winds seem to be the best for migration.

Mammals

October Highlights

All Month Long

- Deer Mice seek out winter accommodation. Human habitations are often chosen. Cavities such as a woodpecker hole or even a man-made birdhouse are favourite winter shelters, but human habitations are often chosen as well.

- Watch for White-tailed Deer feeding along the edges of corn fields and woodlots at dawn and dusk. By now the fawns have been weaned and their white spots are gone.

- Buck White-tails make digs on the forest floor in preparation for the upcoming rut.

- Fall is often the time of year when people come across bats in buildings such as schools, churches and older homes. These are usually Big Brown Bats looking for wintering sites or animals that have been disturbed during their dormancy.

Early October

- Groundhogs and jumping mice start their long period of hibernation. ◇

Mid-October

- The first of the two bow seasons for deer begins on October 15 and lasts until early November.

- The moose hunt in northern Peterborough County opens in the middle of the month and generally lasts for five days.

Late October

- Chipmunks retreat to their secure, well-provisioned dens. Unlike the Groundhog, chipmunks are unable to store enough body fat to get them through the winter without eating.

- Porcupines mate from late October through December and employ an elaborate dance. They can look quite comical as they roll and tumble, stand up on their hind legs and actually box and cuff each other. Fortunately for the male, the underside of the female's tail does not have quills, so he is able to lean against her and mate in typical mammal fashion.

White-tailed Deer are often seen along the edge of cornfields.

Our True Hibernators: Groundhogs and Jumping Mice

Some time in late September or the first half of October, Groundhogs begin their five-month hibernation period. The winter den is often built along the forest edge or even in the forest itself. Being one and a half to two metres in depth, it is well below the frost line. Unlike most other members of the squirrel family, the Groundhog does not store food for winter consumption but relies on a substantial layer of fat to provide nourishment during hibernation. The Groundhog's heart rate falls from 100 beats per minute to 15 and its body temperature will eventually drop from 35°C to 6°C!

The only other true hibernators that we have in the Kawarthas are the Woodland Jumping Mouse and Meadow Jumping Mouse. They retreat to their winter quarters at about the same time as the Groundhog. They dig a special winter hole of about one metre in depth and then prepare a bed of dried vegetation. To ensure complete privacy, the animal then plugs the entrance to the hole. Jumping mice are very profound hibernators and will not be seen again until May.

Eastern Chipmunk.

Amphibians and Reptiles

October Highlights

All Month Long

- Frogs and toads are often found sitting motionless on warm road pavement on wet, mild fall nights. The River Road between Trent University and Lakefield is a good place to see this phenomenon. ◇

- Sporadic calling from Spring Peepers can still be heard on warm days.

- Red-backed Salamanders are born in late summer and early fall. The species is easy to find at this time of year. Look under flat rocks, patio stones and logs, particularly in rural areas.

- Eastern Garter Snakes are still active and can be seen basking in the mid-fall sun. They are the last of the snakes to retreat to winter quarters.

- Turtles are seen only rarely after mid-October. The shorter days and weak fall sun do not provide the necessary warmth to raise their body temperature sufficiently. Consequently, many turtles begin hibernation.

Red-backed Salamander.

Soaking Up the Heat

If the weather remains warm, amphibians are still active for most of October. You can still hear the sporadic, lonely calling of Spring Peepers this month and scare up frogs along wetland borders. And, as in the spring, amphibians are also seen on warm, wet autumn nights. Warm daytime temperatures followed by an evening rain often attract large numbers of Leopard Frogs, Green Frogs and American Toads to road surfaces adjacent to wetlands or rivers. The temperature difference between the cooler ambient air and the heat-retentive road surface probably explains their popularity with amphibians. It is also probable that some of these species, such as the Leopard Frog, are migrating towards their wintering sites. Strangely enough, the frogs and toads seem to just sit and soak up the warmth and will allow you to pick them up with almost no attempt to get away. The River Road between Peterborough and Lakefield is a good location to see this phenomenon. When you find an area with frogs, park your vehicle, grab your flashlight and walk.

*American Toad and
Leopard Frog on pavement.*

Fishes

October Highlights

All Month Long
- With the "autumn turnover" in the weather and cool water temperatures, some species such as bass are becoming less active.
- Muskies continue to feed heavily. This can make for great fishing.

Early October
- Lake Trout are spawning along lake shores. They usually lay their eggs about two weeks before Brook Trout. ◇

Mid-October
- The fishing season for bass ends on October 15 in northern Peterborough County (division 15). The season continues for another month in the south (division 6).

Late October
- Brightly-coloured Brook Trout spawn at gravel-bottomed sites in stream headwaters and along lakeshores. They only choose areas where spring water wells up through the gravel. ◇

Spawning Trout

For our native trout, the spawning season usually extends from October into the middle of November. Lake Trout are the first off the mark. They prefer to spawn along shorelines with exposed areas of rock rubble. Spawning activity takes place solely at night, when water temperatures are between 10° C and 12° C. The depth of the water can range anywhere from 30 centimetres to 20 metres. No attempt is made by the adults to guard the eggs.

Brook Trout spawn about two weeks later in gravel-bottomed sites in the shallow headwaters of streams. Occasionally, they will also spawn along lake shorelines. They can sometimes be seen making their way upstream towards spawning sites and even stopping briefly to sun themselves by resting over submerged rocks or logs. The lower flanks of the male glow with a vivid reddish-orange blush in the fall, providing one of nature's last colour spectacles of the year.

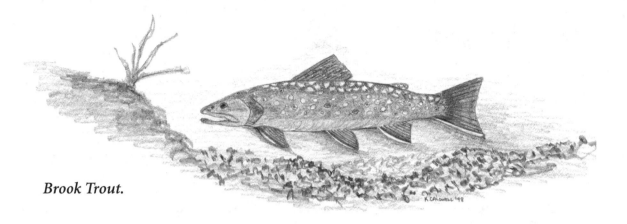

Brook Trout.

Because the fish spawn during the day in water that is often only about 30 centimetres deep, it is possible to observe their spawning behaviour. The female constructs a shallow depression in the gravel, in which she lays her eggs. After they are fertilized by the male, she stirs up the sand and gravel in such a way as to cover the eggs and protect them from would-be predators. There is one final requirement for successful spawning. There must be an upwelling of spring water under the spawning beds. The spring water, which is warmed by geothermal heat from the earth, keeps the eggs at a warmer temperature during the winter months. Without this warming effect, successful development would not be possible. This water also flushes away waste products from the nest and provides fresh oxygen.

For anyone wanting to see the spawning behaviour of Brook Trout, it is sometimes possible to observe the fish in Cavan Creek (also called Cavanville and Trout Creek in places) upstream from the village of Cavan, and in the upper reaches of Baxter Creek, Jackson Creek and the Ouse River. You should always ask permission, however, before going on private property.

Insects and Other Invertebrates

October Highlights

All Month Long
- Sulphur butterflies are active throughout October. The occasional Monarch, too, can usually be seen until late in the month. Watch also for Mourning Cloaks and Compton Tortoiseshells.

- The odd mosquito still puts in an appearance. These are species of the genus *Culex* and they overwinter as adults. They require a blood meal in order to survive until next spring.

- Mating clouds of midges are still common, even on days when the temperature is just above freezing. It is amazing that these delicate insects are able to fly at such low temperatures when much larger and more robust insects such as butterflies are unable to coax their wing muscles into action.

- Some darners, as well as dragonflies of the genus *Sympetrum*, are still active.

Early October
- Snowy Tree Crickets can still be heard until the first heavy frosts.

Mid-October
- Killing frosts usually bring the cricket and grasshopper chorus to an end and terminate most insect activity in general.

- Cluster Flies start looking for cracks and crannies in buildings, where large "clusters" of them will spend the winter. They are similar to houseflies but have whitish hairs on the thorax. ◊

Late October
- Wasps, flies and ladybird beetles gather on the sun-warmed sides of buildings in an effort to warm their flight muscles. It is not uncommon to see birds such as migrating Yellow-rumped Warblers feeding on these insects.

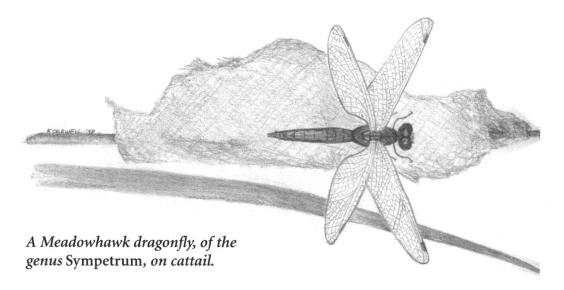

A Meadowhawk dragonfly, of the genus Sympetrum, *on cattail.*

Seeking Out Warmth and Shelter

Cluster Flies are drawn to human habitations in the fall. Slightly larger than a housefly, these bristly grey insects have numerous fine whitish hairs on their back. To endure the winter, they hibernate by jamming themselves in large numbers into cracks and crannies in the siding and window sills of cottages, houses and other buildings. On mild, sunny, winter days, the flies often wake up and try to move to where it is warmest, namely inside. If successful at gaining entrance, they then congregate in large "clusters" on window panes and buzz crazily as they try to get out!

Cluster Flies have an interesting life cycle. Adult females lay their eggs in the soil. After the eggs hatch, the larva seeks out an earthworm to parasitize. The larva burrows into the worm and feeds on it for up to a month. It then leaves the worm, pupates and emerges as an adult which feeds on flowers until it's ready to hibernate.

Plants

October Highlights

All Month Long

- Flowers continue to go to seed and use many ingenious strategies for dispersal. Airborne milkweed seeds floating on a silky parachute are a common sight on fall days. ◇

- Trees are shedding their leaves, each species following its own timetable. Even when there is no wind, the warming effect of the morning sun is sufficient to cause many leaves to fall.

- Soybeans are still being harvested until the middle of the month.

- Butternut and Ironwood seeds are ripe and can be collected this month.

Early October

- The fall colours are at their height. Quite often the peak coincides with the weekend before Thanksgiving. The Sugar, and especially the Red Maples, give the best show. The spectacle quickly declines afterwards, however, especially if there is wind and rain.

- When the leaves change colour, the identity of individual trees is often instantly apparent, even from a distance. Trees that were simply part of the "green blur" all summer long, suddenly stand out in their own unique fall colour and boldly advertise what species they are.

- Different trees of the same species do not always turn the same colour in the fall. A range of colours can often be seen. The White Ash is famous for its wide variety of fall colours. ◇

Mid-October

- With maples now quickly shedding their leaves, aspens and oaks stand out as at no other time of year. As the oranges and reds of the maples fall to the ground, the yellows of the aspens take over, interspersed here and there with the browns and burgundies of the oaks.

- Although we spend a great deal of time raking, the rich, spicy fragrance of the leaves and the cool, invigorating air make the effort worthwhile. Vistas previously hidden by the leaves now become visible again. ◇

- Because they are still mostly green and fully-leaved, the extent of non-native trees and shrubs becomes evident. Norway Maple and European Buckthorn stand out in particular. ◇

- Farmers turn their attention to hard corn, used in such diverse ways as cattle feed, ethanol, corn starch and liquor. It is harvested from mid-October until well into December.

Late October

- The last of the asters bring the year's wildflower parade to a conclusion.
- The smoky, golden-yellow of Tamaracks lights up wetland borders like so many candles. They represent the final act in the annual fall colour extravaganza.

Casting their Genes to the Wind

Many of the fall and summer flowers are spreading their seeds at this time. Since adult plants have no choice but to remain rooted where they are, their embryos must do the travelling. The special adaptations that seeds have developed for travel are fascinating. Some wrap themselves in a bright, tasty fruit in order to move by way of a bird's digestive system. Others are sticky or bristly and are able to hitch a ride on a mammal's fur or a walker's pants. Many are designed for flight, either by way of a silky parachute or thanks to a winged appendage. There are even some that have a waterproof coating that allows the embryo to float with the current and to end up on some silty shoreline where it can take root.

The pods of the milkweed open and release the silky parachute-born seeds to the wind.

Milkweed pod spilling its seeds.

The seeds are arranged in such a manner that only a few are released at a time. Another very noticeable change takes place in the Queen Anne's Lace, better known to some as Wild Carrot. When the seeds mature, the flower bracts curl in and hold the seeds in what looks like a bird's nest. Goldenrod and aster flowers take on the appearance of greyish brown wool, as do the cattail flowerheads that are now breaking apart.

Colour Diversity Within Species

There is often amazing diversity in the colour of the leaves within the same species of tree. This is especially true for White Ash, Red Maple and Red Oak. Ash leaves cover a colour spectrum from bronze-yellow to eggplant purple with every imaginable shading and mixture in between. As for Red Maple, the female tree usually turns a brilliant yellow in the fall whereas the male becomes a bright, vermilion red. On some maples all of the leaves are uniform in colour, while on others it looks as if a frenzied artist has been at work dabbing the leaves with blotches of red, pink, orange, yellow and purple. In terms of intensity and variety of colour, the Red Maple definitely steals the fall foliage show.

Red Oak is also a master in variety of colour. Its most impressive autumn apparel is a deep, long-lasting, reddish burgundy. However, oranges, brownish yellows and rusty browns are also common. It is reassuring to note that, in all this diversity of fall colour, there just may be an underlying rule of uniformity. Bernd Heinrich, a zoology professor at the University of Vermont, compared the colour of individual trees over several years and found that they turned a similar colour each fall. A yellow maple became yellow again and a purple ash tended to be purple once more. Confirming these observations with one's own trees would be an interesting experiment.

Table 10.2: **The Leaf Drop Timetable**

The following chart shows the approximate time when the more common trees, shrubs and vines have shed most of their leaves.

early October	White Ash, Red Maple, Staghorn Sumac, Virginia Creeper
mid-October	Sugar Maple, Black Walnut, American Basswood, American Elm, Pin Cherry, Red-osier Dogwood
late October	White Birch, Trembling Aspen, Bitternut Hickory, American Beech (mature trees), Speckled Alder, Black Locust, Silver Maple
early November	Tamarack, Norway Maple, Red Oak, European Buckthorn, Common Lilac, native willows
mid-November	Siberian Elm, Weeping Willow

Why Are Some Trees Still Green?

As the month advances, it quickly becomes apparent that many trees in the city and around country homes are still completely green and seemingly unaware that fall has arrived. These trees and shrubs are almost all non-native species or "exotics," and they are still operating on their ancestral European or Asian timetable. Some of the common species include Norway Maple, King Crimson Maple (a variety of the Norway), Weeping Willow, Little-leaved Linden, Siberian Elm, Carolina Poplar, Common Lilac and European Buckthorn. The buckthorn in particular has become very widespread and is now the most common wild shrub (or small tree) in the City of Peterborough, in the understorey of woodlots and along hedgerows bordering on agricultural lands. Its abundance is immediately apparent at this time of year because it is still green when just about everything else is leafless.

Although some people may feel that non-native species allow us to hang onto the greenery of summer just a little longer, they also tend to stick out like a sore thumb at this time of year and take away from the "sense of place" that our native species provide.

Rich Smells and New Vistas

Hastened by wind and rain, the leaves of most trees fall surprisingly fast and turn brown within a few days. They gather everywhere and can make cycling and even driving treacherous, especially when they are wet. All of this means many hours spent raking. Fortunately, our labour is rewarded by the rich, spicy smell of the leaves which can instantly transport us back to the autumns of our childhood. To truly appreciate this wonderful aroma, however, allow some time for a walk in the autumn woods. At no other season of the year is our sense of smell so fully engaged as when walking through a deep carpet of fallen leaves on a mild, damp October day.

Our eyes and ears will also notice changes in the woods. Looking around, it's as if a curtain has been opened, allowing us to see distant objects that were hidden from view since last spring. Most years, the leaves quickly dry and curl up and you can hear every creature that dares walk about. If you sit and listen carefully on a calm day, you soon become aware of a steady rustling as chipmunks, squirrels, mice and voles go about their work gathering food.

Although it is far less common today, burning the fall leaves was always considered a rite of fall. Like the smell of burning grass in the spring, the aromatic smoke of a leaf fire can communicate the time of the season as accurately as any calendar.

Weather

October Highlights

All Month Long

- Generally warm weather is still with us for most of October. As a matter of fact, an extended period of days above 20° C occurs most years. When this warm weather comes after the first "hard" frost, it is referred to as Indian Summer.

- On warm, sunny October days, the light often has a hazy, almost dream-like quality. This is due to the large amount of water vapour in the air in the fall and the fact that the sun is lower in the sky. The two factors combine a feeling of reverie and stillness.

- The "fall turn-over" re-oxygenates the lakes. ◇

- This is usually the month of the first killing frosts and the first strenuous scraping of the car windshield.

Late October

- The first snowfall usually whitens the ground for a brief period by month's end.

- Daylight Saving Time ends on the last Sunday of October. Set your clocks back an hour.

- Total darkness is upon us by 5:30 p.m.

Table 10.3: **October Weather Averages, 1961-1990**

Daily Maximum	13.2° C
Daily Minimum	1.6° C
Extreme Maximum	28.9° C
Extreme Minimum	- 9.4° C
Rainfall	68.4 mm
Snowfall	1.8 cm
Precipitation	70.8 mm

The Fall Turnover

The long, cool nights of fall bring about an interesting phenomenon in our lakes. The surface waters cool down to the same temperature (4° C) as the uniformly cold deeper waters below. All of the water now has the same resistance to currents and no longer does the lake function as two separate lakes with a warm lake on top of a cold one. The currents, which are caused by wave action, can therefore thoroughly mix and oxygenate the entire lake just as in the spring. This phenomenon is known as the fall turnover, and it will continue until early December, when ice seals the water off from the effects of the wind. At times, the mixing even brings dead weeds and other debris from the lake bottom to the surface. This "breath of air" will have to last all winter, since ice will soon cut off the waters from further oxygenation.

Table 10.4: **Approximate Twilight, Sunrise and Sunset Times (DST)**

Date	Twilight Begins	Sunrise	Sunset	Twilight Ends
Oct. 1	6:43 a.m.	7:12 a.m.	6:53 p.m.	7:22 p.m.
Oct.10	6:53 a.m.	7:22 a.m.	6:37 p.m.	7:06 p.m.
Oct. 20	7:06 a.m.	7:35 a.m.	6:20 p.m.	6:50 p.m.
Nov. 1	6:21 a.m. (EST)	6:51 a.m. (EST)	5:03 p.m. (EST)	5:33 p.m. (EST)

The Night Sky

October Highlights

All Month Long

- Major constellations and stars visible (October 15, 9:00 p.m. DST)

  Northwest: Ursa Major (low in N) with Ursa Minor (with *Polaris*) above; "Summer Triangle" made up of *Vega* (in Lyra), *Deneb* (in Cygnus) and *Altair* (in Aquila) high in W

  Northeast: Cassiopeia with Andromeda to right and Pleiades to lower right

  Southeast: Pegasus (with the Great Square) and Andromeda (with M31 galaxy)

  Southwest: Sagittarius at W horizon; *Altair* (in Aquila) above and to left; Milky Way runs up from the horizon through Sagittarius and Aquila

- The Orion constellation looms in the southern sky as we head off for work in the early morning darkness. Like the falling leaves, Orion's arrival is a sure sign that winter is fast approaching.

- At any given time of year, at least one of the planets is visible in the night sky. The planet parade is made up of Venus, Jupiter, Saturn, Mars and sometimes Mercury. Because there are relatively fewer bright stars in the fall, any planets that may be visible tend to stand out more now than in the other seasons. ◇

- The full moon in October is known as the Hunter's Moon. Like the Harvest Moon, it rises only about 30 minutes later each evening, bathing the fields and forests in moonlight and allowing hunters of long ago to pursue game late into the evening.

The Planets

In addition to the moon and stars, there is always at least one planet travelling through the night sky. Sometimes, as many as three or four may be seen. The planets we see most often are Venus, Mars, Jupiter and Saturn. Mercury, too, is visible on occasion and Uranus, although quite faint, can also be made out. Neptune and Pluto cannot be seen by the naked eye. The planets do not twinkle like the stars but cast a steady, even light. They always appear along the ecliptic—the apparent path of the sun through the sky. Any bright objects along the ecliptic that do not appear in star charts are probably planets. The planets do not follow the east-west rotation of the stars and constellations but appear to wander along the ecliptic haphazardly. They are not linked to any particular season so a given planet does not necessarily appear at a given time of year. Check astronomy magazines or an astronomy column in a newspaper to find out where and when the planets will be visible.

The brightest and most striking planets are Venus and Jupiter. Never very high up, Venus appears on the eastern horizon as the "morning star" and on the western horizon as the "evening star," but it is never visible more than about three hours after sunset or before sunrise. It is much brighter than any of the true stars. Venus is especially radiant during the twilight hours and adds a lovely touch to the start or finish of the day. Jupiter is the second brightest planet. Shining stronger than any star, Jupiter is particularly interesting because several of its four brightest moons can be clearly seen with binoculars. In fact, their orbits can be followed night after night around the planet.

As for Mars, it can always be told by its reddish colour. Its actual brightness varies a great deal depending on its distance from Earth. Saturn, although not as bright as Jupiter or Venus, is unique because of its famous rings. A telescope, however, is required to view the rings. Jupiter, Mars and Saturn can show up anywhere along the ecliptic—east, south or west—and at any time of the night.

The November woods.

NATURE'S YEAR IN THE KAWARTHAS

CHAPTER 11

November—A Hush Upon the Land

In November a hush settles upon the land. The "seeping" of kinglets and White-throated Sparrows ceases, most crows and robins depart and the last crickets surrender to the cold. Damp cloudy weather, leafless trees, and faded grasses and flowers create a world of greys and browns, punctuated only by the dark green of conifers. Yet sometimes late fall's typical bleakness is pushed aside by a lingering Indian Summer that gently eases us into winter. In other years, the snow comes early and stays until spring.

Like the first Red-winged Blackbirds in March, the arrival of the birds of winter serves to mark the change of season. In addition to the Northern Shrikes and American Tree Sparrows that began arriving in October, Bald Eagles return each year in late November to spend the winter in the Kawarthas. They are often joined by Bohemian Waxwings, Snowy Owls and various winter finches. At the same time, however, Common Loons are departing for the Atlantic seaboard and taking with them the last vestiges of summer. For lakeside residents, it is a melancholy event.

A walk on a late November day seems uneventful, with seemingly little of interest to catch our attention. Yet the relative scarcity of plants and animals allows us to focus on the commonplace—the leafless trees reduced to their elemental form, the intricacy and diversity of the mosses and evergreen ferns, and the beauty of a milkweed pod spilling its last seeds. But, other than the occasional call of a chickadee or woodpecker and the steady rustling of squirrels and mice as they forage for seeds, the woods are nearly devoid of animal sounds. With colder weather, nature's kaleidoscope of smells is also reduced to a minimum. Apart from the scent of decaying leaves or the smoke of a wood stove, there is little to stir our sense of smell. But the cold of late fall does bring renewed appreciation for the warmth and comfort of our homes and anticipation for the holiday season just around the corner. With the yard work done and wood stacked in the garage, we can sit back and enjoy the sound of the north wind as it ushers in winter.

November At a Glance

Bald Eagles and sometimes Golden Eagles start arriving to overwinter in the Kawarthas. These are different birds from those that simply migrated through our area in mid-October. Numbers of Rough-legged Hawks, American Tree Sparrows and Northern Shrikes increase. Most loons depart although a small number will continue to linger on local lakes with diving ducks and grebes. Uncommon gulls such as the Glaucous and Iceland Gull often show up at Little Lake and at the Bensfort Road landfill. Except for a small number that regularly spend the winter here, the last American Robins head south.

Muskrats build cone-shaped homes of mud and vegetation. Coyotes continue to call frequently. With White-tailed bucks in rut, the deer hunt begins on the first Monday of the month. Snowshoe Hares and weasels acquire their white winter coats. Skunks, raccoons and bears retreat to their winter quarters but will come out on warm days.

The last amphibians and reptiles begin hibernation. A variety of different strategies is used to survive the winter season.

Whitefish begin spawning just as Brook Trout are finishing. Fishing season for Northern Pike, Walleye, Muskellunge and bass ends on November 15.

The last Sympetrum dragonflies and tortoiseshell butterflies are seen. Most other insects are now inactive. Depending on the species, they are overwintering as eggs, nymphs, larvae, pupae or adults. Monarch butterflies arrive in large numbers on their Mexican wintering grounds.

Roadsides are bordered by the monotonous browns and greys of dead or dormant herbaceous plants. Evergreen forest-floor plants become conspicuous. These include mosses, club-mosses and various ferns. Red Oaks, Silver Maple and Tamarack are the only native deciduous trees that may still have foliage.

The days are short but Indian Summer conditions are still possible. The first significant snowfall usually occurs. Average daily temperatures are a maximum of 6° C and a minimum of -2° C. In mid-November sunrise occurs at about 7:10 a.m. and sunset is at about 4:45 p.m.

The Great Square of Pegasus is almost at the zenith. Orion is low in the east with the spectacular Pleiades (Seven Sisters) above it. The Big Dipper is low in the north.

Birds

November Highlights

All Month Long

■ Most Red-tailed Hawks leave the Kawarthas for more southern destinations. On a good day, hundreds can be seen migrating along the north shore of Lake Ontario. Some will spend the winter along the lakeshore but most will migrate south into the United States.

■ Snowy Owls may begin to arrive. Numbers of American Tree Sparrows and Northern Shrikes increase. Birders also hope for an influx of winter finches such as Pine Grosbeaks, Pine Siskins and Common Redpolls.

■ As long as there is open water, diving ducks and small numbers of loons will continue to linger on local lakes including Little Lake in Peterborough. Freeze-up may occur, however, by late November.

■ Feeder activity tends to slow down as migrant sparrows have now left. If you have a crabapple tree, however, you may receive a visit from a flock of Pine Grosbeaks or Bohemian Waxwings. The latter appear almost every year but numbers fluctuate greatly.

■ With ducks, gulls, eagles and the possibility of northern finches and owls, November can be an excellent month for birding. Species that have strayed off their usual migration route or have wandered north of their normal range may show up as well.

Early November

■ Most of our loons and robins head south. However, a small number of robins regularly overwinter in Peterborough, especially in years when wild food is plentiful. ◇

Mid-November

■ Glaucous, Iceland and Great Black-backed Gulls, three species which are uncommon in the Kawarthas, sometimes show up at Little Lake, on the larger Kawartha Lakes and at the Peterborough landfill on Bensfort Road.

■ Although most of our crows depart about now, an increasing number is remaining to spend the winter here. Canada's largest winter crow roost is in Essex County near Windsor, where over 50,000 birds gather each winter. Whether crows from the Kawarthas end up there as well is anyone's guess.

Late November

- Male Great Horned Owls stake out breeding territories and begin to call.

- Bald and sometimes Golden Eagles begin to arrive. The Kawarthas have become known as one of the best places in Ontario to see eagles in late fall and winter. ◇

Table 11.1: **November Departures and Arrivals**

early month

departures	Common Loon (most), Great Blue Heron, Snow Goose, Green-winged Teal, Killdeer, Greater Yellowlegs, White-rumped Sandpiper, Pectoral Sandpiper, Dunlin, Common Snipe, Red-tailed Hawk (w), Northern Saw-whet Owl (w), American Robin (w), American Pipit, Yellow-rumped Warbler, Fox Sparrow,
arrivals	Common Merganser (b), Snowy Owl,* Bohemian Waxwing,* Common Redpoll*

mid-month

departures	Mallard (w), American Black Duck, Ruddy Duck, Redhead, Canvasback, Greater Scaup, Lesser Scaup, Ring-necked Duck, White-winged Scoter, Black Scoter, Surf Scoter, Red-breasted Merganser, Northern Harrier, Rough-legged Hawk (w), American Coot, Long-eared Owl (w), American Crow (w), Golden-crowned Kinglet (w),
arrivals	Iceland Gull,* Glaucous Gull,* Great Black-backed Gull

late month

departures	Long-tailed Duck, Bufflehead (w), Hooded Merganser
arrivals	Bald Eagle, Golden Eagle (overwintering birds)

Robins and Loons Depart

Our most familiar summer bird, the American Robin, leaves the Kawarthas in late October or early November. Every year, however, there are always a few dozen birds that will try their luck at overwintering in the area, especially when the fruits of European Buckthorn, Riverbank Grape, European mountain-ash and ornamental crabapples are abundant. Robins are especially fond of European Buckthorn berries, particularly after the berries have had a chance to freeze for a period of time. Freezing sweetens the berries and makes them the equivalent of an avian ice wine.

Most loons also leave in early November, although some will have departed earlier. A few will even stay into December, provided there is open water. Dressed in their gray and white winter plumage, Common Loons could almost be mistaken for a different species at this time of year. Immature birds acquire this plumage during the summer, while adults moult to their winter garb in the fall. Adult loons tend to leave the breeding range in the fall before their young. When loons are occasionally trapped by early ice formation, they are usually young-of-the-year birds. They are probably late-hatching individuals not yet capable of sustained flight. Iced-in loons are often preyed upon by eagles.

The Eagles Arrive

The northern half of Peterborough County has acquired a reputation since the mid-1980s as an excellent place to see Bald Eagles and occasionally Golden Eagles in the late fall and winter. As many as 12 Balds are present most years. They begin to arrive in late November, presumably from nesting territories in northern and northwestern Ontario. When northern lakes and rivers freeze, Bald Eagles can no longer find food and are forced to winter elsewhere. Primarily scavengers, eagles are attracted to this area in part because of the high deer population and the relative abundance of carcasses. Deer often fall prey to Coyotes, wolves, road traffic, thin ice and the adversity of winter. Where there is open water, eagles will also feed on dead fish and dead or injured ducks and loons. Hunting is made easier when waterfowl become frozen in the ice, or when overnight freezing makes it impossible for birds to run on the water to take off. Bald Eagles will occasionally try to capture live prey such as Muskrats and ducks. A bird was regularly observed pursuing ducks on Little Lake and on the Otonabee River one winter.

Many of the Bald Eagles seen in the Kawarthas are dark-plumaged immatures which lack the white head and tail of the adult. First-year birds are especially dark and show white only on the underwing and tail. They are easily confused with the much less common immature Golden Eagle. Bald Eagles do not attain full adult plumage until four or five years of age. Care must be taken in the identification of these dark birds so as not to confuse them with Common Ravens, Turkey Vultures (not here in winter), Golden Eagles or some unrecognized kind of hawk.

There are often sightings in late fall of eagles sitting on the ice or in a tree close to areas of open water. Jack Lake, Upper Stoney Lake, Gannon's Narrows, Deer Bay and Buckhorn Lake in the vicinity of the Curve Lake First Nations Reserve are all good locations to look for early-winter eagles.

Once the lakes freeze over, the birds can often be found at local dumps such as those at Anstruther Lake Road, Apsley, Kasshabog Lake and Haultain. If you want to see the eagles, it is important to arrive early in the morning before human activity at the dump begins. Later in the day, eagles can often be seen soaring, especially in the area between Stony Lake and

Bald Eagle with Common Goldeneye.

Apsley. Open locations along the Kawartha Nordic Ski Club trails at Haultain can also be good viewing spots. Occasionally, an eagle will even follow the Otonabee River south into Peterborough and scare up the ducks in and around Little Lake.

Mammals

November Highlights

All Month Long

- Muskrats build cone-shaped homes and feeding platforms of cattails, rushes and mud. They are only about one metre in height, making them much smaller than Beaver lodges. Both Beavers and Muskrats are fairly easy to observe this month. ◇

- In what has been termed the "fall shuffle," young Muskrats disperse from their parents' territory and are often forced to travel considerable distances to find an unoccupied territory of their own for the winter. Many fail to survive this adventure.

- Coyotes continue to call frequently.

- Early snowfalls reveal the nocturnal world of mammal movements. Coyotes, deer, squirrels, mice and voles are just a few of the many species that leave their tracks for us to decipher.

- The high-pitched squeaking and peeping of shrews can be heard in woodlands on calm days. The sound is not unlike that of baby birds softly begging in the nest.

- Striped Skunks, Raccoons and Black Bears retreat to their winter quarters but will come out on warm days. They are not true hibernators. ◇

- Snowshoe Hares and weasels are acquiring their white winter coats. In the case of the hare, the ears and feet turn white first while the back is the last section of the body to change colour. Except for the black ear tips, Snowshoes are usually pure white by early December.

Early November

- With the arrival of the breeding season, White-tail bucks are now in rut. This also marks the beginning of the annual deer harvest by rifle and shotgun. The hunt constitutes a veritable "flight to the woods" for men and boys in rural areas. Car accidents involving deer are common now as well. ◇

- The deer hunt begins on the first Monday of the month and lasts for about two weeks in most parts of the Kawarthas. The second archery season for deer starts later in the month and, depending on the district, may last until the end of December.

Late November

- The hunting season for Black Bear ends on November 30 throughout Peterborough County.

The Retreat to Winter Quarters Continues

As the weather becomes colder and food disappears, many mammals retire to sheltered dens, where they spend most of their time sleeping. Unlike true hibernators, which enter a death-like state of extremely low body temperature and heart rate, mammals which simply sleep for extended periods maintain nearly normal body temperature and awaken frequently.

Chipmunks sleep two or three days, awaken to visit a food chamber to eat, go to another chamber to get rid of body waste, and then return to sleep. Raccoons and skunks do not store food but rely on body fat to get through the winter. When temperatures are below freezing, both of these species sleep for extended periods. However, they often become active again during mild spells. For their winter quarters, Raccoons will choose abandoned burrows, caves, hollow logs, culverts and buildings. Skunks usually prefer a chamber in the ground such as an old Groundhog burrow. They often take refuge under buildings as well. Skunks are generally more active than raccoons in the winter.

Muskrat with lodge in background.

Black Bears stay close to their denning site in November and will retire with the onset of cold weather. They usually dig out their own den on the side of a hill or under an uprooted tree. Sometimes, however, the den consists of nothing more than the shelter of a brushpile or a rock crevice. In fact, about one-third of adult male bears sleep directly on the ground, often on a pile of bunched up grasses or conifer branches. In winter, a sleeping bear's body temperature decreases only a few degrees while its heart rate slows to about eight beats a minute. Bears can be easily aroused from their winter sleep.

The Flight to the Woods

For many area residents, November is synonymous with the annual deer hunt. In some parts of the Kawarthas there is a veritable "flight to the woods" with businesses shut down and every able-bodied man between 16 and 90 away on the hunt. The White-tails' peak breeding season in central Ontario is the second and third weeks of November. The buck's antlers have matured and hardened by this time and they are "in rut," or at the peak of their sexual readiness. Since September, the bucks have been rubbing and polishing their antlers on saplings. These small trees actually serve as signposts of a buck's presence in the area. Special glands in the animal's forehead deposit scent on the wood. Antler rubs are smooth in appearance, show no teeth marks and are located 30 centimetres to 1.5 metres above the ground.

Bucks also make scrapes in the leaf litter with their antlers. The buck urinates on its hind legs in such a way that the urine runs over the hock glands and carries the scent down to the scrape in the ground. Like rubs, scrapes use scent to advertise a buck's presence, readiness to breed and possibly even his social rank. To find scrapes, look carefully in open areas of the forest, around ponds or Beaver dams or where a deer run passes under overhanging branches that appear broken and frayed. Female deer visit both rubs and scrapes during the breeding season. The dominant male in a given area may mate with as many as seven does.

Throughout the late fall and winter, deer can often be seen at both dawn and dusk. The Northey's Bay Road between Highway 28 and Petroglyphs Provincial Park can be especially good for seeing deer. Caution must be taken, however, when driving in deer country at this time of year. More collisions involving deer take place in late October and November than in any other month. With this being the mating season, the animals are much more active and are moving around more than usual. Watch for dark shadows along the side of the road and the bright green reflection of the deer's eyes in your headlights. If you do see a deer on or near the road, slow down immediately because there will almost certainly be more nearby, and they easily become disoriented and unpredictable when confronted with an automobile. Most accidents involving deer occur at dusk.

Amphibians and Reptiles

November Highlights

All Month Long
- Most amphibians and reptiles have already begun hibernating by early November.
- Frogs either become frozen "frogsicles" in the leaf litter or snuggle into the mud at the bottom of rivers or wetlands. Toads opt for retreating to warmer climes below the frost line. ◇
- Snakes go for the same strategy as toads and head down below the frost line.
- Turtles choose to overwinter at the bottom of lakes and wetlands.
- Most salamanders retreat deep into the ground in winter. Some aquatic species, however, remain relatively active all winter.

Frogsicles and Other Overwintering Strategies

By November most reptiles and amphibians have moved to their wintering quarters. Usually the last "herptile" to remain active is the Eastern Garter Snake. Frogs and toads use a number of different strategies to survive the onslaught of winter. Contrary to popular belief, the majority of species do not burrow into the mud at the bottom of wetlands. Many of our frogs actually spend the winter in the leaf litter of the forest floor. This group includes the Spring Peeper, Chorus Frog, Gray Treefrog and Wood Frog. They literally become small blocks of ice. Surprisingly enough, the ice crystals do not damage the animals because they form in the body cavities outside of the cells. In the fall, the cells manufacture glycerol, a sugar substance not unlike antifreeze, which inhibits freezing. Even though more than half the water in the frog's body may be frozen, there is no damage done to internal organs. During this long period of suspended animation, there is no breathing, blood circulation or heartbeat. Researchers have dug up these blocks of batrachian ice or "frogsicles" and let them thaw out. Within less than an hour, the frogs became active! When you consider that these species spend the winter frozen, thaw out in spring and then proceed to sing their hearts out before even eating, the resilience of life is extraordinary.

Green Frogs, Bullfrogs and Mink Frogs overwinter in the mud at the bottom of ponds and marshes. They are able to take the little oxygen they need directly through their skins. Leopard Frogs prefer moving water and will often migrate to streams and rivers in the fall. The fast-flowing water provides plenty of oxygen. It is not uncommon to see diving ducks on the Otonabee River come up with a hibernating Leopard Frog that they have plucked from the river bottom.

The American Toad has a completely different strategy for winter survival. The toad retreats to below the frost line, either by burrowing down into loose soil or by taking up winter residence in ready-made burrows or crevices. Toads need to retreat deep enough in the ground to escape temperatures below freezing. Terrestrial salamanders such as the Red-backed Salamander use the same strategy in winter. Several aquatic salamanders remain semi-active during the winter and are occasionally seen swimming under the ice.

Snakes must also descend below the frost line in order to survive. Rock piles, crevices and rodent burrows are all common hibernacula. Many species move to these sites during cool weather in October, although Eastern Garter Snakes may wait until well into November. It is not uncommon to find a number of different snake species using the same wintering site. This is probably explained by the scarcity of good sites. There are also reports of garter snakes hibernating in cisterns and even being immersed in water.

Aquatic turtles use a strategy similar to many frogs to survive winter. The Snapping,

Midland Painted and Musk Turtles sink down into the mud at the bottom of small lakes and wetlands. They enter a state of true hibernation in which heartbeat can slow to less than one per cent of the summer rate and active breathing may cease entirely. This allows them to survive for extended periods of time when there is no oxygen available in the water at all. Some turtles, however, are able to absorb oxygen during hibernation through blood vessels in the anal opening.

As mentioned in the chapter on August, some baby turtles actually overwinter in the nest and do not burrow out until the following spring. How do they survive in a nest that is only six centimetres deep when ground temperatures drop below freezing? As with treefrogs, only body fluids outside of the cells freeze. The water within the cells remains liquid, thanks to the production of a special protein which stimulates the formation of tiny ice crystals. These crystals remain small enough that no cellular damage occurs. However, the rest of the hatchling's body freezes to such a degree that there is no heartbeat, no blood flow and no breathing. Yet when the turtle is thawed, it quickly returns to normal activity. Interestingly enough, evolution has not conferred this amazing ability on adult turtles. Although adults are unable to withstand freezing, they can, as mentioned above, survive oxygen deprivation. These adaptations on the part of turtles are being closely studied by medical researchers in the hope of using the knowledge to enhance human survival.

Eastern Garter Snake.

Fishes

November Highlights

Early November

- Whitefish are the last species of the year to spawn. The small Stony Lake population spawns in Perry Creek in Burleigh Falls when the water temperature is below 7° C. The young fish hatch out in April or May.

- Many anglers contend that early November offers the best Muskie fishing of the year.

Mid-November

■ Fishing season for Northern Pike, Walleye, Muskellunge and bass ends November 15 in southern Peterborough County and, with the exception of bass which ends in October, on November 30 in the north.

■ Except for Lake Scugog, all fishing is prohibited on the Kawartha Lakes (Rice, Katchewanooka, Clear, Stony, Buckhorn, Chemong, Pigeon, Sturgeon) from November 16th to the Friday before the last Saturday in April in any year. There is, however, ice-fishing permitted on some of the lakes in northern Peterborough County.

Late November

■ Walleye begin to move upstream along large rivers such as the Otonabee. They remain in the rivers over the course of the winter in anticipation of the early spring spawn. Walleye feed in extremely shallow water at night during this time.

Insects and Other Invertebrates

November Highlights

All Month Long

■ Monarch Butterflies are arriving in large numbers on their wintering grounds in the pine forests of the Sierra Madre mountains near Mexico City.

■ The familiar, ball-shaped swellings on goldenrods become very visible. ◇

■ Winter survival is now the name of the game. Whether overwintering as eggs, nymphs, larvae, pupae or adults, the strategies insects use are both fascinating and ingenious. ◇

■ A few hardy Field Crickets may still be heard on warm days.

Early November

■ The last dragonflies and butterflies are seen. Some species that are usually still active, albeit in very small numbers, include the Yellow-legged Meadowfly (dragonfly), Clouded Sulphur and Compton Tortoiseshell.

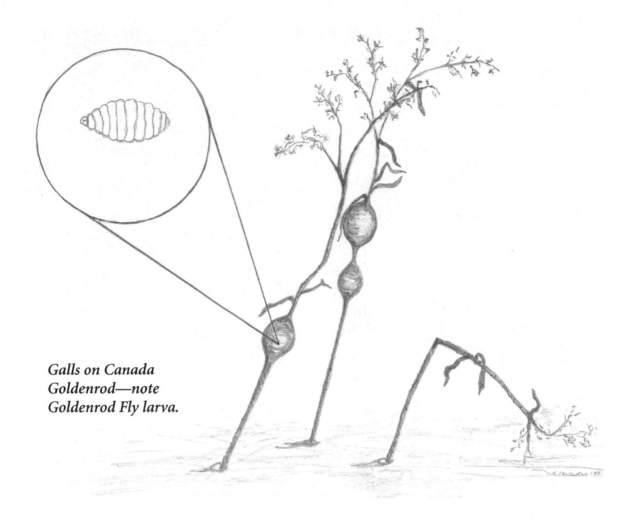

Galls on Canada Goldenrod—note Goldenrod Fly larva.

Goldenrod Galls

Most people are familiar with the ball-like swellings on the stems of goldenrod plants. These are actually caused by a common roadside fly, the Goldenrod Gall Fly. In early summer, the female fly lays her eggs on the stems of developing goldenrod plants. The eggs hatch and the larvae burrow into the stem and create a chamber in which to feed. The plant responds to this intrusion by growing a spherical deformation around the insect chamber. If you open the gall with a pen knife, you will find a small white larva with a dark head. The larva spends the winter in this cozy enclosure.

In the spring, the larva becomes active again and chews out an escape route, almost to the outer surface of the gall. It then moves back toward the centre and pupates in a hard, cocoon-like puparium made from the larval skin. The adult escapes from the puparium and from the gall itself by inflating a spiny, balloon-like structure out through the front of its head. This structure presses a circular hole through both the puparium and the surface of the gall. It then retracts back into the head.

If you open a gall in the spring, you should be able to see the exit tunnel created by the larva before it pupates. Old galls usually show a small hole on the outside through which the fly escaped. Adult Goldenrod Gall Flies are about half a centimetre in length, have a light brown head and thorax and have attractive dark patterns on otherwise clear wings.

Getting Through the Winter

Depending on the species, insects can be found overwintering in every stage of their life cycle. Many insects synthesize glycerol in the fall, a substance similar to the ethylene glycol we put in our radiators. Since glycerol also acts as an antifreeze, an insect's body temperature can fall to below - 30° C. without the tissues freezing solid. In fact, if you touch an insect larva at this temperature, it is still pliable. Bernd Heinrich, in *A Year in the Maine Woods* describes the taste of overwintering carpenter ants as "candy-sweet."

The following list provides examples of how some familiar species survive the ordeal of winter:

Mourning Cloak Butterfly

It waits out the winter as an adult, taking refuge in tight, dark holes or crevices in trees, rocks, buildings, etc. It may, however, emerge and take wing on mild days.

Canadian Tiger Swallowtail Butterfly

Tiger Swallowtail butterflies overwinter as a grey pupa or chrysalis. They are attached to twigs and bark by a silk button at the posterior end and a silken noose in the middle.

Isabella Moth

It hibernates in plant debris as a larva. This is the well-known Woolly Bear caterpillar. It can sometimes be seen walking over the snow on mild winter days.

Eastern Tent Caterpillar

The eggs of these voracious caterpillars can be found cemented to the twigs of cherry trees. The egg mass is covered with a varnish-like substance and forms a ring around the twig.

Common Green Darner Dragonfly

There appear to be two separate populations of this species in Ontario. One population matures quickly from egg to adult and migrates south in the fall, returning in the spring. A second population, indistinguishable in appearance, matures more slowly and spends the winter in ponds and wetlands as a nymph.

Band-winged Grasshoppers (locusts)

Like most grasshoppers, these insects overwinter as eggs deposited in the ground.

Field Cricket

Almost all of the crickets overwinter as eggs.

Praying Mantid

This species overwinters as eggs in a buff-coloured, foam-like case attached to weeds or twigs.

Bumble Bee

Pregnant adult queen bees overwinter in decaying vegetation and underground holes. while the males and workers die. The queens emerge to start a new colony in the spring.

Honey Bee

The entire bee colony survives the winter in the adult stage. They are the only insects to maintain an elevated body temperature all winter. They do so by clustering and vibrating their flight muscles. They feed on stored honey.

Yellowjacket Wasp

Pregnant adult queen yellowjackets overwinter in holes and crevices in rocks and wood. The males and workers die.

Mosquitoes

Most mosquitoes, such as those of the genus *Aedes*, overwinter as eggs laid in the soil at the margin of ponds. They will hatch in the spring meltwater. Those of the genus *Culex*, a variety often seen in the fall, overwinter in locations such as basements and sewers as adult, mated females. One mosquito species even overwinters as larvae in the cup-like leaves of the Pitcher Plant. It spends the winter frozen in the ice.

Blackflies

The blackflies that assail us in early May actually hatch in late fall and spend the winter as slowly growing larvae. They can be seen all winter on rocks in unfrozen streams. Those that bite us in June and July overwinter as eggs on the river bottom.

Ladybird Beetles

These insects overwinter in the leaf-litter and in crevices as adults. They are frequently found in large groups.

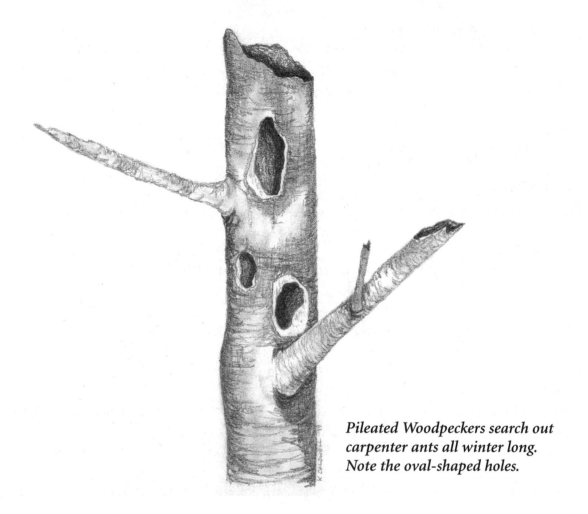

Pileated Woodpeckers search out carpenter ants all winter long. Note the oval-shaped holes.

Spiders

Depending on the family, some spiders overwinter as eggs covered by thick, silken sacs and attached to plants or hidden under loose bark. Crab spiders overwinter as adults behind loose bark. Hunting spiders, too, spend the winter months in the adult stage and can sometimes be seen walking on the snow on mild days. Wolf spiders survive as sub-adults and actually remain active throughout much of the winter in the sub-nivean space under the snow. When spring arrives they molt to the adult stage.

Carpenter Ants

Adult carpenter ants hibernate in clusters in the centre of both dead and living trees. They are often found in logs that have been split for firewood. Carpenter ants quickly become active when temperatures rise above freezing.

Plants

November Highlights

All Month Long

- The year's flower parade has come to an end. Roadsides now are bordered by the browns and greys of dead or dormant plants. Although they appear dried and lifeless, most of these species are perennials. Beneath the ground the roots are strong and healthy and will send up new stalks in the spring.

- In our woodlands, the only trees still clinging to their foliage are young American Beech, Sugar Maple and Ironwood. Many will retain at least some leaves all winter.

- During a walk in the woods, look for the rich purple leaves of Bunchberry as well as the tan wrinkled leaves and shrivelled red berries of Canada Mayflower. The evergreen leaves of various wildflower species are also conspicuous. These include Trailing Arbutus, Pipsissewa, Partridgeberry and Bog Laurel.

- The seeds and fruit of a wide variety of trees, shrubs and vines attract birds and provide some rare November colour. The orange and yellow fruits of Bittersweet and the red berries of Wintergreen Holly are especially attractive. Ornamental varieties of crabapple, mountain-ash and hawthorn are usually heavy with fruit as well, and attract robins, waxwings and Pine Grosbeaks.

- Eastern Hemlocks shed their seeds from late fall to late winter. It is not uncommon to see the snow beneath these trees literally powdered with seeds.

- Mosses, club-mosses, lichens and several species of evergreen ferns stand out against the brown leaf litter and deserve close observation. Ground Pine, a type of club-moss, releases little puffs of yellow spores when your foot brushes up against it. ◇

- Aldo Leopold, one of America's greatest conservationists and ecologists, called November the "month of the axe" and judged it the best time of the year to cut firewood. The weather is comfortable for physical labour and wood cut in late fall and winter has a lower moisture content. ◇

- Hard corn is still being harvested this month and green fields of young wheat stand out noticeably. The smell of manure is often in the air as farmers spread it to fertilize their fields in the fall.

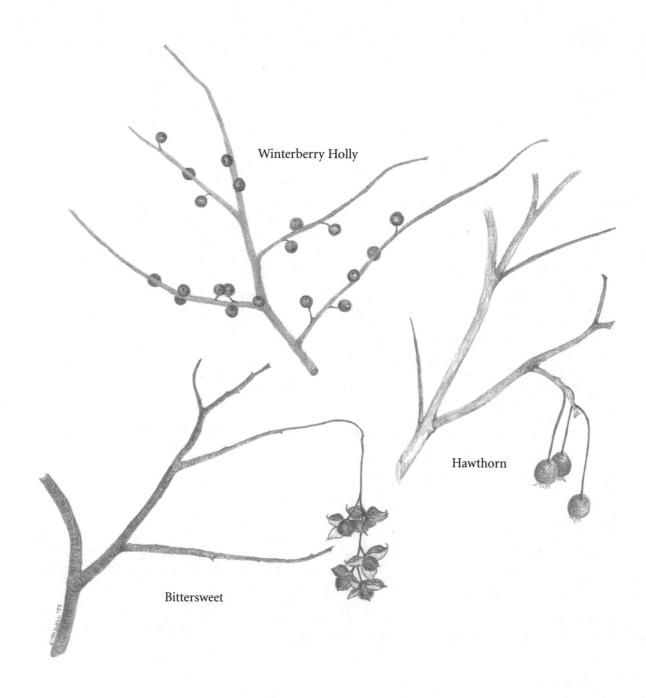

Winterberry Holly

Hawthorn

Bittersweet

Three conspicuous November fruits.

Early November

- A few dandelions are still flowering on suburban lawns.

- Red Oaks, Weeping Willows, Tamaracks, and Silver Maples are the only mature deciduous trees that still have foliage. Some oaks will hold their leaves until the end of the month and a few leaves all winter long. A particularly attractive stand of Red Oak is located at the south entrance to the village of Bridgenorth.

- Still clothed in leaves, non-native trees and shrubs are quite conspicuous and look very much out of place in the late fall landscape. The Norway Maple stands out in particular. Most trees turn a bright yellow and often still have their leaves by Remembrance Day. Given this maple's European origins, the concurrence of the two events is fitting.

Mid-November

- Some Silver Maples that have been planted keep their yellow-beige leaves until the middle of the month. These trees may be a different genetic stock that originated outside of Ontario. As a general rule, however, all tree species planted in the city hold their leaves longer than those growing wild in rural areas.

Turning Our Attention to the Non-flowering Plants

Nearly all of the mosses remain fresh and green during the late fall and winter. They are much more conspicuous now since they are one of the few green plants around. It is worth the effort to get down on your hands and knees to examine the mosses closely. It is like entering a miniature green forest that until now was just part of the green "blur." The intricate design and distinct form, colour and texture of the different species suddenly become evident. In conifer swamps, sphagnum (peat moss) dominates. There are many different species but all are spongy and often form carpet-like mats and large hummocks. Other groups of mosses include the upright mosses such as Juniper Moss and the creeping mosses such as Shaggy Moss.

Even more noticeable in many areas are the club-

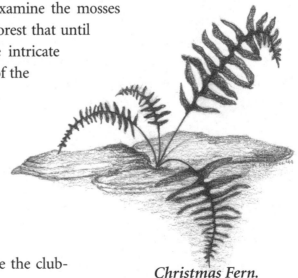

Christmas Fern.

mosses, close relatives of the ferns. One species, the Ground Pine, sometimes covers large areas of the forest floor. In November, it releases little clouds of spores when it is brushed up against. These spores were once used in the manufacture of fireworks and as a source of illumination in early photography. They are inflammable, water-repellent and nearly weightless.

Several species of ferns also remain green in the winter. The most common are Christmas Fern, Rock Polypody and Marginal Wood Fern. Christmas Fern can be found in Mark S. Burnham Provincial Park and Peter's Woods. Rock Polypody and Marginal Wood Fern are common everywhere on the Shield, such as along the High Falls Trail at Petroglyphs Provincial Park.[1]

The Month of the Axe

Aldo Leopold, in *A Sand County Almanac,* referred to November as " the month of the axe." The weather is cool enough to make strenuous outdoor work comfortable and, because the leaves have fallen, a clear view is possible of how the branches of neighbouring trees intertwine. By late fall, there is also less sap in the wood since it becomes more concentrated in the roots. By cutting, splitting and stacking the wood between now and the end of February, late winter freezing and thawing will cause cracking and allow drying air to enter. Sap, not rainwater, is the main concern when drying wood. The logs should, however, be stacked with the bark side up in order to shed precipitation. The wood should be allowed to dry at least until the following autumn.

Before cutting down dead trees, however, it is important to remember that a large number of birds and mammals use tree cavities as nesting or den sites and many species will accept no substitutes. Natural cavities are also important roosting sites that provide crucial shelter for animals during wet or cold weather. Unless an old snag is an obvious threat to human safety, it should be allowed to stand. "Tidying up" a woodlot by removing dead trees will only make it poorer as wildlife habitat.

Weather

November Highlights

All Month Long
- The days are short and the weather is often cool and damp. However, Indian Summer

conditions are also possible, with temperatures in the high teens and lots of sunshine.

■ Most people would probably be surprised that total precipitation for November is only slightly above the year's monthly average, and that the average number of days with rain is no more than during the summer months.

■ A taste of winter usually comes to the Kawarthas in November. The first significant snowfall occurs and permanent snow cover is sometimes with us by month's end.

■ Frost is recorded an average of 20 days this month.

Table 11.2: **November Weather Averages, 1961-1990**

Daily Maximum	6.2° C
Daily Minimum	-2.3° C
Extreme Maximum	22.8° C
Extreme Minimum	-17.6° C
Rainfall	62.2 mm
Snowfall	14.3 cm
Precipitation	77.3 mm

Table 11.3: **Approximate Twilight, Sunrise and Sunset Times (EST)**

Date	Twilight Begins	Sunrise	Sunset	Twilight Ends
Nov. 1	6:21 a.m.	6:51 a.m.	5:03 p.m.	5:33 p.m.
Nov. 10	6:32 a.m.	7:03 a.m.	4:51 p.m.	5:22 p.m.
Nov. 20	6:44 a.m.	7:16 a.m.	4:42 p.m.	5:14 p.m.
Dec. 1	6:57 a.m.	7:29 a.m.	4:36 p.m.	5:08 p.m.

The Night Sky

November Highlights

All Month Long
■ Major constellations and stars visible (November 15, 9:00 p.m. EST)

Northwest: Summer Triangle made up of *Vega* (in Lyra), *Deneb* (in Cygnus) and *Altair* (in Aquila)

Northeast: Ursa Major low in N with Ursa Minor (with *Polaris*) above; Auriga (with

Capella) Cassiopeia near Zenith; Pleiades star cluster (due E); Gemini just above horizon

Southeast: Orion (with *Betelgeuse* and *Rigel*) low in E; Taurus (with *Aldebaran*) high to its right

Southwest: Pegasus (with the Great Square) and Andromeda (with M31 galaxy) almost at zenith

■ The Pleiades (Seven Sisters) adorn the evening sky.

Early November

■ The South Taurid meteor shower peaks about November 3 and can be seen in the northeast between Taurus, Auriga and Perseus. Under ideal conditions, it is possible to see about 15 meteors per hour.

Late November

■ On November 17, the Leonid shower peaks at about 10 p.m. It is seen in the Leo constellation, low in the northeastern sky, and produces about 15 meteors per hour.

■ Orion's arrival in the southeast seems to make November nights all the colder.

The Pleiades

If you are out for an evening walk this month, look for a beautiful cluster of stars in the eastern sky. These stars are known as the Pleiades or Seven Sisters. Viewed from the city, at least six stars are visible to the naked eye while country residents with keen eyesight may see as many as 12. To be able to count them is considered a good test of eyesight. A pair of binoculars will reveal several dozen stars while a good telescope will show several hundred. Astronomers estimate their distance from Earth at about 400 light-years and their age at a relatively young 100 million years old. To the Greeks, this cluster of blue-white stars represented the seven daughters of Atlas, the giant who supported the world on his shoulders. In Central America, streets were oriented to line up with the point where the star cluster appears to set on the western horizon.

Winter

Snowy Owl on fence post.

Black-capped Chickadees in hawthorn.

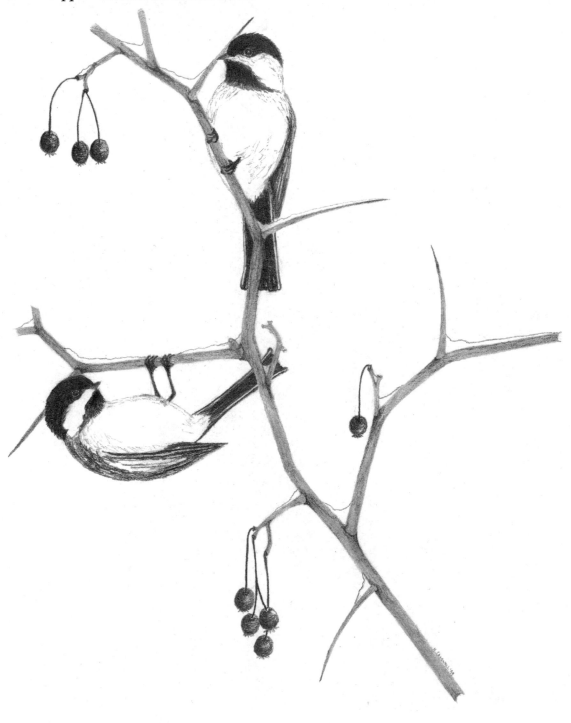

NATURE'S YEAR IN THE KAWARTHAS

CHAPTER 12

December—The Sun Stands Still

Despite what the calendar might say, December 1st heralds the beginning of winter, a season of unadorned fundamentals. The half-hearted sun casts a pale light as it traces its lowest trajectory of the year through the southern sky. With nights as long as June days, it's no wonder that ancient peoples feared the sun's total disappearance. So it was with great joy and relief that they celebrated the winter solstice, the day that the sun literally "stands still" and stops its march southward. For the next six months, the days will grow longer. In fact, the first spring bird song is a mere eight weeks away.

With the arrival of December, naturalists look forward to the camaraderie and friendly competition of the Christmas Bird Count. Spending an entire day outside simply counting and looking for birds is the ideal antidote to the pressures, excesses and mad rush of the holiday season.

As attractive as our holiday decorations may be, nature itself provides the most enduring Yuletide adornments: festive Winterberry Holly fruits, radiant cardinals, fluffy chickadee baubles, hoar-frosted windows, and shimmering icicles. The Christmas tree, symbolic of life's vigour in the face of winter, fills our homes with the resinous fragrance of the northern forest. Nature also supplies its own array of sounds for the festive season—the cracking and rumbling of ice forming on the lakes, the shrill scolding of Red Squirrels, and the croaking of ravens patrolling the Shield.

Although December sees the year come full circle, it is neither an end nor a beginning. Like every other month, it is simply part of an indivisible whole.

December At a Glance

Small numbers of loons and ducks linger on area lakes until freeze-up. On lakes such as Buckhorn and Stony, eagles are often seen sitting on the ice near open water. Watch for hawks and sometimes Snowy Owls in open fields. Between mid-December and early January, Christmas Bird Counts are held.

The coat of the Red Squirrel becomes a brilliant russet. Muskrats continue to build piles of vegetation in holes they have broken in the ice. Before the snow gets too deep, try identifying and interpreting mammal tracks and various signs such as "nip twigs."

With a little practice, all conifers and most mature hardwoods can be identified by shape alone. Pines shed their cones in the late fall and early winter. Choosing a Christmas tree? Consider a Balsam Fir.

The winter solstice marks the beginning of winter. The Kawartha Lakes are frozen most years by December 12. Average daily temperatures for the month are a maximum of -1° C and a minimum of -10 C. Snowfall averages 42 centimetres. For the Kawarthas, the chances of having a white Christmas are over 80%. In mid-December, the sun rises at about 7:40 a.m. and sets around 4:35 p.m.

Clear December evenings make for excellent stargazing. Cassiopeia looms high in the north sky and resembles an "M." In the southeast, look for the Winter Six: Orion, Taurus, Gemini, Auriga, Canis Major and Canis Minor. The Big Dipper is low in the north.

Books on Ontario's natural history make great Christmas gifts. A family outing to a Christmas tree farm provides a welcome break from the rush of the holiday season. Ice and snow this month offer up all sorts of photographic possibilities.

Birds

December Highlights

All Month Long

- Migratory birds that breed in the Kawarthas are now on their wintering grounds, where they must compete with the resident bird community of the area for food resources.

- Great Black-backed, Glaucous and Iceland Gulls may still turn up at the Bensfort Road landfill, at Little Lake and on open patches of water on the larger Kawartha Lakes. These gulls often appear at the landfill all winter long whenever the temperature is around 0° C for more than a day.

- As a general rule, winter birds are most often found around human habitations, open water and farmland. ◇

- On area lakes such as Jack, Katchewanooka, Buckhorn and Stony, eagles are often seen sitting on the ice near open water or perched in nearby trees.

- The number of species and individual birds visiting feeders in winter often fluctuates dramatically. People often ask: "Where are all the birds?" ◇

- December is the peak calling month for both Eastern Screech and Great Horned Owls.

Early December

- Ducks lingering until freeze-up usually include Common Goldeneye, Common Merganser, Hooded Merganser and American Black Duck. A small number of Common Loons, too, stay until the ice comes. As climate change continues, we will most likely see a shift to later departure dates. Our large, resident Mallard population will remain to winter along open sections of the Otonabee River.

- Loons sometimes become trapped in the ice when a pool of open water freezes overnight. Even if some open water remains, loons require a large expanse of water on which to run in order to take off. Iced-in birds regularly fall prey to eagles at this time of year.

- For listing purposes, December 1st marks the beginning of the official winter birding season. It ends on the last day of February. In the Kawarthas, it is possible to see at least 60 species of birds during this period.

Mid-December

- Between mid-December and early January, Christmas Bird Counts take place both locally and across North and South America. ◇

Glaucous Gull.

NATURE'S YEAR IN THE KAWARTHAS

Table 12.1: December Departures and Arrivals

early month

departures	Common Goldeneye (w), Common Merganser (w), Ring-billed Gull

late month

departures	Giant Canada Goose (may overwinter)
arrivals	Great Gray Owl*

Finding Birds in Winter

There are several rules-of-thumb that make finding birds in winter easier. First of all, many species tend to be associated with human habitations. Rural neighbourhoods with lots of feeders are a good place to start. Anywhere there is open water is also worth investigating. Such areas can include Gannon's Narrows, Burleigh Falls, Young's Point, Lake Katchewanooka, Lakefield, the Otonabee River and Little Lake. Gulls, eagles, kingfishers, herons, ducks and other waterfowl are all possible. Birds can also be found in habitats which afford good cover such as thick stands of coniferous trees, brushpiles, shrubby areas, and around farm buildings. The presence of chickadees often indicates that other species are around as well. Pishing (see September) can be quite effective in drawing the birds in for a closer look.

When driving through farmland and near airports, watch the open fields for Snowy Owls, Red-tailed Hawks, and possibly a lingering Rough-legged Hawk. All three species often perch in trees, on telephone poles and also on hay bales. Snowy Owls will also choose a knoll as an observation point. Once a Snowy Owl has found a productive hunting area—which usually means a good supply of Meadow Voles—it usually remains there until its departure in early spring for the Arctic. Farmland habitat is also good for Snow Buntings and, later in the winter, for Horned Larks. In overgrown fields with small trees, watch for Northern Shrikes.

In the northern parts of Peterborough County, keep an eye open for birds foraging right on the road. Winter finches in particular are attracted by the grit used in sanding operations. The Jack Lake Road and County Road 507 north of Flynn's Corners are often good places to see this. For those who like cross-country skiing, the Kawartha Nordic Ski Club trails provide opportunities to see species often associated with Algonquin Park. These include Black-backed Woodpeckers, Gray Jays and both White-winged and Red Crossbill. The trails are located on Highway 28, 40 kilometres north of Peterborough at Haultain.

In the city, keep an eye skyward. Cooper's and Sharp-shinned Hawks are fairly common in the winter and can be identified at considerable distances by their unique "flap-flap-glide" flight pattern. The large number of feeders attracts both of these raptor species, which dine almost exclusively on songbirds.

Why is There Nothing at My Feeder?

Many people often wonder why the number of birds visiting their feeder fluctuates so much. There are several possible explanations. Winter finches, for example, are highly nomadic and will wander great distances over the course of the winter. Human offerings of bird seed do not appear to be enough to make them stay. The availability of natural food is the determining factor. Secondly, many species such as House Finches, House Sparrows, American Goldfinches and sometimes even Northern Cardinals now travel in flocks and may frequent only a small number of feeders. If your feeder is not on their list, you may find things very quiet. Also, with the number of people feeding birds these days, there are relatively fewer birds to go around. Finally, the presence of a raptor in the neighbourhood may also explain why, on a given day, there are fewer birds. Hawks, of course, are drawn by the fact that people are feeding birds in the first place.

I always feel privileged when a Sharp-shinned or Cooper's Hawk makes an appearance in my yard. In addition to being beautiful birds in their own right, they allow me to observe first-hand the food chain at work as the sun's energy passes from sunflower seed to Mourning Dove to hawk.

Counting Birds at Christmas

December is an eventful month for birding. One reason is the annual Christmas Bird Count. The "counts" take place throughout North, Central and South America between mid-December and early January. There are two counts held in the Kawarthas, one centred in Peterborough and a second centred in Petroglyphs Provincial Park. They are both organized by the Peterborough Field Naturalists and anyone can participate regardless of experience.

A Christmas Bird Count takes place during a single calendar day and covers the area of a circle measuring 24 kilometres in diameter. The circle is divided up into a number of sectors, with each sector being covered by a different group of observers. The birders are out from dawn until dusk recording not only the different species seen but also the number of individual birds. Many observers actually start before dawn in the hope of hearing owls.

Evening Grosbeak.

Considerable time is also spent tactfully peering into people's yards to see what is coming to their feeder. So, if you notice a group of suspicious-looking characters sitting in a car and scrutinizing your property with binoculars, you don't need to call the police. Rather, go out and tell them what birds have been coming to your yard. At the end of the day, the various groups gather for a much-appreciated hot meal and to compile the results.

Depending on what sort of weather has prevailed during the fall and on the availability of natural foods such as berries and cones, the number of species counted changes considerably from year to year. A mild fall means more species, since some birds will linger in our area before heading south or perishing. A heavy wild grape crop will probably allow greater numbers of robins and waxwings to overwinter, while plentiful pine and spruce cones might attract various species of winter finches. The weather on the day of the count can have a major impact as well, especially if there is heavy snow or rain. On average, the Peterborough count records about 50 species, the Petroglyphs count about 35 and Presqu'ile about 60. In comparison, a Christmas Bird Count held in Panama each year usually tallies over 300 species!

You do not have to be an expert to take part in a bird count. Simply having extra eyes and ears in the group invariably leads to more birds being counted. You can also participate as a "feeder watcher." If you can devote at least two hours to watching your feeder on count day, your sightings can be phoned in and included.

The count results are submitted to the National Audubon Society in Washington, D.C., which supervises the counts and publishes the results in the journal *American Birds*. This data, collected over a long period of time, can provide valuable information on the relative abundance and distribution of bird species. A Christmas Bird Count, however, is other things as well. It serves as a welcome break from the stress and consumerism of the holiday season and as an excuse to get together with other birders for some friendly competition and camaraderie.

Commonly Recorded Species on the Peterborough and Petroglyphs Christmas Bird Counts

Mallard,* Common Goldeneye,* Common Merganser,* Sharp-shinned Hawk,* Cooper's Hawk,* Red-tailed Hawk,* Bald Eagle,** Ruffed Grouse, Ring-billed Gull,* Herring Gull,* Rock Dove, Mourning Dove,* Great Horned Owl, Barred Owl,** Downy Woodpecker, Hairy Woodpecker, Black-backed Woodpecker,** Pileated Woodpecker, Northern Shrike, Blue Jay, Gray Jay,** American Crow, Common Raven,** Black-capped Chickadee, Red-breasted

Nuthatch, White-breasted Nuthatch, Brown Creeper, Golden-crowned Kinglet, American Robin,* European Starling, Bohemian Waxwing, Cedar Waxwing, American Tree Sparrow, Dark-eyed Junco, Snow Bunting, Northern Cardinal,* Pine Grosbeak, House Finch,* Purple Finch, Pine Siskin, Common Redpoll, American Goldfinch, Evening Grosbeak, House Sparrow*

* usually found on Peterborough count only
** usually found on Petroglyphs count only

Table 12.2: **Where Are They Now?**

When the National Audubon Society publishes the results of the Christmas Bird Counts each year, it is interesting to note some of the locations where large concentrations of "our" birds spend the winter months. All of these species actually winter over a large area.

Common Loon:	436,	Morehead City, North Carolina
Great Blue Heron: 3	59,	Freeport, Louisiana
Common Merganser:	39,640,	Point Pelee, Ontario
Turkey Vulture:	3,000,	Dade County, Florida
Osprey:	237,	Merritt Island, Florida
Killdeer:	7,187,	Crowley, Louisiana
American Woodcock:	124,	Cape Charles, Virginia
Ruby-Throated Hummingbird:	181,	Jaco, Costa Rica
Barn Swallow:	5,540,	Manaus, Brazil
Tree Swallow:	250,000,	Lake Placid, Florida
Eastern Bluebird:	701,	Palmetto, Texas
American Robin:	1,000,000,	Piedmont, South Carolina
Yellow-rumped Warbler:	11,759,	Gulf Shores, Alabama
Yellow Warbler:	71,	Cabo Rojo, Puerto Rico
Indigo Bunting:	30,	El Naranjo, Mexico
White-throated Sparrow:	3,170,	Lower Kent County, Maryland
Baltimore Oriole:	422,	Jaco, Costa Rica

Mammals

December Highlights

All Month Long

- The Red Squirrel's coat is now a brilliant russet. It is also much thicker than the summer coat and will provide better protection from the cold.

- "Nip twigs" on the ground below conifers are a sure sign of Red Squirrel activity. ◇

- Throughout the late fall and winter, Gray Squirrels are often seen high up in Manitoba and Norway Maples, where they feed on the keys.

- Deer carcasses are an important food source for eagles wintering in this area.

- Identifying and interpreting mammal tracks is a fascinating pastime and adds a great deal to a winter outing. ◇

- If you are fortunate, you may have a family of flying squirrels providing nightly entertainment at your birdfeeder. They are usually quite tame and don't seem to be bothered by floodlights or people sitting quietly outside. Both Northern and Southern Flying Squirrels occur in Peterborough County. The latter is a provincially rare species.

Taking a Nip to Get Through the Winter

In late fall and winter, Red Squirrels are a common sight in mixed and coniferous woodlands. In addition to their agitated calls, Red Squirrels leave behind a number of other signs of their presence. Among these are "nip twigs" scattered on the ground under spruce and other conifers. In order to get at the cones and terminal buds that are an integral part of their diet, squirrels nip off the tips of conifer branches allowing the twig to fall to the ground. They then scurry down from the tree and remove the cones and buds, leaving the rest of the twig on the ground. While the buds are consumed immediately, the cones are often stored in hollow logs, under the roots of dead trees and in spaces between rocks. They are later taken to a favourite eating spot such as a tree stump. Only the seeds, however, are actually consumed. A pile of cone scales and shafts accumulates at the eating site. It is called a midden and can sometimes measure half a metre deep!

Red Squirrel with "nip twigs."

Mammal Tracks

To the great frustration of many naturalists, mammals are often shy, nocturnal and difficult to see. Fortunately, however, they do leave behind a record of their comings and goings in the form of tracks. Although the art of "tracking" requires considerable practice, it does allow the observer to enter the often secret world of mammal activity. Being able to read tracks also adds a great deal to any winter outing.

The best conditions for tracking are fresh, damp, shallow snow or soft, damp mud or sand. As a beginner, you will have more success and less frustration if you limit your efforts to tracks laid down in these conditions. Tracks that are incomplete, faint or badly worn are best left for another day. An excellent introductory lesson to tracking is to watch how tracks are laid down by your cat, dog or resident squirrels. When you understand how these common but representative animals move (a dog provides an introduction to the canine family), the patterns of the tracks they leave behind make a lot more sense. Get yourself a good guide book.[1]

Fishes

December Highlights

- Fishing season for most species is closed.
- Travel on lakes and rivers can become treacherous as waterways begin to freeze.
- This is a time for anglers and fishes to have a rest.

Plants

December Highlights

All Month Long
- Red and White Pine shed their cones during the late fall and early winter. ◇
- Balsam Fir makes the perfect Christmas tree—symmetrical shape, long-lasting needles and a wonderful fragrance. ◇
- You may still see farmers harvesting hard corn this month. Even though the plants are dry, withered and frozen, they still have excellent food value.

Casting Off Cones

Each species has its own timetable for releasing seeds and shedding cones. For many conifers such as White Spruce and Eastern Hemlock, both of these events happen during the late fall and winter. In fact, it is not uncommon to find the snow beneath these two species powdered with seeds. Spruce cones drop from the trees during this same period but the cones of the hemlock remain on the branches over the entire winter. White Cedar cones also open in the fall and release the seeds over a period of several months. The cones slowly fall off during this same period as well. Tamaracks and pines also choose the fall for casting off their seeds. The cones of White Pine drop from the tree in late fall or winter while those of Red Pine usually stay on until spring. Tamarack cones also remain on the tree long after the seeds are released.

The cones of the Balsam Fir follow a slightly different pattern from the other conifers. First of all, you will almost never find a Balsam Fir cone on the ground. The scales are shed while the cone is still on the tree, so all we see in winter is the stick-like core. Fir cones grow

Five distinctive cones.

White Pine

Northern White Cedar

White Spruce

Balsam Fir

in dense groups near the top of the tree and stand straight up like candles. The scales begin to fall away in September, thereby releasing the seeds. The bare axis of the cone usually remains on the tree for several years.

The Best Christmas Tree

Among the many tasks to be completed during the holiday season is the purchase of a Christmas tree. What species do you choose? For many, the best choice is the traditional favourite, Balsam Fir. They have a wonderful balsamic fragrance that immediately evokes memories of Christmases past. The fir is not only easy to decorate but it holds its needles longer than most other species. It is also one of the most perfectly symmetrical evergreens. Although you may have to pay a little more for this species, it is worth the extra expense. On the farm, choosing and cutting down a fir tree was a much anticipated event because it meant that the work to ready the farm for winter was finished and Christmas celebrations could finally begin in earnest.

Weather

December Highlights

All Month Long
- The different winter air masses that affect the Kawarthas cause considerable variability in winter weather. Air masses originating over the Pacific tend to be cool and raw, while Arctic air brings frigidly cold conditions.

- Above-freezing maximums are quite common. On average, however, December is only a slightly milder month than January and February.

- A huge bank of clouds along the horizon is a common winter sight when you look south from Peterborough on a clear day. These clouds form over Lake Ontario as a result of water vapour rising from the relatively warm lake and condensing in the cold air above.

Mid-December
- During most years, all of the Kawartha Lakes are frozen by December 12. ◇

Late December
- The winter solstice marks the shortest day of the year as the sun traces its lowest and shortest arc through the sky. It is also the official beginning of winter. ◇

- Even though the days do grow longer after the solstice, the increase in daylight is in the afternoon, not in the morning. On January 20, the sun rises only two minutes earlier than it did on December 20. Sunset, however, is about 30 minutes later.

- The chance of having a white Christmas in the Kawarthas is over 80%.

Table 12.3: **December Weather Averages, 1961-1990**

Daily Maximum	-1.0° C
Daily Minimum	-10.4° C
Extreme Maximum	19.2° C
Extreme Minimum	-33.9° C
Rainfall	33.9 mm
Snowfall	41.5 cm
Precipitation	76.2 mm

The Lakes Freeze Over

The Kawartha Lakes are usually frozen by mid-December. The speed at which freezing can occur is amazing. One day the whole lake is open; the next it's completely frozen. There is no intermediate stage between water and ice—it's one or the other. How this comes about is interesting. When water cools to 4° C, something remarkable occurs. Instead of becoming denser and sinking, it actually begins to expand and becomes lighter. Being colder—and lighter—than the water below, it stays on the surface of the lake. As the water is cooled even more, the expansion continues until 0° C is reached. At this point, the molecules lock into the pattern of a solid and form ice. In his book *Winter*, Doug Sadler writes: "To the physicist as to the layperson, the suddenness of the metamorphosis is truly astonishing. It is as if tension builds up to an unbearable point where it has to be released in a sudden, orgasmic moment of creation."[2] This process of molecular bonding and ice formation goes ahead even in the presence of waves. The expansion of the water from 4° C up to the point of freezing means that the ice is 10% lighter than the water below and therefore floats on the surface.

The Mystique of the Winter Solstice

Caught in the mad rush of the holiday season, most of us are unaware that a profound celestial event takes place this month. December is the month of the winter solstice, the shortest day of the year, and the first official day of winter. At the solstice, the Northern Hemisphere is tipped farthest away from the sun. The sun therefore traces its lowest and shortest arc through the sky making it the shortest day of the year.

The solstice has always been a time of awe and amazement. It is an event that was noticed and celebrated by ancient cultures on every continent and, in the opinion of some, was a precursor to faith. Just when the world appeared to be on the brink of utter darkness and oblivion, the sun seemingly stopped moving further and further south each day and essentially "stood still." It then proceeded to move northward once again and to climb higher and higher into the sky. For people of northern climes, the winter solstice represents the assurance that the days will once again grow longer and spring indeed will come. Many people are once again celebrating these spiritual and symbolic dimensions of the winter solstice.[3]

Comparative sunrise points at summer and winter solstices.

Table 12.4: **Approximate Twilight, Sunrise and Sunset Times (EST)**

Date	Twilight Begins	Sunrise	Sunset	Twilight Ends
Dec. 1	6:57 a.m.	7:29 a.m.	4:36 p.m.	5:08 p.m.
Dec. 10	7:05 a.m.	7:38 a.m.	4:34 p.m.	5:08 p.m.
Dec. 20	7:12 a.m.	7:45 a.m.	4:37 p.m.	5:10 p.m.
Jan. 1	7:16 a.m.	7:49 a.m.	4:45 p.m.	5:18 p.m.

The Night Sky

December Highlights

All Month Long

- Major constellations and stars visible (December 15, 9:00 p.m. EST)

    Northwest: Cassiopeia near Zenith; Summer Triangle with *Vega* and *Altair* just above horizon and *Deneb* in mid-sky

    Northeast: Ursa Major low in N with Ursa Minor (with *Polaris*) above it; Auriga (with *Capella*) near Zenith; Gemini (with *Castor* and *Pollux*) in mid-sky;

    Southeast: Pleiades near Zenith; Orion (with *Betelgeuse* and *Rigel*), Taurus (with*Aldebaran*) high to its right; Canis Major (with *Sirius*) low to its left; Auriga (with *Capella*) high above

Southwest: Pegasus (with the Great Square) high in W; Andromeda (with M31 galaxy) almost at Zenith

■ Seeing the Northern Lights, or Aurora Borealis, is a rare but memorable experience. Try to get in the habit of glancing up at the northern sky on clear nights. ◇

■ In the southeast, look for the Winter Six: Orion, Taurus, Gemini, Auriga, Canis Major and Canis Minor. The winter constellations shine brightly and are easy to pick out.

■ The December moon rises about 30 degrees north of due east and sets 30 degrees north of due west.

The Aurora Borealis

Although the Aurora Borealis, or Northern Lights, can occur at any time of the year, they somehow seem more impressive on a cold winter night. *Aurora* is Latin for "dawn," and *Borealis* means "north." The term is appropriate because the light appears to fan out from the north and can be strong enough to suggest the coming dawn. The light can take many forms, appearing like arcs, rays, clouds or just a glow. The colours can range from a transparent white, through hues of green and purple, to a brilliant display of deep primary colours. The Aurora often appears like clouds moving about in a strange manner and then suddenly swinging out across the sky in a new direction.

The current theory explaining the Aurora Borealis is that it results from sunspots spewing out electrically charged particles that interact with gases high in the Earth's ionosphere and create light. It is believed that these particles follow the earth's magnetic field towards the poles, becoming more concentrated and therefore more visible.

The winter sky looking southeast.

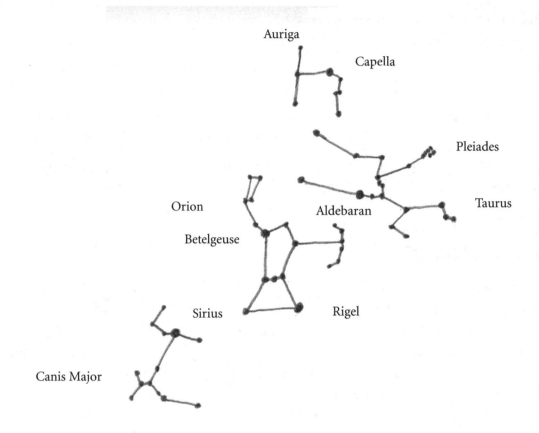

Auriga

Capella

Pleiades

Orion

Aldebaran

Taurus

Betelgeuse

Rigel

Sirius

Canis Major

K. CALDWELL '02

NATURE'S YEAR IN THE KAWARTHAS

Appendix 1: Where to go?

As Doug Sadler says in *Our Heritage of Birds,* "Birds are where you find them." In other words, interesting sightings of birds or any other plants or animals can be had just about anywhere. There are, however, some locations that seem to be consistently better than others, and most are probably not known to the visitor or casual observer. The groups of plants or animals that are of special interest in these areas are indicated in italics. The location numbers correspond to the numbers on the map on page 307.

South from Peterborough to Lower Otonabee River and Rice Lake

★ 1 **Peterborough Airport and Vicinity:**

Take Airport Rd. (Cty. Rd. 11) south from Highway 115—*good birding all year long.*

★ 2 **Briar Hill Pond:**

Located at corner of County Roads 21 and 28—*waterfowl and shorebirds.*

★ 3 **Pleasant Point Road:**

From Cty. Rd. 21, take Fourth Line 2 km east to Pleasant Point Rd. Follow to river—*Screech Owls possible.*

★ 4 **Pengelley Landing on Rice Lake:**

Take Cty. Rd. 2 east from Bailieboro. Turn south at Scriven Road and follow to lake—*ducks in spring and late fall.*

★ 5 **Rainbow Tallgrass Prairie Restoration Site:**

Continue north on Cty. Rd. 2 and turn east at Second Line. Follow signs to Rainbow Cottages Resort—*tallgrass prairie, waterfowl on river.*

★ 6 **Bensfort Bridge:**

Follow Cty. Rd. 2 to where it crosses Otonabee River—*ducks and gulls in winter and spring.*

★ 7 **Bensfort Road Landfill:**

Located on Bensfort Road just north of Cty. Rd. 2 and 6 km south of By-pass—*late fall and winter gulls.*

★ 8 **Kent's Bay Road to Otonabee River:**

Follow Hiawatha Line (Cty. Rd. 31) south from Cty. Rd. 2 to Hiawatha First Nation. Take Kent's Bay Rd. west to river—*ducks in spring.*

★ 9   **Herkimer Point Road:**

Turn east off Cty. Rd. 31 at Hiawatha First Nation—*good birding in spring, summer and fall; variety of habitats.*

★ 10   **Harrick Point:**

Located at end of Paudash St. at Hiawatha First Nation—*ducks in spring at mouth of Otonabee River.*

★ 11   **Mather's Corners:**

Take Drummond Line just south from Mather's Corners on Cty. Rd. 2—*ducks in spring in flooded field.*

★ 12   **Indian River at Keene:**

Large wetland located just east of village. Canoe recommended—*wetland birds.*

★ 13   **River Road:**

Take Second Line of Asphodel south from Cty. Rd. 2. River Road is first road on left. Follow across to Sixth Line of Asphodel—*birds, spring flowers, ferns, trees.*

★ 14   **Old C.N. Railway Bed:**

One section between Drummond Line and Cty. Rd. 34 (north of Base Line). Second section east of Indian River between Base Line and Cameron Line—*excellent butterfly-watching*

City of Peterborough and Vicinity

★ 15   **Mark S. Burnham Provincial Park:**

Located on north side of Highway 7, just east of Peterborough—*rich and diverse flora in remnant stand of mature forest; also ferns, sedges, spring wildflowers.*

★ 16   **Lock 19 on Otonabee River:**

Take Sherburne St. south from Lansdowne St. Turn left at Morrow and follow to Lock 19 parking lot—*spawning Walleye and suckers in spring.*

★ 17   **Little Lake:**

Located in the middle of Peterborough, the lake is best viewed from Little Lake Cemetery on Crescent St., Lock 20 on Maria St. and the Mark St. Wharf—*early spring and late fall waterfowl; land migrants in cemetery.*

★ 18 **Jackson Park:**

Located at junction of Parkhill Rd. and Monaghan Rd. in Peterborough—*migrant land birds in spring and fall.*

★ 19 **Jackson Creek Wetlands and Lily Lake:**

From Ackison Rd., follow the rail-trail east through the wetlands for about 1 km to Lily Lake—*wetland birds and mammals.*

★ 20 **Trent University Nature Areas:**

Numerous trails traverse a variety of habitats on both sides of the Otonabee River. These include the Trent Wildlife Sanctuary trails off University Rd., the trail to the Trent Canal Wetlands starting west of University Rd. and the Promise Rock Trail, which extends north from the Science Complex parking lot. The pond at the Archaeological Centre is also worth a visit in the spring—*birds, butterflies, plants, amphibians, etc.*

★ 21 **University Road wetland:**

Located just north of the Warsaw Road (Cty. Rd. 4) on University Rd.—*impressive frog and toad chorus in the spring, wetland birds.*

★ 22 **University Heights Woodland:**

Located along Hetherington Dr. in north end of city—*spring flowers, birds, amphibians.*

★ 23 **Rotary-Greenway Trail:**

Hunter St. East north to Nassau Mills Rd.—*butterflies (especially at north end), birds, lilacs in spring.*

★ 24 **Peterborough Ecology Park and Beavermead Park:**

Located on Ashburnham Dr. just south of Maria St.—*birds (including winter bird feeder trail), butterflies, demonstration gardens including native plants, prairie restoration.*

★ 25 **Meade Creek to Downer's Corners Wetland:**

Located between Ashburnham Rd. and Television Rd.—*wetland birds, amphibians, plants.*

★ 26 **Kawartha Heights Park:**

Located between Kawartha Heights Blvd. and Redwood Dr. Access from south end of Crestwood Ave.—*birds, plants, butterflies.*

★ 27 **Coldsprings Wetland:**

Follow Ashburnham Dr. south of by-pass. Wetland begins just south of C.P.R. tracks—*wetland birds, amphibians, mammals, plants.*

★ 28 **Parkway (proposed) Corridor:**

The section between Hilliard St. and Cumberland Ave. is particularly interesting—*birds (including robins in winter).*

West of Peterborough

★ 29 **Cavan Swamp:**

Can be accessed from Mount Pleasant Rd. (Cty. Rd. 9), Hooton Drive and Hayes Line (Parkhill Road West)—*wetland plants (including orchids), birds, mammals.*

★ 30 **Omemee Sewage Lagoons:**

Follow County Road 7 north from lights in Omemee. Turn left at Beaver Road and continue 500m.—*waterfowl and shorebirds during migration.*

★ 31 **Emily Provincial Park:**

Located in Victoria County. Take Cty. Rd. 10 north from Highway 7 almost to Cty. Rd. 14—*interesting marsh boardwalk, sphagnum island, Ospreys common.*

★ 32 **Emily Tract:**

Located on Victoria Cty. Rd. 14, west of Cty. Rd. 10 and Pigeon Lake—*large Red and White Pine, extensive wetland, spring wildflowers, good birding.*

North and East of Peterborough

★ 33 **River Road:**

Also called Cty. Rd. 32. Located on east bank of Otonabee River between Peterborough and Lakefield—*winter, spring and fall waterfowl, migrating swallows in spring, eagles possible in winter.*

★ 34 **Lakefield Sewage Lagoons:**

On south edge of Lakefield. Turn east off Cty. Rd. 32 (River Road) onto Cty. Rd. 33. Entrance on right but gate usually closed—*ducks and shorebirds.*

★ 35 **Lakefield Marsh:**

Located at south end of Lake Katchewanooka. Near Lakefield Secondary School, turn north off Cty. Rd. 29 onto Clement Street. Turn right on D'eyncourt St. Follow signs. Observation tower and short boardwalk—*wetland birds (including Black Terns and Least Bitterns), plants, migrant ducks.*

★ 36 **Lynch's Rock Rd and Sawer Creek Wetland:**

Follow Highway 134 north almost to Lakefield. Turn east on Strickland Rd., then north on Douro Fifth Line and east on Lynch's Rock Rd. Follow to Sawer Creek Wetland and south along Douro Third Line—*good birding, Sandhill Cranes possible.*

★ 37 **Buckley Lake:**

Located east of Highway 134 and north of Douro Centre Road. Private property as of 1999—*wetland birds (including Sandhill Cranes) and plants.*

★ 38 **Warsaw Caves Conservation Area:**

Take Cty. Rd. 4 north from village of Warsaw. Turn east at Cave Rd. Follow signs—*geologic formations, fossils, birds, plants (including Walking Fern).*

★ 39 **Havelock Sewage Lagoons:**

Turn south in Havelock at junction of Highways 7 and 30. Take the first road on the left (Old Norwood Rd.) Lagoon entrance is the gated gravel drive about 1 km on right—*ducks, shorebirds.*

★ 40 **Sandy Lake Road:**

Turn east off Cty. Rd. 46 just north of Twin Lakes—*birds, butterflies (especially in sedge marshes); moose possible.*

★ 41 **West Kosh Road:**

Take Cty. Rd. 6 north past Northey's Bay Rd. Turn east on West Kosh Rd. just south of Nephton. Follow to Kasshabog Lake—*birds, butterflies, eagles possible at dump.*

★ 42 **Petroglyphs Provincial Park:**

Located on Northey's Bay Rd. (Cty. Rd. 56) just west of Cty. Rd. 6—*birds (including eagles and Gray Jays), butterflies, deer, plants, Five-lined Skinks, etc.*

★ 43 **High Falls Trail:**

Extends from Petroglyphs Provincial Park to High Falls on Eels Creek—*birds, plants (including ferns).*

★ 44 **Northey's Bay Rd.:**

Located between Highway 28 and Cty. Rd. 6 along north shore of Stony Lake—*birds (including eagles in winter), butterflies, deer.*

★ 45 **Haultain Dump:**

Located on east side of Highway 28 just south of Haultain and Eels Creek—*eagles in winter if garbage is available.*

★ 46 **Kawartha Highlands Signature Site:**

Located north of Buckhorn Lake between County Road 507 and Highway 28, covering 35,000 hectares, the Local Stockholder Committee has recommended that the area be given "operating provincial park status" (no decision as of summer 2002)—*a rich array of special features including vast rock barrens high quality bogs, ferns and alvars, rare flora, older forest stands.*

★ 47 **Kawartha Nordic Cross-Country Ski Trails:**

Located on east side of Highway 28 just north of Haultain and Eels Creek—*deer, birds, butterflies, eagles possible in winter.*

★ 48 **Anstruther Lake Road:**

At south end of Apsley, turn west off Highway 28. Follow for several kilometres to dump and beyond—*birds including eagles possible at dump.*

★ 49 **Jack Lake Road:**

Turn south off Cty. Rd. 504 on east side of Apsley. Follow to Jack Lake and then west and south again to gravel pits at end of road—*birds (eagles possible over lake, crossbills in Tamaracks), butterflies, deer.*

★ 50 **The Gut Conservation Area on Crowe River:**

Take Cty. Rd. 504 east to Lasswade. Continue east for about 7 km. Watch for signs—*gorge in basaltic rock, Shield birds, spring wildflowers, etc.*

★ 51 **Oliver Ecological Centre (Trent University):**

From Cty. Rd. 36, turn south onto Mill Line Rd. (about 5.5 km east of Bobcaygeon). Watch for signs—*birds (including Northern Saw-whet Owls in October), plants, etc.*

★ 52 **Galway-Cavendish Forest Access Road:**

Turn west off Cty. Rd. 507 just north of Mississauga Dam Rd.—*excellent butterfly habitat, birds.*

★ 53 **Salmon Lake Road:**

Continue north on Cty. Rd. 507 past Pencil Lake Rd. Turn west on Salmon Lake Rd.—*birds, butterflies, Moose possible.*

★ 54 **Miller Creek Conservation Area:**

Take Seventh Line of Smith about 2 km west from Cty. Rd. 24 or East Communications Rd. 2 km east from Bridgenorth. Observation tower and trails—*wetland birds (including Black Terns, bitterns and rails), amphibians, plants, butterflies, dragonflies.*

★ 55 **Brumwell Street:**

Located south of East Communication Rd (Seventh Line) on east edge of Bridgenorth. Walk from gate down to gravel pit—*birds, butterflies, amphibians, late-summer flowers.*

★ 56 **Ennismore Inn on Pigeon Lake:**

Take Cty Rd. 16 north of Ennismore village to Kerry line. Turn west and follow to lake—*spring and fall waterfowl.*

★ 57 **Gannon's Narrows:**

On Cty. Rd. 16 at junction of Pigeon and Buckhorn Lakes—*waterfowl in winter, spring and fall, eagles possible, otters on ice.*

★ 58 **Six Foot Bay Road to Buckhorn Lake:**

Take Six Foot Bay Rd. south from Lakehurst Rd. near Sandy Lake—*waterfowl in spring and fall.*

★ 59 **Perry Creek on Highway 28:**

On north edge of Burleigh Falls. Creek flows under the first bridge south of junction of County Road 36 and Highway 28—*whitefish spawning in early November.*

★ 60 **Millage Road:**

Turn north off Highway 28 just north of Young's Point onto North School Road. Follow north past the 15th line of Smith to Millage Road—*salamanders at night in spring.*

★ 61 **Clear Lake Road to Clear Lake:**

Turn east off Highway 28 on Clear Lake Rd. 2 km north of Young's Point. Follow to lake—*waterfowl in spring and fall.*

★ 62 **South Beach Road to Clear Lake:**

Turn east off Highway 28 at south end of Young's Point. Check stand of White Pines. Follow road to lake—*waterbirds on lake in spring and fall, land birds in pines.*

★ 63   **Camp Kawartha:**

Turn east off Highway 28 at Birchview Rd. and follow signs to Camp Kawartha. Walk through fields on east side of Birchview Rd. (across from Camp entrance)—*whip-poor-will, Eastern Towhee, American Woodcock, alvar habitat.*

★ 64   **Lake Katchewanooka:**

The water can be viewed from Cty. Rd. 25 on west side of lake and from the bottom of Stenner Rd. off Highway 28 on east side—*waterbirds in fall, winter and spring; eagles in winter.*

A Little Further Afield

Peter's Woods Provincial Nature Reserve:

Rd. 29 to second road on right. Go 2 km south to the reserve—*rich and diverse remnant stand of mature forest with ferns, orchids, spring wildflowers, birds (southern species possible).*

Red Cloud Cemetery:

Located near Warkworth, travel east from Bewdley on Cty. Rd. 9 to Northumberland Cty. Rd. 45. Cross highway and continue east (Cty. Rd. 29) to Dawson Rd. Go south to Red Cloud School Road. Turn east and follow to cemetery on north side of road—*small remnant of original Rice Lake Plains Tallgrass Prairie.*

Carden Plains:

Located northeast of Beaverton, take Cty. Rd. 48 to Kirkfield and then Cty. Rd. 6 north towards Dalrymple. Explore concession roads north and south of the highway—*one of top 10 birding destinations in Ontario, especially for grassland birds (Eastern Bluebird, Upland Plover, etc.); unique alvar plant communities.*

Port Perry Sewage Lagoon:

Located on Scugog Line 8, just north of Port Perry. (Note: permit required – phone 905-985-7973.) —*One of the best locations in Southern Ontario to see shorebirds.*

Presqu'ile Provincial Park:

Located at Brighton on Lake Ontario—*great birding all year long, unique plant communities, staging area for migrant Monarch Butterflies, huge waterfowl concentrations in late winter and early spring.*

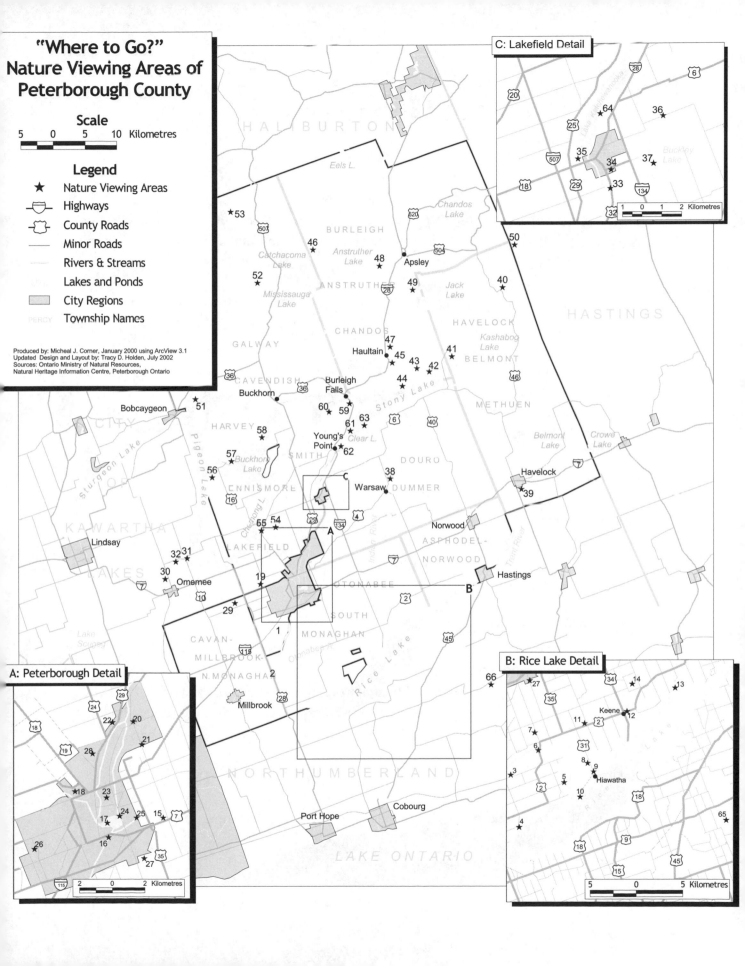

"Where to Go?" Nature Viewing Areas of Peterborough County

Scale

5   0   5   10   Kilometres

Legend

★ Nature Viewing Areas
🛡 Highways
🛡 County Roads
— Minor Roads
— Rivers & Streams
Lakes and Ponds
City Regions
Township Names

Produced by: Micheal J. Corner, January 2000 using ArcView 3.1
Updated Design and Layout by: Tracy D. Holden, July 2002
Sources: Ontario Ministry of Natural Resources,
Natural Heritage Information Centre, Peterborough Ontario

C: Lakefield Detail

1   0   1   2   Kilometres

A: Peterborough Detail

2   0   2   Kilometres

B: Rice Lake Detail

5   0   5   Kilometres

Appendix 2: **Additional Resources**

Federation of Ontario Naturalists

355 Lesmill Rd., Don Mills, ON M3B 2W8   tel. 416-444-8419

web site: www.ontarionature.org   1-800-440-2366

The F.O.N. is a not-for-profit nature and conservation organization that was founded in 1931 to protect and conserve the natural heritage of Ontario. They publish an excellent magazine, *Seasons*, four times a year.

Natural Heritage Information Centre (NHIC)

300 Water St., 2nd Floor, North Tower   tel. 705-755-2159

Peterborough, ON K9J 8M5   fax 705-755-2168

Web site: www.mnr.gov.on.ca/MNR/nhic/nhic.html

The NHIC compiles, maintains and provides information on rare, threatened and endangered species and spaces in Ontario. It is located in the Ministry of Natural Resources building in Peterborough.

Peterborough Field Naturalists

P.O. Box 1532, Peterborough, ON K9J 7H7   tel. 705-742-8644

Web site: www3.sympatico.ca/jbyoung/pfnhome.htm

The Peterborough Field Naturalists hold regular field trips and monthly indoor meetings on a wide variety of topics relating to natural history and conservation. A newsletter, *The Orchid*, is published each month from September to June.

Peterborough Green-Up and Ecology Park

383 George St. N., Peterborough ON K9H 3R2   tel. 705-745-3238

Web site: www.greenup.on.ca

The Green-Up is a non-profit charitable organization with a focus on environmental issues such as waste reduction, water and energy conservation, greenspace enhancement and CO_2 reduction. The Peterborough Ecology Park is a project of the Peterborough Green-Up.

Trent University Nature Areas

tel. 705-748-1011

There are 16 nature areas on this large and ecologically diverse campus. Regular interpretive events are scheduled.

Web site: www.trentu.ca/biology/tna

Otonabee Region Conservation Authority

250 Milroy Drive, Peterborough, ON tel. 705-745-5791

Web site: http://otonabee.com/

O.R.C.A. manages approximately 30 conservation areas in the Otonabee, Indian and Ouse River watersheds. Many of these are of considerable interest to naturalists.

Web Sites of Interest

Amphibians

Amphibians of Ontario—"Frogs and Toads"

www.torontozoo.com/adoptapond/aoo/aoo.html

Ontario amphibian and reptile distribution maps (results of the Ontario Amphibian and Reptile Atlas Project)

www.mnr.gov.on.ca/MNR/nhic/herps/ohs.html

Astronomy

Earth and Sky Homepage

www.earthsky.com/

"This Week's Sky at a glance"

www.skypub.com/sights/sights.shtml

Birds

"Bird Studies Canada"

www.bsc-eoc.org/bscmain.html

"OFO—Ontario Field Ornithologists"

www.interlog.com/~ofo/

General Interest

"Quid Novis Peterborough and Central Ontario" (information source)

www.quidnovis.com

Insects
"Butterfly Watching in Ontario"
www.web-nat.com/Butterfly/

"ODE News Home Page (dragonflies and damselflies)
www.odenews.net

Phenology (seasonal change)
"Journey North 2001"
www.learner.org/jnorth/

"Plantwatch"
www.devonian.ualberta.ca/pwatch/

Wisconsin Phenological Society
www.naturenet.com/alnc/wps/

Plants
"North America Native Plant Society"
www.nanps.org/index.shtml

"The Arboretum—University of Guelph"
www.uoguelph.ca/~arboretu/

Weather
Climate Normals (climate normals for 1971-2000 should appear at this site in late 2002)
www.msc-smc.ec.gc.ca/climate/climate_normals/index_e.cfm

Notes

Chapter 1: January—Silence and Survival

1. Source of 10 most common feeder birds (1999-2000) is Project FeederWatch. Project FeederWatch is a winter-long survey of birds that visit feeders at backyards, nature centres, community areas and other locales in North America. FeederWatchers periodically count the highest numbers of each species they see at their feeders from November through early April. FeederWatch helps scientists track broadscale movements of winter bird populations and long-term trends in bird distribution and abundance. Project FeederWatch is operated by the Cornell Lab of Ornithology in partnership with the National Audubon Society, Bird Studies Canada, and the Canadian Nature Federation.

2. Source of January Weather Averages (1961-1990), Environment Canada. Averages for beyond 1990 were not yet available at the time of publication. All monthly weather averages are from Environment Canada. Canadian Climate Normals 1961-1990, Environment Canada.

Chapter 6: June—Endless Day and the Urgency of Life

1. Hal Borland was an outdoor writer for the *New York Times* from 1941 to 1978. Hal Borland, *Twelve Moons of the Year* (New York: Alfred A. Knopf, 1979) 166.

2. Instructions for building nesting platforms can be obtained from Bird Studies Canada (see Web Sites of Interest in Appendix 2).

3. E.H. Dunn, C.M. Downes and B.T. Collins, "BBS Population Trend Analyses," *BBS Canada: A Newsletter for Cooperators in the Bird Breeding Survey of Canada* (Hull: Canadian Wildlife Service, Winter 2000) 6.

Chapter 7: July—Summer at Its Height

1. A pish is a sound birders make in order to draw birds in closer. You make the sound as though you're saying "Pssst" to someone to get their attention, but draw the sound out and repeat it. Be persistent because it is often very effective.

2. One of the best field guide presently available is a small booklet called *The Dragonflies and Damselflies of Algonquin Provincial Park* published by the Friends of Algonquin

Park and illustrated by Peter Burke, a well-known illustrator and naturalist who grew up in Peterborough. Another more recent publication is Sidney Dunkle, *Dragonflies Through Binoculars: A Field Guide to Dragonflies of North America*. New York: Oxford University Press, 2000.

Chapter 8: August—Summer Becoming Fall

1. For information on available commercial tapes of the calls of crickets, grasshoppers and locusts, see the Bibliography in Georges Pelletier, *Insectes chanteurs du Québec* (L'Acadie, QC: Editions Broquet, 1995). This includes a tape and booklet, available in French only. The only English-language insect song resource found is the following Web site: http://buzz.ifas.ufl.edu/, "Singing Insects of North America."

Chapter 9: September—Mists and Melancholy Joy

1. To contact the province-wide information line regarding Fall colour spots in September and October, call 1-800-567-1140. You may also call 1-800-ONTARIO.

Chapter 11: November—A Hush upon the Land

1. *Forest Plants of Central Ontario*, listed in the Bibliography, is an excellent field guide for identifying the mosses, club mosses and ferns. See Chambers, B.

Chapter 12: December—The Sun Stands Still

1. *Animal Tracks of Ontario* by Ian Sheldon is a useful beginner's guide. See Bibliography for listing.

2. Doug Sadler, *Winter: A Natural History* (Peterborough, ON: Broadview Press, 1990) 20.

3. The Internet is an excellent source of ideas on how to make the winter solstice part of your holiday celebrations. Two excellent sites are:
   http://www.religioustolerance.org/winter_solstice.htm
   http://www.circlesanctuary.org/pholidays/WinterSolstice.html
   The first site, religioustolerance.org, provides information on December celebrations by religions all over the world. The second site, circlesanctuary.org, offers numerous ideas for celebrating not only the winter solstice but other seasonal events as well.

Bibliography

Many of the observations sighted and various comments in the text come from personal communications. Published sources for the book appear below.

Books:

Adams, P. and Taylor, C., ed. *Peterborough and the Kawarthas*. Peterborough, Ontario: Heritage Publications, 1985.

Alsheimer, Charles J., *Whitetail: Behaviour Through The Seasons*. Iola, Wisconsin: Krause Publications, 1996.

Bates, J.A., *Northwoods Companion: Fall & Winter*. Mercer, Wisconsin: Manitowish River Press, 1997.

Bennet, D. and Tiner, T., *Up North Again*. Toronto: McClelland & Stewart, 1997.

Bennet, D. and Tiner, T., *Up North Daybook 1995*. Markham, Ontario: Reed Books, 1995.

Borland, Hal, *Book of Days*. New York: Alfred A. Knopf, 1976.

Borland, Hal, *Twelve Moons of the Year*. New York: Alfred A. Knopf, 1979.

Cadman, M., Eagles, P. and Helleiner, F., *Atlas of the Breeding Birds of Ontario*. Waterloo, Ontario: University of Waterloo Press, 1987.

Chambers, B., *Forest Plants of Central Ontario*. Edmonton: Lone Pine Publishing, 1996.

Connor, Jack, *The Complete Birder*. Boston: Houghton Mifflin Co., 1988.

Dunkle, Sidney, *Dragonflies Through Binoculars. A Field Guide to Dragonflies of North America*. New York: Oxford University Press, 2000.

Heinrich, Bernd, *A Year in the Maine Woods*. Don Mills, Ontario: Addison-Wesley, 1994.

Jauss, Anne Marie, *Discovering Nature the Year Round*. New York: E.P. Dutton & Co., 1955.

Lawrence, R. D., *The Place in the Forest*. Toronto: Natural Heritage, 1998.

_____, *Where the Water Lilies Grow*. Toronto: Natural Heritage, 1999.

Layberry, Ross A. *The Butterflies of Canada*. Toronto: University of Toronto Press, 1998.

Leopold, Aldo, *A Sand County Almanac*. New York: Ballantine Books, 1970.

Logier, E.B., *The Snakes of Ontario*. Toronto: University of Toronto Press, 1958.

Nelson, Roger, *A Dales Naturalist*. Skipton, North Yorkshire, UK: Dalesman Publishing Co., 1993.

Pelletier, Georges, *Insectes chanteurs du Québec.* L'Acadie, Québec: Editions Broquet, 1995.

Peterborough Field Naturalists. *Kawarthas Nature.* Erin, Ontario: Boston Mills Press, 1992.

Rey, H.A., *The Stars.* Boston: Houghton Mifflin, 1980.

Sadler, Doug, *Winter: A Natural History.* Peterborough, Ontario: Broadview Press, 1990.

Scott, W.B., *Freshwater Fishes of Eastern Canada.* Toronto: University of Toronto Press, 1967.

Serrao, John, *Nature's Events.* Harrisburg, Pennsylvania: Stackpole Books, 1992.

Sheldon, Ian, *Animal Tracks of Ontario.* Edmonton: Lone Pine Publishing, 1997.

Stokes, D. and Stokes, L., *A Guide to Bird Behaviour: Volume III.* Toronto: Little, Brown and Company, 1989.

Stokes, Donald, *A Guide to Nature in Winter.* Toronto: Little, Brown and Company, 1976.

Stokes, Donald, *A Guide to Observing Insect Lives.* Toronto: Little, Brown and Company, 1983.

Strickland, Dan and Rutter, Russ, *The Best of the Raven.* Whitney, Ontario: The Friends of Algonquin Park, 1993.

Teale, Edwin Way, *A Walk Through the Year.* New York: Dodd, Mead, and Co., 1987.

Theberge, John B., ed., *Legacy: The Natural History of Ontario.* Toronto: McClelland & Stewart, 1989.

Magazines, periodicals, newspapers:

Burke, P., Jones, C., Line, J., Oldham, M. and Sorrill, P., *1998 Peterborough County Natural History Summary.* Peterborough Field Naturalists: Peterborough Natural Heritage Information Centre, and Trent University, 1999.

Carpentier, Geoff, *The Mammals of Peterborough County.* Peterborough, Ontario: Peterborough Field Naturalists, 1987.

Dunn, E.H., Downes, C.M. and Collins, B.T., "BBS Population Trend Analysis," *BBS Canada, A Newsletter for Cooperators in the Breeding Bird Survey of Canada.* (Hull: Canadian Wildlife Service, Winter 2000) 6.

Leopold, A. and Jones, S.E., "A Phenological Record for Sauk and Dane Counties, Wisconsin, 1935-45" *Ecological Monographs.* Vol. 17, No. 1 (1947).

Marsh Monitoring Program—Training Kit. 2001 Revised Edition. Published by Bird Studies Canada in cooperation with Environment Canada and the U.S. Environmental Protection Agency.

Marsh Monitoring Program—Training Tape (Amphibians and Birds). 2001 Revised Edition. Produced by Bird Studies Canada in cooperation with Environment Canada and the U.S. Environmental Protection Agency.

Ministry of Natural Resources (Ontario). 1997. *Deer Conservation in Winter.*

Monroe, Burt. "Summary of highest counts for individuals for Canada and the United States." *American Birds*—90th Christmas Bird Count. Vol. 44, No. 4 (1990).

Philipp, D.P. and M.R. Gross, "Genetic Evidence for Cucklodry in Bluegill Lepomis marcrochirus," *Molecular Ecology* (3): 1994, 563-569.

Sadler, Doug, *Our Heritage of Birds.* Peterborough, Ontario: Peterborough Field Naturalists, 1983.

Sadler, Doug, "The 1995-1997 Great Gray Owl Invasions in the Peterborough Area" *Ontario Birds*, Volume 16, Number 2 (1988).

Whelan, Peter, "Birds" (column) *Globe and Mail*, 1985-1999.

Whittam, B. and Francis, C.M., "Project Feeder Watch Canadian Summary 1999-2000." *Birdwatch Canada*, No. 14. Port Rowan, Ontario: Bird Studies Canada, Fall 2000, 1.

Personal Communication:

■ Brock Fenton, January 2, 2001.
■ Brad White, March 20, 2000.

Index

Page numbers in bold face type refer to tables or illustrations

A

Air masses, 176, 294
Air Quality Index (AQI), 200
Alavar habitat, 304-306
Algae: 147
    late summer bloom of, 196
    spring bloom of, 147
    Aphanizomenon flos-aquae,
      147
    blue-green, 147, 196
    filamentous, 147
    Microcystis, 196
Algonquin Park, 96, 101, 182,
    188, 189, 222, 228, 285
American Birds, 288
Amphibians (see frogs and
toads; salamanders)
Andromeda Galaxy, 232
Anstruther Lake Road, 304
Anthony, Anne, 240
Ant(s): 58, 120
    flying, 218
    carpenter, 272
Apsley (ON), 3, 27, 146, 228,
    261, 262, 304
Armour Hill (Peterborough),
    154
Aurora Borealis (see Northern
Lights)

B

BBS (see Breeding Bird Survey)
Badger(s), 38, 39
Bancroft (ON), 182, 228
Bats: 7, 28, 74, 126, 131-134,
    164, 206, 214
    Big Brown, 132, 182, 213,
      214, 241
    birth of young, 126, 132
    cleansing flights of, 7
    Eastern Pipistrelle, 215
    Eastern Small-footed, 215
    echolocation by, 132
    hibernation of, 7, 74, 182,
      213-215
    Hoary, 214
    Little Brown, 132, 134, 188,
      213, 214
    mating, 182, 206, 215
    migration of, 213, 214
    Northern Long-eared, 215
    observing bats, 132
    Red, 132, 213, 214
    Silver-haired, 214
    swarming of, 215
Baxter Creek, 246
Bear, Black: 2, 8, 74, 75, 83, 117,
    131, 160, 164, 165, 188, 213,
    258, 263, 264
    bear's nests, 188
    birth of cubs, 2, 8
    den of, 264

dependence on berries, 75,
    165
emergence in spring, 74, 75
how to see, 75
mating, 132, 160
Beaver(s): 2, 7, 74, 101, 126, 131,
    213, 262
    mating, 7
Beavermead Park, 323
Beaverton (ON), 306
Bee(s): 55, 58, 60, 66, 150
    Honey, 11, 117, 218, 271
    overwintering of, 11, 271
Beetles: 141, 190
    bark, 12
    firefly, fireflies, 126, 141, **143**,
      144, 168
      how to see, 141, 144
      mating strategies of, 144
    June, 96, 107, 141, 143
    ladybird, 55, 247, 271
    long-horned, 218
    soldier, 218
    whirligig, 167
Belleville (ON), 215
Belmont Lake, 81
Bensfort Bridge, 299
Bensfort Road landfill, 258, 259,
283, 299
Bewdley (ON), 306
Birchview Road, 141
Bird Studies Canada, 129
Birding (birders) (See also each

of months): 97, 99, 100, 240, 259, 286, 288, 299, 300, 302, 306

August opportunities, 186

finding birds in winter, 285

identifying fall warblers, 207, 211

November, 259

pishing, 161, 207, 210, 211, 285

winter birding season, 254

Birds: 99, 110, 120, 191, 235, 257, 281, 287, 301-306

arrivals and departures of (tables), 26, 46, 68, 98, 128, 162, 185, 208, 239, 260, 285

bird song (see vocalizations)

Bitterns: 305

American, 47, **68, 239**

Least, **98, 185, 303**

Blackbird(s): 26, 160, 206, 207, 209, 236, 237, 240

Red-winged, 23, **43-46**, 47, 60, 61, **130**, 161, 163, 209, 238, 239, 257

post-breeding flocks of, 163

Rusty, **46, 208**, 209, **239**

Bluebird(s): 4, 239

Eastern, xv, 45, 46, 128, **239, 289**, 306

Bobolink, **95, 131**, 147, **208**

Breeding Bird Survey(s) (BBS), 126, 127, 129, 130

Bufflehead, **46**, 49, **68, 70, 239, 260**

Buntings:

Indigo, **94**, 97, **98**, 122, **131, 158**, 183, **208, 289**

Snow, 25, 28, **47, 239**, 285, **289**

calls (see vocalizations)

Canvasback, **46**, 49, **68, 239, 260**

Cardinal(s): 23, 24, 26, 65, 67

Northern, **6, 22**, 25, 47, **131**, 240, 286, **289**

Catbird, Gray, **98, 130, 131, 209**

Chickadee(s), 1, 3, 4, 23, 24, 26, 59, 210, 257, 285

Black-capped, 3, **6**, 11, 25, 26, 49, **130, 131**, 240, **280, 288**

Boreal, 5

Christmas Bird Count, 281, 282, 283, 286, 288, **289**

Christmas Bird Count Species (table), **289**

Coot, American, **68, 239, 260**

Cormorant, Double-crested, **68, 239**

Cowbird, Brown-headed, 46, 47, **209**

Crane(s): 26

Sandhill, **46, 239, 303**

courtship dance of, 46

Creeper, Brown, 25, **68, 208, 239, 289**

Crossbill(s): 3, 13, 27, 304

nesting of, 27

Red, 5, 27, 285

White-winged, 5, 27, 207, **208**, 285

Crow, American, 23-**26**, 28, 45, 49, 128, **131**, 161, 186, 209, 236, 237, 240, 257, 259, **260, 288**

Cuckoo, Black-billed, 98, 111, 185

Dawn chorus (see vocalizations)

Dove(s):

Mourning, **6**, 25, 26, 47, 49, 65, 92, 128, **131**, 183, 240, 286, **288**

Rock, 131, **288**

Dowitcher, Short-billed, **98**, 186

diving ducks, 108, 236, 238, 258, 259, 266

Duck(s): 185, 235, 259, 261, 262, 282, 284, 285, 299, 300, 302, 303

American Black, **46, 68, 70, 239, 260**, 283

Long-tailed, **98**, 238, **239, 260**

Ring-necked, **46**, 49, **68, 70**, 108, **185, 260**

Ruddy, **68, 98, 239, 260**

Wood, **46, 50, 70, 239**

Dunlin, **98**, 128, **239, 260**

Eagle(s): 259-261, 262, 282-285, 290, 302-304

Bald, xv, 2, 3, 46, 47, 75, **239**, 257, 258, **260-262, 288**

nesting of, 46

feeding behaviour of, 261

how to see, 261

Golden, 46, **239**, 258, **260**, 261

Egret, Cattle, 240

Falcon, Peregrine, **209, 239**

Feeder(s), 283, 286, 288, 290

feeder birds (table), **6**

Finch(es): 2, 3, 5

House, 25, 47, 49, **131**, 240, 286, **289**

Purple, 5, 25, **130, 185**, 208, 240, **289**

Flicker, Northern , **46, 131, 208, 239**

Flycatchers: 97, 128, 207

Alder, **98, 208**

Great Crested, **98, 130, 131, 208**

Least, **98, 130, 208**

Olive-sided, **98, 185**

Willow, **98**

Yellow-bellied. **98, 185, 208**

Gadwall, **46, 68, 185, 239**
Geese: 26, 185, 205, 235, 236, 239
  Canada, 25, 45, 66, 72, 73, 96, 209, 237, 239
    nesting of, 45
    sub-species of, 73
  "Giant" Canada, **26**, 46, 68, 73, 97, 208, 239, **285**
    moult migration of, 97, 98
  Hutchins' Canada, 73
  "Northern" Canada, 68, 73, 97, 208, **209**, 237, 239, 240
    fall migration of, 208, 237
    spring migration of, 68
  Snow, **46**, 49, **68**, 73, **239**, **260**
Goshawk, Northern, 5
Goldeneye(s): 27
  Barrow's, 3
  Common, 2, 3, 25, **26**, 49, **68, 70**, 238, **239**, **262**, 283, **285, 288**
    courtship behaviour of, 25
Goldfinch, American, 5, **6**, 131, 185, 240, 286, **289**
Grackle, Common, **46**, 47, 67, 128, **130**, 161, 163, 209, **239**
    nesting of, 67
Grebes: 258
  Horned, **68, 98, 239**
  Pied-billed, **46**, 49, **50, 70, 239**
  Red-necked, **68, 98, 208, 239**
Grosbeak(s):
  Evening, 5, 65, **98**, 238, **287, 289**
  Pine, 5, **46**, 238, **239**, 259, 273, **289**

Rose-breasted, 47, 97, **98, 130, 209**
    at feeders, 97
groundings of, 99
Grouse: 4, 65
  Ruffed, 3, 18, 45, 51, 67, 208, 237, **288**
    drumming of, 51, 67, 237
    strange behaviour of, 237
Gulls: 129, 236, 237, 240, 258, 259, 283, 285, 299
  Bonaparte's, **185, 239**
  Glaucous, 47, 258-**260**, 283, **284**
  Great Black-backed, **47**, 259, **260**, 283
  Herring, **26, 46, 68, 131, 239, 288**
  Iceland, 47, 258-**260**, 283
  Ring-billed, **46, 131, 162**, 187, 209, 210, **285, 288**
Harrier, Northern, **46**, 147, **239, 260**
Hawk(s): 207, 261, 282, 286
  Broad-winged, **68**, 207, **208**
    fall migration of, 207
  Cooper's, **46, 239**, 286, **288**
  Red-shouldered, **46, 239**
  Red-tailed, 27, **46, 48, 259, 260**, 285, **288**
    courtship behaviour of, 27
    fall migration of, 259
  Rough-legged, 5, 238, **239**, 258, **260**, 285
  Sharp-shinned, **68**, 208, 286, **288**
Herons: 285
  Great Blue, **46, 260, 289**
  Green, **68, 239**
Hummingbird (s), 96, 97, 127, 161, 163
  Ruby-throated, 36, 85, **98**, 126, **208, 289**

at feeders, 97
at sapsucker drillings, 85, 97
courtship flight of, 126, 127
emptying crop, 163
Broad-billed, 240
Ibis, Glossy, 240
Jay(s):
  Blue, xx, **6**,47, 49, 67, **98, 128, 130, 131**, 183, 187, **204-207, 208**, 240, **288**
    calls of, 183, 187, 207
    exodus southward, 207
    nesting of, 67
  Grey, 5, 45, 285, **288**, 303
Junco, Dark-eyed, **6**, 47, 67, **68**, 207, **209**, 212, **239**, 240, **289**
    April abundance of, 67
Kestrel, American, **46**, 208
Killdeer, **46**, 47, 92, **131**, 183, 207, **260, 289**
Kingbird, Eastern, **98, 130, 131, 208**
Kingfisher, Belted, **46, 239**, 285
Kinglet(s): 66, 210, 257
  Golden-crowned, **46**, 208, 237, 240, **260, 289**
  Ruby-crowned, **68**, 95, **98, 208**, 237, **239**
Lark(s):
  "Northern" Horned, **209**, 285
  "Prairie" Horned, 23-**26**, 28
Longspur, Lapland, **239**
Loon, Common, 67, 68 **70**, 97, 100, 127, 128, **131**, 183, 185, 257-**260**, 261, 282, 283, **289**
    April arrival of, 67, **68**
    baby loons, 127, 129
    convocations of, 183, 185, 186

calls and displays of, 100, 186

protection of, 129

trapped by ice, 261, 284

Mallard, **46**, 49, **68**, **70**, 127, **162**, **260**, 283, **288**

Martin, Purple, **68**, **131**, **185**

Meadowlark, Eastern, 45, **46**, **131**, 147, 208, **239**

Mergansers: 238

Common, 2, 3, 25, **26**, **26**, 49, **68**, **70**, 161, **260**, 283, **285**, **288**, **289**

family groups of, 161

Hooded, xx, **46**, 49, **50**, **68**, **70**, **239**, **260**, 283

Red-breasted, **239**, **260**

Merlin, **68**, **185**, **239**

Migration (migrants) of, 24, 26, 28, 61, 96-100, 122, 125-128, 181, 183, 185, 186, 205-207, 236, 241, 259

fall migration, 159, 161, 162, 163, 210, 211

Moorhen, Common, **68**, 208

moulting of, 97, 98, 160, 161, 185

nests (nesting) of, 126, 128, 185

Nighthawk, Common: **98**, 110, **131**, 159, 161, 183, 186, **187**, **208**

migration of, 182, 183, 186

Nuthatch(es), 3, 4, 210

Red-breasted, 5, 25, 47, **185**, 187, 240, **289**

White-breasted, **xxii**, 1, 3, 6, 25, 26, 240, **289**

Oldsquaw (see Long-tailed Duck)

Oriole: 97

Baltimore, xx, **98**, **131**, **185**, **289**, 302

Osprey(s): 61, **68**, 127, **131**, 162, **208**, **289**

hatching of, 127

Ovenbird, 47, **98**, **130**, 211

Owl(s): 3, 6-8, 26, 44, 45, 50, 259, 286

Barred, 25, 27, 47, 50, 51, 67, 183

peak calling of, 50, 67, 183

winter wandering by, 25, 27

Boreal, 5

Eastern Screech, 50, 51, 283, 299

Great Gray, 5, 6, 8, 47, 50, 285

Great Horned, 2, 3, 24, 27, 45, 50, 260, 283, **288**

nesting of, 45

Long-eared, **239**, **260**

Northern Hawk, 5, **47**, 50

Northern Saw-whet, **46**, **209**, 237-239, 241, **260**, 304

fall banding of, 241

Snowy, 5, 6, **47**, 50, 257, 259, **260**, 279, 282, 285

pair bonds of, 26, 186

Parula, Northern, **98**, 208

Phalarope, Wilson's, **98**, **128**

Phoebe, Eastern, 45, **46**, 51, **131**, 208

Pintail, Northern, **46**, **68**, 70, 162, **185**, **239**

Pipit, American, **98**, 207, **208**, 209, **260**

Plovers:

Black-bellied, 207, **208**, **239**

Semipalmated, **98**, **128**, **185**, 186

Upland, 306

Rail(s): 66, **305**

Virginia, **68**, 208

Raven, Common, xiv, 25, 27, 45, 261, 281

aerial displays of, 25, 27

Redhead, 46, 49, **68**, **239**, **260**

Redpoll(s): 3

Common, 5, **6**, **68**, 238, 259, **260**, **289**

Hoary, 5

Redstart, American, **98**, **130**, **208**, 211

Robin(s): 3, 26, 44, 65, 67, 127, 130, 207, 210, 237, 240, 257, 259, 273, 287, 302

American, 3, **4**, 18, 26, 43, 45, **46**, 47, 49, 60, 61, 67, 128, **131**, 208, 210, 258, **260**, **288**, **289**

fall flocks of, 210

first of spring, 44-46

overwintering of, 3, 18

Sandpipers:

Baird's, 186

Least, **98**, **128**, **162**, 186, **208**

Pectoral, **68**, **98**, **162**, 186, 207, **260**

Semipalmated, **128**, **162**, **185**, 186

Solitary, **98**, **162**, 186, **208**

Spotted, **98**, **185**

Stilt, 186

Upland, **68**

White-rumped, **239**, **260**

Sapsucker, Yellow-bellied: 64, 67, **68**, 84, 85, 97

courtship drumming of, 67

drillings of, 97

Scaup: 108, 238

Greater, **46**, 49, **68**, **70**, **239**, **260**

Lesser, **46**, 49, **50**, **70**, **208**, **260**

Scoters: 238

Black, **239**, **260**

Surf, **239**, **260**

White-winged, **98, 239, 260**

shorebirds, 66, 127, 159, 160, 161, **163**, 178, 182, 183, 186, 207, 299, 302, 306

Shoveler, Northern, **46, 68, 70, 185, 239**

Shrike, Northern, xx, 5, **68, 239**, 257-259, 285, **288**

Siskin, Pine, 5, 27, **98**, 238, **239**, 259, **289**

Snipe, Common: 45, **46**, 51, 65, 67, 69, **239, 260**
    courtship flight of, 67

Sora, **68, 208**

Sparrow(s): 66, 67, 92, 205, 206, 235-237, 259
    American Tree, 46, 47, 67, **68, 239**, 257-259, **289**
    Chipping, **68, 131, 239**
    Clay-coloured, **98**
    Field, **68, 131, 239**
    Fox, **68**, 236, 237, **239, 240, 260**
    Grasshopper, **98, 185**
    House, 26, 45, 49, **131**, 286, **289**
    Lincoln's, **98, 208**
    Savannah, **68, 131**, 147, **239**
    Song, 41, 45, 46, 47, **131**, 183, **239**
    Swamp, **68, 130, 239**
    Vesper, **68, 239**
    White-throated, **68**, 95, 205, **208**, 212, 237, **239**, 240, 257, **289**
        at feeders, 207, 212
        fall singing of, 205, 208, 237
    White-crowned, xx, **98**, 207, **208**, 212, 237, **239**, 240

Starling(s): 23, 45, 160, 163
    European, 3, **6**, 25, 49, **131**, 209, **288**

survival in cold weather, 4

Swallow(s): 66, 67, 110, 160, 161, 163, 181, 183, 207
    on wires, 160, 161, 181, 183
    Bank, 68, 162, **185**
    Barn, **68**, 131, 180, **185**, 289
    Cliff, **68, 185**
    Northern Rough-winged, 68, 162, **185**
    Tree, xv, 26, 44, **46**, 51, 56, 66, 67, 71, **72, 130, 131, 208, 289**
        first of spring, 44, 46
        huge flocks of, 67, 71

Swan, Tundra, 46, 49, 185

Swift, Chimney, **68**, 126, 127, **131, 208**
    courtship flight of, 126, 127

Tanager: 97
    Scarlet, **98, 209**

Teal:
    Blue-winged, 46, **68, 70**, 162, **239**
    Green-winged, 46, 70, **239, 260**

Terns:
    Black, **98, 185**, 303, 304
    Caspian, **68**, 161, **162, 208**
    Common, **98, 185**

Thrasher, Brown, **68, 131, 208**

Thrush(es): 97, 159, 207, 208
    Gray-cheeked, **98, 208**
    Hermit, **68, 130**, 161, **239**
    night calls of, 208
    Swainson's, **98, 185, 208**
    Wood, **98, 130**, 161, **208**

Towhee, Eastern, 47, **68, 239**, 306

Turkey, Wild, 68

Veery, **98, 130**, 161, **185**

Vireo(s): 97, 205, 207, 210
    Blue-headed, **68, 208, 239**
    Philadelphia, **98, 185, 208**
    Red-eyed, xvi, **98, 130, 131**,

183, **184**, 186, **208**
    Warbling, **98, 130, 131, 208**
    Yellow-throated, **98**

vocalizations of (bird song), 3, 24, 25, 43-45, 47, 126, 127, 130, 159, 160, 161, 168, 183, 208, 210
    calls of August, 181, 183, 187
    contact calls, 210
    dawn chorus, 127, 130
    in March, 43
    in July, 159, 160, 161, 168
    learning bird song, 47, 49

Vulture, Turkey, **46**, 208, **239**, 261, **289**

Wading birds, 67

Warblers: 61, 66, 97, 159, 185, 186, 205, 207, 210, 211, 237
    arrival in May, 61, 97
    Bay-breasted, **98, 185, 209**
    Black-and-white, **98**, 99, **130, 209**
    Blackburnian, **98, 208**
    Blackpoll, xx, **98, 185, 209**
    Black-throated Blue, **98**, 211, **239**
    Black-throated Green, **98, 130**, 211, **239**
    Canada, **98, 208**, 211
    Cape May, **98, 185, 208**
    Cerulean, xix, **98, 185**
    Chestnut-sided, **98, 131, 208**, 211
    fall identification of, 211
    Golden-winged, **98, 185**
    Magnolia, **98**, 128, **239**
    Mourning, **98, 208**
    Nashville, **98**, 211, **239**
    Orange-crowned, **209, 239**
    Palm, **98, 208, 239**
    peak fall migration of, 183, 211
    Pine, **68, 239**

Prairie, **98, 185**

Tennessee, **98, 185, 239**

Wilson's, **98, 128, 185, 208**

Yellow, **98, 130, 131**, 161, 162, 211, **289**

Yellow-rumped, **68**, 130, **185, 208**, 211, 237, 240, 247, **260, 289**

waterfowl, 26, 44, 49, **50**, 66, 70, 208, 261, 285, 299, 300, 302, 305, 306

waterfowl count totals (table), 70

waterfowl migration, 162, 236

Waterthrush, Northern, **68**, **130, 162, 185**, 211

Waxwing(s): 273, 288
  Bohemian, 5, 6, **68**, 257, 259, **260, 289**
  Cedar, 5, **98**, 185, 187, **209, 289**

Whimbrel, **98**, 183

Whip-poor-will(s), **98**, 159, 161, **208**, 306

Wigeon, American, **46, 68, 70**, 162, **185, 239**

winter destinations of (table), **289**

winter finches, 257, 259, 285, 286, 288

Woodcock, American, xvi, 45, **46**, 51, 65, 67, 69, 92, **239, 289**, 306
  courtship flight of, 67, 69

Woodpecker(s): 3, 25, 65, 67, 257
  Black-backed, 5, 285, **288**
  Downy, 1, **6**, 11, **288**
  Hairy, **288**
  Pileated, 1, 3, **272, 288**
  Red-headed, **98**
  Three-toed, 5

Wood-Pewee, Eastern, 36, **98**, 183, **208**

Wrens:
  House, 26, **98, 131, 208**
  Marsh, **208**
  Sedge, **98**
  Winter, **68, 208, 239**

Yellowlegs:
  Greater, **68, 98**, 162, 186, **260**
  Lesser, **68, 98**, 162, 186, **208**
  Yellowthroat, Common, **98**, **130, 131, 239**

Bird Studies Canada, 129

Blackfly(flies), 11, 12, 96, 107, 108, 169, 271
  blood meals, 108, 109
  in winter, 11, 271
  larvae, 11, 12, 108, 271
  life cycle of, 12, 108

Bobcaygeon (ON), vii, 67, 304

Bogs, 150, 304
  sphagnum, 147

Borland, Hal, 125

Briar Hill Pond, 299

Bridgenorth (ON), 275, 305

Brighton (ON), 49, 306

Buckhorn, 68, 228, 241

Buckhorn Lake, xvii, 49, 67, 70, 261, 268, 282, 283, 304, 305

Buckhorn Wildlife Art Festival, 182

Buckley Lake, 163, 303

Bugs: 190
  ambush, 218
  Giant Water, 141, 143
  Large Milkweed, 190
  Strider, water, 167

Bumblebee: 106, 117, 271
  in winter, 271
  queen, 106, 271

Burleigh Falls (ON), 172, 267, 285

Butterflies: 83-85, 96, 140, 141, 144-146, 190, 219, 246, 247, 268, 301, 303, 304

Admiral:
  Red, 145, **169**, 220
  White, 126, 141, **145, 169**

Arctic, Chryxus, 106, **112**

Azure:
  Spring, 66, 83, **112**
  Summer, **145**

Blue, Silvery, **145**

Brown, Eyed, 45, **169**

Buckeye, Common, 141

butterfly-watching: 141, 144
  in June, 141, 144
  in May, 106
  in September, 219, 220
  Presqu'ile Provincial Park, 219, 220

Checkerspot, Baltimore, **169**

Cloudywing, Northern, **112**, 145

Comma, Eastern, 55, 66, 83, 112

counting of, 146

Crescent, Northern, 144, **145**, **195**

Duskywing:
  Columbine, **112**
  Dreamy, **112**
  Juvenal's, **112**

Elfin: 84
  Eastern Pine, **112**
  Henry's, **112**
  Hoary, **112**

Fritillary(ies): **123**, 160, 167
  Atlantis, **145, 169**
  Great-Spangled, **169**
  Meadow, **169, 195**
  Silver-bordered, **169**

Hairstreak: 123
  Acadian, **169**
  Banded, **145**
  Early, **83**

Lady (Ladies):
  American, **145, 169**, 220
  Painted, 220

Marble, Olympia, 106, **112**
Monarch, 134, 141, **145**, **169**, 182, 190, **195**, **203**, 206, 218, 219, 246, 258, 268, 306
   at Presqu'ile Provincial Park, 219, 220
   caterpillars, 190
   in Mexico, 141, 219, 220, 258, 268
   migration of, 206, 218
Mourning Cloak, 44, 55, 66, 83, **84**, 85, **112**, 145, **169**, 246, 270
Nymphalis, 84
of early spring, 106
of early summer (table), **145**
of late summer and early fall (table), **195**
of May (table), **112**
of mid-summer (table), **169**
Pearly-eye, Northern, **145**, **169**
Peterborough County
butterfly count, 146
   Polygonia, 84
Question Mark, **145**, **169**
Ringlet, Common, **145**, **195**
Skipper: 83
   Arctic, **145**
   Dun, **145**, **169**
   European, 141, 144, **145**, 146
   Hobomok, **112**, **145**
   Least, **169**
   Long Dash, **145**
   Mulberry Wing, **169**
   Peck's, **145**
   Tawny-edged, **145**
Sulphur(s): 182, 190, 219, 236, 246
   Clouded, **145**, **195**, **203**, 219, 268
   Orange, **169**, **195**, 219
Swallowtail(s), 126, 141
   "puddling," 107

Black, 107, **169**
Canadian Tiger, 107, **112**, **145**, 270
   in winter, 270
Sympetrum, 182, 191, 236, 247, 258
Tortoiseshell(s): 55, 83, 258
   Compton, 55, 84, **112**, 246, 268
   Milbert's, **112**, **145**, **169**
Viceroy, **145**, **169**, **195**
White:
   Cabbage, **112**, **145**, **169**, **195**
   Mustard, **112**, **145**, **169**, **195**
   West Virginia, 106, **112**
Wood-Nymph, Common, **169**
Wood-Satyr, Little, **145**, **169**
Butterfly-watching, 112, 160, 300

C

CN railway bed, 145, 300
Caddisflies, 134
Camp Kawartha, 305, 306
Canadian Shield, xvii, xviii, 25, 75, 76, 89, 106, 108, 144, 146, 152, 186, 190, 205, 227, 276, 281, 304
Carden Plains, 306
Caribou, 18
Caterpillars: 107, 110, 190, 195
   American Dagger Moth, 219, 221
   Eastern Tent, 11, **12**, 110, 167, 220, 270
   egg masses of, 11, 12, 110
   life cycle of, 110
   Fall Webworm, 182, 191, 219, **220**
   webs of , 182, 220
   life cycle of, 220
   Forest Tent, 96, 110
   life history of, 111
   predation of, 110, 111

Gypsy Moth, 107, 111-112
   host trees of, 111
   life cycle of, 111-112
   infestations of, 111
Woolly Bear, 83, 219, **221**, 270
   to forecast winter, 221
   in September, 221
   in spring, 83
Yellow Bear, 219, 221
Cavan Creek, 246
Cavan Swamp, xviii, 145, 149, 189, 302
Chandos Lake, 27, 50, 81
Chemong Lake, xvii, 81, 82, 268
Centreton (ON), 89
Chipmunk(s): 8, 44, 51, 132, 213, 214, 236, 242, 252, 263
   Eastern, 214, **243**
   den of, 242
   preparations for winter, 214
Chlorophyll, 224, 225
Christmas tree(s), 281, 283, 292, 293
Cicadas: 160, 168, 181, 182, 190, 191, 192, 194, 219
   Dogday, 194
   Periodical (*Magicada*), 194
   sound of, 181, 190, 191, 194, 219
Clear Lake, xvii, 70, 79, 81, 89, 141, 210, 268, 305
Clear Lake Road, 305
Clouds, 176, 207, 294
Climate change, xvi, 26, 58, 61, 284
Club-mosses, 258, 273, 276
   in late fall and winter, 258, 273, 276
   Ground Pine (*Lycopodium dendroideum*), 273, 276
Coldsprings Wetland, 302
Coltesloe area, 240
Comets:
   Swift-Tuttle, 202

Constellations: 19-21, 39, 40, 62, 63, 91, 122, 155-157, 178, 179, 201, 202, 230-233, 254, 255, 277, 278, 296, 297

Andromeda, 19, 39, 62, 201, 230, 232, **233**, 254, 278, 296

Aquarius, 122

Aquila, 155, 157, 179, 201, 230, 254, 277

Auriga, 2, 19, 24, 39, 62, 91, 122, 277, 282, 296-**298**

Big Dipper, 2, **21**, 24, 39, 40, 44, 62, 63, 91, 96, 122, 126, 160, 179, 182, 206, 236, 258

Boötes, 62, **63**, 91, 122, 155, 178, 201, 230

Canis Major, 2, 19, 24, 39, 40, 62, 91, 282, 296-**298**

Canis Minor, 2, 24, 39, 40, 62, 91, 282, 297

Cassiopeia, 19-**21**, 39, 62, 91, 122, 155, 178, 201, 206, 230, 232, **233**, 254, 278, 282, 296

Corona Borealis, 122

Cygnus, 155-157, 179, 201, 230, 254, 277

Draco, 19

Gemini, 19, 24, 39, 40, 62, 122, 231, 296, 297

Great Square of Pegasus, 19, 39, 178, 206, 230, 232, **233**, 236, 258, 297

Leo (Lion), 19, 20, 39, 43, 44, 62, **63**, 91, 96, 122, 155, 178, 278

Lepus, 40

Little Dipper, 19-21, 39, 62

Lyra, 155, 157, 178, 179, 230, 254

Northern Cross, 179

Orion, xvi, 2, 19, 20, 24, 39, 40, 62, 91, 122, 201, 236, 254, 258, 278, 282, 296, 297, **298**

Perseus, 156, 160, 201, 202, 282, 298

Pleiades (Seven Sisters), 19, 39, 40, 62, 91, 230, 258, 278, 296, **298**

Sagittarius, 155, 156, 178, 201, 230, 254

Scorpius, 40, 201, 231

Summer Triangle, 126, 155, 160, 178, 179, 182, 201, 230, 254, 277, 296

Taurus, 19, 24, 39, 40, 62, 91, 231, 278, 297, **298**

Ursa Major, 19-21, 122, 155, 178, 201, 230, 254, 277, 296

Ursa Minor, 19-21, 122, 155, 178, 201, 230, 254, 277, 296

Virgo, 62, **63**, 91, 96, 122, 178

Winter Six, 2, 19

Cordova Lake, 81

Cottontail, Eastern, 52

mating of, 52

Coyote(s), 2, 7, 8, 29, 31, 44, 52, 53, 188, 189, 214, 258, 261, 262

birth of young, 52

calls of, 7, 189

how to see, 189

hybridization with wolves, 189

mating, 29

Crayfish: 11, 106

Rusty, 106

Cricket(s): 141, 168, 181, 182, 190, 191, 205, 206, 219, 235, 236, 257

description of song (table), **194**

Field (*Gryllus spp.*), **192**, 268, 270

Spring Field, 107

ground (*Nemobiinae*), 192, **194**

Snowy Tree (*Oecanhus fultoni*), 193, **194**, 236, 247

to calcuate air temperature, 191, 193

tree (*Oecanthinae*), 193, **194**

where to hear, 193

Crowe Lake, xvii, 81

Crowe River, 304

Curve Lake First Nation Reserve, 261

D

Damselflies: 96, 106, **113**, 126, 140, 160, 167, 168, 169

Bluet, 113, 142

Boreal, **113**

Hagen's, **142**

Marsh, **142**

Forktail, Eastern, **113**, 142

Jewelwing, Ebony, **142**

mating of, 169

of late spring and early summer (table), **142**

of May (table), **113**

Daylight Saving Time, 253

Deciduous forest(s), 130

Deer Bay, 70

Deer, White-tailed: xix, 1, 2, 7, 17, 18, 24, 29-31, 53, 96, 101, 126, 131, 188, 213, 236, 241, **242**, 258, 261, 262, 263-265, 290, 303, 304

accidents with cars, 263, 265

antlers of, 2, 7, 101, 131, 213, 264, 265

behaviour in rut, 236, 241, 258, 263-265

behaviour in winter, 17, 24, 29, 31

birth of young, 101

carcasses of, 261, 290

coat of, 213

deer yards, 2, 7, 8, 18, 30, 31

how to see, 53, 265

in corn fields, 241, 242

Dorset (ON), 228

Downer's Corners Wetland, 301
Dragonflies: 96, 106, 110, 113,
    126, 140, 141, 160, 167, **168**,
    168, 182, 219, 247, 305
    Baskettail Beaverpond, 141
    Clubtail, Lancet, **142**
    Darner, Common Green, 66,
        106, **113**, **142**, 247, 271
        in winter, 270
    Emerald:
        American, **113**
        Racket-tailed, **142**
    mating of, 168
    Meadowhawk (*Sympetrum*),
        182, 236, **247**, 258
        Yellow-legged, 219, 268
        Whitefaced, 219
    of late spring and early
        summer (table), **142**
    of May (table), **113**
    Pennant, Calico, **142**
    Skimmer:
        Chalk-fronted, **142**
        Four-spotted, **113**, **142**
        Twelve-spotted, **142**
    synchronous emergence of,
        141
    Whiteface:
        Hudsonian, **113**
        Dot-tailed, **142**
    Whitetail, Common, **142**
Dyson, Tim, 6, 241

E

Earthshine, 92
Earthworm(s), 210, 248
Eels Creek, 303, 304
Eel Lake, xvii
El Nino, xvi
Elk, 18
Emily Provincial Park, 302
Emily Tract, 302
Emlen, Stephen, 122

Ennismore Inn, 305
Equinox, fall, 62, 206, 230
Equinox, spring, 62, 92
Essex County, 259

F

Fall leaves (see Trees)
Fens, 150, 157
Fern(s): 2, 196, 222, 257, 258,
    273, 300, 303, 304, 306
    in late fall and winter, 257,
        258, 273, 276
    Bracken, 222, 228
    Christmas, 2, 13, **275**, 276
    Rock Polypody, 276
    Marginal Wood Fern, 276
    Walking, 303
Field Guide to the Birds, 211
Fields, meadows, 131, 224, 225
Firefly (see Beetles)
Fishes: 78, 167, 182, 190, 206,
    245, 292
    Bass: 2, 9, 126, 138-140, 166,
        167, 190, 245, 258, 268
        how to see, 138-140
        spawning, 126, 138, 140,
            166, 190
        Largemouth, 138, 140, 160
        Rock, 138, 139, 160, 166
        Smallmouth, 9, 105, 138-
            140, 160, 166, 167, 190
    Bluegill(s): 126, 138, 139, 166
        mating strategies, 138-139
    Bullhead(s): 2, 9
        Brown, 138
        spawning, 138
    Burbot (Ling) (Freshwater
        Cod): 24, 31, 32
        mating behaviour, 32
    Carp, Common: 2, 9, 137, 166
        how to see, 137
        spawning, 137, 166
    Chub, Creek: **105**, 106

    spawning, 106
    Crappie, Black: 10, 138
        spawning, 138
    Darter, Iowa: 96, 104, **105**
        how to see, 105, 106
        spawning, 105
    Herring, Lake, 10
    minnows, 104
    Muskellunge (Muskies): 66,
        80, 81, 138, 166, 167, 190,
        206, 217, **218**, 236, 245,
        258, 267, 268
        fall feeding, 206, 236, 245
        spawning, 66
        how to see, 66, 80, 81
    non-game species, 96, 104, 105
    Northern Pike: 9, 10, 55, 66,
        80, 81, 96, 104, 268
        spawning, 55, 66, 81
        how to see, 81
    Perch, Yellow: 2, 9, 10, 80, 160,
        166
        spawning, 80
    Pumpkinseed: 105, 126, 138,
        139, 166
        how to see, 166
        spawning, 126
    Shiners, Spottail, 166
    Splake, 9, 10
    Stickleback, Brook: 104, 137
        spawning, 137
    Sucker, White: 66, 80, 81, 83
        how to see, 83
        spawning, 66
    Trout: 80, 206, 246
        Brook, 9, 10, 96, 105, 113,
            190, 217, 236, 245, **246**,
            258
            colour in fall, 217, 245
            spawning, 217, 236, 245,
                246
            how to see, 217, 246
        Brown, 190
        Lake, 9, 10, 32, 55, 177, 190,

236, 245
 spawning, 236, 245
 Rainbow, 9, 10, 66, 80
 spawning, 66
Trout-Perch: 82
 spawning, 82
Walleye: xvi, 2, 9, 10, 32, 55,
 66, 80-**82**, 83, 96, 90, 104,
 190, 206, 217, 258, 268, 300
 fall feeding, 206, 217, 268
 how to see, 80, 82
 spawning, 66, 80-82, 300
Whitefish, 10, 177, 258, 267,
 305
 spawning, 258, 305
Fisher(s), 74
Fishing: 217, 236, 245, 267
 anglers, 267, 292
 fly-fishing, 96, 105
 fishing seasons, 9, 55, 80, 104,
 105, 138, 217, 245, 258, 268,
 292
 ice fishing, 268
Flea, Snow (Springtail), 24, 32,
 33, 34, 44, 55
 behaviour of, 21, 33
Flowers (including Wildflowers):
 Agalinis, Small-flowered, 196,
 198, 222
 Amaranth, Green (Pigweed),
 15
 Anemone, Canada, **149**
 Arbutus, Trailing, **86**, 89
 Arethusa (Dragon's Mouth),
 146, **149**, 150
 Arrowhead, Common, 174
 Aster(s), 16, 205, 206, 218,
 221, 225, 235, 236, 249, 250
 where to find, 16
 Calico, **198**, 227
 Flat-topped White, **198**, 227
 Hairy, **224**
 Heath, **224**, 227
 Large-leaved, **198**

New England, **198**, 203, 225
 Panicled, **224**, 227
 Purple-stemmed, 227
 Smooth, 227
 Sky Blue, **173**
Beardtongue, Hairy, **172**
Beechdrops, **224**
Beggar Ticks, 16
Bellwort, Large-flowered, 114
Bergamot, Wild, 170, **172**, **173**,
 174
Blackberry, Common, **149**,
 170, 193, 198, **225**, 228
Black-eyed Susan, 16, **171**,
 172, 173, 199
Bladderworts, 196
Blazing-Star, Cylindric, **173**
Bloodroot, **86**, 119
Blue Cohosh, **86**, 119
Blueberry(berries), **114**, 164,
 198, 228
Blue-eyed Grass, **149**
Blue Flag, **149**
Boneset, **172**
Bouncing Bet, **172**, 199
Bunchberry, 126, 147, **149**,
 151, 152, 198, 273
 adaptations of, 152
Burdock, Common, 16
Bur Marigold, **198**, 222
Butter-and-Eggs, 172
Buttercup(s): 126, 147
 Common, **114**
 Early, **173**
 Kidney-leaved, **114**
 Prairie, 114, **173**
 Tall, **148**
Butterfly Weed (see Butterfly
 Milkweed)
Calopogon (Swamp Pink), 150
Campion, Bladder, 147, **149**,
 172
Cardinal Flower, 196, **198**
Cattail(s), 11, **149**, 174, 235,

250, 262
Chicory, **149**, 172
Cinquefoil, Rough, **149**
Clintonia, Yellow, 126, **149**
Clover:
 Red, 172
 White Sweet, **149**, 160, 170,
 171, 172, 199
Coltsfoot: 44, 57, 65, 66, 85,
 86, 88
 adaptations of, 88
Columbine, Wild, **114**
Coral-root: 149, 172
 Early, **114**
 Spotted, 174
Cranberry, 35, **149**, 198, 222
Cucumber, Wild, 196, **198**,
 199, 222
Currant(s), **89**, 114
Daisy, daisies: 126
 Ox-eye, 147-**149**, 160, 170,
 172
Dandelion, Common: 75, **86**,
 95, 96, 113, 117275
 attraction of insects by, 117
Dogbane, Spreading, 144, 172,
 228
Dragon-head, False, 222
Dragon's Mouth (see
 Arethusa)
Dutchman's Breeches, **86**, 119
Early Meadow Rue, **114**
Evening Primrose, 16, **172**, 199
Everlasting, Pearly, **172**
Fireweed, 1, 222
first bloom calendars (tables),
 59, 86, 114, 149, 172, 198,
 224
Fleabane:
 Daisy, 16
 Philadelphia, **149**, 172
Forget-me-not, **149**
Gentian:
 Bottle, 197, **198**, 222

Fringed, 197, **198**, 222
Gerardia (see Agalinis)
Goat's-beard, 147, **148**, **149**
Goldenrod(s): 16, 113, 172,
    182, 196, **197**, 205, 206,
    218, 221, 225-227, 250, 268,
    269
    attraction of insects by,
        199, 218
    Blue-stemmed, **226**, 227
    Bog, 227
    Canada, **198**, **203**, **226**, 227,
        269
    Early, **172**, 227
    galls, 268, **269**, 270
    Grass-leaved, **172**, **198**, 199,
        226
    Zigzag, 227
Goldthread, 147, **149**, 152
Gooseberry, Prickly, **114**
Grape, Riverbank, **149**
Grass-of-Parnassus, **198**, 222
Grass Pink, **149**
Harebell, 172, 196
Hawks-beard, Smooth, 172,
    199
Hawkweed:
    Orange, **172**
    Yellow, **148**, **149**
Hepatica(s), xv, 66, **86**, 119
Honeysuckle(s): 160, 171, 198
    Fly, **114**
    Tartarian, 114, **116**
Indian Pipe: 171, **172**, 174
    adaptations to shade, 174
Jack-in-the-Pulpit, **114**, **115**,
    119
Jewelweed, Spotted, **172**, 174,
    175, 182, 196
Joe-Pye-Weed, Spotted, 144,
    172, 174, **175**, 182, 196
Knapweed, Spotted, 172
Ladies'-slipper(s): 146, 150
    pollination of, 150

Pink, 150, **151**, 114
Ram's-head, **114**, 150
Showy, **149**, 150
Yellow, **114**, 150
Ladies'-tresses, orchids: 197,
    222
    Nodding, **198**
Lamb's Quarters, 16
Laurel, Bog, 273
Laurel, Sheep, **149**, 174
leaf-out calendars (tables), **89**,
    116
Leek, Wild: 23, 44, 55, 59
    in March, 55
Lily (lilies):
    Fragrant White Water, 174
    Wood, **149**, **173**
    Yellow Pond, 174
    Yellow Trout, **114**, **115**, 119
Lobelia:
    Great, **198**
    Kalm's, **172**, 222
Loosestrife, Purple, 160, 170,
    174, **175**, 182, 196
Lupine, Wild, **173**
Mallow, Musk, 172
Marigold, Marsh, **86**, **114**
Mayapple, 119
Mayflower, Canada, **114**, **149**,
    151, 273
Meadow Rue:
    Early, **114**
    Tall, **149**, 174
Meadowsweet, 174
Milkweed: **123**, 144, 160, 170,
    172, 173, 248-**250**, 257
    Butterfly, 170, **172**, **173**
    Common, 149, 172, 222
    fragrance of, 159, 160, 170,
        172
    pollinia bodies, 172, 173
    Swamp, 172, 174
Mullein, Common, 16, 172
Mustard(s), **114**, 16, 126, 147

Nightshade, Bittersweet, **149**
Orchid(s) (see also lady's
    slippers): 16, 125, 126, 149,
    150, 170, 302, 306
    our local heritage of, 150
    Rose Pogonia, 146, **149**,
        150, 170, 174
Orchis, Showy, **114**
Paint Brush, Indian, **173**
Partridgeberry, 273
Pickerelweed, 174
Pipsissewa, **13**, 174, 273
Pitcher Plant(s), 174
Poison Ivy: 113, 118, 119, **149**,
    198, 228
    identification of, 118
    allergic reaction to, 118,
        119
Polygala, Fringed, **114**, 147,
    151
Pussytoes, **114**
Queen-Anne's Lace (Wild
    Carrot), 16, 160, 170, **171**,
    172, 196, 199, 250
Ragweed, Common, 16, 181,
    182, 196, **198**, 199
    cause of hayfever, 181, 182,
        196, 199
Raspberry(berries), 159, 164,
    170, 193
    Purple-flowering, 172, **198**,
        228
    Red, **149**, 198, **225**
Rattlesnake-plantain, **172**
Roadside flowers, 88, 126, 147,
    159, 160, 170-172, 181, 182,
    196, 197, 224, 227, 258, 273
Rocket, Dame's, **148**, **149**
Rose, Wild, **149**
Sarsaparilla:
    Bristly, 198
    Wild, **149**, 152
Saxifrage, Early, **114**
Shinleaf, 174

Skunk Cabbage, 58-60
Snakeroot:
    Seneca, **173**
    White, **198**, 222
Solomon's Seal, **149**
Solomon's Seal, False, **114**
Sorrel, Wood, **149**, 151, 174
spring ephemerals
    (adaptations of), 151, 152
Spring Beauty, **114**, 119
Squirrel Corn, 119
Starflower, 147, **149**, **151**, 152
St. John's-wort, **149**, 172
Strawberry(berries): 126, 159,
    228
    Barren, **114**
    Wild, **114**
Sunflower, Woodland, 196,
    198
Swamp Pink (see Calopogon)
Sweetgale, **114**
Thistle(s), 172, 196, 199, 222
Tick Trefoil:
    Canada, **175**
    Showy, **172**, **173**, 196
Toothwort, Two-leaved, **114**,
    119
Trefoil, Birdsfoot, **149**
Trillium(s): 16, **115**, 119
    Painted, **114**
    Red, **114**, 119
    White, 95, **114**
Turtlehead, **198**
Twinflower, **149**, 152, 174
Vetch(es): **149**
    Purple, 172
Violet(s): **86**, 119
    Arrow-leaved, **173**
Viper's-bugloss, 147, **149**, 172
Virgin's Bower, 196, **198**, 199,
    222
wetland flowers, 160, 175
Wintergreen, 2, 13, 151, 174
woodland wild flowers, 85,

174
Yarrow, **149**, 172
Fly (flies): 60, 66, 247
    Cluster, 247, 248
        in windows, 248
        life cycle of, 248
    Deer, 160, 167, 169
        behaviour of, 169
    flower fly larvae, 141
    Goldenrod Gall, 2, 12, 269
        formation of galls, 12, 269
        life cycle of, 269, 270
    Horse, 160, 167, 169
    March, 44, 55
    syrphid, 218
    Tachinid Flesh, 111
    wingless scorpion-flies, 32
    wingless winter crane, 32
Flynn's Corners, 285
Forest Plants of Central Ontario,
    36
Fossils, 303
Fox(es): 2, 44, 135, 165, **102**
    Red, 8, 29, 52, 53, 126, 132,
        164
        birth of young, 44, 52, 101,
            102
        fox-watching, 101
French River, 188
Froghoppers (see Spittlebugs)
Frogs (and toads): 44, 65, 76, 92,
    103, 167, 206, 215, 217, 236,
    240, 243, 244, 265, 266, 301
    Bullfrog, 54, **79**, 103, 126, 134,
        159, 160, 165, 166, 167, 266
    breeding periods of (table), **79**
    calls: 65, 76
        amphibian chorus, 76, 165,
            166, 301
        descriptions of (table), 54
        in fall, 216
        learning of, 53, 54
    Frogsicles, 266
    Green, 54, **79**, 103, 126, 134,

160, 165, 166, 189, 216, 244,
    266
    (Midland) Chorus, 53, 54, 66,
        76-79, 194, 266
    migrations of, 215, 216
    Mink, 54, **79**, 103, 126, 134,
        160, 165, 266
    (Northern) Leopard, 54, 66,
        76, 77, **79**, 167, 182, 189,
        216, **244**, 266
        in fields, 189, 216
    on warm roads, 243, 244
    overwintering strategies of,
        266
    Peeper, (Northern) Spring, xv,
        xvi, 53, 54, 66, 69, 76-**79**,
        134, 165, 189, 194, 206, 215,
        236, 243, 244, 266
        how to see, 134
    Pickerel, 54, 76, **79**
    Toad, (Eastern) American: 53,
        54, **79**, 96, 103, 165, 182,
        189, 193, 194, 216, **244**,
        265, 266
        call of, 103
        mating, 103
        winter survival of, 266
    Treefrog, Gray, 54, **79**, 103,
        126, 134, 136, 137, 206, 215,
        266, 267
        how to see, 136
    Wood, 54, 66, 76, **77**, **79**, 134,
        165, 189, 215, 266
Frost(s), 16, 96, 111, 113, 120,
    191, 206, 214, 222, 228, 229,
    235, 236, 247, 252, 253, 277
Fruits (see Trees)
Fungi (see mushrooms)

G

Galls (see Goldenrod)
Galway-Cavendish Forest Access
Road, 112, 146, 304

Ganaraska River, 80
Gannon's Narrows, 45, 49, 70, 75, 82, 261, 285, 305
Glen Alda, 222, 228
Glycerol, 266, 270
Glycogen, 136
Goldenrod Gall Flies:
    larvae, 11
Gooderham (ON), 27
Grass(es): 113, 117, 118, 147, 222
    Big Blue Stem, **173**
    Crab, 16
    identification in fall, 222
    Indian, 173
    Meadow Fescue, 147
    Mountain Rice (*Oryzopsis asperifolia*), **86**, 118
    of June, **147**
    of spring, 8, 16, 31, 33, 75, 81, 86, 89, 113, 114, 117, 118, 120, 147, 149
    of prairie, xviii, 173, 299
    Orchard, 147
    Sweet (Vanilla) (*Hierochloe odorata*), 118
    Timothy, 147
    Woodland Poa (*Poa alsodes*), 113, 118
Grasshoppers: 160, 168, 181, 182, 190-192, 205, 219
    description of song (table), 194
    band-winged grasshoppers (*Oedipodinae*), 193
    bush-katydids (*Scudderia* spp.), 193, **194**
    long-horned (*Tettigoniidae*), 191, **192**, 193
    Melanoplus femurrubrum, 193
    production of sound, 191
    short-horned (locusts) (*Acrididae*), 191, 193
    spur-throated (locusts) (*Melanoplus*), 193

true katydids (*Pseudophyllinae*), 193
    where to hear, 192
Great Lakes, xvii, 25, 61, 72, 162
Groundhog(s): 29, 38, 39, 44, 52, 66, 101, 126, 132, 164, 206, 214, 236, 242, 243, 263
    Groundhog Day, 23, 24, 36, 38
    hibernation of, 38, 66, 206, 214, 236, 243
    mating of, 44, 52
    young emerge from burrows, 132
Gut Conservation Area, The, 304

H

Haliburton, xv
Haliburton County, 6
Hare(s): 18
    European, 52
    Snowshoe, 17, 18, 52, 258, 263
        winter coat of, 18, 258, 263
        mating of, 52
Harrick Point, 299
Hastings (ON), xvii, 68
Hastings County, 6
Havelock (ON), 112
Havelock Sewage Lagoons, 186, 303
Haultain (ON), 3, 101, 261, 285
Haultain Dump, 261, 304
Havelock (ON), 129
Havelock-Belmont-Methuen Township, 89
Heber Rogers Conservation Area, 89
Heinrich, Bernd, xvi, 251, 270
Herkimer Point, 100
Herkimer Point Road, 300
Hiawatha Reserve, xviii, 100, 173, 299, 300
High Falls Trail, 276, 303
Honey, 117, 170

Hornet (see Wasps)
Horsetail, Common, 113
Hudson Bay, 73
Hudson Bay Lowlands, 73
Humidity, 170, 176, 179, 200, 229
Hunting (hunters):
    flight to the woods (deer hunt), 263, 264
    fall goose hunt, 239
    hunting seasons, 263

I

Indian Summer, 236, 252, 258, 276
Indian River, 50, 215, 300
Insects (see also individual species): 85, 95, 105, 117, 125, 132, 133, 134, 141, 165, 172, 173, 181, 182, 199, 206, 215, 218, 236, 258, 268
    aquatic, 140
    at sugar bush, 55-56
    night-time insect sounds (table), **194**
    winter survival of, 268, 270-272
    chorus of, 236
Insect-watching, 141

J

Jack Lake, 10, 261, 283, 304
Jack Lake Road, 27, 146, 285, 304
Jackson Creek, 246
Jackson Creek Wetlands, 301
Jackson Park, 97, 100, 300
James Bay, 66, 68, 73, 97

K

Kasshabog Lake, 3, 261, 303
Kawartha Heights Park, 301
Kawartha Highlands Provincial

Park, xviii
Kawartha Highlands Signature
    Site, 304
Kawartha Lakes, xv, xvii, 70, 81,
    100, 107, 108, 177, 190, 196,
    259, 268, 282, 294
Kawartha Nordic Ski Club, 261,
    285, 304
Keene (ON), 300
Kent's Bay Road, 299
Kirkton (ON), 306
Kiwanis-Jackson Park Rail-Trail,
    145

L
_____

Lady Eaton Drumlin, 145
lake(s): 2, 9, 31, 32, 44, 45, 55, 73,
    81, 83, 89, 90, 105-107, 120,
    121, 132, 138, 140, 147, 174,
    176, 177, 196, 252, 253, 259,
    261, 267, 295
    candled ice, 90
    ice-out of, 67, 89, 90
    fall turnover of, 245, 252, 253
    freeze-up of, 259, 281, 295
    oxygen levels of, 55, 177, 253
    spring turnover of, 120, 121
    in summer, 174, 177, 196
    thermocline of, 177, 182, 190
Lake Catchacoma, 112, 146
Lake Erie, 99, 220
Lake Huron, 161
Lake Katchewanooka, xvii, 45, 49,
    67, 70, 268, 283, 285, 300, 302
Lake Ontario, 80, 161, 207, 220,
    239, 241, 259, 294, 306
Lake Scugog, xvii, 9, 10
Lakefield (ON), 68, 243, 244, 285,
    302
Lakefield Marsh, 70, 302
Lakefield Sewage Lagoons, 186,
    302
Land O' Lakes, xv

Lasswade (ON), 129, 228, 304
Leaves (see Trees)
Legend for Arrival and Departure
    Charts, xx
Lemming(s), 5
Leopold, Aldo, 273, 276
Lichen(s): 24, 35, 273
    British Soldiers, 36
    False Pixie Cup, 36
    in winter, 273
    Lungwort, 36
    Parmelia, 35, 36
    Powder Horn, 36
    Rock Tripe, 36
Liftlock (Peterborough), 139
Lightning, 174, 176, 177
Lily Lake, 75, 301
Little Lake, 45, 46, 49, 51, 67, 258,
    259, 261, 283, 285, 300
Little Lake Cemetery, 72, 100, 300
Locust (see short-horned
    grasshoppers)
Locust, Carolina, 191
Lovesick Lake, xvii, 70
Lower Buckhorn Lake, 49
Lynch's Rock Road, 303
Lyrids (see meteor showers)

M
_____

Mackenzie House Pond, 78
Mantid, Praying, 218, 271
Mark S. Burnham Provincial
    Park, xviii, 80, 89, 118, 227,
    276, 300
Marmora (ON), xvii
Marsh Monitoring Program, 312,
    316
Marten(s), 74
    birth of young, 74
Mather's Corners, 70, 300
Mayflies, 134, 140
McMaster University, 188
Meade Creek, 301

Meteor showers: 201, 202, 278
    Eta Aquarids, 122
    Leonids, 278
    Lyrids, 91
    Perseids, 182, 201, 202
    Quadrantids, 19
    South Taurids, 278
Mice: 5, 7, 18, 252, 257, 262
    Deer, 241
        winter shelter of, 18, 241,
        243
    hibernation of, 236, 243
    Meadow Jumping, 236, 242,
    243
    under the snow, 7, 8
    Woodland Jumping, 243
Midges, 44, 56, 57, 66, 71, 72, 83,
    167, 236, 247
    life cycle of, 56, 57
    swarming, 44, 56, 66, 246
Milky Way, 126, 155, 156, 160,
    178, 179, 181, 182, 231, 232
Millage Road, 79, 305
Miller Creek Conservation Area,
    69, 70, 78, 100, 144, 145, 163,
    169, 304
Ministry of Natural Resources, 31
Mink(s): 2, 24
    American, 28, 29, 74
    mating, 28, 29
    birth of young, 74
Mississauga Dam Road, 304
Mist(s), 206, 229
Mnemonics, 15, 47, 49
Moira River, 215
Mole(s), 7
Moon: 91, 92, 179, 201, 231, 254
    halo of, 91
    Harvest Moon, 206, 231, 254
    Hunter's Moon, 231, 236, 254
    June, 155
    learning phases of, 91-93
Moose: xix, 2, 7, 18, 29, 30, 32,
    96, 101, 165, 206, 242, 303, 304

antlers of, 2, 7
birth of young, 101
how to see, 96
rut of, 206
ticks, 52
Morris, Frank, 149
Mosquitoes: 83, 96, 107, 109, 110, 156,
169, 247, 271
Aedes, 109, 271
in winter, 271
Aedes vexans, 109
Culex, 83, 247, 271
in October, 247
in winter, 271
Culex pipiens (Northern House Mosquito), 109
ecological role of, 110
life history of, 109
Northern House, 109
Mosses: 257, 258, 273, 275
in late fall and winter, 257, 258, 273
Juniper, 275
Shaggy, 275
Sphagnum (peat moss), 275
Moths (see also Caterpillars): 126, 141-143
Arctiidae, 133, 134
Big Poplar, 143
Cattail Borer, 11
larvae, 11
Cecropia, **142**, 143
life cycle of, 142
Eastern Tent Caterpillar, 110, 220
Fall Webworm, 182, 191, 219, 220
Forest Tent, 110, 111
giant silk, 126, 141-143
how to see, 143
mating strategies of, 142
Gypsy, 111, 112
life cycle, 111, 112

Imperial, 143
Infant, The, 83
Io, **142**
Isabella, 83, 221, 270
Luna, 142
Milkweed Tussock, 190
Polyphemus, 142
Promethea, 142
Noctuid, 55, 56
Royal, 143
Sphinx, 126, 141, 143
strategies to avoid bats, 133, 134
underwing (*Catocala*), 191, **195**
how to attract, 191
Virginia Ctenuchid, 141
Woolly Bear, 83, 219, 221, 270
Yellow Bear, 219, 221
American Dagger, 219, 221
Mushroom(s): 170, 182, 196, 206, 214, 222, 227, 228
Brown Hay Cap (*Panaeolus foenisecii*), 113
classification into groups, 227
coral fungi, 227
Cracked Top Mushroom (*Agrocybe dura*), 113
Destroying Angel, 227
Dunce Cap (*Conocybe lactea*), 170
earthstars, 227
Field Mushroom (*Agaricus campestris*), 170
gilled fungi, 227
jelly fungi, 227
morrels, 113, 227
on lawns, 113, 170, 223
polypores, 227
puffballs, 227
quick growth of, 228
Shaggy Mane (*Coprinus comatus*), 223
stinkhorns, 227

Stinking Parasol (*Lepiota cristata*), 223
where to find, 227
Muskoka, xv
Muskrat(s): 44, 51, 74, 258, 262, **264**, 282
fall dispersal of, 262
homes of, 258, 262
mating, 44, 51
Mussel, Zebra, 106-108
life history of, 107, 108

N

National Audubon Society, 288, **289**
National Lightning Safety Institute, 177
Natural Heritage Information Centre, 308, 312
Northern Lights, 2, 297
Northey's Bay Road, 265, 303
Northumberland County, 89
Norwood (ON), 237

O

Oak Ridges Moraine, 80
Odonata (order of insects), 168
Oliver Ecological Centre, 241, 304
Omemee Sewage Lagoons, 302
Orion (see Constellations)
Orion Nebula, 40
Orono (ON), 193
Otonabee College, 78
Otonabee Region Conservation Authority, 309
Otonabee River, xv, xvii, xviii, 3, 27, 49-51, 56, 66, 67, 70-72, 173, 261, 266, 284, 285, 299, 300-302
Otter(s), 2, 66, 73-75, 188
River, 28, **74**, 101
birth of young, 101

how to see, 74, 75
Our Heritage of Birds, 299
Ouse River, 50, 246
Owen Point, 186

P

Parkhill Road West, 145
Parkway (proposed) Corridor,
    301
Pencil Lake, 10
Pencil Lake Road, 304
Pengelley Landing, 299
Perry Creek, 267, 305
Perseid meteor shower, 182, 201,
    202
Peterborough (ON), xvii, 3, 27,
    45, 49, 68, 71, 75, 82, 83, 89,
    100, 139, 149, 173, 215, 240,
    244, 251, 259, 261, 285, 286,
    288, **289**, 294, 299, 300-302
Peterborough Airport, 69, 299
Peterborough County, xv, xvii,
    xviii, xxi, 6, 9, 10, 50, 55, 73,
    80, 101, 130, 138, 144, 146,
    162, 168, 172, 179, 188, 193,
    213, 217, 222, 225, 242, 261,
    263, 268, 285, 290
Peterborough Crown Game
    Reserve, 7, 27, 30
Peterborough Drumlin Field,
    xviii
Peterborough Field Naturalists,
    286
Peterborough Green-Up and
    Ecology Park, 301
Peter's Woods Provincial Park,
    89, 100, 112, 276, 306
Peterson, Roger Tory, 211
Petroglyphs Provincial Park, xviii,
    3, 89, 134, 145, 146, 150, 196,
    265, 176, 286, 288, **289**, 303
Phenology, xvi
Photosynthesis, 24, 35, 55, 58, 59,

120, 151, 152, 177, 224
Phytoplankton, 10
Pigeon Lake, xvii, 70, 81, 241,
    268, 302, 305
Pishing (see Birding)
Planet(s): 254, 255
    Jupiter, 254, 255
    Mars, 254, 255
    Mercury, 254
    Neptune, 254
    Pluto, 254
    Saturn, 254, 255
    Uranus, 254
    Venus, 254, 255
Plants (see trees, flowers, etc.)
    301-303
Pleasant Point Road, 299
Point Pelee, 99
pollen, 86, 114, 119, 149, 150,
    152, 172, 181
pollination (pollinate), 60, 86, 88,
    109, 117, 119, 150, 152
Porcupine(s): 7-9, 74, 101, 236,
    242
    diet of, 7, 8, 74
    mating, 236, 241
    in winter, 7-9
Port Hope (ON), 80, 241
Port Perry sewage lagoons, 186,
    306
Prairie (tallgrass), 173
Precipitation, 17, 38, 61, 90, 121,
    153, 176, 200, 230, 253, 277,
    294
Presqu'ile Provincial Park, 49,
    162, 186, 219-220, 288, 306
Promise Rock Trail, 145, 301

R

Raccoon(s): 24, 28, 29, 66, 74, 78,
    126, 129, 135, 160, 164, 165,
    258, 268
    mating, 28, 29

birth of young, 66, 74
Rain (rainfall), 17, 38, 61, 90, 121,
    153, 176, 200, 230, 253, 277,
    294
Rainbow Tallgrass Prairie
Restoration Site, 173, 299
Red Cloud Cemetery, 306
Renfrew (ON), 215
Rice Lake, xvii, xviii, 49, 50, 70,
    173, 210, 299
Rice Lake Plains Tallgrass Prairie,
    306
Rice Lake Tallgrass Prairie
    Ecosystem (table), **173**
River Road, 300, 302
Roadkill, 74, 102, 160, 164
Rockhouse Gemboree, 182
Rotary-Greenway Trail, 301
Rushes: 113, 117, 118, 262
    of spring, 118
    Pointed Wood (*Luzula
        acuminata*), 118
    Wood (*Luzula multiflora*), 113,
        118

S

Sadler, Doug, 6, 240, 295, 299
Salamander(s): 65, 66, 76, 78, 79,
    165, 265, 305
    Blue-spotted, 78, 165
    Eastern Newt, 78
    Four-toed, 79
    how to see, 79, 243
    mating of, 66, 78
    overwintering of, 266
    Red-backed, 134, 243, **244**
        eggs, 134
    Spotted (Yellow-spotted), 78,
        165
Salmon Lake Road, 304
Sand County Almanac, A, 276
Sandy Lake, 305
Sandy Lake Road, 112, 146, 303

Sawer Creek Wetland, 100, 303
Scott's Plains (later
    Peterborough), 173
Seasonal Occurrences of Natural
    Events of Special Interest
    (table), **xix**
Sedges: 66, 113, 300
    Carex lucorum, 118
    Distant, **86**
    identification of, 89, 113, 117,
        118, 300
    of spring, 118
    Pedunculed (*Carex
        pedunculata*), **86**, 118
    Pennsylvania (*Carex
        pennsylvanica*), 113, 118
    Plantain-leaved (*Carex
        plantaginea*), **86**, 118
Seeds (See individual species)
Seed dispersal, 249
Shield (see Canadian Shield)
Shooting stars (see Meteor
    Showers)
Shrews: 7, 8, 18, 262
    squeak of, 262
Shrubs (see Trees, Shrubs and
    Vines)
Silent Lake Provincial Park, xvii
Six Foot Bay Road, 305
Skink, Five-lined: 76, 134, **135**,
    303
    how to see, 76
    mating, 134
Skunk(s): 23, 24, 78, 135, 165,
    258
    Striped, 28-30, 51, 53, 101,
        126, 132, 164, 262, 263
    digs of, 263
    mating of, 28, 29, 51
    spray of, 29
    young emerge, 132, 160, 164
Smell(s): 257, 273
    American Basswood flowers,
        159, 160, 170

Balsam Fir, 292, 293
Balsam Poplar, 15, 43, 57, 95,
    120, 124, 125
boiling maple sap, 43
fallen leaves, 235, 252
freshly cut hay, 125, 126
grass fires, 252
June air, 124
lilac blossoms, 120, 124, 125
manure, 273
mowen grass, 120, 124, 125
milkweed, 159, 160, 170, 172
skunk, 23, 24, 29
Skunk Cabbage, 59, 60
thawing earth, 43
Wild Bergamot, 181
windfall apples, 205
Snake(s): 265, 266
    Eastern Garter, 53, 66, 76, 79,
        80, 96, 160, 165, 243, 266,
        267
    birth of young, 160, 165
    mating, 66, 76, 79, 80, 96
    overwintering, 266
    Milk, 134
    Northern Water: 96, 103, 160,
        165
    birth of young, 160
    mating, 96, 103
    Ringneck, 134
Snelgrove Creek, 78
Snow (snowfall), 8, 17, 18, 23, 29,
    34, 38, 55, 59, 61, 75, 89, 90,
    121, 153, 176, 200, 230, 253,
    258, 277, 283, 294
Solstice, summer, 125, 126, 153,
    154, 295
Solstice, winter, 95, 281, 283, 294,
    295
South Beach Road, 100
Soybeans, 113, 147, 223, 237, 239
Sphagnum (peat moss) (see
    Mosses)
Spider(s): 140, 182, 206, 215, 219,

272
    ballooning of, 140, 219
    Crab, 272
    Grass, 12
    Hunting, 272
    overwintering, 272
    Wolf, 272
Spittlebugs, 107
Springtails (see Snow Flea)
Squirrel Creek Conservation
    Area, 100
Squirrel(s): 7, 24, 35, 55, 213, 214,
    252, 257, 262, 291
    Gray, 28, 29, 52, 188, 213, 214,
        290
    birth of young, 29, 52, 188
    mating, 28
    preparation for winter, 213,
        214
    Northern Flying, 52, 90, 101
    at bird feeders, 290
    mating, 52
    Red, 7, **42**, 44, 52, 101, 213,
        214, 281, 282, 290, **291**
    coat of, 282, 290
    mating, 44
    nip twigs, 42, 52, 55, 290,
        291
    preparation for winter, 212,
        214
    Southern Flying, 52, 101, 290
    at bird feeders, 290
    mating, 52
Stars: 19, 254, 255, 277, 278, 296
    Aldebaran, 19, 39, 40, 62, 63,
        91, 296-**298**
    Altair, 155, 157, 178, 179, 201,
        230, 254, 277, 296
    Arcturus, 62, **63**, 91, 96, 96,
        122, 126, 155, 178, 179, 201,
        230
    as directional clues, 20, 22
    Betelgeuse, 19, 39, 40, 62, 63,
        91, 277, 296, **298**

Capella, 19, 39, 62, 63, 91, 122, 277, 296-**298**

Castor, 19, 39, 62, 63, 91, 122, 296

change of through seasons, 20

Deneb, 155, 157, 178, 179, 201, 230, 254, 277, 296

Pointers, The, 20

Polaris (North Star), 19-21, 39, 62, 91, 122, 155, 178, 201, 230, 254, 277, 296

Pollux, 19, 39, 62, 63, 91, 122, 296

Procyon, 62, 63

Regulus, 19, 39, 62, **63**, 91, 122, 155, 178

Rigel, 19, 39, 40, 62, 63, 91, 277, **298**

Sirius (Dog Star), 19, 39, 40, 62, 63, 91, 178, 200, 296-**298**

Spica, 62, **63**, 91, 96, 122, 155

Vega, 155, 157, 178, 179, 201, 230, 254, 277, 296

Stargazing, 178, 179

Stoneflies: 32, 44, 55
life history, 34
Small Winter, **34**
how to see, 34

Stony (Stoney) Lake, xvii, 30, 143, 146, 149, 165, 186, 261, 267, 268, 282, 283, 303

Strickland, Samuel, 173

Strider, water (see Bugs)

Sturgeon Lake, xvii, 268

Sugar bush, 55, 59, 84

Sunrise and sunset times (see also monthly table), 2, 18, 39, 44, 61, 66, 90, 120, 155, 160, 176, 177, 182, 201, 206, 230, 236, 255, 258, 277, 283, 296

T

Tapes (of animal sounds), 27, 49, 50, 53, 192, 312

Temperature(s), 2, 24, 44, 66, 96, 126, 160, 182, 206, 229, 236, 244, 258, 283, 294

Tennessee Valley, 73

Thaws, 17, 43

Thoreau, Henry David, 181

Thunderstorms, 176, 177

Ticks, 52

Toads (see Frogs and Toads)

Township of Asphodel, 75, 300

Township of Dummer, 75

Tracks, tracking, 291

Trees, Shrubs and Vines:
Alder, Speckled, 58, 65, 66, 85, **86, 87, 251**
Apple, 31, 167
Arrow-wood, Downy, 198
Ash: 113
Red, 222
White, xviii, 15, 31, **116**, 146, 206, 222, **223, 225, 229**, 249, 250, **251**
colour diversity in, 206
Aspen(s): 44, 57-**59**, 74, 75, 83, **86**, 228, 249
Bigtooth, 14, **116**, 225, **229**
Trembling, 14, 85, **87**, 114, **116, 225, 229**
Basswood, American, xviii, 1, 15, 31, **116**, 159, **160, 223, 225, 229, 251**
Beech, American, xviii, 14, 15, 24, 35-**37, 149, 223, 225, 229**, 273
Birch(es), 18, 57, 83
White, 14, 57, 85, 111, 222
Yellow, xviii, 14, 31, **225**
Bittersweet, **149**, 198, 273, **274**
Buckthorn, European, **149**, 198, 210, 249, **251**, 260

invasiveness of, 198
buds, 14-15
Butternut, 248
Catalpa, **149**
Catkins, **58**, 74, 85-88
Cedar, White, xviii, 13, 31, 57, 150, 222, **292**
Cherry: 96, 107, 109, 113, 125, 160, 167, 171, 270
Black, 14, **149**, 198, 210
Choke, 115, 117, **124, 198, 225**
fruit, 164
Pin, **114, 115**, 117, 198, **225, 229**
Crabapple, 259, 260, 273
Dogwood(s): 126, 147, 160, 171, 198, 210, 222, **225**, 228
Red-osier, 14, 57, **114**, 196, **197-199**
Alternate-leaved, **149**
Elder, Red-berried, 44, 57, **89**, **114**, 170, **175**, 198
Elderberry, Common, **149**, 174, **175**, 198
Elm(s): 65, 66, 86, 114, 147, **225**
American, xviii, **86, 116**, 147, **184, 229, 251**
Siberian, **251**
Fir, Balsam, 14, 27, **114**, 149, 222, 283, **292**, 293
first bloom calendars (tables), **59, 86, 114, 149, 172, 198**
Grape, Riverbank, 198, 228, 260
Hawthorn(s), 114, 126, 147, 273, **274**, 280
Hemlock, Eastern, xviii, 7, 8, 27, 31, 85, 214, 273
Hickory, Bitternut, xix, 15, **225, 229**
Highbush-Cranberry: 35, **149**, 198

American, 222

Hobblebush, **114**, 198

Holly:

Mountain, 198

Winterberry, 198, 273, **274**, 281

Horse Chestnut, 15, 120

identification in winter, 13-15

Ironwood (Hop-hornbean), 36, 248, 273

Juneberry (see Serviceberry)

Juniper, xviii

Leatherleaf, 114

Leatherwood, **86**, 89

Leaves: 221, 224, 252

autumn leaf colour (table), **225**

beech, 36, 37

colour change of, 221, 224, 225

colour timetable of (table), **229**

colour diversity within species, 225, 249, 250

leaf-drop timetable (table), **251**

leaf-out calendars (tables), **89**, **116**

of June, 146

seeing the fall colours, 222, 228, 229

shedding of, 224, 225, 235, 236, 248, 252

Lilac, Common, 44, 57, 95, 96, 112, **114**, **116**, 120, **124**, 125, **251**

Linden, Little-leaved, **251**

Locust, Black, **149**, **251**

Maple(s), 1, 65, 85, 86, 205, 249

King Crimson, **229**, **251**

Manitoba, **86**, **116**, **234**, 290

Norway, 114, **116**, **225**, **229**, 249, **251**, 275, 290

Red, 15, 31, **41**, 57-**59**, 85, **86**, **87**, **116**, 147, 182, 196, 199, 222, **225**, 228, **229**, **234**, 248, 250, **251**

colour diversity in, 196, 199

Silver, 57-**59**, 114, 147, 149, **225**, **229**, **234**, **251**, 258, 275

Striped, 86, **225**, **234**

Sugar, xviii, 36, 44, 57, 74, 114, **116**, 198, 199, 222, **223**, **225**, 228, **229**, **234**, 248, **251**, 273

masting, 5

mountain-ash, 4, 210, 273

American, 198

European, 260

Nannyberry, **149**, 198

non-native species in fall, 251, 252, 275

Oak(s): 36, 111, 113, **225**, 228, 229

Red, 15, **116**, **149**, **229**, 235, 250, **251**, 258, 275

colour diversity in, 228, 251

White, **149**, **229**

Pine(s): 2, 7, 89, **114**, 149, 150, 152, 282, 292, 305

Red, 152, 222, 223, 292, 302

(Eastern) White, xviii, 5, 8, 13, 100, **149**, 152, 223, 292, 293, 302, 305

pollen showers from, 152

Poplar(s): 65, 66, 86-88, 111, 147, 235

Balsam, 15, 43, 57, 75, 95, 120, **124**, 125, 147, **225**, **229**

fragrance of, 15, 43, 57

Carolina, **251**

Serviceberry(berries)

(Juneberry) (shadbush), 113, **114**, 116, 117, 149, 198

Spruce(s): 114, 146, 214, 290

Black, xix

White, 5, 13, 14, 27, 85, 222, 292, 293

Shadbush (see Serviceberry)

Sumac, Staghorn, 31, 35, **149**, 182, 196, 198, **225**, **229**, **251**

Sweet-fern, 205

Tamarack, 7, 8, 27, **116**, 222, **229**, 235, 236, 249, **251**, 258, 275, 292, 304

in late October, 235, 236, 249

twig(s), 14, 15

Viburnums, 126, 147

Viburnum, Maple-leaved, 35, 198, **225**, 228

Virginia Creeper, 182, 196, 198, 199, 206, 222, 228, **251**

Walnut, Black, **149**, **225**, **229**, **251**

Willow(s): 14, 57, 66, 85, **86**, 88, **116**, 147, **225**, **251**

Pussy, 23, 43, 44, 57, **58**, **59**, 88

Weeping, **251**, 275

Yew, Canada, 31

Trent Canal Wetlands, 301

Trent University, 51, 71, 78, 89, 100, 144, 188, 241, 243, 304

Trent University Nature Areas, 301

Trent University Wildlife Sanctuary, 69, 301

Turtle(s): 53, 66, 76, 78, 104, 126, 135, 136, 182, 189, 206, 215, 236, 243, 265, 266

basking of, 103, 104

egg-laying of, 104, 126, 135, 160, 165

hatching of eggs, 136, 182, 189, 206, 215

hibernation of, 236, 243, 267
Map, 65
Musk, 267
(Midland) Painted, 96, 103,
104, 134, 135, 267
Snapping, 134-136, 160, 165,
216, 267
Twin Lakes, 146

U

University Road wetland, 78, 301
University Heights Woodland,
301
University of Vermont, 251
Upper Buckhorn Lake, 49
Upper Stoney Lake, 261

V

Victoria County, 10, 302
Vines (see Trees and Shrubs)
Vole(s): 5, 7, 8, 18, 152, 162
Meadow, 285

W

Warkworth (ON), 306
Warsaw Caves Conservation
Area, 146, 150, 215, 237, 303

Wasps: 83, 194, 206, 218
Hornet, Bald-faced, 194, 219
paper nests of, 194
Vespids, 195
Vespula, 194
Yellowjacket, 182, 191, 194,
195, 219, 271
life cycle of, 195
Waterfowl Viewing Weekends
(Brighton), 49
Weasel(s): 53, 66, 258, 263
winter coat of, 258, 263
Short-tailed, 74
Long-tailed, 74
Weather: 26, 76, 99, 100, 112, 120,
160, 178, 181, 182, 200, 211,
229, 230, 245, 252, 253, 263,
294
averages (monthly table), 17,
38, 61, 90, 120, 121, 153,
200, 277
influence on bird migration,
61, 186, 211
Webworm, Fall (see Caterpillars)
West Kosh Road, 303
West Nile Virus, xxi
wetland(s), 66, 76, 78, 103, 110,
130, 147, 162, 170, 174, 182,
183, 196, 199, 206, 209, 216,
222, 227, 244, 249, 267, 270,

300-302
wetland flowers, 175
Wheat, 222
White, Brad, 188
Wilberforce (ON), 222
Wildflowers (See Flowers)
Wilson, Paul, 188
Windsor (ON), 173, 259
Winter, 295
Wolf, wolves: 7, 18, 24, 29, 31, 44,
52, 182, 188, 261
birth of young, 44, 52
Eastern, 29, 101, 188, 189
Gray, 188
hybridization of, 189
identity of, 188
mating, 29
Red, 188

Y

Year in the Maine Woods, A, 270
Young's Point (ON), 3, 82, 100,
141, 285, 305

Z

Zebra Mussel (see Mussels,
Zebra)
Zooplankton, 10

About the Author

As a youngster, Drew Monkman's interest in nature began with frogs and turtles but soon grew to include birds and, eventually, all of the rest. He is a board member and past president of the Peterborough Field Naturalists and popular field trip leader. Drew also participates in a

number of wildlife monitoring programs such as the Breeding Bird Survey, the Marsh Monitoring Program and the new Ontario Breeding Bird Atlas. As an educator, Drew emphasizes environmental education in all his teaching and strives to develop in his students a basic literacy in the workings of the natural world. Drew has also been involved for the past twelve years in schoolyard naturalization and has written several articles on this topic. A journalism graduate from Université Laval in Quebec City, Drew is married with four children. *Nature's Year in the Kawarthas* is the result of twenty years of careful observation of natural phenomena in the Peterborough area where he has lived for almost his entire life.

About the Illustrator

Kimberly Caldwell, born and raised on the prairies, received a degree in Ecology from the University of Manitoba. She then spent six years living in the Peterborough area acquainting herself with the Kawarthas. She now resides in Sault Ste. Marie, Ontario, with her husband and two children. Sketching has been a lifelong hobby and these are her first published illustrations.